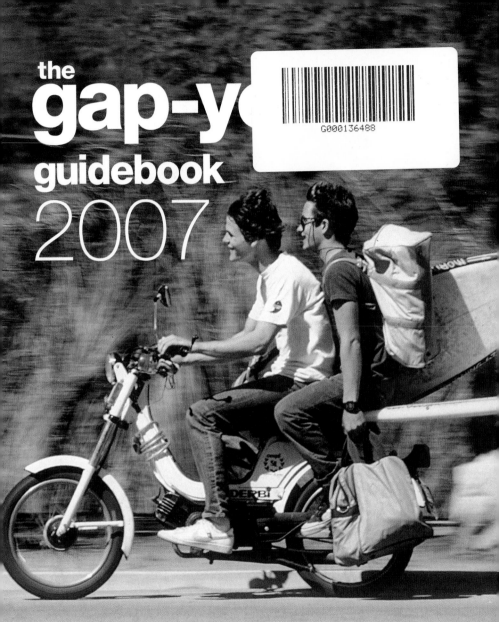

the gap-year guidebook 2007

Consultant Editor: Alison Withers
In-house Editor: Lizzy Bacon

John Catt Educational Ltd

Consultant Editor	Alison Withers
In-house Editor	Lizzy Bacon
Production Supervisor	Neil Rogers
Design Assistant, Illustrator	Scott James
Web Developer	Chris Woods
Advertising Sales	Nicola Coote
	Andrew Ducksbury
	Harriet Rayner
	Michael Ridley
Copy Clerk	Wendy Bosberry-Scott
Accounts Administrator	Sarah Green
Distribution	Ian Morphew
Director – General Manager	David Ahier
Information Director	Christine Evans
Publishing Director	Derek Bingham
Managing Director	Jonathan Evans

Published in 2007 by John Catt Educational Ltd,
Great Glemham, Saxmundham, Suffolk IP17 2DH, UK
Tel: 01728 663666   Fax: 01728 663415
E–mail: info@gap-year.com   Website: www.gap-year.com

First published by Peridot Press in 1992; Fifteenth edition 2007
© 2007 John Catt Educational Ltd

British Library Cataloguing in Publication Data.

ISBN: 1 904724 34 5
      978 1 904724 34 6

Designed and typeset by John Catt Educational Limited, Great Glemham, Saxmundham, Suffolk IP17 2DH.

Printed and bound in Great Britain by MPG Impressions Ltd, The Gresham Press, Old Woking, Surrey GU22 9LH

contents

Prepare for take-off!

Your gap-year abroad

contents... continued

Your gap-year in the UK

Preface

WE live on a beautiful planet of amazing abundance and variety – but it's also a very messed-up world.

It would be foolish to pretend since 9/11, and more particularly since the Iraq war, that the world isn't becoming a pretty unstable place.

In 2005 as the last edition of the **gap-**year guidebook was being prepared, Live8 had forced third world debt poverty into the spotlight. A year on and the Independent, August 14, 2006, reported that Africa had become the top destination for volunteer gappers.

It seems hardly a day has gone by since then without another horrible statistic on global warming, or news of another outbreak of strife or breakdown in negotiations in places where there was tension already.

Violence escalates in Iraq and Afghanistan and there have been bombings in London and Mumbai. At the time of writing near-war had broken out between Israel and Lebanon's Hizbollah, peace talks had broken down in Sri Lanka bringing back strife and bombings - and a tsunami had hit Indonesia.

Yet still the number of people who take time out to do something far outside their normal lives continues to grow. Is it because the powerless, no matter whether it is the environment, animals or people, are the ones most damaged by all this, and that touches a nerve in most of us, whatever our age or circumstances? Exasperation at the slow pace of political change? A feeling that time's running out if you want to explore the world's glorious diversity?

A **gap-** can be whatever you want it to be: a chance to go and see, to test yourself, your stamina, your organisational skills, to do something meaningful, give something back, take a break from the rat race, add an extra dimension to the CV or even change career direction.

However you choose to spend it, a **gap-** is a guaranteed life-changing experience, a chance to learn, grow and clear out the cobwebs.

Sounds good? Then this guidebook is for you or anyone in your family, who is considering a **gap-.**

You'll find sections covering work, study or volunteering – in the UK or abroad, plus general chapters on travel and on staying safe, on special issues for mature gappers to consider and, this year, a new chapter on handling your return to complete the picture.

If you're thinking of taking time out, whatever your age, you can use the **gap-**year guidebook to sort through the possible options and find contacts for organisations that can help make it real.

contents... continued

Back to earth

Appendices

Appendix 1

Appendix 2

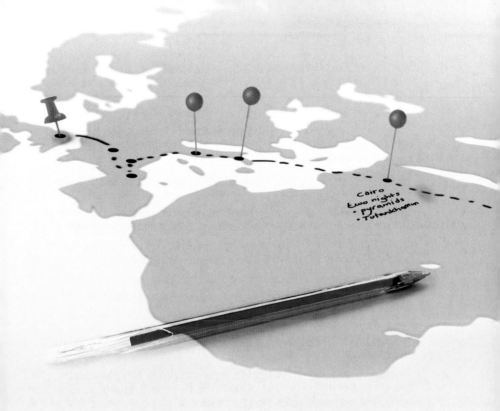

Introduction

Any time you take time out from the normal pattern of your life to do something completely different –
that's a gap-

Mariel's 18, lives in Canada, and has decided to take a break after her first year at Uni to go travelling. She's been keeping us up to date with her money-raising activities and gap- preparations on www.gap-year.com.

"I'm an eighteen year old girl with dreams of seeing the world and conquering it. I want to climb the highest mountains and sail through the trees of the rainforest.

"For years, I've left all of this to daytime fantasy, mostly during classes, labs and lectures.

"Now it is all that I can ever feel my heart would be satisfied in doing, and all that I can consciously pursue to make a life worthwhile for myself.

"There is nothing here that I am trying to escape and I know I will miss my home as I journey through the places I've only ever imagined."

Mariel's currently working at two jobs and living independently – already learning a lot about organising time, budgeting and preparing for a **gap-**year:

"Trust me, this is DEFINITELY not my idea of a great work situation, but hey, money is money when you are planning one of these gap year adventures.

"That being said and understood I'm in no position to turn away anything that will further me on my trek. "Due to this flaw in my present situation I am now a part time sales clerk, a master of price-gun use and cash register trickery, and to be completely honest, I hate it."

"Even though I'm just beginning this process of getting things in order to go, everything is snowballing on me already. I've just sent off my Working Holiday in New Zealand application, I've got another job interview lined up later in the week, and I've got to notify my boss that I'm leaving. I haven't even gotten my first paycheck there yet! Can you hear the resounding echo of my fearful "What was I thinking!"?

"Costs are coming forward already, my main application fee, so far, is $120 Canadian. Then there is the $4200.00 that I need to have saved to be eligible for acceptance (it goes to your cost of living while in NZ), and the guarantee that I can support the cost of a plane ticket home throughout the entire process. That, ladies and gents, is an additional $1800-$2000."

"Please tell me I'm just dreaming… this is going to be tough. Goodbye shopaholic tendencies, hello sales racks, coupon cutting and diy. "

Introduction

Taking a **gap-**year is a whole new world - this guide book helps prepare you for take-off, but also this year you'll find a new chapter, 'Re-entry', on how to cope when you get back.

So who goes on a gap-year?

Anybody and everybody, people from all walks of life. A **gap-**year doesn't have to cost a fortune, and there are ways to make your year out pay for itself.

Teenagers, mid-career 30-somethings, early retirers, mums and children, even whole families have shared their experiences with us at www.**gap-**year.com.

And do you know what? Whatever they've done they all say it has been a life-changing experience.

What is it?

Time out of the normal routine to do something different, challenging, fulfilling, memorable – that's a **gap-**.

Why take a gap-?

Time out before further study? A break from the daily work routine? A memorable experience? To give something back? To learn something new? Tick all that apply!!

For whatever reason you decide to take your year out, no one should think a **gap-**year is an easy option. You can use this guidebook to help you organise your thoughts, your options and then take the steps to make them real.

When should you go?

Traditionally **gap-**years have been taken after A levels, and provided a welcome and deserved rest from the hard slog of study and the anxiety of exams, exam results and applying for university places.

Most universities (not necessarily all) think **gap-**years are great because gappers come to them fresher, wiser, more mature, and able to cope with looking after themselves not to mention being less jaded about more studying.

However, some universities, especially if you're applying to a very popular course, don't welcome **gap-**years. So some students opt to take a year out after graduating before getting a 'proper' job. These gappers can take a year out secure in the knowledge that their studies are over, their degree is in the bag and now they have a chance to cut free before a career and adult responsibilities take over.

visit: www.gap-year.com

Older gappers taking a career break will have different reasons and choices, depending on such things as where they are in life, where any children they have are at in school or whether their employer encourages career breaks and has schemes in place to help employees. There's more on all this in our chapter on career breaks and mature travellers.

You're going where? To do what?.......

If you're going to make the most of a **gap-**, whatever you want from it, then you need to make sure you do end up doing something that you find exciting, fun and challenging.

This may mean travelling to Thailand, helping with conservation work in Scotland or learning to snowboard. With a whole year ahead of you, you could even manage all three if you wanted. The point is to do what you think is right (don't just follow your friends to the nearest beach), something that gives you a sense of achievement.

One good tip for the early stages of making a plan is to cut out and keep anything you find in magazines, brochures or newspapers that appeals to you – an article, a picture, an activity – and to make a note of anything you find interesting on the internet.

These will help you gradually build up a picture of where you want to go and what you might want to do.

They will also help you decide what you want from your **gap-**year: do you

want relevant work experience? Something that relates to your course at uni? To study/learn something new? Or an adventure that would be a completely different experience from any of the things you might normally do? From this you can draw up a rough plan, start searching for organisations that can help you. The **gap-**year guidebook and website are good places for this as well as for ideas of what you can do – and to get an idea of how much it will cost.

How to get the most out of your gap-year

Your cuttings and notes have helped you decide what you want from your **gap-**year, where you might go and you have a rough plan. Maybe you've narrowed down the organisations that can help you and have some idea of the costs.

Now you're at the stage of nailing down the details. The trick to having a good **gap-**year is to get the organisation sorted.

That doesn't mean you can't be spontaneous, but it would be a real let-down if you got to the border of Nepal and found you hadn't got the right visa to get in! Or, while you're in Australia, you get the chance of a great job working with a local TV company but they can't take you on because you couldn't be bothered to get a work permit sorted before you left the UK.

Your **gap-** has already started........and it's months before you'll get on that plane. Organising your **gap-**year is an opportunity to look forward to the exciting 12 months to come – and as you're doing it you might come across new things that help you refine your plans.

14

It's inevitably going to be a busy time, organising stuff at home, storing possessions, letting a house or flat if you own one, arranging finance and perhaps doing some fund raising or extra work.

It may sound like a recipe for stress but putting in the extra effort truly is all worth it once you're on the road - and you can use it to demonstrate organising ability on your CV when you get back.

How do you pay for it?

It depends on what you want to do, your interests, age, skills and qualifications.

For younger gappers the options range from voluntary work, maybe after working and saving money for part of their **gap**-year, to paid work using existing skills, for example teaching English or working as an au pair, to adding to skills and qualifications by doing an internship or perhaps doing a sports or sailing course.

Some people work for a while to raise money for, say, a three-month activity, then come back to earn some more so they can go off again and do something different.

For career break gappers who already have professional skills to offer, the United Nations Volunteer Programme is a good place to start looking at the options.

UNV has links to local charities, NGOs (Non Governmental Organisations) and projects in countries all over the world. Some will be looking for people willing to work with them for living expenses, others will be looking for volunteers.

See our chapter (p.77) for career breakers for contact links.

the gap-year guidebook 2007

Is a gap-year safe?

There is no denying the world has become a less stable place in recent years.

Bombs targeted in urban areas have included London and Mumbai so it's no longer necessarily true that it's safer to stay at home.

However, in some parts of the world terrorists have targeted places known to be frequented by First World travellers, so you should always check with the Foreign Office whether a country is safe to travel to and if there are any areas you should avoid.

Although traffic accidents, random acts of God and the weather can happen anywhere, we're not saying you shouldn't take your personal safety seriously – it should always be your number one priority.

You should not put yourself in danger by agreeing to anything about which you have misgivings because you don't want to risk someone thinking that you're stupid or scared. There's one rule: If in doubt – don't.

We highly recommend that you take a gappers' safety course before you go. It's not as dull as it sounds – the companies we know about (see page 60) have staff who are ex-SAS! How cool is that? They will teach you how to recognise danger (from people as well as natural disasters), and how to look after yourself in a bad situation – it could be the thing that saves your life.

While political and environmental instability shouldn't stop you from taking a **gap-**year they may influence where you choose to go and there's plenty of information in this guidebook for things you can do closer to home if you prefer.

We would say that as long as you have done all you can to be well prepared with travelling essentials and knowledge, then go for it!

Whoever heard of a totally safe adventure?

Editor's note

Thanks to Reeds, HBOS, BT, Minesh Tanna, Chetal Patel, MondoChallenge and others for their contributions and help and to all those gappers who shared their stories and pictures, their experience and their wisdom – and generally kept the ed from nervous breakdown.

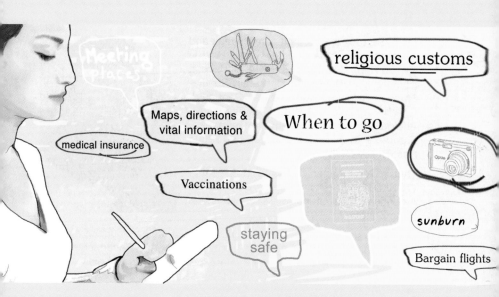

Chapter 1

Tips for travellers

Mich, 34, took a 20-month career break and went off around the world covering: Prague (Czech Rep), UAE-Dubai & INDIA, Budapest, (Hungary); EUROPE incl. inter-rail: Spain - France - Belgium - Netherlands - Germany - Czech Republic - Austria - Switzerland - Austria - Hungary - Austria - Germany - France – Spain (Jul 2005 - Sep 2005 Rest/Break in UK).

Then Copenhagen (Denmark) - Mini-WORLDTOUR (Oct 2005 - Jun 2006): Argentina, Chile, Uruguay, US, Japan, Hong Kong & India.

During his **gap-** he: "Lived a little again, without the handcuffs of the 9am - 5pm (which in London is now in reality 8am - 8pm) - Reconnected with friends & family around the world and experienced more of places that I love - discovered new places I had never seen and did things that I had never done."

He'd been back two months and at first found it all: "Overwhelming! The intensity of London hit all at once ... the old world of 'home' had changed: those I had left behind had moved on in their lives ... as had I ... but to varying degree & direction ... A lot to take in all at once!

"... then the latent frustration generated from delayed tubes & trains, need for money & pace of life surfaced ... deep breaths needed!..."

He'd left his job in the corporate world with a global communications technology company and gone travelling with no clear plans for his return.

Here's what he learned: "Life can be as simple or as complicated as you make it! ... the last 20 months plus has also reinforced my feeling that you don't need much to be happy, but money helps ... though an open mind & open heart helps more! ... relationships & time are the most valuable commodities."

And now? "Short-term: Corporate prostitution – work to rebuild the bank balances for the next 12 – 18 months while I find my feet back in the UK. Medium-term: Build my own business using my skill-set & experiences in a place like Edinburgh perhaps, i.e. a city that is smaller & more relaxed than London - perhaps a cafe or guesthouse, places of social interaction where I can put to use my interest in food, travel & culture, design, art, photography, film & music...and much more... Something that's mine, not working for 'the Man', my own blank canvas to do what I may... Longer-term: Would love to have something set up in India, Argentina & somewhere in mainland Europe"

Right now he's pursuing his short-term plan back with his former company as a "Synergy Manager".

This section covers travel in general. No matter whether you're planning to join specific projects or travel independently, if you do the basic preparation in advance you should have a problem-free trip. We have lots of practical advice for those who haven't been on long trips abroad before, covering everything from taking care of essential documents and planning what to pack to how to stay safe in-country and avoid offending local sensibilities.

You'll find information on useful internet sites – take a look at www.**gap-yearshop.com** at the back of the book for kit and accessories you might need to take with you.

The next chapter lists travel companies and you'll find useful information about individual countries, including embassy phone numbers in Appendix 2: Country info.

Getting organised

Leave someone in charge at home

Make sure you have someone reliable and trustworthy in charge of sorting things out for you – especially the official stuff that won't wait. Get someone you really trust to open your post and arrange to talk to them at regular intervals in case something turns up that you need to deal with. But some things you just have to do yourself, so make sure you've done everything important before you go and won't need to sign or apply for anything crucial while you're away.

Know where you're going

The more you know about your destination, the easier your trip will be: India, for example, is unbearably hot in April and May. It's also worth finding out when special events are on. It would be a shame to turn up in Hong Kong for example and have just missed the annual Dragon Boat race.

Check out **http://www.whatsonwhen.com** - It's a great site, which lists all sorts of events around the world.

Before visiting any country that has recently been politically volatile or could turn into a war zone check with the FCO for the current situation (Tel: 0870 606 0290 / **www.fco.gov.uk**) for up-to-date information.

Identity crisis

If you do need to get yourself a passport for the first time, application forms are available from Post Offices. A standard adult ten-year passport costs £51 and you'll need your birth certificate and passport photos. It should take no more than a month from the time you apply to the time you receive your passport, although it's sensible to allow some leeway.

You can send the form direct to the Passport Office or use their 'Check and Send' service at one of the 2300 Post Offices and Worldchoice travel agents throughout the UK. The 'Check and Send' service gets your application checked for completeness (including documentation and fee) and given priority by the UK Passport Services (UKPS) – they are usually able to process these applications in two weeks.

If your passport application is urgent you can use the guaranteed same-day (Premium) service or the guaranteed one-week (Fast Track) service. Both services are only available by appointment (phone the UKPS Adviceline on +44 (0) 870 521 0410), and both are expensive (£96.50 for Premium, £77.50 for Fast Track). The Premium service is only available for renewals and amendments.

This may seem complicated, but the UKPS website, **www.ukps.gov.uk**, is very helpful. It's a good idea to leave a complete photocopy of your passport at home before you go travelling and also to keep a photocopy with you, including any pages with visa stamps – this can make a lost or stolen passport much easier to cope with.

Passport Agency Globe House, 89 Eccleston Square
London SW1V 1PN, UK
Tel: +44 (0) 870 521 0410
www.ukps.gov.uk

It can be useful to join the International Youth Hostels Association (YHA). They run over 4,500 hostels in 60 countries offering reasonably priced accommodation. The basic YHA membership for an individual is £15.95, but there are several alternatives – from £9.95 for a year's membership for under 26-year-olds to £22.95 for a joint family membership. You can join online, by phone or by post and membership applications are only accepted from an address within Europe. Non EU residents can buy membership at a hostel in their home country or take out international membership on arrival at a hostel. Remember that a year's membership is valid only from the date of issue and cannot be post-dated.

YHA Trevelyan House, Dimple Road, Matlock, Derbyshire DE4 3YH, UK
(England & Wales) Tel: +44 (0) 1629 592600
Fax: +44 (0) 1629 592702
www.yha.org.uk

An ISIC (International Student Identity Card – **www.isiccard.com**) costs £7 (valid for 15 months from September to the following December). Simply pick up the application form from your local Students' Union, Student Travel Office, college or school. You can also download an application from the ISIC website.

The ISIC card identifies you as a student and entitles you to over 900 student discounts in the UK alone.

Discounts include everything from museum entrance and restaurant bills to flights and international phone calls. You also get access to a 24-hour ISIC travel helpline. You qualify for an ISIC if you are in full-time education (15 hours per week, 26 weeks per year). If you are on a **gap**-year and have a confirmed place in higher education you are eligible for a card in the calendar year in which you are due to start your higher education place. If you don't qualify for an ISIC, then the IYTC (International Youth Travel Card, £7) is valid for a year and offers similar discounts to anyone under 26, and is available from the same places as an ISIC.

Planning the route

Do you feel lured to a particular area? Latin America? Scandinavia?... or to a particular climate? Snow? Monsoon?... or to unexplored territory? Mongolia via the Trans-Siberian Express?... what about a particular purpose? Surfing? Learning a language?... or all these ingredients, wrapped up in one journey? You need to get a framework clear in your mind – or let a cheap round-the-world ticket decide the framework for you. Bear in mind that it's safer to travel with someone you know and having contacts lined up along the route is a big help.

The more remote a place is, the more useful it is to have company. If you have six months or so to spare, you can arrange travel that takes you all the way round the world, although you may find it interesting to spend more than half your time in one region, like Africa or the USA.

Following the herd

There are well-trodden backpacking routes: through south-east Asia and Australia; across Russia to China and Hong Kong by rail; from the USA to central America; or through Spain and Africa and back to the UK. You may feel that following the same routes everyone else is taking is boring – but there's probably a reason that they've become popular over recent years – they're interesting, exciting and varied.

If you want to be more explorer than follower of fashion, then why not try countries that have recently opened up to foreign visitors, such as Cambodia, – though they tend to charge a lot for visas (check visa costs through a travel agent, who may be able to arrange it for you).

Obviously avoid danger zones and check with contacts who know a country, as well as the Foreign Office (**www.fco.gov.uk**). The political situation around the world as we go to press is serious stuff and can't be ignored. The point of your **gap**-year travels is to have fun, experience different cultures, meet new people – not to end up in the middle of a war zone with your life in danger. The Foreign Office updates its danger list regularly as new areas of unrest emerge, but it's not, and never can be, a failsafe.

Two particularly useful sections on the FCO website are "know before you go" and the travellers' checklist.

Travel guides

The Rough Guide and Lonely Planet books are probably the best-known guides and are excellent, as are the Footprint and Thomas Cook guides. Whatever your interests, these books will give you relevant information about the places you are going to – as well as copious information on towns, travel routes and budget hotels in the countries they cover. They are all updated regularly but bear in mind the time it takes to gather, write and print the information. It's possible some details will have changed when you get where you are going.

Religious customs, behaviour and dress codes

Men and women should dress modestly in Muslim countries. Women in particular should wear long sleeves and cover their legs. Uncovered flesh, especially female, offends Islam.

In most Asian and African countries don't wear a bikini top and shorts in city streets if you don't want to attract the wrong kind of intrusive male attention. In any case an all-over light cotton covering will better protect you from sunburn and insect bites.

Similarly in Buddhist countries the head is sacred and so it is unconventional to touch it.

Before entering temples and mosques throughout India and S Asia, you must remove your shoes. There are usually places at the entrances where you can leave them with attendants to look after them. Usually women are also expected to cover their hair – and in Jain temples wearing or carrying anything made of leather is also forbidden.

Even in Europe you'd be expected to cover your head, and be dressed respectfully if you go into a church. Each culture or religion has its own holy 'laws' and codes of behaviour.

Open gestures of affection, kissing or even holding hands between married couples can be shocking to some cultures. This is particularly true of India, though it seems to be relaxing a little in the cities. However, you will often see men or boys strolling around hand in hand or with arms around each other's shoulders in India – don't misinterpret: they are friends, NOT gay couples!!

Sitting cross-legged with the soles of your feet pointing towards companions is another example of a habit regarded as bad manners or even insulting in some places and actually if you think about it it's pretty logical if you're in a place where people walk around less than clean streets either barefoot or in sandals.

It's worth remembering that in most places – even the so-called First World – rural communities are usually far more traditional and straight-laced than city ones and casual Anglo-Saxon dress codes and habits can offend.

If you don't want to find yourself in real trouble do some research first.

Insurance

Your insurance needs to be fixed before you go, but it's a far from simple matter. The range of policies is vast – and they all cover different things. The basic things to check if an insurance policy covers are: medical, legal, passport loss, ticket loss, cash loss, luggage, cancellation, missed flights, working abroad, hazardous sports, medical conditions. Also see if they provide a 24-hour helpline.

It is important to make sure that you are covered for the activities you are likely to take part in. Be aware that companies may make a distinction between doing a hazardous sport once (e.g. going skiing during your brief trip to the Stubai Glacier) and spending your whole time doing them (e.g. six months intensive skiing in the Rockies). Some insurance policies also have age limits.

Some banks provide cover for holidays paid for using their credit cards, but their policies may not include all the essentials. Banks also offer blanket travel insurance (medical, personal accident, third party liability, theft, loss, cancellation, delay and more). You may be able to get reductions if you have an account with the relevant bank or buy foreign currency through it. Beware of 'free' insurance provided with your ticket. 'Free' can mean 'not very useful'.

Medical insurance

If you're going to Europe you can get a European Health Insurance Card (EHIC), which allows for free or reduced cost medical treatment within Europe should you need it. You can apply online on:

http://www.dh.gov.uk/PolicyAndGuidance/HealthAdviceForTravellers/fs/en

Your card is valid for three to five years and should be delivered in seven days.

Or you can telephone EHIC applications, Newcastle on Tyne, on 0845 606 2030. The EHIC card only covers treatment under the state scheme in all EU countries, plus Denmark, Iceland, Liechtenstein, Norway and Switzerland. You can also pick up application forms at your post office.

Countries with no health care agreements with the UK include Canada, the USA, India, most of the Far East, the whole of Africa and Latin America.

Wherever it happens, a serious illness, broken limb or injury you cause someone else can be very expensive.

Medical insurance is usually part of an all-in travel policy. Costs vary widely by company, destination, activity and level of cover. Make sure you have generous cover for injury or disablement, know what you're covered for and when you've got the policy read the small print carefully (for example, does it cover transport home if you need an emergency operation that cannot be carried out safely abroad?).

Some policies won't cover high risk activities like skiing, snowboarding, bungee jumping, etc. so you'll need to get extra specific cover. If you have a condition that is likely to recur, you may have to declare this when you buy the insurance. Also, check whether the policy covers you for the medical costs if the condition does recur.

Already covered?

If you're going abroad on a voluntary work assignment you may find that the organisation arranging it wants you to take a specified insurance policy as part of the total cost. You may also find you have a 'clash of policies' before you even start looking for the right policy. For example, if your family has already booked you a one-year multi-travel insurance policy to cover travel with the family at other times of the year, you may find you are already covered for loss of life, limb loss, permanent disablement, some medical expenses, theft and so on. These multi-trip policies can be basic as well as quite cheap, so it's essential to check the small print of what the policy covers.

You could find you need extra cover if you'll be doing sports or anything dangerous. In this case you can start by finding out (through the broker or agent who sold you the policy) if any additional cover can be tacked on to your existing policy, though this can be expensive and most off-the-shelf policies won't do it.

Try to find a policy that doesn't already duplicate what is covered by an existing policy (they don't pay out twice), but some duplication is unavoidable and it's obviously better to be covered twice than not at all.

Making a claim

Read through the small print carefully before you travel and make sure you know what to do if you need to make a claim – most policies will insist that you report a crime to the police (often within a certain time period) and send in the police report with your insurance claim. What you don't want to happen is to have a claim dismissed because you don't have the right paperwork to back it up.

Insurers are unlikely to trip over themselves to pay you money and many travel policies impose conditions which are virtually impossible to meet.

For example, some policies demand that you report not only theft of items but also loss of items. Fine, but the police are likely to be pretty reluctant to write a crime report because you think you may have accidentally left your camera in the loo! The Foreign Office website, **www.fco.gov.uk/travel**, has a good page about insurance and is worth checking out for advice and links.

27

Who to choose?

Since travel agents were banned from making you buy their favourite insurance policy as part of a travel package, there has been intense competition between insurance companies. There are now several insurers offering tailor-made insurance policies for **gap**-year students.

Companies offering gap-year insurance

24Dr Travel
Great Strudgates Farm,
Ralcombe, West Sussex RH17 6RB

www.24drtravel.com
Tel: +44 (0) 1444 811 700
Fax: +44 ((0) 1444 811 900
Email: Insurance@24drtravel.com

£156.33, 12 months, Australia/New Zealand. £217.97, 12 months, USA/Canada (Wintersports available). £97.80, 12 months in Europe.

ACE European Group Ltd
Customer Services, Ashdown House,
125 High Street
Crawley, West Sussex RH10 1DQ

www.gapyeartravel.com
Tel: +44 (0) 1293 726 225

Email: ace.traveluk@ace-ina.com

Boots Insurance
www.bootsinsurance.com
Tel: +44 (0) 845 840 2020

Either buy online, by phone or by visiting larger Boots stores. Website has area dedicated to Gap Year and offers policies from 3 to 12 months.

Dogtag Ltd
6 Magellan Terrace, Gatwick Road,
Crawley, Surrey RH10 9PJ
www.dogtag.co.uk
Tel: +44 (0) 8700 364 824

Email: enquiries@dogtag.co.uk

Downunder Worldwide Travel Insurance
Downunder Insurance Services Ltd,
PO Box 55605, Paddington
London W9 3UW
www.duinsure.com

Tel: +44 (0) 800 393 908
Fax: +44 (0) 207 402 9272
Email: info@duinsure.com

Save up to 60% on High St prices plus a further 10% discount if you book online. Comprehensive travel insurance for the adventurous traveller. Working holidays covered, plus over 80 adventurous sports or activities. Medical Emergency and money back guarantee. All their operators are seasoned travellers, so book with the experts on freephone 0800 393908 or check out their website at www.duinsure.com. They are a 'know before you go' preferred supplier to the backpacker market.

Endsleigh Insurance Services Ltd
Endsleigh Park, Shurdington Road,
Cheltenham Spa, Gloucestershire GL51 4UE
www.endsleigh.co.uk
Tel: +44 (0) 800 028 3571

Have backpackers and gap year insurance policies.

Flexicover Direct
109 Elmers End Road,
Beckenham, Kent BR3 4SY
www.flexicover.com
Tel: 0870 990 9292
Fax: 0870 990 9298
Email: info@flexicover.com

Gap Year travel insurance for the 18-45s. Europe, Aus/NZ & worldwide cover including medical, cancellation and optional baggage cover plus working holidays and a host of sporting activities.

Go Travel Insurance
West Wing, Miles Gray Road,
Basildon, Essex SS14 3GD
www.gotravelinsurance.co.uk/
Tel: +44 (0) 870 421 1521

Email: enquiries@gotravelinsurance.co.uk

Go Travel Insurance offers a flexible backpacker policy.

Insure and Go
Maitland House, Warrior Square,
Southend on Sea, Essex SS1 2AA
www.insureandgo.com
Tel: 0870 901 3674

Email: information@insureandgo.com

29

Great value gap year travel insurance from specialist provider Insure and Go, for trips from 31 days to 18 months. Visit www.insureandgo.com or call 0870 901 3674.

MRL Group Ltd
Enterprise House, Station Parade,
Chipstead, Surrey CR5 3TE

www.mrlinsurance.co.uk
Tel: 00 353 91 745 890

Offers Gap Year polices of between 4 and 12 months to people under the age of 35.

Navigator Travel Insurance Services Ltd
19 Ralli Courts, West Riverside,
Manchester, Lancashire M3 5FT

www.navigatortravel.co.uk
Tel: +44 (0) 161 973 6435
Fax: +44 (0) 161 973 6418
Email: enquiries@navigatortravel.co.uk

£100, 6 months worldwide budget policy; £140, 6 months worldwide gold policy; £179, 12 months worldwide budget policy; £265, 12 months worldwide gold policy. Navigator Travel Insurance offers specialist policies for long-stay overseas trips, with an emphasis on covering adventure sports. These policies also cover casual working. Cover is available up to 18 months, with no excesses on a gold policy of

6 months duration or longer. Though there are cheaper policies around, these features make the Gold policy an ideal cover for a gap year trip, as many of the lower priced policies do not offer cover for these activities.

Options Travel Insurance
Lumbry Park, Selborne Road,
Alton, Hampshire GU34 3HF

www.optionsinsurance.co.uk
Tel: +44 (0) 870 876 7878
Fax: +44 (0) 1420 566 321
Email: optionswebsite@inter-group.co.uk

They offer cover for backpackers aged 39 years and under for trips of between 4 and 12 months. Cover from £30.

Planet Travel Insurance
PO Box 3798,
Westbury, Wiltshire BA13 4WY

www.planet-travel.uk.com
Tel: +44 (0) 845 458 4587

Email: mail@planet-travel.uk.com

Offers backpacker cover for gappers aged under 39.

Round the World Insurance
Travel Nation
The Courtyard, 61 Western Road, Hove
East Sussex BN3 1JD

www.roundtheworldinsurance.co.uk
Tel: +44 (0) 845 3444 225
Fax: +44 (0) 845 3444 226

This is specialist travel insurance designed for people on round-the-world or multi-stop trips. We offer an excellent cover, premiums and claims handling service. The people at the end of the 24/7 medical emergency hot-line are an outfit called Specialty Assistance. In addition to a world-wide control centre in London, Specialty Assistance operates through three centres in the USA, South Africa and Thailand. Specialty Assistance boasts a worldwide network of over 150 agents and 500 correspondents who are able to provide on-the-spot assistance and reassurance.

Snowcard Insurance Services Limited
Lower Boddington,
Daventry, Northamptonshire NN11 6XZ

www.snowcard.co.uk
Tel: +44 (0)1327 262805

Email: assistance@snowcard.co.uk

Travel & Activity insurance including long stays up to 18 months. Activcard Backpacker. Activcard Explorer.

Worldwide Travel Insurance Services Ltd
The Business Centre,
1-7 Commercial Road, Paddock Wood
Tonbridge, Kent TN12 6YT

www.worldwideinsure.com
Tel: +44 (0) 870 428 6500

Email: customerservices@worldwideinsure.com

What to take

Start thinking early about what to take with you and write a list – adding to it every time you think of something. Then sit down and rationalise – cross off everything you don't really need. Pack the essentials and enough clothes to see you through – about five changes of clothing should last you for months if

31

Here are one former gapper's 20 tips for packing!

A side-opening backpack is easier than a top-opening one

Put all the clothes you think you'll need on the bed then halve the pile!!

Pack in reverse order – first in, last out

Heavy stuff goes at the bottom

Pack in categories in plastic bags – easier to find stuff

Use vacuum pack bags for bulky items

Ziplock bags are good for undies and bits and pieces

Store toilet rolls and dirty undies in side pockets – easy for thieves to open and they won't want them!

Take a small, separate backpack for day hikes etc. You can buy small, thin folding ones

Keep spares (undies, toothbrush, water bottle, important numbers and documents) in hand luggage

Take a sleeping bag liner – useful in hostels

Take a sarong (versatile: can be a bedsheet, towel, purse, bag)

Camping towels are lightweight and dry fast

Take a first aid kit

Remove packaging from everything but keep printed instructions for medications

Shaving oil takes less space than cream. Put liquids in squashy bottles

You can never have too many baby wipes or rolls of gaffer tape!

Fill shoes, cups etc with socks and undies to save space

Tie up loose backpack straps before it goes into transit

Take a good pocket guidebook, camera, and a notebook to write in.

you choose carefully. Don't take anything that doesn't go with everything else and stick to materials that are comfortable, hard-wearing, easy to wash and dry and don't crease too much. Make sure you have clothes that are suitable for the climates you are visiting. And relax – you can't prepare for every eventuality if you're living out of a rucksack. The best way to know what you need is to ask someone who's already been what they took, what they didn't need and what they wished they had taken.

And remember most places have cheap markets, not to mention interesting local clothes, so you can always top up or replace clothes while you are travelling.

Adventure Centre
240 Manchester Road,
Warrington, Cheshire WA1 3BE

www.cheaptents.com
Tel: +44 (0) 1925 411 385
Fax: +44 (0) 161 927 7718
Email: tents@cheaptents.com

Unless you're going trekking you won't need anything too flash: the maps in guidebooks are usually pretty good. A good pocket business diary can be very useful – one that gives international dialling codes, time differences, local currency details, bank opening hours, public holidays and other information.

Take a list with you of essential information like directions to voluntary work postings, key addresses, medical information, credit card numbers (try to disguise these in case everything gets stolen), passport details, contact numbers in case of loss of travellers cheques and insurance and flight details – and leave a copy with someone at home as well.

Another way of keeping safe copies of your vital documents (even if everything you have is lost or stolen) is to scan them before you leave and email them as attachments to your internet-based email address.

Tickets and money

Leave photocopies of serial numbers of tickets, passports and credit cards at home. It's also worth keeping copies on you, separate from the rest of your valuables, and one travellers cheque separate from the others (useful if all the rest get stolen). Waist money pouches worn under clothes are really good.

Take widely-accepted travellers cheques like those issued by big international banks – but don't make the mistake of taking American Express travellers cheques to Cuba or any other country on less than friendly terms with the US – and don't carry much cash. Cheques in pounds sterling are widely accepted, but US dollars more so. You should also record the numbers of the travellers cheques that you spend, as it helps if you need to replace lost or stolen ones.

It can help to arrive with some local currency in notes and coins. You can often change travellers cheques in banks at airport arrivals halls. Be careful at foreign exchange shops or kiosks: they often charge extortionate commissions or make the equivalent amount of money on very wide exchange rates.

Credit cards

Essential back-up. Both Visa and Mastercard are useful for getting local currency cash advances, sometimes from a cash dispenser, at banks abroad.

You can then use the cash to buy more travellers cheques – safer than walking around with suitcases of money. If you're using your credit card to get money over the counter then you're likely to need some form of ID (e.g. passport). The problem with a credit card is losing it or having it stolen – keep a note of the numbers and how to report the loss of the card.

If you are paying for goods or restaurant meals by using your card you should insist on signing bills/receipts in your presence and not allow the card to be taken out of your sight. This way you'll have no unpleasant surprises or mysterious purchases when you see your card statement.

33

Wiring money

If all else fails and you find yourself stranded with no cash, no travellers cheques and no credit cards, then having money wired to you could be a lifesaver. Two major companies offer this service: MoneyGram (**www.moneygram.com**) and Western Union (**www.westernunion.com**). Both have vast numbers of branches worldwide – MoneyGram has 55,000 in 155 countries and Western Union has 140,000 in 185 countries.

The service allows a friend or relative to transfer money to you almost instantaneously. Once you have persuaded your 'guardian angel' to send you the money, all they have to do is go to the nearest MoneyGram or Western Union, fill in a form and hand over the money (in cash). It is then transferred to the company's branch nearest to you, where you in turn fill in a form and pick it up. Both you and the person sending the money will need ID, and you may be asked security questions.

Where to buy your kit

Some overseas voluntary organisations (such as SPW) arrange for their students to have discounts at specific shops, like the YHA. The best advice on equipment usually comes from specialist shops, although they may not be the cheapest: these include YHA shops, Blacks, Millets and Camping and Outdoors Centres. Take a look at www.**gap-**yearshop.com for a specialist selling over the internet.

Rucksacks

Advice from students who have collapsed under the weight of 65- to 70-litre rucksacks: think carefully before buying so big. There is no need to look like a walking sack of coal, sweating under the weight of bottles of shampoo that will take two months to use. Thailand does have shampoo. For hot countries a 30- to 35-litre rucksack (excluding sleeping bag) is usually big enough. In cold countries you are obviously going to need a bigger rucksack, but you can keep bags light by packing clothes made of special lightweight fabrics.

Try not to set off with a totally full bag – you're bound to buy stuff along the way and you don't want to be trekking across the world with a handful of plastic bags. If you really can't resist and end up buying too many souvenirs to carry you can always post them home, but be warned: postage is expensive, so that 'cheap' souvenir could end up costing more than you bargained for. You could always start off with a bigger bag, but remember, the longer you walk the heavier it gets.

Really useful are rucksacks that take a sleeping bag at the bottom and open laterally like suitcases so you don't have to pull out all your worldly possessions just to find a pair of socks. You might want to go for one with zips and tiny padlocks for security, but remember that this doesn't give real protection, as a determined thief will happily slash your bag open.

34

Prices for a well-stitched 65-litre rucksack can vary greatly. Remember, the most expensive is not necessarily the best – get what is most suitable for your trip.

You can get all sorts of trendy attachments such as 'an integral pocket for your hydration bladder' but don't hand over money for stuff you won't need. If you go to a good outdoor store, they should be able to advise you on exactly what you need for your particular trip. Most of these stores have websites with helpful hints and lists of 'essential' items. Best of all talk to someone who's been before and ask them what they wish they'd taken or left at home.

A must is an extra small day bag or rucksack to carry valuables and things you need in a hurry, as well as bottles of water, guidebooks, camera and so on.

You should be able to leave your rucksack in most hostels or guest houses if you are staying for more than a day (most thieves won't be interested in nicking your socks), or in a locker at the train station. ALWAYS take camera, passport, important papers and money with you everywhere, zipped up, preferably out of view.

Footwear

It's worth investing in something comfortable if you're heading off on a long trip. In hot countries, a good pair of sandals is the preferred footwear for many and there's a great range of sports sandals available. They might seem a bit pricey but a good strong pair will last and be comfortable. If you're going somewhere cheap, you could just pick up a pair out there, but you're likely to be doing a lot more walking than usual – even if you're only sightseeing – so comfort and durability are important.

Some people like chunky walking boots, others just their trainers, but it's best to get something that won't fall apart when you're halfway up Mount Kilimanjaro. Take more than one pair of comfortable shoes in case they don't last, but don't take too many – they'll be an unnecessary burden, and take up precious space in your rucksack.

Sleeping bags

First, are you sure you even need one? For hot countries you may just want to take a sheet sleeping bag (basically just a sewn-up sheet). If you do take a sleeping bag, think about what you'll be doing. The more active your holiday, the more you need a decent bag; go to a specialist shop where you can get good advice.

Take into account weight and size and the conditions you'll be travelling in – you might want to go for one of those dinky compression sacs that you can use to squash sleeping bags into. Sheet bags are useful, and you can usually rent down bags for treks in, say, Nepal – but don't assume you'll always be able to do this. For cold countries, you need bulky heat-retaining materials. If you're going to be doing a lot of sleeping outdoors, a roll-mat is probably a good idea too.

35

The main thing is that you can carry it and that you will be comfortable. No way are you going to have enough energy to look around art galleries, let alone trek through jungle or up mountains (however comfortable your shoes are), if you're not getting any sleep.

Prices vary hugely and you can sometimes find a four-season bag cheaper than a one-season bag – it's mostly down to quality: at the cheaper end expect to pay around £10 for a sheet bag; £30 for a one-season sleeping-bag (suitable to 5°C); £30-40 for a two-season sleeping-bag (suitable to 0°C); £45 for a three-season sleeping-bag (suitable to -5°C). You can pay more than two or three times as much for better gear.

First-aid kit

There is no need to take a whole chemist's shop with you. Ask your GP for advice, but useful basics are rehydration sachets (to use after diarrhoea); waterproof plasters; TCP; corn and blister plasters for sore feet; cotton buds; a small pair of straight nail scissors (not to be carried in your hand luggage on the plane); safety pins; insect repellent; antiseptic cream; anti-diarrhoea pills (only short term; they stop the diarrhoea temporarily but don't cure you); water sterilisation tablets; and anti-histamine cream.

You can get a medical pack from most chemists or travel shops, by mail order from MASTA (Tel: +44 (0) 113 238 7575; **www.masta.org**). Homeway (see www.**gap**-yearshop.com) also specialises in medical kits for travellers: the contents vary from sting relief, tick removers, blister kits, sun block and rehydration sachets to complete sterile medical packs with needles and syringe kits (in case you think the needle someone might have to inject you with may not be sterile).

You can also buy various types of mosquito net, water purification tablets and filters, money pouches, world receiver radios, travel irons and kettles. Not to mention a personal attack alarm. If you take too much kit though, you'll need a removal van to take it with you.

Handy items

The list of useful things to take varies from person to person, but the following are generally considered very helpful: string that can double as a washing line and is handy for putting up mosquito nets; a universal sink plug; a torch; and a padlock and chain to secure your rucksacks on long journeys and double lock hostel rooms.

There are mixed views about those security wire mesh covers you can buy for rucksacks. Some prefer a simple padlock and chain and say the security mesh covers are an open invitation to a thief armed with wire cutters since they imply you're carrying something valuable. Others say the point is that they're slash proof so useful as a short-term deterrent against thieves armed with a knife when you're doing something where you might be distracted – like making a phone call.

A penknife with different functions is also extremely useful. Remember that since 11 September 2001 sharp items have been banned from your hand luggage when travelling by plane. Hand-luggage restrictions have been changed again recently in response to perceived security threats, so make sure you check with your departure airport as close to when you're due to leave as possible for the current restrictions on bag size and what you can carry.

Airport security varies around the world. For example, outbound from Delhi international airport if you are carrying matches or cigarette lighters in pockets or hand luggage they will be confiscated.

Water purifying tablets are useful but won't deal with all the possible water-borne parasites – sometimes boiling water and adding iodine are also necessary. It's best to stick to bottled mineral water if available – even for brushing your teeth - but always check that the seal is intact before you buy. That way you will be sure it's not a bottle of mineral water refilled with the local dodgy supply.

Remember it's easy to get dehydrated in hot countries so you should always carry a bottle of water with you and drink frequently – up to 8 litres a day.

Masking tape has also been recommended to us as a vital piece of survival kit; apparently it's handy for mending slashed rucksacks, sealing ant nests, fixing doors, sticking up mosquito nets...

Cameras

Today's traveller has never been better served for recording their precious memories and sharing them with friends and relatives. With a digital camera, not only can you check every photograph you have taken by replaying them on the screen on the camera back, but you can also email your images back home via internet cafés which are springing up globally – even in the remotest of places you are likely to find one. Alternatively, internet service providers offer photo storage space where you can store or share your memories with others.

Digital cameras not only offer the advantage of being able to send your photographs home in a quick and convenient way but many cameras accept high capacity memory cards that can hold several hundred photographs. And don't forget that being able to view each photograph on your camera's screen means that you can delete the dud photographs and reuse the space on the memory card. It's advisable to carry a fully charged spare battery and ensure that you can recharge your camera batteries during your travels – remote areas with no electricity will prove a problem!

Film still offers a convenient way of recording your journey. Film cameras require less battery power than digital cameras, but always take a few spare batteries with you. Films can be processed on a regular basis enabling you to note on the back of each print when and where you took the picture.

Camcorders now offer an inexpensive way of bringing your travels to life in sound and vision. Today's camcorders now record direct onto an internal hard drive. Mini DV and Mini DVD tapes still offer good value though, as you can always post your tape or disc to those back home to view while you continue your travels, and Mini DVDs will fit most DVD players for instant playback. You

37

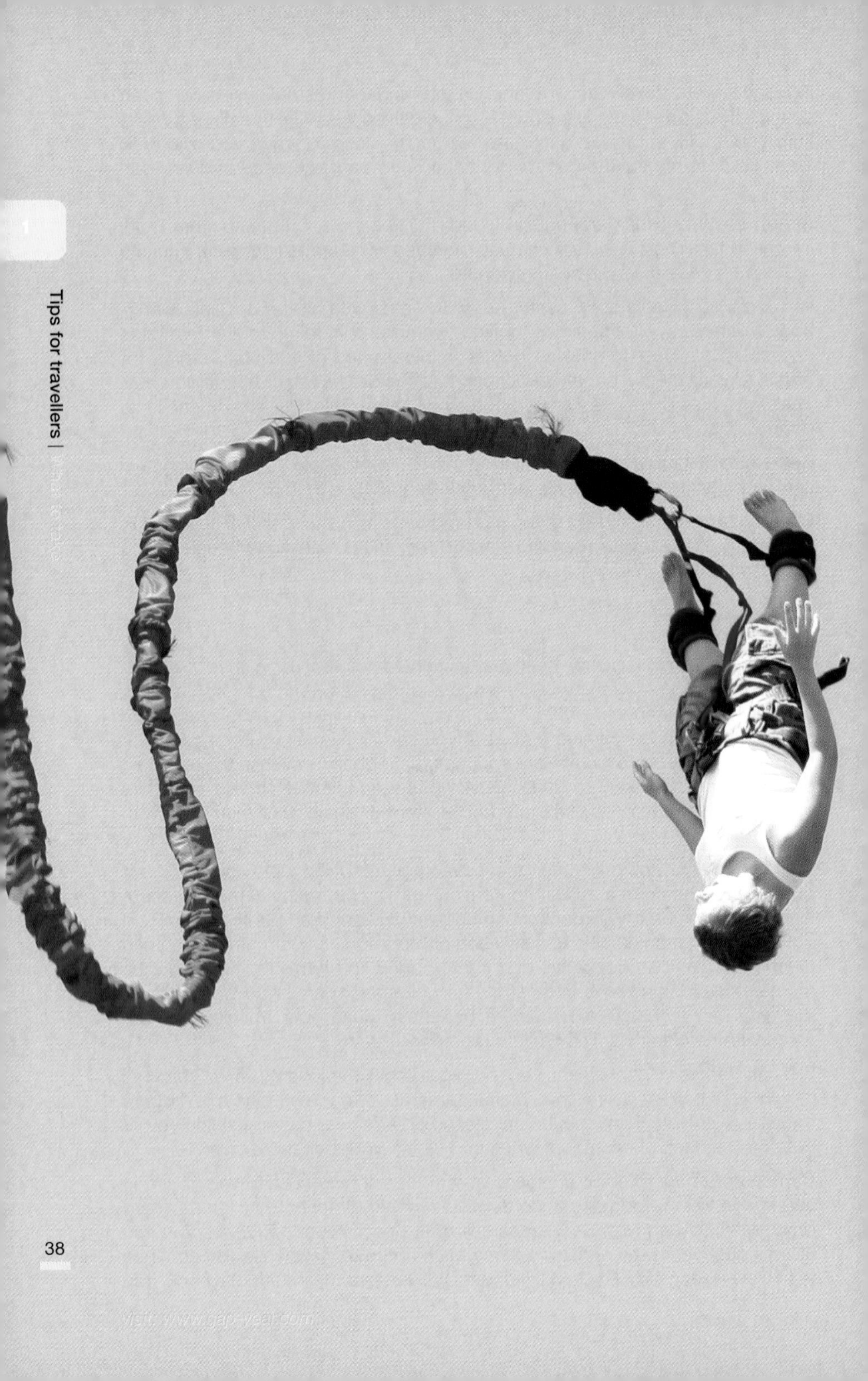

can edit footage taken on your camcorder on your computer back home and produce a really entertaining film of your exploits. Camcorders will also take a still photograph either direct to the media used or a separate removable storage card.

When planning your trip remember to seek advice from your local photographic dealer about which camera will suit your requirements best. Always buy a camera case to protect your precious equipment from knocks, dust and moisture; and most importantly don't buy the cheapest you can find. Cheap equipment will invariably let you down, and with inexpensive digital cameras you might suffer from software compatibility/connection problems.

Health & safety

Note: Although we make every effort to be as up-to-date and accurate as possible, the following advice is intended to serve as a guideline only. It is designed to be helpful rather than definitive, and you should always check with your GP what you need for your trip, preferably at least eight weeks before going away.

It's not only which countries you'll be going to, but for how long and what degree of roughing it: six months in a basic backpacker hostel puts people at higher risk than two weeks in a five-star hotel. Tell your doctor your proposed travel route and the type of activities you will be doing and ask for advice not only about injections and pills needed, but symptoms to look out for and what to do if you suspect you've caught something. Some immunisations are free under the NHS but you may have to pay for the more exotic/rare. Some, like the Hepatitis A vaccine, can be very expensive, but this is not an area to be mean with your money – it really is worth being cautious with your health.

If you are going abroad to do voluntary work, don't assume the organization will give you medical advice first or even when you get there, though they often do. Find out for yourself, and check if there is a medically-qualified person in or near the institution you are going to be posted with. People who've been to the relevant country/area are a great source of information.

It is important to keep a record of any treatment, such as courses of antibiotics, that you have when overseas and to tell your doctor when you get back. Also be wary of needles and insist on unused ones; it's best if you can see the packet opened in front of you, or you could take a 'sterile kit' (containing needles) with you. Also, many people recommend that you know your blood type before you leave the country, to save time and ensure safety.

Your GP might have it on record – if not, a small charge may be made for a blood test.

Some travellers prefer to go to a dedicated travel clinic to get pre-travel health advice. This may be especially worthwhile if your GP/practice nurse does not see many travellers. British Airways has three travel clinics in London where you can get jabs – call 020 7606 2977 for more information about this service.

The Medical Advisory Services for Travellers Abroad (MASTA) has travel clinics around Britain. To find your nearest clinic check the website **www.masta.org** or contact the Location Line (Tel: 01276 685 040).

39

Alternatively you can do your own research and take the information to your doctor or nurse. MASTA has a 'Travellers Health Line' on 0906 8224 100.

Travellers leave details of their proposed journey to obtain a health brief by first class post. This brief provides information on the recommended vaccines, malaria tablets, disease outbreak information and safety advice. Calls cost 60p/min and last approximately 4-5 minutes depending on how many countries you request details on.

www.e-med.co.uk   http://www.fitfortravel.scot.nhs.uk/

www.travelhealth.co.uk

For safety advice try the Foreign and Commonwealth Office: www.fco.gov.uk/travel

Department of Health Freefone Health Information Service (Tel: 0800 665 544) and their website: www.dh.gov.uk/home/fs/en

Make sure you have a sensible first aid kit with you, organise your medical insurance and, if you don't speak the language, have the basic words for medical emergencies written down so you can explain what is wrong.

Accidents / Injuries

Accidents and injuries are the greatest cause of death in young travellers abroad. Alcohol/drug use will increase the risk of these occurring. Travellers to areas with poor medical facilities should take a sterile medical equipment pack with them. As highlighted earlier, make sure that you have good travel insurance that will bring you home if necessary.

AIDS

The HIV virus that causes AIDS is caught from: injections with infected needles; transfusions of infected blood; sexual intercourse with an infected person; or possibly cuts (if you have a shave at the barber's, insist on a fresh blade, but it's probably best to avoid the experience altogether). It is NOT caught through everyday contact, insect bites, dirty food or crockery, kissing, coughing or sneezing. Protect yourself: always use condoms during sex, make sure needles are new (you can take your own sterile pack for medical emergencies) if you need a blood transfusion make sure blood has been screened, and don't get a tattoo or piercing until you're back home and can check out the tattoo shop properly.

Remember this is a fatal disease and though medical advances are being made there is no preventive vaccination and no cure.

Asthma and allergies

Whether you are an asthmatic or have an allergy to chemicals in the air, food, stings, or antibiotics, ask your GP for advice before you go. You will be able to take some treatments with you.

Allergy sufferers, If you suffer from severe shock reactions to insect bites/nuts

40

or any other allergy, make sure you have enough of your anaphylactic shock packs with you - you may not be able to get them in some parts of the world.

Chronic conditions

Asthmatics, diabetics, epileptics or those with other conditions should always wear an obvious necklace or bracelet or carry an identity card stating details of their condition. Tragedies do occur due to ignorance, and if you are found unconscious, a label can be a lifesaver. See **www.medicalert.org.uk/** for information on obtaining these items.

You should also keep with you a written record of your medical condition and the proper names (not just trade names) of any medication you are taking. If you are going on an organised trip or volunteering abroad, find out who the responsible person for medical matters is and make sure you fully brief them about your condition.

Contraceptives

If you are on the pill it is advisable to take as many with you as possible. Remember that contraceptives go against some countries' religious beliefs so they may not be as readily available as you might think. Antibiotics, vomiting and diarrhoea may inhibit the absorption of the pill, so use alternative means of contraception until seven days after the illness. Condoms: unprotected sex can be fatal, so everyone should take them even if they are not likely to be used (not everyone thinks about sex the whole time). Keep them away from sand, water and sun. If buying abroad, make sure they are a known make and have not been kept in damp, hot or icy conditions.

Dentist

Pretty obvious but often forgotten: get anything you need done to your teeth before you go. Especially worth checking up on are wisdom teeth and fillings - you don't want to spend three months in Africa with toothache.

Diabetics

Wear an obvious medical alert necklace or bracelet or carry an ID card stating your condition (preferably with a translation into the local language). Take enough insulin for your stay, although it is unlikely that a GP will give you the amount of medication needed for a full year of travelling – three to six months is usually their limit, in which case, be prepared to buy insulin abroad and at full price. Ring the BDA Careline to make sure the brand of insulin you use is available in the particular country you are planning to visit. Your medication must be kept in the passenger area of a plane, not the aircraft hold where it will freeze.

41

Diabetes UK 10 Parkway, London NW1 7AA, UK
Tel: +44 (0) 207 424 1000
Careline: 0845 120 2960
email: careline@diabetes.org.uk
www.diabetes.org.uk

Diabetes UK produces a general travel information booklet as well as specific travel packs for about 70 countries. Ring or email the careline (Mon-Fri 9am-5pm) or check out the website for expert advice and all information for diabetic travellers, including info on travel insurance.

Diarrhoea

By far the most common health problem to affect travellers abroad is travellers' diarrhoea. This is difficult to avoid but it is sensible to do the best you can to prevent problems. High risk food/drinks include untreated tap water, shellfish, unpasteurised dairy products, salads, peeled fruit, raw/undercooked meat and fish. Take a kit to deal with the symptoms of travellers' diarrhoea (your doctor or nurse should be able to advise on this). Remember to take plenty of 'safe' drinks if you are ill and rehydration salts to replace lost vitamins and minerals.

Eyes

Wearers of contact lenses should stock up on cleaning fluid before going, especially if venturing off the beaten track, and be careful what water is used for cleaning; ask your optician for advice.

Dust and wind can be a real problem, so carrying refreshing eye drops to soothe itchy eyes and wash out grit can be really useful. Also most supermarket pharmacies, plus travel and camping shops sell plastic bottles of mildly medicated hand cleanser that dries instantly and are small and light to carry. You only use a small amount each time so it's worth packing a couple. They're really useful for cleaning hands before putting in contact lenses if the local water supply is suspect. It's also worth making sure you have glasses as a back-up, as it's not always possible to replace lost or broken contacts.

If you wear glasses consider taking a spare pair – they don't have to be expensive and you can choose frames that are flexible and durable. Keep them in a hard glasses case in a waterproof (and more to the point sandproof) pouch.

Malaria

This disease is caught from the bite of an anopheles mosquito, and mosquitoes are vicious and vindictive. Highest risk areas are tropical regions like Sub Saharan Africa, the Solomon Islands and Vanuatu (Pacific), the Amazon basin in South America and parts of Asia. There's no jab, but your GP will give you a course of pills to take.

It may sound obvious, but try to avoid getting bitten as much as possible. Use insect repellent, preferably containing either at least 30% DEET (diethyltoluamide), or extract of lemon eucalyptus oil. Keep your arms and legs covered between dusk and dawn and use a 'knockdown' spray to kill any mosquitoes immediately.

Mosquito nets are useful, but they can be hard to put up correctly. It is often worth carrying a little extra string and small bits of wire so that the net can be hung up in rooms that don't have hanging hooks. Ideally the net should be impregnated with an insecticide, you can buy nets that are already treated from specialist shops and travel clinics (see www.**gap**-yearshop.com for a full range). For a long trip, the pills can cost a lot. And some people, particularly on long trips, stop taking their pills, especially if they're not getting bitten much. Don't. Malaria can be fatal.

Your GP, practice nurse or local travel clinic should know which of a variety of antimalarials is best for you, depending on your medical history (e.g. for epileptics) and the countries you are visiting. Your travel health adviser will also be able to tell you what the symptoms of malaria are, and that you must seek treatment quickly. The combination of paludrine plus chloroquine is recommended for some countries. In areas where the malaria shows significant drug resistance, mefloquine, doxycyline or Malarone will be recommended.

All the anti-malarial tablets have various pros and cons, and some of them have rather significant side-effects. If you are going to try the weekly mefloquine tablets, MASTA recommends that you start taking the course two and a half to three weeks before departure. Most people who experience unpleasant side effects with this drug, will notice them by the third dose. This trial will allow you time to swap to an alternative regime before you go, if you do have problems.

Doxycycline can also be started two days before departure and is taken every day until one month after return. For paludrine and chloroquine start the course one week before you leave and continue it for four weeks on your return. Don't think that this means you can leave it until a week before you go - the earlier you see your GP the better.

As there are a number of different antimalarials, it's important to make sure you're taking the right variety. Visit your GP or travel clinic a couple of months before you go to discuss the options.

It's worth doing a little research of your own before going to your GP or practice nurse! Very occasionally we hear stories of unsuitable drugs being recommended – this can be from the GP, practice nurse, travel agent or pharmacist.

For some places dual-voltage mosquito killer plugs are a good idea. Tests carried out for Holiday Which? by the London School of Hygiene and Tropical Medicine (published in September 2005) found four that gave 100% protection – Boots Repel, Jungle Formula, Lifesystems and Mosqui-Go Duo.

Another good idea is to spray clothes with permethrin – which usually lasts up to two weeks, although Healthguard has a product that works for three months or 30 washes. Visit **http://www.healthguardtm.com/** to find out more or call them on 0208 343 9911.

SAFETY TIPS:

Travel in pairs if you can

Never hitch-hike or accept lifts from strangers

Avoid badly-lit streets after dark

Never discuss your own or your family's financial situation with strangers

Never try unknown substances

Never carry unopened parcels for people, especially when you fly

Always let people know where you are going and stay in touch with people back home regularly

Don't swim in strong currents or heavy waves or crocodile-infested waters: several **gap-**year students have died this way

Check fire exit routes in hostels or other buildings where you plan to stay

Shake out clothes and shoes before you put them on: snakes, scorpions or allergy-causing plants may have got inside

If you don't like the look of some of the other people in a hostel, put your bed against the door at night

Keep windows open if you are in a room with a gas water heater or other source of carbon monoxide to let gases escape if the equipment is faulty

Sunburn

Avoid over-exposure, especially on first arrival in a sunny country, and use sun creams and sun-block frequently.

Latest figures from Cancer Research UK show that 1,777 people die from melanoma each year and melanoma is the second most common cancer among people aged 20-39.

Don't think you're safe if you're spending three months as a skiing instructor either – snow can increase the amount of exposure to the sun's harmful rays significantly.

Vaccinations

Hepatitis (A&B), Japanese Encephalitis, Meningitis, Polio, Rabies, Tetanus, Tuberculosis, Typhoid, Yellow Fever. Ask your GP for advice on vaccinations/precautions at least six to eight weeks before you go (some may be available on the NHS). Keep a record card on you of what you've had done. Certain countries won't admit you unless you have a valid yellow fever certificate.

Seeking medical advice abroad

You can expect to be a bit ill when you travel just due to the different food and unsettled lifestyle (paracetamol and loo paper will probably be the best things you've packed). But if vomiting and/or diarrhoea continue for more than four to five days or you run a fever, have convulsions or breathing difficulties (or any unusual symptoms), get someone to call a doctor straight away. Seek advice on the best doctor to call, the British Embassy or a five-star hotel in the area may be able to offer some advice here.

If the doctor advises being sent home for treatment and you have an insurance policy with a repatriation arrangement, get someone to call the insurance company's headquarters or office in the relevant country for help as soon as possible. If your treatment is not free you should be able to pay by credit card, but check first with your insurers – they may cover the costs upfront. If you do pay yourself, make sure the details are written out on a receipt and keep all bills or receipts so you can claim on your insurance policy when you get home.

Staying safe

Before you do anything or go anywhere think about the consequences – this isn't about not having a good time, or being boring – it's about getting through your **gap-**year alive and not getting mugged, raped or murdered. If people hassle you, you can usually crack a joke and move on. If you are offered strange drinks or drugs be sensible and think about your safety first.

One of the biggest dangers in accepting a drink is that someone can slip in the so-called "date rape" drug (Rohypnol). It doesn't taste of anything and you won't know you're taking it. Combined with alcohol, it can induce a blackout with memory loss and decrease your resistance, leaving you open to attack.

About ten minutes after ingesting the drug, you may feel dizzy and disoriented, simultaneously too hot and too cold, or nauseous. You might have difficulty speaking or moving and then pass out. Victims have no memory of what happened while under the drug's influence. Another drug that can be used in a similar way is GHB (gamma-hydroxybutate) also known as "liquid ecstasy", "somatomax", "scoop" or "grievous bodily harm".

If you are tempted to try the local variety of cannabis in the belief that it is relatively harmless and universal, know what the local drug laws are and don't take risks. In many places in South Asia, for example, it is illegal and possession carries stiff penalties in prisons where conditions are not remotely like they are in the UK.

Remember also, that if you are speaking English with a local inhabitant, they may not understand or use a word with the same meaning as you do. Particularly in the fraught area of emotional relationships and dating, remembering this and understanding the local religion, customs and morality can save a lot of misunderstanding, misery and heartache.

If someone keeps pestering you with unwanted sexual advances after you have said no, get to somewhere where there are other people within earshot.

Only use violence as a last resort – it's not worth fighting back against violent muggers. They're likely to be stronger than you and may be carrying a gun or a knife.

45

Remember in many countries of the developing world, where there are no social security or welfare systems, life can be extremely tough and people close to despair. What may seem like a cheap trinket to you may be enough to buy them a square meal for which they are desperate enough to steal from you violently, so it is sensible not to wear too much jewellery.

Another good tip is to try to always carry a supply of small change and small notes in a pocket (trousers or jeans with deep pockets can be very useful) and not reveal that you are carrying larger notes. Do not keep all your money in one place, distribute it between, say, a small daytime backpack, your rucksack or suitcase and a hidden belt bag so that if you are robbed, you still have some money in reserve.

If you use a flat belt bag worn inside clothes try to loop the strap through trouser belt loops or use some safety pins. Thieves have got wise to travellers using these for passports and travellers cheques and techniques for relieving you of them have become more sophisticated. One solution could be to buy some stick-on Velcro™ (or the stitch-on variety – more time-consuming but ultimately more secure) and attach a strip to the waistband inside all your trousers with the matching strip on the back of the belt bag.

If someone tries to snatch your bag throw it at them – it keeps as much space between you and them and puts them off guard, giving you time to get away.

Anyway you'll have wisely hidden any money, passports or tickets in a bag under your clothes. Stick close to other people while you get back to base.

Safety courses have been available for business travellers for years – companies are now offering courses specifically designed for gappers. These are by no means boring – you won't be sitting at a desk taking notes!

Companies offering safety equipment & training

Adventure First Aid
14 Pennsylvania Road,
Torquay, Devon TQ1 1NX

www.adventurefirstaid.co.uk
Tel: +44 (0) 845 658 8928

Email: info@adventurefirstaid.co.uk

Immediate Temporary Care Overseas Travel First Aid and Crisis management courses over two days. Practical - Interactive - Dynamic courses delivered by experienced professional trainers.

British Red Cross
44 Moorfields,
London EC2Y 9AL

www.redcross.org.uk
Tel: +44 (0) 870 170 7000
Fax: +44 (0) 207 7562 2000

The Red Cross offers first aid courses around the UK lasting from one to four days depending on your experience and the level you want to achieve. Contact them directly to find your nearest course.

Geography Outdoors

Royal Geographical Society (with IBG),
1 Kensington Gore,
London SW7 2AR

www.rgs.org/eac
Tel: +44 (0) 20 7591 3000
Fax: +44 (0) 20 7591 3001

Geography Outdoors (formerly the Expedition Advisory Centre) provides information, training and advice to anyone involved in expeditions, field research or outdoor learning in the UK and overseas.

International Remote Trauma

Pegaxis House, Suite 144, 61 Victoria Road
Surbiton, Surrey KT6 4JX

www.remotetrauma.com
Tel: + 44 (0) 208 398 4242
Fax: + 44 (0) 208 398 4242
Email: admin@remotetrauma.com

International Remote Trauma - specialist medical support and first aid training.

Intrepid Expeditions

3 Chapel Court Cottages, Broadclyst,
Exeter, Devon EX5 3JT

www.intrepid-expeditions.co.uk
Tel: +44 (0) 1392 882 445
Fax: +44 (0) 1392 882 445
Email: nigel@intrepid-expeditions.co.uk

Formerly known as I-survive, Intrepid Expeditions runs many different survival courses, including a first aid course, ranging from 2-day courses to a two-week trip to Sweden.

Objective Travel Safety Ltd

Bragborough Lodge Farm, Braunston,
Nr Daventry, Northants NN11 7HA

www.objectivegapsafety.com
Tel: +44 (0) 1788 899 029
Fax: (0)1788 891 259
Email: office@objectivegapsafety.com

A fun one-day safety course for travellers, designed to teach them how to think safe and prepare for challenges they may face.

Sim4travel Ltd

Brunel Science Park, Gardiner Building,
Kingston Lane
Uxbridge, Middlesex UB8 3PQ

www.sim4travel.co.uk

Tel: +44 (0) 8700 62 66 63
Fax: +44 (0) 845 890 22 88

Stay in touch for less overseas. Use your own mobile and save up to 85% off standard call charges.

St John Ambulance

National Headquarters, 27 St John's Lane,
London EC1M 4BU

www.sja.org.uk
Tel: +44 (0) 8700 10 49 50
Fax: +44 (0) 8700 10 40 65

The St John Ambulance Association runs first aid courses throughout the year around the country. Courses last a day and are suitable for all levels of experience.

Suffolk Sailing
Unit 75, Claydon Business Park,
Gipping Road, Great Blakenham
Ipswich, Suffolk IP6 0NL

www.suffolk-sailing.co.uk
Tel: +44 (0) 1473 833010
Fax: +44 (0) 1473 833020
Email: Liferafts@suffolk-sailing.freeserve.co.uk

Although mainly suppliers of sailing safety equipment, Suffolk Sailing does offer a one-day RYA/DOT Basic Sea Survival Course for Small Craft.

The Instant Mosquito Net Company Ltd
25 Berkeley Close,
Rochester upon Medway, Kent ME1 2UA

www.mosinet.co.uk
Tel: +44 (0) 1634 303 874
Email: steven.spedding@instantmosquito.net

The Instant Mosquito Net - Fully portable, self supporting mosquito net. Lightweight, easy to use mosquito net that folds into its own carry bag.

TravelPharm
Unit 10 D, Mill Park Industrial Estate,
White Cross Road
Woodbury Saiterton, Devon EX5 1EL

www.travelpharm.com
Tel: +44 (0) 1395 233771
Fax: +44 (0) 1395 233707
Email: info@travelpharm.com

Provides travellers with a range of medication and equipment at very competitive prices to make your journey both healthier and safer!

Ultimate Gap Year
5 Beaumont Crescent,
London W14 9LX

www.ultimategapyear.co.uk
Tel: + 44 (0) 20 7386 9101

Email: info@ultimategapyear.co.uk

Ultimate Gap Year aims to provide students with essential safety advice and knowledge before they embark on a gap year or remote travel to developing countries.

Meeting places

Your first impression of some countries will be the swarm of people that descends on you, hassling you to take a taxi or buy something – at night it can be quite scary. Remember, anyone can get lost. When you are on the road don't panic. Always agree meeting places before you go somewhere and play safe by having a double back-up plan. "If I don't see you outside the Latino Roxy at 1.00, I'll see you at the Lufthansa office at 4.00. Then I'm going back to the hostel." Try looking behind you occasionally.

Stop thief!

If you have money, a camera or a passport stolen abroad (and the chances of this are high), report the theft immediately to the nearest police station and make sure you have some written record from them giving the date that you did so with all relevant details.

Police in popular budget destinations may have had to deal with hundreds of

48

insurance scams in the past and may not be sympathetic. Dress smartly (and cover up; going in a bikini is not a good idea), stay polite and calm, but firm. It is very unlikely anyone will catch the thief or get your stuff back – all you need is a record of the police report for your insurance claim. Ask someone back home to notify insurers and post or fax a copy of the police notification home. Many insurers will not pay up for loss or theft unless the police are notified (some policies won't pay out if you don't do this within 24 hours). This also applies if you are involved in any accident likely to result in an insurance claim. Keep records of everything that might be important – better to throw it away later than not to have it when needed.

Getting about

Trains

Inter-railing

If you want to visit a lot of countries, one of the best ways to travel is by train on an InterRail ticket. With InterRail you have the freedom of the rail networks of Europe (and a bit beyond), allowing you to go as you please in 28 countries.

From the northern lights of Sweden to the kasbahs of Morocco, you can call at all the stops. InterRail takes you from city centre to city centre – avoiding airport hassles, ticket queues and traffic jams, and giving you more time to make the most of your visit. InterRail passes are available for both under and over 26s, but you need to have lived in Europe for at least six months. Overnight trains are available on most major routes, saving on accommodation costs, allowing you to go to sleep in one country and wake up in another! Supplements apply so ask when you book. You will have to pay extra to travel on some express intercity trains or the Eurostar. Most major stations such as Paris, Brussels, Amsterdam and Rome have washing facilities and left luggage.

InterRail divides Europe into eight zones: you can opt to travel in as many zones as you want (see the table below), but your ticket won't include travel in the UK.

Zone A: Republic of Ireland

Zone B: Norway, Sweden, Finland

Zone C: Austria, Denmark, Germany, Switzerland

Zone D: Croatia, the Czech Republic, Hungary, Poland, Slovakia, Bosnia-Herzegovina

Zone E: Belgium, France, Luxembourg, The Netherlands

Zone F: Spain, Portugal, Morocco

Zone G: Italy, Greece, Turkey, Slovenia

Zone H: Bulgaria, Romania, Macedonia, Yugoslavia.

49

InterRail Prices

	Under 26	Over 26
Any 1 zone 16 days	£145 €195	£215 €286
Any 2 zones 22 days	£205 €275	£295 €396
All zones 1 month	£285 €385	£405 €546

For further details on how to buy an Inter-Rail pass, visit their website **www.inter-rail.co.uk.**

Prices quoted here are only valid until Dec 31 2006 and are for guidance only. **Please note details differ slightly on the UK and European versions of the Inter-Rail website and we would strongly advise you contact them directly to double check details.**

Call the Rail Europe Call Centre: 08708 371 371 or visit their travel centre 178 Piccadilly, London W1J 9AL.

Eurostar

The Eurostar train is a quick, easy and relatively cheap way to get to Europe. You can get from London to Calais from £30, and the trains are comfortable and run frequently. Tickets can be purchased online at **www.eurostar.com**, in an approved travel agency, or at any Eurostar train station.

Trans-Siberian Express

If you're looking for a train adventure then you're unlikely to beat the Trans-Siberian Express. It will cost you from £509 for train transport only. On top of this you will need some money for food and drink, visas, air fare, etc. For China, Russia and Mongolia you'll need to have a visa for your passport to allow you into each country. Contact each relevant embassy to find out what type of visa you will need (i.e. visitor's or transit). It's probably easiest to arrange for all your train tickets, visas and hotel accommodation through a specialist agency, about six months before you leave. Your journey will be a lot easier if you have all your paperwork in order before you leave – although it will cost you more to do it this way.

The trains can be pretty basic, varying according to which line you're travelling on and which country owns the train. On some trains you can opt to upgrade to first class for about an extra $200. This should give you your own cabin with shower, wash basin and more comfort – though you'll be more comfortable, you may find it more interesting back in second class with all the other backpackers and traders.

If you're travelling in autumn or winter make sure you take warm clothes – the trains have rather unreliable heating. If you travel in late November/December you may freeze into a solid block of ice, but it will be snowing by then and the views will be spectacular. If you go in September it will be warmer and a bit cheaper.

If you want to read up about it before you go, try the Trans-Siberian Handbook by Bryn Thomas. It is updated frequently and it has details about the towns you'll be passing through and the timetables. But go to www.transsiberia.com for the best and most comprehensive information about the Trans-Siberian

Express anywhere. It will answer all your questions and give you useful hints. It's run by someone who has personally travelled on the trains, so he knows what he's talking about.

Buses/Coaches

Getting on a bus or coach in a foreign country, especially if you don't speak the language, can be a voyage of discovery in itself. UK bus timetables can be indecipherable, but try one in Patagonia! Get help from a local you trust, hotel/hostel staff, or the local police station if all else fails. In developing countries, locals think nothing of transporting their livestock by public transport, so be prepared to sit next to a chicken! That said, some buses and coaches can be positively luxurious and they do tend to be cheaper than trains.

Greyhound International Greyhound Lines Inc
PO Box 660689, MS490 Dallas
TX 75266-0689, USA
Tel: +1 800 229 9424
www.greyhound.com

Greyhound buses now have air conditioning, tinted windows and a loo on board, as well as a strict no smoking policy. Greyhound also arranges a 'GoHostelling' package that combines bus travel and hostel accommodation, see **www.yha.com.au** (Australia) and **www.norcalhostels.org** (USA). They have a Discovery Pass which allows 7, 15, 30 and 60 days unlimited travel.

There's the usual 10% discount for ISIC and Euro 26 ID cardholders. The bus company operates outside America too, with Greyhound Pioneer Australia (**www.greyhound.com.au**) and Greyhound Coach Lines Africa (**www.greyhound.co.za**). Check out their website or contact them for information about their various ticket options.

Planes

There's been a great deal in the news about the contribution of CO_2 emissions from airplane fuel, especially for long-haul flights. If you're going to be travelling a lot and time's limited you're not likely to be able to avoid planes altogether. But if you're concerned about global warming and want to do your bit you can pay a small "carbon offset" charge on your flight. If you want to know more try **http://www.offsetters.com/.**

The site has a calculator so you can work out how much to pay and your money goes towards sustainable development projects around the world.

Travel is one area where the internet is invaluable – you can search for ticket information, timetables, prices and special offers whether you're travelling by air, sea, train or bus. Often you can book and pay online and pick up your ticket at the airport. Make sure you read the 'Terms and Conditions' to see what you're paying for and whether you can get your money back.

Because the internet gives customers so much information to choose from, travel companies have to compete harder to win your booking.

51

The internet also shows you what flexibility is possible (a lot), so you could also find your decision making turned upside down.

Instead of planning a round-the-world trip, for example, by deciding on your destinations and then finding the cheapest flight path through them, you could look at the special offers available first, see how far in advance you can book a ticket, and decide what to do with the destinations you've got when you've booked. One of the destinations – for example, a voluntary work assignment beginning in Tanzania in February – may have to be on a fixed date; the others may not. The route you have in mind may be different from the samples on offer, but you can usually have one tailor made for you and the prices you find on the web, with simple maps, can act as a benchmark.

Make sure you check out the company making an offer on the web before you use internet booking procedures (does it have a verifiable address and phone number?), and read all the small print in a booking contract before you agree to buy – just as you would outside the virtual world.

Bargain flights

Scheduled airlines often offer discount fares for students under 26, so don't rule them out. Other cheap flights are advertised regularly in the newspapers and on the web (see above). All sorts of travel agents can fix you up with multi destination tickets, and student travel specialists often know where to find the best deals for **gap-**year students.

Above all, travel is an area where searching the internet for good deals should be top of your list – though it works best for single-destination trips rather than complex travel routes where you have to change several times. Here are some useful websites – the prices are examples we found in December 2005:

Bargain transport

Airline Network
The Trident Centre, Portway Ribble Docklands,
Preston, Lancashire PR2 2QA

www.airline-network.co.uk
Tel: +44 (0) 870 700 0543

Flight search engine and booking service for low cost scheduled flights. Sample flight: London, Gatwick to Los Angeles, California, from £476.

Austravel
Wigmore House, Wigmore Place, Wigmore Lane
Luton, Bedfordshire LU2 9TN

www.austravel.net
Tel: +44 (0) 870 166 2020

Combines scheduled and charter flights to produce RTW itineraries. Information about and flights to Australia, New Zealand, Asia and the South Pacific. Sample flight: London to Sydney open ticket; where you can use your return ticket any time within the year, £741.

British Midland Airways Ltd
Donington Hall,
Castle Donington, Derbyshire DE74 2SB

www.flybmi.com
Tel: +44 (0) 1332 64 81 81
Fax: +44 (0) 1709 314 993

Low cost flights to Europe and America. Sample flights: return flights from Heathrow to Dublin from £60.

Cheap Flights
49 Marylebone High Street, London W1U 5HJ

www.cheapflights.co.uk

Flights and destinations, special deals, holiday offers, round-the-world tickets, last minute bargains. Sample flight: Edinburgh to Barcelona for £105.

Deckchair.com
Travelcoast Ltd, Victoria Gate, Chobham Road
Woking, Surrey GU21 6JD

www.deckchair.com
Tel: +44 (0) 870 888 1730

Aims to find you the best available fare. Key in where you want to leave from and go to, plus dates and other details, and wait to see what happens! We keyed in London Heathrow to Delhi and found it for £426 including tax.

EasyJet Plc
Easyland, London Luton Airport,
Luton, Bedfordshire LU2 9LS

www.easyjet.co.uk
Tel: + 44 (0) 871 244 2366

Easyjet offers cheap flights to European destinations with further reductions if you book over the internet. Sample flight: a one-way ticket to Amsterdam from Liverpool, £50.99.

Ebookers (Flightbookers Ltd)
6th Floor, Hamlyn House, Macdonald Road
London N19 5PR

www.ebookers.com
Tel: +44 (0) 800 082 3000

Cheap online flights can be booked from this site. They also offer many deals, such as one-way from Gatwick to Bangkok for £256.

Florence by Bike
Via San Zanobi, 91/R - 120-122/R,
Firenze, 50129, Italy

www.florencebybike.it
Tel: +39 055 488 992
Fax: +39 055 488 992
Email: info@florencebybike.it

International Rail
Chase House, Gilbert Street,
Ropley, Hampshire SO24 0BY

www.interrail.com/
Tel: 0870 0841411

Email: feedback@interrail.com

InterRail Pass provides unlimited travel in 29 European countries with prices starting at only £140 for 16 days – that is less than £9 a day for unlimited travel on the sophisticated European Rail network. The pass is very flexible allowing you to choose either one or all zones - you decide how much of Europe you want to explore! Check prices and buy your InterRail Pass securely online in the UK and save yourself up to £12 per pass compared to other student travel sites. Alternatively call our National Call Centre who will also be able to assist you with your reservations.

One World Alliance
www.oneworld.com

Corporation Trust Center, 1209 Orange Street, Wilmington, Newcastle County DE 19801 USA

Alliance between Aer Lingus, American Airlines, BA, Cathay Pacific, Finnair, Iberia, LanChile & Qantas (Japan Airlines will join in early 2007 and Malév and Royal Jordanian are also planning to join in 2007). Their programmes include 'oneworld explorer' and 'circle trip explorer' both of which are good if you want to cover lots of miles and stopovers.

Ryanair
www.ryanair.com
Tel: 0871 246 0000 (UK reservations)

Satellite 3, Stansted Airport, Essex CM24 1RW

Low cost airline to European destinations – many outward flights are actually free! – but make sure you check how much the return flight will be.

Stray Ltd
www.straytravel.co.nz
Tel: +64 (0) 9 309 8772
Fax: +64 (0) 9 307 5759
Email: enquiries@straytravel.co.nz

31 Beach Road, Auckland Central, New Zealand

Stray is New Zealand's fastest growing backpacker bus network - designed for travellers who want to get off the beaten track.

Thomas Cook
www.thomascook.com
Tel: +44 (0) 1733 417 100

The Thomas Cook Business Park, Coningsby Road, Peterborough, Northamptonshire PE3 8SB

General travel agent with high street branches offering flights and late deals.

Travellers Contact Point
www.travellers.com.au
Tel: +44 (0) 207 432 7475
Fax: +44 (0) 20 7432 7400
Email: info@travellersuk.com

85 Shaftesbury Avenue, Soho, London W1D 5DX

Travelocity
www.travelocity.co.uk
Tel: +44 (0) 870 273 3273
Fax: +44 (0) 870 876 1122

Western House, Cambridge Road, Stansted Mountfitchet, Essex CM24 8BZ

Key in destination and budget and see what Travelocity's search engine finds. Also has destination guide, flight timetables, maps and weather. Sample flight: London to Boston for £218 plus tax.

54

Travelsupermarket.com
Moneysupermarket House,
St David's Park, Ewloe
Chester, Cheshire CH5 3UZ

www.travelsupermarket.com

Tel: +44 (0) 845 345 5708

Email: customerservice@moneysupermarket.com

Searches a wide range of websites looking to find the cheapest flights available.

www.cheaponlineflights.com
5 Harvest Rise, Barrow on Humber,
Lincolnshire DN19 7SU

www.cheaponlineflights.com

Email: info@cheaponlineflights.com

Great travel website offering some very low prices, especially if you are prepared to go last minute. Sample flight: London to Oslo for £85.

www.germanwings.com
Terminalstraße 10,
51147 Köln Germany

www.germanwings.com
Tel: +44 (0) 870 252 12 50
Fax: +49 (0) 2203 1027-300

Cheap onway flights all across Europe. See website for direct call centre numbers in a wide variety of countries.

Car

Another popular option is to travel (mostly around Europe) by car. It means you can kip in it when necessary, save money on train fares and you don't have to lug your rucksack into cafés.

Make sure you know the motoring regulations of the countries you'll be visiting – they vary from country to country. Check that you are insured to drive abroad and that this is clear on the documentation you carry with you. The AA advises that you carry your vehicle insurance, vehicle registration documents and a current tax disc in the car and, of course, take your driving licence with you. If you still have an old paper licence you might want to consider getting it updated to a photo licence before you go, but make sure you leave enough time for this – the DVLA isn't known for its speedy processing. You can pick up a DL1 form from most Post Offices, your local Vehicle Licencing office or call the DVLA on +44 (0) 906 185 8585.

It is also advisable to take an International Driving Permit (IDP) as not all countries accept the British driving licence. In theory you don't need one in any of the EC member states, Iceland, Liechtenstein or Norway, but the AA recommends having an IDP if you intend to drive in any country other than the UK. And as it only costs £5.50 it's better than getting into trouble and being fined for driving without a valid licence.

An International Driving Permit is valid for 12 months and can be applied for up to three months in advance. Applying is easy – The AA and RAC issue the permits – you must be over 18 and hold a current UK driving licence. You'll need to fill in a form and provide your UK driving licence, passport and a recent passport-sized photo of yourself, which you can take to a participating Post Office or post them to the AA or RAC (see below for address), allowing

55

at least ten working days. Both the AA and RAC websites have loads of info about the permit and driving abroad in general, and you can even download the application form.

It's a good idea to put your car in for a service a couple of weeks before you leave and, unless you're a mechanic, it is worth getting breakdown cover specifically for your trip abroad with any of the major recovery companies such as the AA, RAC or Green Flag. If you end up stuck on the side of the road it could end up an expensive experience.

The RAC recommends taking a first aid kit, fire extinguisher, warning triangle, headlamp beam reflectors and spare lamp bulbs. These are all required by law in many countries and make sense anyway.

The Automobile Association
Fanum House, Erskine
Renfrewshire PA8 6BW, UK
Tel (IDP): +44 (0) 800 55 00 55
(Other motoring enquiries): +44 (0) 8705 500 600
www.theaa.com

The RAC Motoring Services
Travel Administration
PO Box 1500
Bristol BS99 2LH, UK
Tel (IDP): +44 (0) 800 550055
(Other motoring enquiries): +44 (0) 906 471740
www.rac.co.uk

Ships

If you want to get to the continent, then taking a ferry across to France or Belgium can be cheap – but why not sail free as a working crew member on ships? Contact head offices of shipping companies to find out the procedures before you leave the UK and find out how to book a passage from a foreign port.

A couple of useful sites where you can register – for a fee - if you like this idea are **http://www.yachtcrew-cv.com** (they charge $45.95, just over £24 to register your CV for life) and **http://www.globalcrewnetwork.com**, (registration fee: £35 for 6 months and £45 for 12 months).

A useful book on this subject is *Working on Yachts and Super Yachts*, price £10.99 (plus £1.50 p&p), published by Vacation Work Abroad, 9 Park End Street, Oxford OX1 1HJ, Tel: +44 (0) 1865 241 978, Fax: +44 (0) 1865 790 885. **http://www.vacationwork.co.uk/book.builder/1-85458-295-X.html.**

Bicycles

Of course, if you're feeling hyper-energetic, you could cycle around the place. This is really popular in north Europe, especially Holland, where the ground tends to be flatter. Most travel agents would be able to point you in the right direction, or you can just rely on hiring bikes while you are out there – make sure you understand the rules of the road.

Accommodation

Hostels are to backpackers what eggs are to bacon, and there are masses to choose from. How safe they are (from fire, flood, drugs, prostitution, theft, ripoff scams, etc.) obviously varies widely and gappers often rely on Rough Guide or Lonely Planet guidebooks or the word-of-mouth recommendations from other backpackers to find a suitable one. Check out **www.hostelworld.com** for hostels pretty much anywhere.

No-one expects five-star conditions and most backpackers don't care too much about the usual drawbacks (from cockroaches to back-breaking beds) as long it's cheap – most hostels would have to double their prices to conform to rigorous health and safety regulations.

Use your common sense and always check where the fire exits are when arriving at a hostel – it's too late to look if there's already a fire and you're trying to get out of the building. This may sound odd, but don't have a bath without some ventilation – faulty water heaters give off lethal and undetectable carbon monoxide fumes and will kill you without you realising it as you fall gently to sleep, never to wake up again. Use your instincts – if you the think the hostel's dodgy or simply not up to scratch, go and find another one.

Accommodation

Accommodation Stockholm Stockholm, Sweden	www.acco.nu Tel: +46 8 651 5224 Email: acco@chello.se
Hostelbookers.com 52-54 High Holborn, London WC1B 6RL	www.hostelbookers.com Tel: +44(0) 20 7406 1800 Fax: +44(0) 2074061801 Email: support@hostelbookers.com
International Youth Hostel Federation 2nd floor, Gate House, Fretherne Road Welwyn Garden City, Hertfordshire AL8 6RD	www.hihostels.com Tel: +44 (0) 1707 324170 Fax: +44 (0) 1707 323980 Email: iyhf@hihostels.com

IYHF represents 4000 Hostelling International youth hostels run by member associations in 90+ countries, and co-ordinates quality, international marketing, and the **www.hihostels.com** global booking system.

Keeping in touch

Spare a thought for those you're leaving behind – friends as well as family. Not only will they be worried about your safety, but they may actually be interested in your travels – most are probably jealous and wish they could go too.

You might find your family are panic-stricken at the thought of you going off into the wide world without them, especially if you are travelling under your own steam rather than on an organised project. Their way of showing they care may be to treat you like you're six years old again – they can't help it – humour them. Try to reach a compromise about how often you will get in touch with them – once a fortnight seems reasonable.

It's not just about keeping them happy: make sure you tell them where you are and where you are going – that way if something does happen to you, at least they know where to start looking. Backpackers do go missing, climbers have accidents, trekkers get lost; at least if someone is concerned by you not getting in touch when expected they can then alert the police. Of course, if you don't stick to what you agreed, don't be surprised if the international police come looking for you.

On the receiving end

You probably can't wait to get away, but you'll be surprised how homesickness can creep up on you when you're thousands of miles away.

Getting letters or emails can be a great pick-me-up if you're feeling homesick, weary or lonely, so distribute your address widely to friends and family before you go, in order to ensure a steady supply of mail. If you're not able to leave behind an exact address then you can have letters sent to the local Poste Restante, often at a main post office, and collect them from there. Also, parcels do usually get through, but don't send anything valuable.

Phone

Use a credit card if you can. If you walk into any international hotel you should be able to use a Visa or Mastercard to pay for an international phone call, but watch out for overcharging. Or you can reverse the charges: if the international operator doesn't understand, try using the American term 'collect call'.

One alternative is to take a chargecard with you. This avoids having to get to grips with local phonecards, operators who don't speak your language and having enough local currency coins to feed the payphone. If you do a search on the internet you will find various offers and schemes – check what you're getting before you give your credit card details.

You can use BT's Chargecard to phone home from abroad from any phone – just call the operator and quote your pin number. The calls are charged to your BT phone account back home and are itemised on the bill; weekly limits can be set in advance. There are different types of Chargecard accounts you can set up, including limiting card use to one number or a set of numbers. For further details on BT Chargecards call: Freephone +44 (0) 800 345 144.

Mobiles

If you're one of those people who needs to be attached to your mobile day and night, you'll probably want to take it with you. Make sure you've set up your account to allow you to make and receive calls and text messages in all the countries you'll be travelling to (and emails if you've got a WAP phone).

Try to limit use of your mobile to emergencies – they usually cost a fortune to run abroad as you pay for all the incoming calls at international rates too. It's worth insuring the handset as mobile theft is common and if it's the latest model, try not to flash it around. But don't rule out using your mobile phone as **gap**-year kit; it might save your life if you break your leg half way up a mountain and need to call for help (make sure you keep the battery charged).

If you are staying in one country for several weeks, consider getting either a cheap local mobile phone or a local SIM card for your UK mobile. Don't forget to alert friends back home to the new number! Local texts and calls tend to be very cheap and incoming calls from abroad are free, which avoids the massive charges when using your UK mobile.

Snail mail

Aerogrammes are a cheap way of writing from most countries. Registering letters usually costs only a few pence (or equivalent) from Third World countries, and is definitely worthwhile. Postcards are quick, cheap and easy – though not very private.

Email

Really useful technologies are rare, but emailing is one of them. What's more, you can now send emails free from almost any web-connected computer to almost any other, using services like Hotmail or Yahoo. These are usually free because they are being paid for by advertising or telephone line rental charges.

All you do is get the free email website up on a computer screen before you leave the UK and key in your registration details to get a free account.

Then, if you can get to a cybercafé or internet kiosk in an airport, hotel, university, office or home when you're abroad you can simply log in to your mailbox (remember your 'User ID' and password if these are part of the package) and receive messages or send them back home.

It beats picture postcards for speed, and you can write much more. If you're a techie with a digital camera and access to computer equipment, you can send your photos 10,000 miles home as email attachments minutes after you've taken them. Here are the most well-known free email providers:

www.altavista.com

www.excite.co.uk

www.freeserve.co.uk

www.hotmail.com

www.lycos.co.uk

www.postmaster.co.uk

www.talk21.co.uk

www.yahoo.co.uk

59

Hotmail is the best known of these, although in practice there is little difference between the services. Most give the opportunity to redirect mail from other email addresses, so you don't need to worry about telling everyone what your new email address is.

If you think getting to a cybercafé is going to be hard there are always WAP phones (you need to register your email address before you leave). Air Mail (**www.airmail.co.uk**) will forward emails to you as text messages on your mobile, and you can send emails by simply sending them a text message which they will forward as an email. Check their website for their up-to-date tariff. In practice, however, if there are no internet facilities in the area then the chances are there won't be a mobile phone signal either, and you may have to resort to more traditional methods of communication.

Having said that, thousands of cybercafés now sprinkle the globe, and internet connections can be difficult in Delhi but perfectly OK in Bolivia, so you'll probably find somewhere that you can email home at some point. This has got to be the quickest and most reliable way to communicate.

Preparation

Adventure Centre
240 Manchester Road,
Warrington, Cheshire WA1 3BE

www.cheaptents.com
Tel: +44 (0) 1925 411 385
Fax: +44 (0) 161 927 7718
Email: tents@cheaptents.com

Ants Media Group
Currumbin Sands Building,
71/995 Gold Coast Highway,
Palm Beach, QLD 4221 Australia

www.gapdownunder.com

Tel: +61 (0) 412 195 102

Email: contact@antsmedia.tv

Ecobrands
3 Adam & Eve Mews,
London W8 6UG

www.ecobrands.co.uk
Tel: +44 (0) 207 460 8101
Fax: +44 (0) 207 565 8779
Email: info@ecobrands.co.uk

Gear Zone
8 Burnet Road, Sweetbriar Road Industrial Estate,
Norwich, Norfolk NR3 2BS

www.gear-zone.co.uk
Tel: +44 (0) 1603 410108
Fax: +44 (0) 1603 413537
Email: info@gear-zone.co.uk

The Year Out Group
Queensfield, 28 King's Road,
Easterton, Wiltshire SN10 4PX

www.yearoutgroup.org
Tel: +44 (0) 7980 395789

Email: info@yearoutgroup.org

yourtraveljournal.com

www.yourtraveljournal.com

Email: sales@yourtraveljournal.com

Online travel journal for only £9.99 annually.

Chapter 2
Travel companies

Chetal, 22, completed her law degree, organised her future job, then took six months off for travel and volunteer work:

She covered: "India – Gujarat, Rajasthan, Agra, Varanasi, Chennai, Kerela, Goa, Mumbai; Africa – Kenya, Tanzania, Malawi, Zambia, Namibia, South Africa, Mozambique"

Chetal had thought through what she wanted from the experience: "My year out was meant to provide me with an insight into different cultures. It was primarily a backpacking experience, but we did do some work experience (legal work in Gujarat) and voluntary work (working in an orphanage that looks after homeless children with disabilities and Aids in Kenya) along the way."

Like everyone who takes a **gap-** she found her insight into the world and herself had expanded: "It opened my eyes to the world we live in today. It made me realise what little people have in developing countries like India and Africa. People back at home, in the UK are so materialistic and always want more. They are never satisfied with what they have. In comparison, locals I met travelling live for the day and make the most of what they have, however, big or small. They have no regrets.

"The last week of my travels, I was counting down the days until I returned home; I couldn't wait! I was longing for my home comforts, seeing my family and friends and most of all sleeping in my bed. I had a grin from ear to ear when I returned, I was on such a high from my travels it was unreal. I was on cloud nine. So many stories and tales had accrued from the last 6 months of my life, memories that would be with me for a lifetime. I could not wait to share my experiences.

"The experience has altered the way I look at things in life. No longer am I pre-occupied with the smaller things in life rather I have an appreciation and real understanding of the world as it is today. I know it sounds rather cliché, but travelling has made me a bigger and better person."

Travel companies

There are any number of exotic travel agents to be found in advertisements in the national daily and Sunday newspapers or online.

As **gap**-years become more popular and so become big business, more travel companies are offering travel deals specifically aimed at gappers.

But do be careful – remember they are businesses set up to make a profit and their advertising is designed to be as exciting and attractive as possible.

Make sure you get references and talk to a gapper who has finished their **gap**-year before you hand over hard cash or sign up for anything.

If you're not sure about a company you can contact the Year Out Group and see if they're a member or if the YOG have heard of them – **www.yearoutgroup.org**, Tel: +44 (0) 7980 395 789.

The following travel companies are just some of the ones we found that are used to dealing with independent travellers and students:

Travel companies, tour operators & expedition organisers

A-Apex Mountain
Nepal Trekking & Expedition
PO Box 12205, Thamel,
Kathmandu, Nepal

www.mountainnepal.com
Tel: +977 1 357135
Fax: +977 1 357135
Email: info@mountainnepal.com

Alliance Abroad Group LP
1221 South Mopac Expressway, Suite 250,
Austin, TX 78746 USA

www.allianceabroad.com
Tel: +1 (512) 457 8062
Fax: +1 (413) 460 3502
Email: info@allianceabroad.com

Alliance Abroad Group offers customised internship, work, teaching and volunteer experiences around the world. Our services include guaranteed placement and 24/7 personal assistance.

Blue Dog Adventures
Amwell Farm House, Nomansland,
Wheathampstead
St. Albans, Hertfordshire AL4 8EJ

www.bluedogadventures.com
Tel: +44 (0) 1582 831302
Fax: +44 (0) 1582 834002
Email: info@bluedogadventures.com

Blue Dog offers a variety of adventures, but focuses mainly on equestrian adventures catering for all levels of horsemanship.

65

the gap-year guidebook 2007

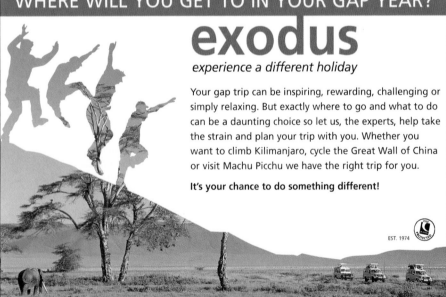

BSES Expeditions

at The Royal Geographical Society,
1 Kensington Gore,
London SW7 2AR

www.bses.org.uk

Tel: +44 (0) 20 7591 3141
Fax: +44 (0) 20 7591 3140
Email: info@bses.org.uk

This charitable organisation runs four week summer expeditions to wilderness areas abroad to conduct scientific research on behalf of universities, research institutes or host nations. It also runs conservation and environmental projects combined with exciting adventurous activities from ice climbing to canoeing.

Bukima Expeditions

43a Riffel Road,
London NW2 4PB

www.bukima.com

Tel: +44 (0) 870 757 2230
Fax: +44 (0) 870 757 2231
Email: adventure@bukima.com

Bukima operates overland expeditions and safaris from 10 to 28 days across Africa, South America and the Middle East.

Camps International Limited

Unit 1 Kingfisher Park, Headlands Business Park,
Blashford, Ringwood
Hampshire BH24 3NX

www.campsinternational.com

Tel: +44 (0) 870 2401843,
Fax: +44 (0) 1425 485398
Email: info@campsinternational.com

Camps International organises expeditions and safaris based in Kenya and Tanzania.

Classic Journeys

33 High Street, Tibshelf,
Alfreton, Derbyshire DE55 5NX

www.classicjourneys.co.uk

Tel: 01773 873497
Fax: 01773 590243
Email: info@classicjourneys.co.uk

Classic Journeys are in their nineteenth year of operating quality adventure holidays throughout the Indian subcontinent and beyond. We are passionate about our destinations and our professional and friendly approach, providing well organised, enjoyable and successful holidays over many years has given us many satisfied clients.

Dorset Expeditionary Society/ Leading Edge Expeditions

Lupins Business Centre, 1-3 Greenhill,
Weymouth, Dorset DT4 7SP

www.dorsetexp.co.uk

Tel: +44 (0) 1305 775 599
Fax: +44 (0) 1305 775 599
Email: admin@leadingedge.org.uk

Dorset Expeditionary Society promotes adventurous expeditions to remote parts of the world. Open to all. May qualify for two sections of the Duke of Edinburgh's Gold Award.

Travel companies | Travel companies

Exodus Travels
Grange Mills, Weir Road,
London SW12 0NE

www.exodus.co.uk
Tel: +44 (0) 20 8675 5550
Fax: +44 (0) 20 8673 0779
Email: sales@exodus.co.uk

Your gap trip can be inspiring, rewarding, challenging or simply relaxing. But exactly where to go and what to do can be a daunting choice. Exodus pride themselves on their travel expertise and knowledge, offering active and adventurous trips that are not only value for money but also operated responsibly to help benefit the host destinations they visit. This philosophy has won them several awards and accolades from highly respected independent panels. Climb Kilimanjaro, cycle the Great Wall of China, join an expedition to the Antarctic, visit Machu Picchu. With over 500 trips to almost 100 destinations, it's your chance to do something different!

Four x 4 Safaris
PO Box 312,
Strubensvalley, 1735 South Africa

www.fourx4safaris.co.za
Tel: + 27 11 958-1746
Fax: + 27 11 958-1084
Email: info@fourx4safaris.co.za.

Four x 4 Safaris arranges guided, self-drive safaris in Botswana game reserves. You should get to see the 'safari big five' (lions, leopards, buffaloes, elephants, rhinos) as well as lots of other species.

Gecko Travel
Hidden Places Adventures Tours Ltd,
94 Old Manor Way,
Portsmouth, Hampshire PO6 2NL

www.geckotravel.com
Tel: +44 (0) 2392 258 859
Fax: +44 (0) 2392 259 121
Email: frontdesk@geckotravel.com

Global Adventures Project
38 Queens Gate,
London SW7 5HR

www.globaladventures.co.uk
Tel: +44 (0) 800 085 4197
Fax: +44 (0) 207 7590 7444
Email: info@globaladventures.co.uk

Goa Way
111 Bell Street,
London NW1 6TL

www.goaway.co.uk
Tel: +44 (0) 20 7258 7800
Fax: +44 (0) 20 7224 6694
Email: sales@goaway.co.uk

Goaway specialises in organising travel to India, which has a population of over one billion people and diversity like you've never seen before.

Greyhound Lines Inc
PO Box 660691, MS 470,
Dallas, TX 75266-0691 USA

www.greyhound.com
Tel: +1 214 849 8100

Email: ifsr@greyhound.com

visit: www.gap-year.com

Guerba World Travel Ltd
Wessex House, 40 Station Road,
Westbury, Wiltshire BA13 3JN

www.guerba.co.uk
Tel: +44 (0) 1373 826 611

Email: info@guerba.co.uk

High & Wild
Compass House, Rowden's Road,
Wells, Somerset BA5 2RR

www.highandwild.co.uk
Tel: +44 (0)1749 671777
Fax: +44 (0)1749 670888
Email: adventures@highandwild.co.uk

High and Wild plan some of the most unusual and exciting adventures to destinations worldwide.

HnH Travellers Australia
18 Withington Street,
East Brisbane, QLD 4169 Australia

www.hnh.net.au
Tel: +61 7 3411 5955

Email: enquiry@hnh.net.au

Inside Japan Tours
Park House, 10 Park Street,
Bristol, Gloucestershire BS1 5HX

www.insidejapantours.com
Tel: +44 (0) 870 746 1044
Fax: +44 (0) 870 746 1047
Email: info@insidejapantours.com

Journey Latin America
12-13 Heathfield Terrace,
Chiswick, London W4 4JE

www.journeylatinamerica.co.uk
Tel: +44 (0) 20 8747 3108
Fax: +44 (0) 20 8742 1312
Email: flights@journeylatinamerica.co.uk

JLA is the UK's major specialist in travel to Latin America. Its 'Open-Jaw' transatlantic tickets permit you to fly into one country and out of another.

Jungle Surfing Canopy Tours
Keydane Pty Ltd, 24 Camelot Close,
Cape Tribulation, QLD 4873 Australia

www.junglesurfingcanopytours.com
Tel: +617 409 80090
Fax: +617 409 80065
Email: enquire@junglesurfingcanopytours.com

Kumuka
40 Earls Court Road,
London W8 6EJ

www.kumuka.com
Tel: +44 (0)207 937 8855
Fax: +44 (0)207 937 6664
Email: adventuretours@kumuka.com

Kumuka offers over 150 tours in 52 different countries, ranging from 4 days to 35 weeks. They hold film nights around the UK to give you a taste of the sort of tours they offer: anywhere from Johannesburg to Cancun in Mexico. Prices tend to be the good side of £1000 for around a month, but do not include flights.

Madventurer	www.madventurer.com
The Old Casino, 1-4 Forth Lane,	Tel: T: +44 (0) 845 121 1996
Newcastle upon Tyne, NE1 5HX	Fax: F: +44 (0)191 269 9490
	Email: team@madventurer.com

Madventurer programmes, specifically for gappers, university students and career breakers, take you on a fully-equipped 4x4 overland vehicle, to explore those out-of-the-way places that you would otherwise not be able to reach safely on your own either in East and West Africa or Latin America.

Mountain Beach Activity Holidays	www.mountain-beach.co.uk
13 Church Street,	Tel: +44 (0) 115 921 5065
Ruddington, Nottinghamshire NG11 6HA	Fax: +44 (0) 115 921 6182
	Email: andy@mountain-beach.co.uk

Find the mountain biking holiday of your dreams with Mountain Beach.

Oasis Overland
The Marsh, Henstridge,
Somerset BA8 0TF

www.oasisoverland.co.uk
Tel: +44 (0) 1963 363400
Fax: +44 (0) 1963 363200
Email: ceris@oasisoverland.co.uk

Oasis Overland operate adventure camping trips using our own expedition trucks. Expeditions from 2 to 40 weeks in Africa, South America, Middle East and along the Silk Route.

On The Go Tours
68-70 North End Road,
West Kensington, London W14 9EP

www.onthegotours.com
Tel: +44 (0) 207 371 1113
Fax: +44 (0) 207 471 6414
Email: info@onthegotours.com

Come to Africa for an incredible overland journey with On The Go tours. Cross barren deserts, lush jungles, highlands and lowlands on roads that vary from paved to dirt or sand. Get up close & personal with Africa's ever-changing landscapes, meet tribal peoples, witness wildlife roaming free and have the time of your life all the way to Cape Town at the tip of Africa.

Overland Club
PO Box 755, Sedgefield,
Stockton on Tees, County Durham TS21 1BG

www.overlandclub.com
Tel: +44 (0) 1740 629 648
Fax: +44 (0) 1740 629 304
Email: info@overlandclub.com

Overland Club provide the ultimate in adventure style group tours and expeditions.

Real Gap Experience
First Floor, 1 Meadow Road,
Tunbridge Wells, Kent TN1 2YG

www.realgap.co.uk
Tel: +44 (0) 1892 516 164
Fax: +44 (0) 1892 523 172
Email: info@realgap.co.uk

One of the larger organisations providing gap year travel opportunities.

Scenic Air AG
P.O. Box 412,
3800 Interlaken, Switzerland

www.scenicair.ch
Tel: +41 (0) 33 821 00 11
Fax: +41 (0) 33 821 64 14
Email: info@scenicair.ch

Thinking of spending time in Switzerland? Fancy scenic flights, glacier trekking, sky-diving or other adventurous activities?

Southern Cross Tours & Expeditions
Rua Felício dos Santos,
54A / 201 Santa Tereza,
Rio de Janeiro, CEP 20240-240 Brazil

Tel: +55 (21) 2252-6793

Email: southerncross@uol.com.br

STA Travel

52 Grosvenor Gardens,
Victoria, London SW1W 0AG

www.statravel.co.uk
Tel: +44 (0) 870 166 2642
Fax: +44 (0) 20 7881 1299
Email: victoria@statravel.co.uk

STA Travel have Travel Help branches or agents in over 85 countries worldwide and if you can't get into a local STA Travel branch, then there is a Help Desk telephone service, which provides you with essential backup for travellers on the move. With over 450 branches worldwide, with 65 of those in the UK, and well-travelled, experienced staff, STA Travel can assist you with all your travel plans for your trip.

The Bush Academy

PO Box 1399,
Thabazimbi, 380 South Africa

www.bushacademy.co.za
Tel: +27 (0) 14 777 6911
Fax: +27 (0) 14 777 6910
Email: enquiries@bushacademy.com

The Bush Academy courses are ideally suited to gappers wanting an introduction to conservation in Southern Africa and those wishing to pursue a conservation oriented career, as well as improving their personal knowledge of wildlife.

The Oriental Caravan

35 Vanburgh Court,
Kennington, London SE11 4NS

www.theorientalcaravan.com
Tel: +44 (0) 207 582 0716

Email: info@theorientalcaravan.com

The Oriental Caravan is a truly independent adventure tour operator specialising in escorted small group travel in the Far East.

Travel Inspirator

5 Clementine Road, Oakhurst,
Swindon, Wiltshire SN25 2JS

www.travelinspirator.com
Tel: +44 (0) 8703 89 23 45
Fax: +44 (0) 7986 00 88 18
Email: info@travelinspirator.com

Travel Inspirator offers a personal travel advice and trip planning service from an experienced and widely travelled expert, geared towards career breaks and gap years.

Travel Nation

The Courtyard, 61 Western Road,
Hove, East Sussex BN3 1JD

www.travelnation.co.uk
Tel: +44 (0) 845 344 4225
Fax: +44 (0) 845 344 4226
Email: quote@travelnation.co.uk

Travel Nation is an independent specialist travel company providing expert advice and the best deals on round-the-world trips, multi-stop itineraries, overland/adventure tours and Trans-Siberian rail journeys. The staff at Travel Nation have each spent many years in the travel industry and are extremely well travelled. Travel Nation gets rave reviews in the travel blogs. We also have an excellent travel insurance product called **www.roundtheworldinsurance.co.uk**.

TrekAmerica

Grange Mills, Weir Road,
London SW12 0NE

www.trekamerica.co.uk
Tel: +44 (0) 870 444 8735
Fax: +44 (0) 870 444 8728
Email: sales@trekamerica.co.uk

Offering more than 60 itineraries from one to nine weeks, TrekAmerica's fun, free, and flexible small group adventure tours are the ideal way to explore North America.

Truck Africa

22 Craven Terrace,
Paddington, London W2 3QH

www.truckafrica.com
Tel: +44 (0) 207 402 9171
Fax: +44 (0) 207 706 2673
Email: sales@truckafrica.com

Truck Africa aims to provide adventurous travel at realistic prices without compromising on quality of vehicle, equipment or crew.

Walks Worldwide

12 The Square, Ingleton,
Carnforth, Lancashire LA6 3EG

www.walksworldwide.com
Tel: +44 (0)1524 242000

Email: Ssles@walksworldwide.com

Walks Worldwide offers different types of walking expeditions around the world, from walking across the Swedish coastal peninsulas to trekking to Everest base camp. They can help groups organise their own trip or you can join one of the existing groups.

Wild at Heart Youth Adventures

Suite 7A, Cowell Park, 47 Old Main Road
Hillcrest, KwaZulu-Natal 3610 South Africa

www.wah.co.za
Tel: +27 31 765 2947
Fax: +27 31 765 7245
Email: info@wah.co.za

Wild at Heart Youth Safari is a well-established South African Based Youth Adventure company. From helping at a monkey sanctuary to working at a reptile farm there are many different opportunities available.

World Challenge Expeditions

Black Arrow House, 2 Chandos Road,
London NW10 6NF

www.world-challenge.co.uk
Tel: +44 (0) 20 8728 7200
Fax: +44 (0) 20 8961 1551
Email: welcome@world-challenge.co.uk

Organises placements and expeditions to some of the most remote and culturally diverse places on Earth.

Travel companies, tour operators & expedition organisers

Alpine Exploratory
9 Copperfield Street,
Wigan, Lancashire WN1 2DZ

www.alpineexploratory.com
Tel: +44 (0) 1942 826 270
Fax: +44 (0) 1942 233 829
Email: info@alpineexploratory.com

Borneo Anchor Travel & Tours/Sabah Divers www.borneoanchortours.com
G27, Wisma Sabah,
Kota Kinabalu, Sabah 88000 Malaysia

Tel: +60 88 256 483
Fax: +60 88 255 482
Email: divers@streamyx.com

Considering Borneo? Check us out! We offer both PADI and SSI scuba diving courses and various wildlife, nature and adventure packages all over Sabah, Malaysian Borneo.

BridgeClimb, Sydney
5 Cumberland Street, The Rocks,
Sydney, NSW2000 Australia

www.bridgeclimb.com
Tel: +61 (0) 2 9240 1100
Fax: +61 (0) 2 9240 1101
Email: admin@bridgeclimb.com

Companions2travel
The Hub, off London Road,
Corwen, Denbighshire LL21 0DD

Companions2travel.co.uk
Tel: 01490 413513

Dragoman Overland
Camp Green,
Debenham, Suffolk IP14 6LA

www.dragoman.co.uk
Tel: +44 (0) 1728 861133
Fax: +44 (0) 1728 861127
Email: enquiries@dragoman.co.uk

Dragoman Overland, the leading Adventure Travel Company, now has something for everyone. With trips from 2 - 52 weeks you can either take a short 'escape', an amazing chance to fit in a real adventure during your annual leave or give it all up and head off overland on one of the 'ultimates'. We will take you through the landscape and culture of Latin America, Africa, Central Asia and the Far East. Our fully equipped overland vehicles mean life on the road is flexible and fun and you get the chance to see the real sights others miss.

Experience Holidays
Park View House, 19 The Avenue,
Eastbourne, East Sussex BN21 3YD

www.experienceholidays.co.uk
Tel: +44 (0) 845 230 2131
Fax: +44 (0) 1323 410864
Email: info@experienceholidays.co.uk

Global Village Backpackers
460 King Street West,
Toronto ON, M5V 1L7 Canada

www.globalbackpackers.com
Tel: +1 416 703 8540
Fax: +1 416 703 3887
Email: info@globalbackpackers.com

Go Differently Ltd
19 West Road,
Saffron Walden, Essex CB11 3DS

www.godifferently.com
Tel: +44 (0) 1799 521950

Email: info@godifferently.com

We offer small-group, short-term volunteering and tailor-made holidays based on the appreciation and respect of the local environment and people throughout India and SE Asia.

Grayline Travel
5/F, Cheong Hing Building,
72 Nathan Road, Tsim Sha Tsui
Kowloon, Hong Kong

www.grayline.com.hk

Tel: +852 2368 7111
Fax: +852 2721 9651
Email: info@grayline.com.hk

Hello Africa Travel
132 Lavender Hill,
Tonbridge, Kent TN9 2AY

www.helloafricatravel.com
Tel: +44 (0) 1732 771 755

Email: info@helloafricatravel.com

High Places Ltd
Globe Centre, Penistone Road,
Sheffield, West Yorkshire S6 3AE

www.highplaces.co.uk
Tel: +44 (0) 114 275 7500
Fax: +44 (0) 114 275 3870
Email: treks@highplaces.co.uk

Himalayan Kingdoms Ltd
Old Crown House, 18 Market Street,
Wotton-under-Edge, Gloucestershire GL12 7AE

www.himalayankingdoms.com
Tel: +44 (0) 845 330 8579
Fax: +44 (0) 1453 844422
Email: info@himalayankingdoms.com

Hostelbookers.com
52-54 High Holborn,
London WC1B 6RL

www.hostelbookers.com
Tel: +44(0) 20 7406 1800
Fax: +44(0) 20 7406 1801
Email: support@hostelbookers.com

Intrepid Travel
11 Spring Street,
Fitzroy, VIC 3065 Australia

www.intrepidtravel.com
Tel: +61 3 9473 2626
Fax: +61 3 9419 4426
Email: info@intrepidtravel.com

Kande Horse Trails
Kande Horse Trails,
Kande, Nkhata Bay South, Box 22
Malawi

www.kanderhorse.com
Tel: 2658500416

Email: kandehorse@africa-online.net

Live Travel
120 Hounslow Road,
Twickenham, Middlesex TW2 7HB

www.live-travel.com
Tel: +44 (0) 208 894 6104
Fax: +44 (0) 870 138 6931
Email: phil.haines@live-travel.com

75

Palmar Voyages

Alemania 575 (N31-77), Mariana de Jesús, Quito, Ecuador

www.palmarvoyages.com
Tel: +593 (2) 2569 809

Email: info@palmarvoyages.com

Proposed tailor-made program in Ecuador, Peru, South America further to your budget. Big choice of programs (conventional, adventure...), Galapagos cruises, Amazon trips, air tickets, etc.

Selective Asia

19 Rymer Street, London SE24 0NG

www.selectiveasia.com
Tel: +44 (0) 845 370 3344
Fax: +44 (0) 207 274 7131
Email: contact@selectiveasia.com

Selective Asia offers a range of unique, privately guided tours and adventure holidays in Cambodia, Laos, Vietnam and Thailand.

Times Travel

71 Oxford Street, London W1D 2EN

travel.timesonline.co.uk
Tel: +44 (0) 20 7447 5000

Email: students@timestravel.co.uk

Student travel specialists offering adventure tours, worldwide flights, budget accommodation, rail and coach passes and student travel cards, insurance, budget car rental and lots of other travel stuff.

Travelbag Ltd

373-375 The Strand, London WC2R 0JE

www.travelbag.co.uk
Tel: +44 (0) 870 414 4444
Fax: +44 (0) 20 7497 2923

Bridge the World organises tailor-made RTW trips and has experience with gap year travellers. If you're interested in visiting Australia, there's a 'wine and canapé' meeting on the first Thursday of every other month at their West End office (4 Regent Place, W1B 5EA) where you'll get the chance to discuss your plans with consultants. Phone in advance as places are limited.

Travellers Connected.com

48 Queen St, Queensgate House, Exeter, Devon EX4 3SR

www.travellersconnected.com
Tel: 08450 291616

Email: info@travellersconnected.com

Worldwide Experience

Ashley Adams Travel (UK) Ltd, Guardian House, Borough Road Godalming, Surrey GU7 2AE

www.worldwideexperience.com

Tel: +44 (0) 1483 860 560
Fax: +44 (0) 1483 860 391
Email: info@worldwideexperience.com

Chapter 3
Career breaks and mature travellers

Michael was 63 and retired when he left for Ngaramtoni, near Arusha, Tanzania.

"I helped Hope Trust, which is financed by Mondo Challenge from UK, but led by two local Tanzanian directors. Hope Trust exists to give elementary finance & marketing/selling skills, plus give small grants & loans, to small businesses, often family units, many of whom are suffering from HIV/AIDS."

He'd done a stint of VSO (Voluntary Service Overseas) in Nigeria 40 years before, so had an idea of what he was getting involved in. He'd also been involved in "helping organisations like VSO, Action Aid, Save the Children etc. I knew what to expect in the developing world."

It took him about three weeks to adjust on his return, he said, and four months on he had taken up family and "non-executive business life" as he'd planned.

He also remains involved with Hope Trust and he and his wife talk to groups about the Trust and raise funds for its work.

His comments and advice for anyone contemplating time out volunteering: "Prepare thoroughly by reading & by meeting returned volunteers from your likely work area, and tell yourself you will need patience, patience, patience - it's hot! When it rains it can block roads & flood, water supply can be intermittent, electricity supply can be intermittent, so pcs pack up!, life is hassle, you will be ill, you will be tired, but carry people along with you rather than lecture them.......& you will value the experience.....

"I continue to aid in a number of ways, and I may volunteer again."

Career breaks and mature travellers

Taking a career break for three months to a year is the fastest-growing sector of **gap-**year activity and the signs are that this will continue.

Another group increasingly taking time out to do something completely different is people of 50-plus and it may be worthwhile considering doing something like this if you have been made redundant or taken early retirement. You never know, it could lead to a whole new career!

Several organisations that arrange places for people on projects abroad have told us that more than half their activity is now focused on helping place people who are taking a career break and mature travellers. Among them is Midlands-based Mondo Challenge.

Anthony Lunch, Managing Director, has some thoughts on the phenomenal growth in the popularity of career breaks, which now account for more than 65% of his organisation's placements – up from 52% last year.

He said: "Many people are looking to do something totally different from their normal job and are keen to teach or work in orphanages despite coming from a business background.

"Although they may be able to use the skills they have acquired in their day to day work, the placements will be totally new and in a challenging environment.

"Many volunteers talk about giving something back. After a few years in the rat race people feel refreshed after having done something they feel has had a positive impact in the developing world. It can make a change to have done something because you believe in it and have seen the impact of your efforts, rather than having been motivated by a possible promotion or a bigger salary."

This brings us to the first of several aspects that would-be career breakers, unlike younger gappers, may have to consider in making their plans – "What effect will it have on my career?"

In fact Mr Lunch said : "Employers are more and more seeing the benefits of offering staff a sabbatical and probably one of the greatest changes I have seen since working in this sector is that businesses themselves are starting to approach us to arrange placements for their staff.

"But in reality, undertaking a challenge of this kind is more of a career development experience than just a break in one's normal routine. New skills are learned in a very short space of time. Teaching in a small school in India, for example, when one has never taught before, provides daily practice in planning and rapidly hones communication skills.

"For women, the ability to work effectively in what is often a male orientated society provides a sharp focus on negotiating skills and on the art of diplomacy."

Volunteers taking part in small business programme face other challenges.

79

"They can forget the excel spreadsheets and 3 year plans. It's today's actions and tomorrow's plan that really matter when trying to create livelihoods".

In this chapter we'll be looking at the sorts of things career breakers and mature travellers will need to consider when making their plans – including the effects on careers, what to do about the house and mortgage, finance and whether or not to take the children.

Big decisions

So how much risk are you taking if you decide to take a break? Well, it seems many employers these days recognise their value and some have well-organised schemes to let their staff take a career break.

Mr Lunch argues that taking part in a volunteer placement is a great addition to any CV and for the employer, letting a member of staff go off for a short break of this kind brings the prospect of them returning with new energy, batteries recharged and creativity enhanced. He goes further – suggesting career break could be re-named career development.

He quotes a Proctor & Gamble marketing manager who "likened his experience on our HIV programme in Tanzania to a 'six week MBA programme'. How's that for career development!

Inquiries to some of the UK's major employers support the positive view they take of staff taking time out to do something else.

BT actually calls its sabbatical policy 'Time Out'.

A spokesman told us: "At BT, we actively encourage our people to live a fulfilling life outside of work and our sabbatical policy known as 'Time Out' has been in place for over four years now. We provide career breaks and time out as part of our suite of flexible working options. We are currently working with several organisations so that we can expand our policy on career breaks, to offer some organisations that may be able to help in planning a career break/voluntary work overseas."

Caroline Waters, director of People and Policy at BT, said:

"Once we had linear careers; now they move in zigzags. We're continually moving in and out of various forms of paid and unpaid employment. Offering career breaks is a critical attraction and retention tool in the highly competitive people market. It gives us a competitive edge over other companies and improves our employer brand."

Catherine Redmond, Head of Employee Benefits at Barclays Bank, said the needs and priorities of their employees were increasingly diverse: "Employees today rightly expect more from the employer than a monthly pay slip... While valuing financial remuneration they are also focused on achieving a real work life balance, developing themselves as people and giving something back to the communities in which they live and work."

Barclays has recognised this with career break schemes open to all employees who have had two years' continuous service. A short-term break (up to 12 months) means a guaranteed return to the company and, if possible, to the same job. Staff also keep staff banking facilities such as staff loans and mortgages.

A longer-term break (12 months to 5 years) means they have to resign from their job, but Ms Redmond said Barclays makes every effort to re-employ them in the future.

It was a similar story at the Royal Bank of Scotland, which has systems in place for staff to take short breaks (8-13 weeks) and longer ones (up to a maximum of 3 years).

Recruitment consultants Reeds also have systems in place for staff wanting to take a career break and offer all employees a sabbatical to pursue other interests outside work after they have been with the company for five and ten years.

A spokeswoman for HBOS (Halifax Group) said:

"HBOS offers career breaks of up to five years to its colleagues, whereby upon the colleague's return to work HBOS would look to re-employ the colleague in a suitable job, at the same grade and at the same place of work. Colleagues requesting a career break would need to discuss this option with their line manager.

"HBOS also offers its colleagues up to 18 weeks unpaid Lifestyle Leave which can be taken for various purposes, such as study or travel.

"Any period of Lifestyle Leave requires approval from the colleague's line manager and is subject to business requirements, organisational needs and effective colleague performance. The 18 week period can be extended according to an individual line manager's discretion.

"Colleagues must provide the business with a minimum of 12 weeks notice prior to the Lifestyle Leave starting.

"The colleague will return to the same job at the end of the Lifestyle Leave."

She offered this advice to people considering a career break:

- Decide what you want to achieve from your lifestyle leave and what you would like to do. Think about what you require from life, any additional skills that you would like to acquire and what you see yourself doing in five years time. This will determine the length of the leave you require.

- When applying to your employer for lifestyle leave think about the positive benefits to them that would arise from your break, especially those who are taking a longer leave. Would it be a development opportunity for you?

- Give a full handover to the person who will be covering your area whilst you are away and be on hand to answer any questions they may have before you leave. A good handover will also make it easier for you when you return to work.

- Those taking a longer period of leave may also want to consider acquiring new skills and to continue networking during their career break.

- Make sure that you are familiar with any notice that you need to give before you return to work.

HBOS also has its own foundation and during 2005 and 2006, sent more than 80 staff to Sri Lanka for a week to help out in Galle, a region devastated by the tsunami, in the South West of Sri Lanka.

During their time there, the HBOS people were working with international housing charity Habitat for Humanity, which had secured land and materials to rebuild family homes.

They worked alongside local families under the direction of Habitat for Humanity and expedition organiser Charity Challenge, doing everything from digging foundations, clearing rubble, mixing concrete or mortar, moving and laying blocks, making windows, landscaping, plastering or painting.

Each complete house was allocated to families who were victims of the tsunami.

The Foundation bore the costs of the volunteering trip and volunteers received a week's paid leave from HBOS. However, they were asked to raise £500 in sponsorship, to be used to build more houses, which the HBOS foundation matched pound for pound.

In the four separate weeks that HBOS volunteers were in Sri Lanka, sixteen houses were built and sufficient funds were raised to build at least 300 new homes or rebuild 1500 damaged ones.

If you can't arrange a sabbatical and you're willing to quit and take your chances what about finding work when the break's over?

Joanna Roberts, head of communications, said in Reeds' experience: "As long as you can demonstrate that you have done something constructive with your time, many employers will look favourably on the extra skills and experience you obtain from a **gap**-year.

"The sheer fact that you have given up a secure job to take a year out and do something else demonstrates that you possess valuable skills such as confidence, determination and a willingness to adapt to new situations."

She said that at the end of a career break, people should take some time to think about what they have learned and how an employer could benefit from this: "A career break is an excellent talking point at an interview and may even serve as a distinct advantage as it will set you apart from other candidates who apply."

Her general advice for anyone considering taking a career break was to think carefully about what you want out of it and to plan activities accordingly. She said it was an ideal opportunity to learn new skills and fill any gaps in your CV and added: "It is always worth talking to your existing employer about the possibility of being re-hired on your return. From an employer's point of view this makes good business sense as not only will you have relevant experience and be familiar with the organisation but you will also be able to bring back a fresh perspective to the job."

Linda Whittern, Director of Careers Partnership (UK), a careers counselling service, echoes this view, but she is more cautious about the benefits of a career break.

Ms Whittern advised: "Take a long hard look at the value to you of such a break, at this stage in your career and home life.

"Put a value on your time (multiply the salary you'd be earning during that period by 133% to take into account your employee benefits – holiday pay, pension rights, etc); assess the opportunities (e.g. promotion prospects) you might be losing; and see whether the benefits you'd obtain (personal and financial) from the break will outweigh these costs.

"Your career break could directly benefit your future career (whatever it is) if what you do during the break:-

- improves your CV by giving you the opportunity to work at a more demanding or more senior level than would be feasible in your home environment (e.g. your day job involves managing neighbourhood disputes and you work as a Peace volunteer protecting civilians against soldiers who are armed and out of control)

- enables you to develop relationships with key organisations and groups of people relevant to your work (e.g. you work in a bank and use your career break to train new entrepreneurs in business skills)

- gives you the 'space' and encouragement to review your career development, management style, etc.

"Taking 'time out' in the early stages of your career can have disproportionate costs – the 20s and 30s are normally times when promotion is relatively easy and rapid, when professional skills are being enhanced and important qualifications gained. Put yourself behind the competition at this stage and you may have to work a lot harder to catch up with your contemporaries."

However, Ms Whittern added: "Taking 'time out' in the middle and later stages of your career is often seen by employers as evidence of 'oldies' continuing initiative and career commitment."

She suggested that there are quicker, more efficient and more informative ways of exploring career choices than taking a career break: "Your first step should be proper careers counselling – this provides self-insight, guidance on the career strategy right for you and information on the careers to which you are best suited. A career review can be completed within half a day or a whole day. The cost of good quality careers counselling is usually within the range £300–£700.

"You might follow up this careers counselling by 'work shadowing' – the time investment per career choice being only days.

"It would be difficult to move into a new career at the right level if you were only prepared to spend some months in the new post. Working below the level you're capable of is rarely much fun."

She was much more cautious about the idea of a career break following redundancy: "A short, active holiday (e.g. rambling or sailing) lasting perhaps a week could be a good idea..

"Unless job hunters are very, very confident of gaining a new position quickly or have enough money not to need to work again, they are generally too anxious to enjoy a career break at this time."

Finance

So you've talked to your employer, perhaps also worked out what you hope to do – there are plenty of contact organisations to help you plan your chosen activities in the various sections throughout this book. The next crucial question is finance.

Obviously the amount of money you'll need depends on where you want to go, what you want to do, and how long you want to be away for. At this point drawing up at least a rough budget for how much it will cost would be a good idea.

Once you have this it's worth talking to your building society or bank to see whether they have any schemes that can meet your needs.

Barclays has student and graduate advisers who can advise on what to do about everything from travel insurance to suspending direct debits and deferring loan payments. Although the banks don't seem yet to have reached the stage of having advisers for career breakers specifically, they are increasingly aware of the trend to take a career break and may well be able to use their experience of advising younger gappers to help you think the finances through.

Maximise your funds: Have you been thinking about clearing out all that unwanted and unused stuff that the average household accumulates? You could use your planned career break as an opportunity to finally get around to it and raise some cash to finance your career break.

Why not consider raising some cash by selling items through eBay, holding a garage sale or taking items to a car boot sale? If you have a car it is likely to devalue in the year you are away, whether anyone is driving it or not, so you could sell it and put the money into your career-break fund. If you've already settled on the kind of project you want to do and it involves raising a specific sum, as volunteer projects often do, you can hold fundraising events to help you raise the cash – the options are as limitless as your imagination! Even simple things like putting all those irritating bits of small change that weigh down pockets and cram purses into a large pot or jar can mount up surprisingly quickly.

Pensions: Check with your employer to see if they offer a pension 'holiday' and, what that might mean to your eventual pension, but it might be possible to stop or reduce your payments while you are away. If you have been with the company less than two years, it could be possible to arrange a refund of pension contributions.

Earning on your career break: It may even be possible to part-fund your career break by using your skills on volunteer and other projects.

United Nations Volunteers sometimes pay modest living or travel costs for people with the skills they need for particular volunteer projects. Have a look at their website:

http://www.unv.org/volunteers/index.htm

There are also organisations that can help with funding for specific projects:

The Winston Churchill Memorial Trust is one of them.

It provides grants for people wanting to travel abroad to work on special projects that they cannot find funding for elsewhere and then use the experience to benefit others in their home communities. Applicants must be British citizens and resident in the UK and must apply by October each year.

The Trust awards travelling fellowships to individuals of all ages wanting to pursue projects that are interesting and unusual. Categories cover a huge range of topics over a three-year cycle. Roughly 100 are awarded each year and they usually provide funds for 4–8 weeks.

The Trust's Director General, Air Vice-Marshal Nigel Sudborough, emphasised that fellowships are not granted to gappers looking to fund academic studies, attend courses or take part in volunteer placements arranged by other organisations.

He advises looking at the WCMT website carefully and says: "The Trust is delighted to receive applications from people taking career breaks for their own projects. We feel that our fellowships may be more appropriate to this group than to younger gappers."

To find out more you can contact the Trust at:
15 Queen's Gate Terrace
London SW7 5PR, UK
Tel: +44(0) 207 584 9315
Fax: +44(0) 207 581 0410
E-mail: office@wcmt.org.uk
Website: http://www.wcmt.org.uk

What about the house?

Some mortgage lenders (including the Halifax) will allow up to six mortgage payment holidays without affecting your scheme.

Another option may be to rent out your house. You may need to check terms and conditions for subletting with your mortgage lender, but it can be a good way of covering the mortgage costs while you are away.

But it is your home and you need to be sure it will be looked after while you are away, so if you decide to rent it's worth using an accommodation agent to take care of things.

A point to consider here is that if you still have some income during your career break, you might have to pay overseas tax. So it would be wise to check with the Inland Revenue to see whether you are eligible for an exemption certificate, which should be given to the accommodation agent.

Many only operate in a local area and we asked Judi Hankins, property manager at Penningtons, Ipswich, Suffolk, for some guidelines.

She said an agent will generally take a six-week deposit from the tenant and will make sure the house is clean and the garden sorted out before you return: "We come across this quite regularly. We see a lot of people thinking about letting their properties because they want to go off and do something different, especially people aged 50-plus. Actually it's very simple. I would say prepare in good time and if you let to the right people who will take care of the property and pay the rent on time you don't have any problem at all."

Firstly, she advised only using an agent who was a member of ARLA, the Association of Residential Letting Agents. They will usually charge 10%-15% of the rental for their services, but they can guide you through the preparation as well as looking after things while you are away.

When letting a house there are some rules to abide by and some safety certificates you must have if you're going to take this route.

Ms Hankins said: "Generally people rent fully-furnished – otherwise think about the storage costs. But any furniture in the house which is made of foam must comply with fire regulations."

A second must-have is a current gas safety certificate for any gas appliances. The gas safety certificate for gas supply to a house costs around £40, but you must have a safety certificate for each appliance in the house – roughly an extra £10 per appliance. The certificate is valid for a year.

the gap-year guidebook 2007

For electricity the regulations are different and Ms Hankins said it was a bit of a grey area, but wiring has to be safe and if your wiring has been installed for 15-20 years it would make sense to have it checked.

Another must is to tell your insurance company what you're planning.

She said: "Some don't like it and you may have to take out specialised cover."

Then there is the question of what to do with your personal property and who to let to. Thorough credit and reference checks are a must to get the right tenant.

Ms Hankins said: "It's important to get the right people and to be realistic. You are going to come back to some wear and tear. Don't expect the house to be exactly as you left it. Things do happen that are not the tenants' fault. But most people with proper references will take care of your property. It's a good idea to meet your tenants, then it becomes someone's home they're renting."

She said leaving ornaments and pictures in place would also reinforce that message but personal possessions and valuables should be packed away and stored – it can be in the attic or basement if you have one and can lock it.

The chance for a good clear out

Is the garage crammed, every drawer and cupboard stuffed? Is it all "file and forget" or "might come in handy" but never has?

Here's another way to look at storage and finance. You haven't touched any of this stuff for years and you've kept saying you'd do a massive clear-out. But the more you add over the years, the more daunting and it's easy to put off. We all do it. And how much house room do some of us give to all that stuff our kids have no space for but have sentimental attachments to?

Preparing for your year out is the perfect opportunity to de-clutter (feng shui if you like) your life. Have a look at what you need to get rid of – car boot sale? Garage sale? E-bay? There are plenty of places where you can sell all the stuff you felt was "too good to get rid of" and "filed" in the garage/attic/spare bedroom to deal with later.

Now's the time to bite the bullet. You'll create space to store what's left that you don't want to leave around a house you might be letting, you'll add some cash to your travel fund, and you'll come back to a pretty organised home. If you've decided to let your home empty you'll need less rented container space – and save yourself some money.

Household contents – storage

Two things to think about if you really want to clear your house before renting are – do you really want to add this to your list of 'things to do' before you go and can you afford it?

We talked to an independent storage company with sites across the UK and to removals and storage company Pickfords to get some idea of what's involved. Sydney Hyams is managing director of Archival Record Management plc, whose head office is in Camberwell, London.

The company rents 10, 20 and 40ft storage containers on managed sites – i.e. sites where there are security guards and your property is safeguarded from fire, flood and theft.

Mr Hyams said you would need a 20ft container for the contents of the average house. The containers are 'self service' so you would have to pack, move and unpack yourself and therefore need to add the costs of van rental and transport to the container rental costs.

You would also have to arrange your own insurance, but, said Mr Hyams, normally you can extend your household contents insurance to cover property on secured sites.

Prices vary according to distance from the storage site, size of container and length of time but for a 20ft container the normal charge is £3.30 plus VAT per day (£23.10 per week plus VAT) with discounts of 5% for 6 months and 10% for a year. So storage alone would come to just over £1,000.

National removals and storage company, Pickfords, also provides container storage on managed sites, but in 7ft square containers of 300 cu ft capacity each, so you could need three or four for the contents of an average 3-bedroomed house, estimated at around 1,200 to 1,400 cubic feet.

Cost per container is £10-£12 per week plus VAT, and the cost reduces to approximately £9 per week plus VAT for a 6-month period and about £7 per week plus VAT for 12 months. But remember that's per container and you could need at least three.

To that you have to add the packing, loading, removal and unloading costs at each end of your career break. The Pickfords representative we spoke to said on average the process costs £300-£400 more than an ordinary house move and prices vary depending on whether your dates fall into peak season for house removals – such as children's school holidays and the peak times of year for house sales.

What about the kids?

This decision is really up to you as parents. Much will depend on the length of time you plan to be away and the point your children are at in their education. Essentially you need to balance the effects of taking a child out of school against the benefits of the 'education' they will get from seeing something of the world. You also need to think through health and medical issues, but that may mean nothing more than carrying essential medical supplies with you, as all travellers are advised to do when travelling abroad.

It's also possible that you can get your child into a local school for some of the time they are away, or you can organise some basic study for them with the help of their school while you are travelling.

A spokesman for the DfES said the 'official' view was that ultimately it was down to the parents but that they should talk it through with their child's school or local education authority.

But parents who have done it even with very small children say that it has been a very worthwhile experience and brought them closer to their kids.

It's worth remembering that most children are a lot more adaptable than parents think and really don't miss all the trappings of modern civilisation once they are in a new place.

Pre-travel prep checklist:

This list covers the extra responsibilities older people might have to consider. It only covers the basics of what you might have to organise – but we hope it will be a useful start for you to cherry-pick what's appropriate and no doubt add your own extras!

Work: Talk to employer about sabbatical/career break options

Career break:
What do you want from it?
What do you want to do?
Where do you want to go?

Finance:
Paying the bills
Mortgage
Financing the trip
Insurance

The house:
Are you going to let it?
Talk to accommodation agency
Safety Certificates
Insurance
Tax exemption?

Storage of possessions:
What do you want to store?
Can it be stored at home?
The chance for a good clear out?

Children:
Talk to school about taking them
Find out about education where you're going
If they're coming how long will the trip be?

For more general advice about travelling see our first chapter Tips for Travellers.

Career breaks & mature travellers | Checklist

Organisations that cater for career-breakers

Gap Year for Grown Ups

First Floor, 1 Meadow Road,
Tunbridge Wells, Kent TN1 2YG

www.gapyearforgrownups.co.uk
Tel: +44 (0) 1892 701 881
Fax: +44 (0) 1892 523 172
Email: info@gapyearforgrownups.co.uk

Only company specialising in career breaks and volunteer work for the over 30s, hundreds of programmes in 30 countries from 2 weeks to 12 months.

Holidaybreak

Overseas Recruitment Dept, Hartford Manor,
Greenbank Lane
Northwich, Cheshire CW8 1HW

www.holidaybreakjobs.com
Tel: +44 (0) 1606 787522
Fax: +44 (0) 870 366 7640
Email: overseas_recruit@holidaybreak.co.uk

You can be a courier, provide activities for children on a holiday break. Be paid while taking a career break!

i-to-i

Woodside House, 261 Low Lane,
Leeds, Yorkshire LS18 5NY

www.i-to-i.com
Tel: +44 (0) 870 333 2332
Fax: +44 (0) 113 205 4619
Email: uk@i-to-i.com

JET - Japan Exchange and Teaching Programme UK

JET Desk, c/o Embassy of Japan,
101-104 Piccadilly, London W1J 7JT

www.jet-uk.org
Tel: +44 (0) 20 7465 6668

Email: info@jet-uk.org

You can apply to take part in the JET programme if you have a bachelors degree in any subject. JET recruits about 400 UK graduates every year.

Madventurer

The Old Casino, 1-4 Forth Lane,
Newcastle upon Tyne, NE1 5HX

www.madventurer.com
Tel: +44 (0) 845 121 1996
Fax: +44 (0)191 269 9490
Email: team@madventurer.com

Aimed at the 25-45 age group this is for the person who wants a break from a stressful job, is in between jobs or who may be fortunate in persuading their employer to give them a number of weeks off to recharge their batteries. Our placements are usually in the fields of education, health or sanitation, although there are also opportunities for sports coaching. We offer a number of five week attachments but the 'break' can also be bespoke in that the career breaker can choose the length of attachment, while the type of attachment will relate to his/her experience and expertise. Madventurer offers career breaks in Ghana, Kenya, Tanzania, Uganda, Peru or Fiji. See **www.careerbreaker.com** Gaps for Grumpies: Building on the successful combination offered to students of a short (two or five weeks) gap followed by a special holiday - this provides the opportunity for people wanting something very different following retirement or redundancy to take part in a community development project with other people of their own age. While accommodation during the project will involve living fairly simply in the local village, but with cooks provided, the holiday will be focused more on seeing historical sites and wildlife with more upmarket accommodation en route and opportunities to relax. See **www.gapsforgrumpies.com**.

MondoChallenge	www.mondochallenge.org
Malsor House, Gayton Road,	Tel: +44 (0) 1604 858225
Milton Malsor, Northamptonshire NN7 3AB	Fax: +44 (0) 1604 859323
	Email: info@mondochallenge.org

MondoChallenge is a not-for-profit organisation that runs volunteer programmes in India, Nepal, Sri Lanka, Tanzania, Kenya, The Gambia, Senegal, Chile and Ecuador. Projects are mainly teaching or business development, and last between 2 and 6 months. Most volunteers are post-graduate or career breakers. There is no upper age limit and we accept a few select gappers every year. All projects are community based - living and working with local people. The cost of a 3-month project is £1000 but doesn't include travel. Couples or friends applying together receive a 10% discount and all start dates are flexible.

NONSTOP Adventure Ltd	www.nonstopadventure.com
Unit 3B, The Plough Brewery,	Tel: +44 (0) 870 241 8070
516 Wandsworth Road	
London SW8 3JX	Email: info@nonstopadventure.com

On The Go Tours	www.onthegotours.com
68-70 North End Road,	Tel: +44 (0) 207 371 1113
West Kensington, London W14 9EP	Fax: +44 (0) 207 471 6414
	Email: info@onthegotours.com

Raleigh International
aleigh House, 27 Parsons Green Lane,
London SW6 4HZ

www.raleighinternational.org
Tel: +44 (0) 20 7371 8585
Fax: +44 (0) 20 7371 5852
Email: info@raleigh.org.uk

Shumba Experience
6 Coventry Street,
Brighton, Sussex BN1 5PQ

www.shumbaexperience.com
Tel: +44 (0) 845 257 3205

Email: info@shumbaexperience.com

Join our exciting wildlife and marine conservation projects in Africa. Volunteer on game reserves to help conserve lions, elephants, leopards and rhinos.

Teaching & Projects Abroad
Aldsworth Parade,
Goring, Sussex BN12 4TX

www.projects-abroad.co.uk
Tel: +44 (0) 1903 708300
Fax: +44 (0) 1903 501026
Email: info@tprojects-abroad.co.uk

The Year Out Group
Queensfield, 28 King's Road,
Easterton, Wiltshire SN10 4PX

www.yearoutgroup.org
Tel: +44 (0) 7980 395789

Email: info@yearoutgroup.org

ANIMALS, COMMUNITY, CONSERVATION, CULTURE, DRAMA, ENVIRONMENT, RELIGIOUS, RESEARCH/SCIENCE, TEACHING, TRAVEL: Year Out Group is an association of the UK's leading Year Out organisations that was launched in 2000 to promote the concepts and benefits of well-structured year out programmes. In 2005 the 34 members of the Group accounted for over 30,000 structured year-out placements. Year Out Group Membership (January 2006): Courses and Cultural Exchanges: Art History Abroad; BUNAC; Camp America; CESA Languages Abroad; Flying Fish; Nonstopski and Snowboard; Peak Leaders; St James's & Lucie Clayton College; Tante Marie School of Cooking; The International Academy; Year Out Drama. Expeditions: BSES; Blue Ventures; Coral Cay Conservation; Frontier; Greenforce; Quest Overseas; Raleigh International; Trekforce Expeditions; VentureCo; Wind Sand & Stars. Projects: Global Vision International; Oyster Worldwide. Structured Work Placements: The Year in Industry. Volunteering: Africa & Asia Venture; Africa Conservation Experience; Changing Worlds; CSV (Community Service Volunteers); GAP Activity Projects; Gap Sports; Global Adventures; i-to-i International Projects; Madventure; Outreach International; Project Trust; Teaching & Projects Abroad; The Leap; Travellers Worldwide.

Travellers Worldwide
7 Mulberry Close,
Ferring, West Sussex BN12 5HY

www.travellersworldwide.com
Tel: +44 (0) 1903 502595
Fax: +44 (0) 1903 500364
Email: info@travellersworldwide.com

Travellers Worldwide organises voluntary work placements abroad. You can participate in very worthwhile work in Australia, Argentina, Brazil, Brunei, Bolivia, China, Cuba, Ghana, Guatemala, India, Kenya, Malaysia, Peru, Russia, Sri Lanka, South Africa, Zambia, Zimbabwe. You can choose from over 200 projects from teaching and care to conservation work with endangered animals. The conservation projects include rehabilitation and research work. Work experience placements available in journalism, law, veterinary, medicine, architecture, hotel and catering, tourism and more. There are structured opportunities to learn languages and other skills such as capoeira in Brazil, tango in Argentina or meditation on Sri Lanka. Projects are flexible and tailored to suit you (two weeks to one year) running throughout the year. No qualifications required. Prices start: £925 including accommodation, food and full support provided throughout.

Chapter 4
Working abroad

Judith was 42 when she decided to take a career break to spend three months teaching in Tanzania.

"Now when I look back I wish I had planned to stay for longer in Tanzania – I think 6 months would have been really good," she said.

She taught English at Sambasha Primary School mainly to Standard 6 pupils (aged between 11-14) in classes of 60-plus. The pupils were mainly Masai and the area was very rural with no electricity.

The experience certainly made her re-think a lot of things. Judith described her feelings when she first got back to the UK:

"Realisation of how much we have and how much we take for granted in the UK and developed countries. I felt like an alien at first – a sense of disgust at our material world – it was hard going into supermarkets and seeing how easily people buy things. I felt ashamed at having so many possessions which I didn't really need. Have still not really got into watching TV. I missed the human contact which I had out there – so much value was placed on your interaction with people. When I came back to London it was so obvious how most people just get on with their own lives and often don't bother to even make eye contact with others.

"It took me at least 2 months to feel comfortable again. I knew I would need to get a job and earn some money. I started looking for a permanent job in teaching but in the meantime did some supply teaching – a real shock after the experience of teaching 60+ pupils in a class in Tanzania with no behavioural problems!

"I would like to think it has changed the way I look at things but I have to work at keeping hold of the experience and remind myself by looking at my photos of the school, the area and the family I lived with. It's made me more aware of what is really important in life – the things that money can't buy."

Judith was due to start a new teaching job in September:

"ironically am going to work in the Private sector which I've never done before and never thought I would – I've decided I want to teach pupils who WANT to learn and I don't want to be in an aggressive or hostile environment which I think is sadly all too often the case in state schools."

She says if you're thinking of taking a **gap-** : "Go for it!! Have an open mind when you go and be prepared for anything but throw yourself in as a human being and you can't go wrong."

visit: www.gap-year.com

If you desperately want to go abroad, can't really afford it and the bit you have managed to save won't cover much more than an airfare a great way to experience a different culture is to live and work in it.

Most jobs give you enough spare time in the evenings and at weekends to enjoy yourself and make friends and you'll be meeting locals and experiencing what the country is really like.

Plus, not only will you cover at least some of your costs, the work experience will look good on your CV – as well as the specific work experience you gain prospective employers will be reassured that you at least know something about basics like punctuality, fitting into an organisation and organising your time.

If you're lucky, you might even find an internship with pay - which would also look good on your CV.

You don't have to be tied to one place for your whole **gap**-year - you can work for a bit and save up for your travels. That way you can learn more about the place and get the inside information from the locals about the best places to see before you set off.

If the chief aim is to cover your costs then there are plenty of different semi-skilled jobs you can get abroad even if you don't speak any languages: from au pair and ski chalet jobs, waitressing and bar work to summer camp staff and teaching English.

Planning ahead

Choosing your destination

Whatever the state of the global economy there are still pockets of job stability. Seasonal farm work still needs to be done and speaking English is always an advantage for jobs in tourism at ski resorts, beach bars and hotel receptions.

If you are a UK citizen or hold an EU (European Union) passport, you can work in any other EU member country without a visa or work permit and there are countless jobs available to students who can speak the right languages. Not all European countries are EU members - go to the European Union website **http://europa.eu.in** to check.

If you want to be more adventurous and venture outside Europe, then check the Foreign Office website for the list of countries they consider simply too dangerous to even go to.

Getting your paperwork sorted

Before you go, make sure you have all the paperwork you need, including visas and work permits, and that you understand all the regulations and restrictions. You can get into serious trouble if you work without the necessary documents - you probably don't want to be deported during your **gap-**year! Some countries will only grant you a visa or work permit if you can prove you already have a job lined up for when you arrive. The best place to get information is the embassy in London for the country you're going to - there's a link on www.**gap-**year.com to the embassy websites, or look in the country info section at the back of this book for embassy phone numbers.

Take a couple of copies of all your paperwork, leave one copy at home with someone reliable and pack another copy separate from the papers themselves just in case they get stolen or lost. It's a good idea to take photocopies of your relevant qualifications with you, and some spare copies of your CV preferably in the local language. Even if you already have a job set up before you go over there, you might not like it and want to apply for another job.

When you're getting your insurance, remember to check that you'll be covered if you're working. We've heard of at least one person whose stuff was damaged, but his insurance wouldn't pay because he was working at the time.

Finding a job

You'll need to be proactive: only the luckiest people (usually in a totally unrealistic Hollywood movie) walk down the street and get offered a job – and if it does happen to you, be careful, it may be a con! Finding a job may take time and effort. The more places you can send your CV the greater the chances of you getting a job.

Register with all the international employment agencies that are free and make sure you know what the agency fee will be if you get employed.

If you use an agency, always insist on talking to someone who has used them before - that way you'll really find out what the deal is.

If you want to go to a particular place, do a search to see if there's a website for that area and then send or email your CV with a short covering note to any interesting local companies. Don't expect to be flooded with replies. Some companies are simply too busy to respond to every enquiry - but you may get lucky and have exactly the skills or qualifications they're looking for.

Some companies will also advertise vacant posts on specialist employment websites, which often have an international section. You can register with the sites too, usually for free.

Tell everyone you know, including relatives and your parents' friends, that you are looking for a job abroad - someone may know someone who has a company abroad who can help you or let you stay with them.

It's always easier to find employment when you're living locally. Lots of jobs are advertised in the local papers, or by 'staff wanted' notices put up in windows. So if you get there and hate the job you've got, don't put up with it, or come running home - see if you can find something better.

Over the next few pages we've listed ideas on types of employment and any companies we know about that will find you work. Always ask a company to put you in contact with someone they have placed before - if they say no then don't use them: they may have something to hide.

Au Pairing

Being an au pair is a good way to immerse yourself in a different culture, learn a new language and hopefully save some extra cash. You should be given enough time out of work to take some language courses as well as have fun.

If you want to get to grips with a foreign language and don't fancy forking out for food and a dismal flat, being an au pair can be a brilliant solution. It involves living with a foreign family, often in Europe, for several months.

You don't need any qualifications to be an au pair, although obviously some experience with children is a bonus. However, au pairing is not like babysitting for a couple of hours - it is a hard job and a big responsibility.

You should listen to any legal advice you are given by the nanny/au pair agency you use. Many au pair agencies also now require written references, police checks and other proof of suitability – which is as much a protection for you as it is for the parents of the children you might look after.

Finding an au pair agency

The safest bet may be to look for a placement through a UK-based au pair agency. It's also better for the prospective family abroad, since they will be dealing with a UK agency (possibly working together with an agency in the family's own country) that has met you, interviewed you and taken up references. Remember they're going to be taking you into their family home and trusting you with their children.

You can also find information on au pair work worldwide on the internet. You can usually register for free and your name will be matched to the families around the world that have registered on the site that meet your specifications (but make sure you make human contact at home and abroad before you make your final decision).

Check that the au pair agency is a member of either the Recruitment and Employment Confederation (which has a website listing all its members and covering au pair employment in many countries), or of the International Au Pair Association.

There are of course good agencies which do not belong to trade associations, either because they are too small to afford the membership fees, or because they are well-established and have a good independent reputation.

However the growth in use of the internet by families seeking au pairs and by young people seeking placements has been so large that it prompted the IAPA to issue a warning in February 2006 to encourage people not to go it alone but to stick to using established and reputable agencies.

They say the trend, "coupled with a significant increase in the use of newspaper classifieds to recruit au pairs has resulted in many families and au pairs experiencing mismatched and at times, frightening placements with no means for recourse."

International Bredgade 25 H
Au Pair Association DK-1260 Copenhagen K, Denmark
Tel: +45 3317 0066 Fax: +45 3393 9676
www.iapa.org

Agencies should ask for an interview and references, and maybe a medical certificate.

Since April 2004, when the rules in the Employment Agencies Act (Charging Fees to Au Pairs) Regulations 1981(d) were changed, au pair agencies operating in the UK and sending au pairs abroad can no longer, under specified circumstances, charge au pairs for finding them a placement.

If you have a complaint against a UK agency it's best to take it up with the Employment Agency Standards Helpline, Tel: +44 (0) 845 955 5105. It operates Monday-Friday 9.30 am to 4.30 pm

You can find out more about your rights on

http://www.dti.gov.uk/employment/employment-agencies/index.html

Make sure the agency you use has connections where you'll be working, get a list of other local au pairs so you have support when you're out there, and take time finding a suitable family. The fewer children the better, and you should expect your own room. It's also worth checking what there is to do in your free time - you don't want to spend every weekend in your bedroom because you're stuck in the middle of nowhere.

Before you go, check you have written confirmation of the hours, duties and pay agreed as well as copies of important documents such as passport, birth certificate, and translations of any academic certificates to prove your student status. Extra passport photos are a good idea, as is the number and address of the local British Consulate - just in case.

Au pairing in Europe

European law stipulates that au pairs should not be younger than 17 and should provide a current medical certificate for an au pair job (participating in normal family duties); that an employment agreement should be made in writing between the au pair and host family, with conditions of employment clearly defined; that the au pair should receive pocket money (exempt from tax) and have enough free time to study; and that the au pair should not be expected to work more than five hours a day and have at least one full free day a week.

The agreement also set up a 'model contract' for young people placed as au pairs.

This is now the accepted definition for au pair jobs in the EU, but not necessarily in other countries. Some countries have different local rules.

Take a look at: http://conventions.coe.int/treaty/en/Treaties/Html/068.htm for the details of the European Agreement and any local variations.

In return for board, lodgings and pocket money, you'll be expected to look after the children and do light domestic chores like ironing, cooking, tidying their bedrooms and doing their washing, for up to five hours a day (six hours in France or Germany), five days a week, as well as spending two or three evenings a week baby-sitting. If you are asked to work more than this then technically you are not doing the work of an au pair, but of a mother's help (which pays more). Or slave. Remember that an au pair is classified as 'non experienced', and you should never be left in sole charge of a baby. If the family gives you more responsibility than you can handle say so; if they don't stop - quit.

It's important to complete all the necessary paperwork for living and working in another country. Most agencies will organise the paperwork side for you, and make sure the legal documents are in order before you leave. Most French agencies require a set of passport photos, a photocopy of your passport, two references (preferably translated into French), and your most recent academic qualifications, as well as a hand-written letter in French to your prospective family which tells them something about you, your reasons for becoming an au pair and any future aspirations.

The agency may also ask for a medical certificate (showing you are free of deadly contagious diseases, etc.) dated less than three months before you leave, and translated into French. Au pairs also have to have a medical examination on arrival in France.

The French Consulate advises you to check that the family you stay with obtains a 'mother's help' work contract (accord de placement au pair d'un stagiaire aide-familiale). If you are a non-EU citizen you are expected to do this before you leave for France, but British au pairs do not need to.

Au Pair Agencies – Europe

Au Pairs by Pebbles
PO Box 6227,
Leighton Buzzard, Bedfordshire LU7 3YY

www.aupairsbypebbles.com
Tel: +44 (0) 870 0664743

Email: info@aupairsbypebbles.com

Pebbles is a friendly and professional agency with offices in the South of France and the UK.

Delaney International
Bramble Cottage, Thorncombe Street,
Bramley, Surrey GU5 0ND

www.delaney-nannies.com
Tel: +44 (0) 1483 894 300
Fax: +44 (0) 1483 894 700
Email: info@delaney-nannies.com

EF Au Pair
Central Admissions Office, Haldenstrasse 4,
6006 Luzern Switzerland

www.ef.org
Tel: +41 41 417 4550
Fax: +41 41 417 4551
Email: aupair.ww@ef.com

Although EF Au Pair (an affiliate of EF International Language Schools) deals mostly with non-English speaking Europeans, people from Britain have a huge language advantage and are always well-received.

Planet Au Pair
C/Los Centelles 45-6-11,
46006 Valencia Spain

www.planetaupair.com
Tel: +34 96 320 6491
Fax: +34 96 320 7832
Email: info@planetaupair.com

Au pairing in North America

You must be 18 or over and it is considered to be a full-time position - the au pair is often in sole charge of the children. You will receive at least 8 hours of child safety and 24 hours of child development instruction before you take up your placement. Looking after children aged under two is more demanding and therefore most agencies ask that you have at least 200 hours of experience with that age group and are at least 19 years old.

All au pair programmes are legislated and regulated by US law, which means (at the time of going to press), that all au pairs receive pocket money tied to the minimum wage, currently US$139.05 (about £74.19) for 51 weeks, working not more than 10 hours per day or more than 45 hours per week.

http://www.interexchange.org/interexchange/regulations.html

If you complete the 51 weeks you can also receive a 'bonus' payment of US$400.

You can expect a good standard of living, full-board, your own bedroom and use of a car. US government regulations stipulate that au pairs must attend education courses (because au pair work is seen primarily as a cultural exchange) 'putting in a minimum of three hours a week during term-time. This is financed by the host family up to a limit of US$500'.

There are support networks for au pairs once you arrive in the US: agencies should provide assigned coordinators who will act as mediators between the au pair and the family if there are problems - and it is possible to be reassigned to a different family.

British and English-speaking Europeans can go to the USA on a 'cultural exchange' with a J1 visa which is valid for a year. Candidates must be between 18 and 26 years of age, have a secondary education, experience or training in childcare, hold a clean drivers' licence and be in good health. Be careful: the USA has a confusing bureaucratic system, and if you're not careful you risk earning money illegally and even being deported. That's why it is important to go with a good agency that will check you have the right paperwork.

Because of strict government regulations, most agencies that organise au pairs in the USA offer very similar services. However it's worth registering with a number of agencies if only to have a range of 'perfect match' host families to choose from.

EduCare

EduCare places au pairs with families who have school-aged children and need childcare before and after school hours. Au pairs on the EduCare scheme work no more than 30 hours per week in return for US$105 and must complete a minimum of 12 hours of academic credit or its equivalent during the programme year (financed by the host family for up to US$1,000.

You can find out more by visiting the Educare website:
http://www.educareinamerica.co.uk/

The US Department of State website has all the up-to-date legislation and information about the necessary visas:
http://www.unitedstatesvisas.gov/

US Embassy (Visas)
5 Upper Grosvenor Street
London W1A 2JB
Tel: +44 (0) 90 6820 0290

Au Pair Agencies – USA

Au Pair in America (APIA)
37 Queen's Gate,
London SW7 5HR

www.aupairamerica.co.uk
Tel: +44 (0) 20 7581 7322
Fax: +44 (0) 20 7581 7345
Email: info@aupairamerica.co.uk

Childcare International
Trafalgar House, Grenville Place,
London NW7 3SA

www.childint.co.uk
Tel: +44 (0) 20 8906 3116

Childcare International is the UK agent for Au Pair in America and also sends au pairs to Europe, Canada and Australia. Ages 18-30.

Internships & paid work placements

If you want to use your gap year to gain relevant work experience, then why not sign up for an internship? It'll give your CV a competitive edge and give you an insight into what that job is really like. Traditionally internships are one year paid employment postings for undergraduate or graduate students, arranged from a university. These websites are useful:

www.internship-usa.com
www.internabroad.com
http://www.internjobs.com/
search/USA/Internship_Programs/index.html

www.internships-usa.com
www.internshipprograms.com
http://www.studyabroadlinks.com/

Before you sign up make sure you're clear just what your placement will involve. An 'internship' should mean you are able to do interesting paid work

related to your degree studies, current or future, for at least six months. Sitting behind a reception desk for very little money is not an internship, but a badly paid job.

Intern programmes

AgriVenture
Speedwell Farm Bungalow, Nettle Bank,
Wisbech, Cambridgeshire PE14 0SA

www.agriventure.com
Tel: +44 (0) 800 7832186
Fax: +44 (0) 1945 4509999
Email: uk@agriventure.com

AgriVenture offers you paid work placements in Australia, New Zealand, Canada, USA, Japan. If you are aged 18 to 30 we can offer work in either agriculture or horticulture. For a one off payment, we arrange your flights, visa, work and travel insurance, work placement, information meeting in the UK, welcome seminar on arrival in host country. Live on the farm or horticultural enterprise with our host families - full support and back up in your host country. Programmes are for between 4 and 14 months.

Anglo-Polish Communications Limited
Derwent Road, York Road Industrial Park,
Malton, North Yorkshire YO17 6YB

www.a-p-c.co.uk
Tel: +44 (0) 1653 699833

Centro Linguistico Italiano Dante Alighieri
Piazza della Repubblica 5,
I-50123 Florence Italy

www.clida.it
Tel: +39 055 21 0808
Fax: +39 055 28 7828
Email: study@clida.it

Established in 1965, CLIDA (Centro Linguistico Italiano Dante Alighieri) is the oldest private school of Italian for foreigners in Italy as well as an internship centre recognised by the "Regione Toscana". CLIDA offers Language & Internship Programs from 1 to 8 months long. Unfortunately, internships in Italy are by law unpaid, but CLIDA has excellent contacts in many professional sectors. Therefore, students from all around the world will have a great opportunity to improve their skills, so gaining precious experience for future jobs. Internships are offered in Florence and its surroundings, in the following areas: Marketing, International Business, Business Development, Sales, Tourism, Hotel/Restaurant Management, Fashion, Leather/Textile industry, Secretarial, Art and Photography, Architecture, Law, Social Work, Web Design, Graphic Design, Agriculture and Botanic Sciences, Accessory Design and Production, Flowers (nurseries), Jewellery (shops or designers) and Books.

Global Adventures Project
38 Queen's Gate,
London SW7 5HR

www.globaladventures.co.uk
Tel: +44 (0) 800 085 4197
Fax: +44 (0) 207 7590 7444
Email: info@globaladventures.co.uk

InterExchange
161 Sixth Avenue,
New York NY 10013 USA

www.interexchange.org
Tel: +1 212 924 0446
Fax: +1 212 924 0575
Email: info@interexchange.org

InterExchange offers J-1 & H-2B visa programs throughout the US. Options include au pair, internship, seasonal work and travel and summer camp positions.

IST Plus
Rosedale House, Rosedale Road,
Richmond, Surrey TW9 2SZ

www.istplus.com
Tel: +44 (0) 208 939 9057
Fax: +44 (0) 208 332 7858
Email: info@istplus.com

We offer work, travel and cultural exchange programmes to the USA, Canada, Australia, New Zealand, Thailand and China and language study in Europe and Latin America.

Working abroad | Internships & paid work placements

105

Telepassport-Bulgaria
PO Box 1, Floor 1, 41 'Tsar Ivan Shisman' Str
Bourgas Bulgaria

www.agencycrew.com
Tel: +359 900 21 640
Fax: +359 56 833 347
Email: contact@agencycrew.com

Telepassport-Bulgaria is a crew manning agency, so if you're interested in spending your year out on a ship travelling the world then it could be worth your while getting in touch. A huge range of jobs are available.

The Year Out Group
Queensfield, 28 King's Road,
Easterton, Wiltshire SN10 4PX

www.yearoutgroup.org
Tel: +44 (0) 7980 395789

Email: info@yearoutgroup.org

Travellers Worldwide
7 Mulberry Close,
Ferring, West Sussex BN12 5HY

www.travellersworldwide.com
Tel: +44 (0) 1903 502595
Fax: +44 (0) 1903 500364
Email: info@travellersworldwide.com

Work the World
Churchill House, 12 Mosley Street,
Newcastle upon Tyne, Northumberland NE1 1DE

www.worktheworld.co.uk
Tel: +44 (0) 191 230 8256
Fax: +44 (0) 191 261 0200
Email: info@worktheworld.co.uk

Xplor Abroad (Cultural Exchange Group of Argentina)
www.xplorabroad.com
Avenida de Mayo, 4th Floor, Office 43,
Buenos Aires, C1085ABQ Argentina

Tel: +54 11 43847070
Fax: +54 11 43847070
Email: info@xplorabroad.com

Sport instructors

Working as a sports instructor is a great way to use your skills to earn money during your **gap**-year. It's also a good way to finance living in a foreign country and maybe some travel after the job ends.

Ski resorts are probably the biggest sports instructor employers, but for every sport that exists – from kayaking to cricket, from sailing to snowboarding – there will be people who want to learn more, and you might be the person to teach them.

Snowboarding and all watersports are really popular at the moment. The great thing is that there are jobs for sport instructors all around the world – from Bermuda to Belgium; from São Paulo to Senegal.

If you don't already have your instructor qualifications then you could spend the first part of your **gap**-year getting qualified (take a look at Chapter 6 Learning abroad: Sport) – lots of the sports schools will help you get a job, although it's always worth asking before you sign up for the course. Also check that the qualification they are offering is what the resorts want.

You can contact resorts/sports schools direct (find them on the internet) or go through an agency, though some agencies have age restrictions and may want specific qualifications. As always, the internet is a good place to search for jobs.

Take a look at:

www.skiingthenet.com

www.jobmonkey.com

http://www.natives.co.uk/

These are just a few we found after doing a quick search - there are bound to be loads more. If you find a really helpful site you could share your luck by telling other gappers on the www.**gap**-year.com message board.

If you can't find what you're looking for in the list of companies below, try searching the internet for national and international sporting associations - explain to them that you're looking for work using your sports skills and ask for their help - they may be able to put you in touch with companies or local groups. Make sure you have an up-to-date and relevant CV ready to go which lists all your sporting achievements and qualifications and which highlights your leadership skills.

Sport instructor jobs

Allan Dive
Kota Kinabula,
Sabah, Borneo

www.allandive.com
Tel: +60 88 711 715
Fax: +60 88 256 483
Email: allandive@hotmail.com

The Allan Dive School offers PADI and SSI (Scuba School International) Instructors training facilities doing basic training to instructor level, marine conservation projects etc. Course prices range from £1500 to £3000.

Base Camp Group
Unit 30, Baseline Business Studios,
Whitchurch Road
London W11 4AT

www.basecampgroup.com
Tel: +44 (0) 20 7243 6222
Fax: +44 (0) 20 7243 6222

Email: contact@basecampgroup.com

Looking for adventure? Base Camp Group run ski & snowboard instructor courses and offer accommodation-only packages in Europe and North America.

Britannia Sailing East Coast
Victory House, Shotley Marina,
Ipswich, Suffolk IP9 1QJ

www.britanniasailingschool.co.uk
Tel: +44 (0) 1473 787019
Fax: +44 (0) 1473 787018
Email: office@britanniasailingschool.co.uk

Based at Shotley Marina near Ipswich, Britannia Sailing is a well-established company with first-class facilities offering all aspects of sailing instruction and yacht charter.

Crewseekers
Hawthorn House, Hawthorn Lane, Sarisbury Green
Southampton, Hampshire SO31 7BD

www.crewseekers.net
Tel: +44 (0) 1489 578319
Fax: +44 (0) 1489 578319
Email: info@crewseekers.co.uk

Work available as yachting crew cruising, racing, yacht delivering around the world. Beginners welcome.

Flying Fish
25 Union Road,
Cowes, Isle of Wight PO31 7TW

www.flyingfishonline.com
Tel: +44 (0) 1983 280 641

Email: mail@flyingfishonline.com

Taking advantage of some of the best training locations in the world, Flying Fish runs sailing, diving, surfing, windsurfing and kitesurfing instructor courses in Australia, New Zealand, Egypt, Greece and the UK. Ski and snowboard instructor training take place in Canada.

GAP SPORTS Ltd.
Thamesbourne House, Station Road,
Bourne End, Buckinghamshire SL8 5QH

www.gapsports.com
Tel: +44 (0) 870 837 9797

Email: info@gapsports.com

Join sports (and non-sports) community projects in Africa and Latin America, become a ski/snowboard instructor in Canada with paid work experience, play and train at international football, rugby, golf and cricket academies, or become a qualified scuba diver and work in dive schools worldwide.

Gap Year Diver Ltd
Tyte Court,
Great Rollright, Oxfordshire OX7 5RS

www.gapyeardiver.com
Tel: +44 (0) 845 257 3292
Fax: +44 (0) 1608 730 574
Email: info@gapyeardiver.com

We offer a full range of PADI courses from complete beginner to instructor standard and beyond. We also offer TDI / PSA technical diving courses as well as work experience placements. During 2006 we will also be launching a range of language and diving courses so you can practice a language and learn scuba diving at the same time.

Goal-Line Soccer Clinics
PO Box 1642,
Corvallis, OR 97339 USA

www.goal-line.com
Tel: +1 (541) 753 5833
Fax: +1 (541) 753 0811
Email: info@goal-line.com

Goal-Line offers paid soccer coaching vacations for qualified applicants. Their programme operates in a number of communities in the Pacific Northwest (Washington, Oregon) of the USA. Summer camp sessions begin in early July and end mid-August.

Madventurer
The Old Casino, 1-4 Forth Lane,
Newcastle upon Tyne, NE1 5HX

www.madventurer.com
Tel: T: +44 (0) 845 121 1996
Fax: F: +44 (0)191 269 9490
Email: team@madventurer.com

Sportventurer offers opportunities to coach children in two and four week (and longer) projects in seven mainstream sports in five developing countries. While qualifications are helpful, they are not essential. Infectious enthusiasm and basic skills are prerequisites.

For more information see **www.sportventurer.com.**

New Zealand Skydiving School
P O Box 21,
Methven, Christchurch New Zealand

www.skydivingnz.com
Tel: +64 (03) 302 9143
Fax: +64 (03) 302 9140
Email: info@skydivingnz.com

Join the international skydiving industry by completing this unique skydiving qualification in New Zealand, the Adventure Capital of the Southern Hemisphere. The Diploma in Commercial Skydiving includes 200 skydives, a wide range of skydiving skills and knowledge including freefall camera / video, video editing, parachute packing, dedicated coaching camps and organised industry experience. The aim is to make students highly employable in the world of commercial skydiving; current graduate employment rates exceed 95%. The Skydiving School has a team of highly qualified and internationally respected instructors and state of the art equipment. The school is New Zealand Parachute Industry Association and New Zealand Qualifications Authority approved. Career Development Loans are available for UK students.

NONSTOP Adventure Ltd
Unit 3B, The Plough Brewery,
516 Wandsworth Road
London SW8 3JX

www.nonstopadventure.com
Tel: +44 (0) 870 241 8070

Email: info@nonstopadventure.com

NONSTOP Adventure is a family owned company that runs sailing, skiing and snowboarding training courses. All our courses are run by the industry's top professionals and focus on general improvement and in most cases will result in gaining internationally recognised qualifications. NONSTOP Ski & Snowboard Improvement and instructor courses in the Canadian Rockies. Gain internationally recognised qualifications that could see you instructing all around the world. NONSTOP Sail 6-week adventure sails that include: Trans Atlantic crossings, Circumnavigations of Britain and circuits of the Caribbean. 14 week Yachtmaster Fast Track courses. RYA yacht sailing courses from our base in Dartmouth.

PJ Scuba
Mermaids Dive Center S-2694,
PADI 5 Star Career Development Center,
Jomtien Beach Road, 75/124 Moo 12
Nongprue, Chonburi 20260 Thailand

www.pjscuba.com
Tel: +66 (0) 186 444 90
Fax: +66 (0) 382 322 21

Email: pjscuba@gmail.com

P J offers the chance to study scuba diving to instructor level (PADI) and then teach in Thailand, Vietnam or Cambodia. There is no entry qualification apart from good interpersonal skills and the ability to swim.

Plas Menai
National Watersports Centre,
Caernarfon, Gwynedd LL55 1UE

www.plasmenai.co.uk
Tel: +44 (0) 1248 670964
Fax: +44 (0) 1248 673939
Email: info@plasmenai.co.uk

Plas Menai offers a range of courses training people to work as watersports, yachting and adventure instructors abroad and in the UK. Training courses last between 1 and 26 weeks and take place in Spain and UK. Courses for beginners and those with experience. Use your qualifications to train, work and travel in your gap year or longer term.

• Start dates throughout the year
• Weekend, 5 day and longer training courses
• Professional Yacht Skipper: 17 wks
• Dinghy and Windsurf Instructor: 12 wks
• Dinghy Instructor: 8 wks
• Multi-Activity Instructor: 26 wks
• Recruitment + work placements.

Ski Academy Switzerland
Haut-Lac International Centre,
1669 Les Sciernes Switzerland

www.skiacademyswitzerland.com
Tel: +41 269 284 200

Email: info@skiacademyswitzerland.com

Ski Academy Switzerland (SAS) is a provider of quality ski instructor programmes with work opportunities for Gap Year Students and for those persons who are on a Career Break or just fancy a challenge!

Snowboard Instructor Training Co www.snowboardinstructortraining.co.nz
Queenstown, Otago New Zealand

Email: info@snowboardinstructortraining.co.nz

Snowboard Instructor Training Co offers you the opportunity to train for your ski instructor qualification with the New Zealand Snow Sports Instructors Alliance Stage 1 snowboard instructors exam.

Teaching & Projects Abroad
Aldsworth Parade,
Goring, Sussex BN12 4TX

www.projects-abroad.co.uk
Tel: +44 (0) 1903 708300
Fax: +44 (0) 1903 501026
Email: info@tprojects-abroad.co.uk

The Year Out Group
Queensfield, 28 King's Road,
Easterton, Wiltshire SN10 4PX

www.yearoutgroup.org
Tel: +44 (0) 7980 395789

Email: info@yearoutgroup.org

UKSA (United Kingdom Sailing Academy)
The Maritime Academy,
West Cowes, Isle of Wight PO31 7PQ

www.uksa.org
Tel: +44 (0) 1983 294 941
Fax: +44 (0) 1983 295 938
Email: info@uksa.org

The United Kingdom Sailing Academy (UKSA), based in Cowes, trains watersport instructors, professional skippers and crews for yachts. Gap year students train with UKSA for six months, in Cowes and Barbados, to become multi-qualified water sport instructors. Six hundred companies worldwide recruit directly through the Academy.

Teaching English as a Foreign Language

Teaching English as a Foreign Language (TEFL) is the ideal combination of doing something useful (if you're any good) and earning some money whilst enjoying life in another culture.

There are a lot of organisations happy to persuade you that a TEFL qualification is a very useful thing to have. Probably too many, in fact, because it's quite difficult for under-21s to get TEFL work abroad. Ask course organisers if they can help to find you TEFL jobs abroad as well as train you.

TEFL courses are available throughout the UK with many different certificates. CELTA is widely recognised by the industry and the Trinity College Certificate in TESOL (Teaching English to Speakers of Other Languages) is probably the most-recognised by the British Council. Both are open to 18-year-olds.

Courses that do not lead to recognised qualifications are only worth doing if linked to a voluntary work placement, or if it has been recommended by an organisation you'll be working for. But you don't have to have any certificates to teach English informally (or as an au pair) abroad, and a short course will give you some idea of how to teach, increase your confidence and give you some lesson plans. See Chapter 6 (Learning abroad), p.187, for more information on TEFL training.

How to find TEFL work

Availability of work for people who can teach English varies, particularly outside the EU. In most countries it is possible to give private lessons. The best way to find out more about individual countries is to contact the relevant embassy in the UK, which will give you up-to-date details of visas, salaries, qualifications needed and a view about the availability of work. You can find links to embassy websites on www.**gap**-year.com. TEFL jobs are advertised in The Times Educational Supplement (Fridays), the Guardian (Tuesdays), in the education section of The Independent and in the EFL Gazette.

Teaching English in private lessons

Giving private tuition, either formally or in conversation classes, is a good way to earn extra cash. Advertisements can be placed in local schools, universities, newspapers and shops when you've been in a country long enough to know the local language and be streetwise.

Be careful about wording your advertisement, particularly if you are young and female. Do not give any indication of your gender, and never write: 'Young English girl gives English lessons' - you could get some heavy-breathing phone calls.

Try to meet prospective students in a public place before inviting them to your home or going to theirs. Usually, you'll be inundated by friends of friends as word gets round there's an English person willing to give private lessons.

TEFL

Changing Worlds
11 Doctors Lane,
Chaldon, Surrey CR3 5AE

www.changingworlds.co.uk
Tel: +44 (0) 1883 340 960
Fax: +44 (0) 870 990 9665
Email: welcome@changingworlds.co.uk

EF English First
Room 2301-08, 23F, Shell Tower, Times Square
Causeway Bay, Hong Kong

www.englishfirst.com
Tel: +852 2111 2370

EF English First, a world leader in language education with 160 schools worldwide, offers full or part-time TEFL courses leading to guaranteed teaching jobs in EF schools in China or Indonesia - with employment possibilities elsewhere. Candidates wishing to apply for courses in Brighton or Manchester do not need previous teaching experience or foreign language skills but must have qualifications enabling them to enter higher education.

En Famille Overseas
La Maison jaune, Avenue de Stade,
34210 Siran France

www.enfamilleoverseas.co.uk
Tel: +33 (0) 468 914 990
Fax: +33 (0) 468 914 990
Email: marylou.toms@wanadoo.fr

En Famille Overseas arranges for you to stay with a family in France or Spain as a paying guest. You can use your 'homestay' as a springboard for finding a local job and you can stay with a family for a week to a year, with the board and lodging costs negotiable if you stay more than a month. You can also attend a suitable language course nearby or have private coaching from your host.

GAP SPORTS Ltd.
Thamesbourne House, Station Road,
Bourne End, Buckinghamshire SL8 5QH

www.gapsports.com
Tel: +44 (0) 870 837 9797

Email: info@gapsports.com

GatherDragons
York, Yorkshire

www.gatherdragons.co.uk

Email: info@gatherdragons.co.uk

i-to-i
Woodside House, 261 Low Lane,
Leeds, Yorkshire LS18 5NY

www.i-to-i.com
Tel: +44 (0) 870 333 2332
Fax: +44 (0) 113 205 4619
Email: uk@i-to-i.com

MondoChallenge
Malsor House, Gayton Road,
Milton Malsor, Northamptonshire NN7 3AB

www.mondochallenge.org
Tel: +44 (0) 1604 858225
Fax: +44 (0) 1604 859323
Email: info@mondochallenge.org

MondoChallenge is a not-for-profit organisation that runs volunteer programmes in India, Nepal, Sri Lanka, Tanzania, Kenya, The Gambia, Senegal, Chile and Ecuador. Projects are mainly teaching or business development, and last between 2 and 6 months. Most volunteers are post-graduate or career breakers. There is no upper age limit and we accept a few select gappers every year. All projects are community based - living and working with local people. The cost of a 3-month project is £1000 but doesn't include travel. Couples or friends applying together receive a 10% discount and all start dates are flexible.

Saxoncourt Training & Recruitment
59 South Molton Street,
London W1K 5SN

www.saxoncourt.com
Tel: +44 (0) 20 7499 8533
Fax: +44 (0) 20 7499 9374
Email: tt@saxoncourt.com

Saxoncourt is an EFL recruitment consultancy placing over 600 English instructors with private language schools in up to 20 different countries worldwide each year. If you don't yet have your TEFL qualification, Saxoncourt also runs full-time four-week courses in London and Oxford, leading to either the Trinity TESOL diploma or the Cambridge CELTA qualification.

Syndicat Mixte Montaigu-Rocheservière

35 avenue Villebois Mareuil,
85607 Montaigu France

www.explomr.com/english
Tel: +33 (0) 2 51 46 45 45
Fax: +33 (0) 2 51 46 45 40
Email: julie_legree@yahoo.co.uk

This French organisation receives local government funding to teach English in primary schools, offering four posts annually – and it also employs a fifth person to work as a language assistant in a local college and lycée.

Teaching & Projects Abroad

Aldsworth Parade,
Goring, Sussex BN12 4TX

www.projects-abroad.co.uk
Tel: +44 (0) 1903 708300
Fax: +44 (0) 1903 501026
Email: info@tprojects-abroad.co.uk

Village Educational Project

Kilimanjaro Tanzania, Ms Katy Allen MBE,
Mint Cottage, Prospect Road
Sevenoaks, Kent TN13 3UA

www.kiliproject.org
Tel: +44 (0) 1732 743 000

Email: project@kiliproject.org

Students teach English to children in rural primary schools in the Marangu region of Mount Kilimanjaro in Tanzania. It costs about £2500 including airfare but excluding visa, spending money and insurance.

Worldwide Experience

Ashley Adams Travel (UK) Ltd,
Guardian House, Borough Road
Godalming, Surrey GU7 2AE

www.worldwideexperience.com
Tel: +44 (0) 1483 860 560
Fax: +44 (0) 1483 860 391
Email: info@worldwideexperience.com

If you are thinking of taking a gap year or even just want to get away for your summer break, Worldwide Experience will have the placement to suit you. Placements start from 2 weeks up to 12 weeks in length and include placements in South Africa, Kenya, Sri Lanka and Scotland.

The following companies should be able to help you get casual work in Europe, or try doing a search on the internet or using **gap**-year message boards to find out if any other gappers know what's available.

Work opportunities - Europe

Acorn Venture
Acorn House, Prospect Road,
Halesowen, West Midlands B62 8DU

www.jobs-acorn.co.uk
Tel: +44 (0) 870 121 9951
Fax: +44 (0) 870 121 9981
Email: info@acorn-venture.com

Acorn Adventure runs adventure holiday camps from April until September based in eight centres in France, Italy, and the UK – their main customers are school/youth groups and families.

Canvas Holidays
East Port House,
Dunfermline, Fifeshire KY12 7JG

www.gvnrecruitment.com
Tel: +44 (0) 1383 629012
Fax: +44 (0) 1383 629071
Email: campingrecruitment@gvnrecruitment.com

GVN recruit staff for award winning tour operators - Canvas Holidays and Camping Life - providing the highest quality self-drive camping holidays across Europe. • positions at over 100 campsites across Europe • supervisory, childcare and campsite courier jobs available • opportunities available from March-October (2 month minimum term contract) • competitive salary, travel to site and accommodation provided If you are friendly, enthusiastic, independent, resourceful and always ready for a challenge then we want to hear from you. You will need to be at least 18 years old and have 1 year's customer service experience.

Château Beaumont Ltd (UK Office)
Weardale Business Centre, Martin Street, Stanhope
Bishop Auckland, County Durham DL13 2UY

www.chateau-beaumont.co.uk
Tel: +44 (0) 844 8000 124
Fax: +44 (0) 871 2000 125

Chateau Beaumont is a small friendly Language and Activity centre based in the Normandy region of France. We welcome British school groups and undertake a program of activities and excursions with a French language input.

French Encounters
63 Fordhouse Road,
Bromsgrove, Worcestershire B60 2LU

www.frenchencounters.com
Tel: +44 (0) 1527 873645
Fax: +44 (0) 1527 832794
Email: admin@frenchencounters.com

French Encounters recruits Gap Year students as animateurs/animatrices for language study field trips for ten to thirteen year old children, based in two Chateaux in Normandy from mid-February to mid-June. Work includes functioning as tour guides, couriers, entertainers, supervisors and role models. Good, conversational French required, preferably at A level. Experience of working with children is useful. All transport, insurance, full board included, plus about £80

117

Looking for a meaningful and productive year out?

Why not work as an 'animateur' with

French Encounters

the specialists in high level educational and language field trips for schools

Do you want to:

really make a difference?

earn while you learn?

confront exciting challenges and broaden your horizons daily?

develop a variety of essential life and vocational skills?

improve your general communication and presentation skills?

learn to be a guide, courier and entertainer?

perfect your French language skills in France?

use your initiative?

live and work in a château in Normandy?

acquire some practical first aid skills?

work with a great variety of people and as part of a dynamic team?

and, of course, have fun in the process?

What previous animateurs have said of their experience:

"An indication of how much we enjoyed it . . . . we're returning
to the château to get married!" 1999

"The first time I took a group out I was terrified - by the end of the season,
I could cope with anything" 2000

"What a good time we had . . . . we all wish we could do it again" 2002

"Felt valued and gained real experience, often asked for but rarely offered!" 2003

"I couldn't imagine a better way to have spent my GAP year. I'll never forget it.
If future animateurs have half the fun we did, it would still be worth it." 2004

"I'd recommend the experience highly - you'd be hard pushed to find a project as
challenging, as valuable for learning so many skills and acquiring new things.
The trouble is finding something else as good for the rest of the year." 2004

"It surpassed all expectations, season was great and we all made friends for life." 2005

"Recommend it to anyone willing to play hard but work harder. Not only really improved my
French, but gained immensely in historical and cultural knowledge and
acquired an interesting repertoire of alternative jokes!" 2005

Season lasts from mid-February - mid-June
Interested ?
contact: French Encounters
63 Fordhouse Road Bromsgrove Worcs B60 2LU
Tel: 01527 873645 Tel/Fax: 01527 832794
email: admin@frenchencounters.com www.frenchencounters.com

weekly, with weekend allowance. Compulsory comprehensive training given. An ideal opportunity to speak and practice French in a real, working context to perfect linguistic skills required for a successful start to a degree programme.

Holidaybreak

Overseas Recruitment Dept, Hartford Manor,
Greenbank Lane
Northwich, Cheshire CW8 1HW

www.holidaybreakjobs.com
Tel: +44 (0) 1606 787522
Fax: +44 (0) 870 366 7640
Email: overseas_recruit@holidaybreak.co.uk

Holidaybreak (Eurocamp and Keycamp) organises camping holidays throughout Europe (excluding the UK) and employs people of 18 and over to help from April/May to July or September/October. Jobs last for at least two months. You can be a courier, (helping customers plus cleaning accommodation), provide activities for children, put up or take down tents or supervise. A competitive wage is paid. Travel costs, uniform, accommodation and subsidised insurance are also provided.

Interspeak

Stretton Lower Hall, Stretton,
Malpas, Cheshire SY14 7HS

www.interspeak.co.uk
Tel: +44 (0) 1829 250 973
Fax: +44 (0) 1829 250 596
Email: enquiries@interspeak.co.uk

Interspeak organises unpaid work placements from between one and six months. You pay a registration fee up front, then a flat fee for arranging the placement. Interspeak will also organise a family for you to stay with, although you can make your own plans if you prefer. Placement jobs vary widely, but Interspeak says it can find placements in banking, law, marketing, media, hotels and restaurants – citing one student working in a fashion photography studio in France and another for a radio station in Spain.

Jobs in the Alps

17 High Street,
Gretton, Northamptonshire NN17 3DE

www.jobs-in-the-alps.co.uk
Tel: +44 (0) 7050 121648
Fax: +44 (0) 1536 771914
Email: info@jobs-in-the-alps.co.uk

Jobs in the Alps offers seasonal jobs in mountain resorts for gap year students who have good French or German, usually A-level or equivalent, and want to use or improve their language skills whilst enjoying winter skiing or summer sports.

Mark Warner Ltd

George House, 61-65 Kensington Church Street,
London W8 4BA

www.markwarner.co.uk/recruitment
Tel: +44 (0) 8700 330 750
Fax: +44 (0) 8700 330 751
Email: recruitment@markwarner.co.uk

Mark Warner are a leading Tour Operator with vacancies all year round including the Alps, Mediterranean, Aegean and Winter Sun destinations.

Natives
263 Putney Bridge Road,
London SW15 2PU

www.natives.co.uk
Tel: +44 (0) 20 8788 4271
Fax: +44 (0) 8700 626 362
Email: vicky@natives.co.uk

Natives.co.uk is the UK's number 1 seasonal recruitment website. If you would like to work in a ski or summer resort you can find details of what jobs are available, where they are, and you can even apply direct. Natives also run chalet cookery courses and ski/snowboard tech courses - you can give yourself the edge(!) over all the other candidates.

Solaire Holidays
43 Milcote Road,
Solihull, Warwickshire B91 1JN

www.solaire.co.uk
Tel: +44 (0) 870 054 0202

Email: holidays@solaire.co.uk

During the summer months Solaire have a number of holiday jobs on offer in France and Spain.

The Year Out Group
Queensfield, 28 King's Road,
Easterton, Wiltshire SN10 4PX

www.yearoutgroup.org
Tel: +44 (0) 7980 395789

Email: info@yearoutgroup.org

Since the terrorist attacks in September 2001 the US Government has set up the Department of Homeland Security, which has tightened up on visas and regulations for getting into the USA.

Although working for a summer in the USA shouldn't be a problem US bureaucracy is complicated and precise and you don't want to arrive thinking you have the right visa only to find yourself deported because you haven't.

So it is important to get the correct visa and work permit documents and there are many categories.

You can get more information on 09042 450100 (only available within the UK, calls charged at £1.20 per minute) or visit **www.usembassy.org.uk.**

Probably the most popular job for young gappers is working on a summer camp. There are about 10,000 camps and they come in all shapes, sizes and specialisms from single sex to religious to sport to music. Many of the organisations listed below can help you find both work and visas but check out the small print about pay, accommodation and other expenses. The blanket minimum wage in the USA at the time of going to press is $5.15 an hour, which doesn't buy you much. Some states have their own minimum wage and according to the US Department of Labour website

http://www.dol.gov/dol/topic/wages/minimumwage.htm

'in cases where an employee is subject to both the state and federal minimum wage laws, the employee is entitled to the higher of the two minimum wages'. It might be worth checking this with the organizations helping you find work.

If camp life doesn't appeal, there's a broad range of travel and work programmes. Take a look at the section on Internships (p.103) as well.

4

121

Work opportunities - North America

BUNAC (British Universities North America Club) www.bunac.org
16 Bowling Green Lane, Tel: +44 (0) 20 7251 3472
London EC1R 0QH Fax: +44 (0) 20 7251 0722
Email: enquiries@bunac.org.uk

BUNAC is a non-profit, member club which has been offering overseas work and volunteer programmes since 1962. Participants get to take up a variety of paid work and volunteer opportunities worldwide. BUNAC's Summer Camp USA programme can help you spend the summer working as a camp counsellor in the USA and will arrange your job, flight, visa and insurance. Applicants need to have experience of working with groups of children in a leadership role. Summer Camp USA is a low cost way to go on a working holiday. Popular alternatives are BUNAC's Work and Gap Canada programmes which enable you to spend 2-12 months living and working in Canada.

Camp America www.campamerica.co.uk
37A Queen's Gate, Tel: +44 (0) 20 7581 7333
London SW7 5HR Fax: +44 (0) 20 7581 7377
Email: enquiries@campamerica.co.uk

Each year Camp America sends thousands of young people to work on summer camps and resorts in the States between June and August.

CCUSA

www.ccusa.com

1st Floor North, Devon House,
171-177 Great Portland Street   Tel: +44 (0) 20 7637 0779
London W1W 5PQ   Fax: +44 (0) 20 7580 6209

CCUSA works with summer camps in beautiful locations in America. You don't need any experience or qualifications but you do need to be at least 18 years old.

Gap Challenge at World Challenge Expeditions

www.world-challenge.co.uk

Black Arrow House, 2 Chandos Road,   Tel: +44 (0) 20 8728 7200
London NW10 6NF   Fax: +44 (0) 20 8961 1551

Email: wlecome@world-challenge.co.uk

Gap Challenge provides individuals with exciting opportunities to take a well-structured gap year, living and working in one of 12 countries around the world.

Global Adventures Project

www.globaladventures.co.uk

38 Queen's Gate,   Tel: +44 (0) 800 085 4197
London SW7 5HR   Fax: +44 (0) 207 7590 7444

Email: info@globaladventures.co.uk

Oyster Worldwide Limited

www.oysterworldwide.com

Hodore Farm,   Tel: +44 (0) 1892 770 771
Hartfield, East Sussex TN7 4AR

Email: emailus@oysterworldwide.com

Love winter sports? Oyster arranges paid work in some of Canada's top ski resorts. We'll place you with top end hotels or, if you have childcare experience, the Whistler resort crèche. You'll be expected to work hard and remain positive. However, you'll get reasonable pay, accommodation, an excellent social life and the chance to hit the slopes on your days off. Opt for Tremblant resort if you want to improve your French too (course included).

The Year Out Group

www.yearoutgroup.org

Queensfield, 28 King's Road,   Tel: +44 (0) 7980 395789
Easterton, Wiltshire SN10 4PX

Email: info@yearoutgroup.org

Seasonal work in Australia and New Zealand

Australasia is still the most popular destination for gappers, so there will be a lot of other backpackers after jobs too - but there are usually plenty of jobs to go around, and many backpackers travel from one casual job to another as a way of paying for their travel. It's a good way to meet people too.

Just surfing the internet from the UK (using keywords like 'Australia jobs' or 'vacation work Australia') gives you an idea of what's on offer. Here's an Australian job website worth a look:

www.youthjobs.com.au

123

Changing Worlds

**Work
earn
have fun**

**AUSTRALIA
NEW ZEALAND**

telephone: 01883 340960
www.changingworlds.co.uk

You may notice that job adverts often carry a note that 'only people with the right to work in Australia may apply for this position'. You can apply or register online, but your chances of getting it before you have a ticket and a visa lined up are not high.

Australian High Commission Australia House, Strand
London WC2 4LA
Visa enquiries: 090 6550 8900 (£1/min)
http://www.uk.embassy.gov.au/

So getting the right type of visa is a priority. The key point is that to do casual work in Australia you will need a Working Holiday Maker (WHM) visa, which costs £75. It allows you to travel and take occasional work (maximum three months with each employer) for up to a year. The year begins the day you enter Australia, so if you never arrive you don't lose anything.

Since 1 November 2005, Working Holiday Makers who have been seasonal workers in regional Australia for a minimum of three months while on their first working holiday visa, have been eligible to apply for a second working holiday visa and stay for a further 12 months. You will need to provide proof.

To qualify for a WHM you need to be aged between 18-30 with no dependants, and be a citizen of a country with reciprocal work agreements with Australia.

Australia has reciprocal WHM arrangements in effect with the United Kingdom, Canada, the Netherlands, Japan, Republic of Ireland, Republic of Korea, Malta, Germany, Denmark, Sweden, Norway, the Hong Kong Special Administrative Region (HKSAR) of the People's Republic of China, Finland, the Republic of Cyprus, France, Italy, Belgium, Estonia and Taiwan.

You can find out all the conditions you need to fulfil and how to apply on:

http://www.immi.gov.au/immigration.htm

You can find information on all types of visas, including the Student Visa, on the Australian High Commission website:

http://www.uk.embassy.gov.au/

Many organisations arrange paid work placements in Australia and New Zealand, and some also organise voluntary work assignments in those and other countries. Some of these will also sort out your paperwork such as visas and work permits for you - although you may have to pay extra for this service.

Below are listed some useful organisations to check out when you're looking for work in Australasia.

125

Work opportunities - Australia & New Zealand

Au Pair Australia
Stableford House, Alderford Street,
Sible Hedingham, Essex CO9 3HX

www.aupairaustralia.co.uk
Tel: +44 (0) 1787 463 318
Fax: +44 (0) 1787 463 318
Email: info@aupairaustralia.co.uk

Au Pair Australia offers a gap year programme for students who wish to work as an au pair or nanny on a cultural exchange programme with a host family in Australia for up to one year.

Changing Worlds
11 Doctors Lane,
Chaldon, Surrey CR3 5AE

www.changingworlds.co.uk
Tel: +44 (0) 1883 340 960
Fax: +44 (0) 870 990 9665
Email: welcome@changingworlds.co.uk

Changing Worlds offers a variety of paid work placements in New Zealand and Australia. In Queenstown, South Island, NZ, they will organise work in the most prestigious hotels, you will get local rates of pay, accommodation and a hectic social life. Work in the Bay of Islands region of North Island in a hotel, on a farm, or on boats around the bay. Farm workers get paid pocket money and stay with a local family. In Queensland, Australia, there are paid placements in hotels in Cairns – right by the Great Barrier Reef! Prices start at £2395 and include return flights, finding a suitable job, assistance with work permits, a one-day UK briefing and support from the Changing Worlds rep in-country who will meet you and take you to your placement. Relevant work experience is always useful particularly for those wishing to work in hotels. Fundraising advice is available although most workers take UK paid jobs prior to their placement. To be eligible you need to be between 18 and 25 for New Zealand and up to 30 for Australia. Changing Worlds also offers unpaid placements around the world. See their listing under Volunteering Abroad.

Go Workabout
PO Box 606,
Claremont, WA 6910 USA

www.goworkabout.com
Tel: +61 (0) 423 289 286
Fax: +61 (0) 862 678 184
Email: info@goworkabout.com

Go Workabout arranges work in Australia for working holiday makers before they travel to Australia.

Launchpad Australia
PO Box 2525,
Fitzroy, VIC 3065 Australia

www.launchpadaustralia.com
Tel: +61 3 9444 7439
Fax: +61 3 9445 9375
Email: workingholiday@launchpadaustralia.com

Launchpad Australia provide awesome working holiday, gap year and career break adventures in Australia and abroad! See website for details of our exciting courses!

The Year Out Group
Queensfield, 28 King's Road,
Easterton, Wiltshire SN10 4PX

www.yearoutgroup.org
Tel: +44 (0) 7980 395789

Email: info@yearoutgroup.org

Travellers Contact Point
85 Shaftesbury Avenue, Soho,
London W1D 5DX

www.travellers.com.au
Tel: +44 (0) 207 432 7475
Fax: +44 (0) 20 7432 7400
Email: info@travellersuk.com

Visas Australia Ltd
PO Box 1,
Nantwich, Cheshire CW5 7PB

www.visas-australia.com
Tel: +44 (0) 1270 626 626
Fax: +44 (0) 1270 626 226
Email: info@visas-australia.com

Visas Australia Company specialises in processing and issuing all types of visas, particularly for gappers. The Company's service is approved by both the Australian Tourist Board and Australian High Commission.

Visitoz
Springbrook Farm, 8921 Burnett Highway,
Goomeri, QLD 4601 Australia

www.visitoz.org
Tel: +61 (0) 741 686 106
Fax: +61 (0) 741 686 155
Email: info@visitoz.org

Visitoz programmes allow gap year students or graduates with a working holiday visa to get short-term jobs in Australia to earn money so that they can continue their travels.

Work Oz
16 Myrtle Tree Crescent, Sand Bay,
Weston Super Mare, Somerset BS22 9UL

www.workoz.com
Tel: +44 (0) 870 240 7367

Email: info@workoz.com

Work Oz specialises in helping British gappers work, live and play in Oz.

Chapter 5
Volunteering abroad

Kate, 31, has clocked up a total of three years on two gap-years.

She took her first one immediately after university, when she spent a two years combining travel and working: "Backpacking, some trekking, mainly staying in hostels – apart from Oz when I bought car & slept on that, fruit picking in New Zealand."

The first time gave her a break from full time studying before starting work and she said it gave her the "chance to travel to places and get to know several countries really well, and to meet people of different countries."

The second time, when she was 30, she spent a year in S America combining trekking, travelling by bus and boat, with three stints of volunteer work.

This trip: "Living in the mountains. Speaking to indigenous people – many of whom don't really speak Spanish. Learning Spanish from scratch. Seeing a totally different way of life."

Both times, she said, she planned her trips so she would return in the spring. "so that weather should be good. It was nice to come back and see friends and family. But you realise that absolutely nothing has changed at home. 2 years is very little in the lives of normal working people – I have to remember not to talk about travelling too much as they don't understand and get irritated with 'when I was in…, we did/saw etc"

Her impressions? "It makes me a little sad that the people of S America think that we (UK & US) have so much better standards of living than them. Of course there is poverty over there but when you tell them you pay $1000 a month for a grim flat shared with random people in London they are amazed. They see our average wages and think that to buy things are the same as they pay."

Her advice to anyone thinking of taking a **gap-** is: "Do it. Don't put it off, do it now. If there is nobody to go with, go alone. I did & made many more friends because of it."

But she adds: "Make sure that you are doing it for the right reason (more for career breakers rather than gap year after uni). There seemed to be a lot of lost souls who were running away from reality at home rather than going travelling for the positive reasons. The problems will still be there when they get back home, and in many cases putting them off will only make things worse."

130

Voluntary work abroad can be one of the most rewarding ways to spend all or part of your **gap-**year. Most gappers who do it come back with memories they never lose and a new perspective on the world.

You could find yourself working with people living in unbelievable poverty, disease, hunger. It can be a humbling and hugely enriching experience and be warned – it can make you question all the things you've taken for granted in your life.

It can also make you feel very proud to have made a difference – however small. It's no exaggeration to say it can be a life-changing experience. Some people who have done it have ended up changing their planned course of study at university and even their whole career plan.

Career-breakers, too, using their skills in places where they're in short supply, have found that a volunteer **gap-** has not only been a satisfying experience but has given them new ideas about their career direction.

On an organised voluntary project you often live among the local community and get closer to daily life than you do as an independent traveller. Many people who've experienced it come back saying that they have been impressed that people can lead fulfilling lives with so little money or material possessions, and have been immensely touched by the hospitality they've received.

So as a volunteer you make new friends, learn about a different culture and communicate with people who may not understand your way of life let alone your language.

World events, particularly since September 11 2001, the Make Poverty History campaign, Live 8 and the like have increasingly focused people's attention so that volunteering has become ever more popular.

So there's a huge number of people wanting to go on these trips and getting chosen can be tough – you may find you have to prove to them that you should be selected to go before they will accept your money! It helps to be clear about your aims and your skills and then you can show what you can contribute.

The companies have a point: they put a lot of effort into getting you out there and if you can't stick it, everyone loses out, from the community you are meant to be helping to the gapper who could have been chosen instead of you.

Voluntary work can be tough. You may be out in the middle of nowhere, with no western influence to be seen; food, language – the entire culture might be totally different to what you're used to and there may not be many English-speakers around: so you may have to cope with culture shock and feeling lonely, isolated and homesick.

131

The first thing to consider is whether you want to work on the environment, with animals or with people before you look around for an organization to help you.

Idealist or hedonist?

You should also consider how committed a volunteer you want to be.

Because voluntary work is so popular with gappers, commercial companies have started to get in on the act and the idealism associated with voluntary work, though still there, has come under some commercial pressure.

Some companies offer two- to four-week holidays combined with some voluntary work but equally there are many organisations still committed to the idealism of voluntary work and offering placements from a few months up to a year.

However, you may not want or be able to offer more than a few weeks or months of your time, so the combined holiday/short volunteering option might be for you.

There's no point in committing yourself to a whole year then finding after a few weeks there that you hate it and want to come home early.

So it's a good idea to be honest with yourself about what you want – there's nothing wrong with wanting to travel and have a good time.

But, whatever you choose make sure you are clear about what you will be doing before you sign up and part with your money.

When to start applying

Applications can close early, particularly for expeditions and conservation projects needing complex funding or tied in with international government programmes. If you'd like to go on one of these projects, planning should usually start about a year ahead, in the autumn term.

Others can be taken up at very short notice – Gap Challenge, for example, can take in applications during the August period when you are getting A level results or going through clearing and book you on a project that starts in September.

If you don't have much time before your **gap**-year starts (maybe you didn't get the grades you expected, or you've made a last-minute decision to defer uni for a year) it is always worth contacting a voluntary organisation about a project you're interested in, in case they've had a last-minute cancellation.

What to expect

Ranging from placements lasting a couple of weeks to teaching for a whole academic year, most placements provide only free accommodation and food – a very few provide pocket money.

132

Gappers expecting cuddly tiger cubs or cute children, a nice apartment with MTV and one long party will soon be on the next flight home. You'll need to be resourceful, be able to teach, build, inspire confidence, communicate and share what you know. Physical and mental fitness, staying power, and the ability to get on with people are essential.

Peter from Africa and Asia Venture explains: "We are looking for self-motivated and reliable positive thinkers. You need to be self-reliant and able to cope when you turn up at a Nepali school and find a basic room, no curtains and that the loo is a 'long-drop' down the garden."

Some other points are worth emphasizing:

You might feel safer going with a big voluntary organisation because they should be able to offer help in a nasty situation. Experience is certainly important where organisations are concerned.

But often a small, specialist organisation is more knowledgeable about a country, a school or other destination. Size and status have little bearing on competence. A charity can be more efficient than a commercial company, and a commercial company can show more sensitivity than a charity.

There are few general rules – talk to someone who's been. Organisations vary as to how much back-up they offer volunteers, from virtually holding your hand throughout your stay and even after you come back, to the 'sink or swim' method.

If you're going to get the most out of your volunteering **gap**-year, then be honest with yourself about what you need: if you feel patronised at the slightest hint of advice then you might get annoyed with too much interference from the organisation. Though do bear in mind that they probably know more than you do about the placement, what sort of vaccinations you're going to need, what will be useful to take with you, and how to get the visas and permits you will need.

Equally if you're shy or nervous it might be as well to go with an organisation that sends volunteers in pairs or groups.

There's nothing wrong with either type of placement – it's about choosing what's right for you.

Talk to a few organisations before you decide which one to go with and, probably more useful, talk to some previous volunteers. They'll be able to tell you what it's really like; don't just ask them if they enjoyed it, get them to describe what they did, what they liked and why, what they didn't like and what they'd do differently.

Wherever you are sent and regardless of the organisation, you will be going to poor countries where the infrastructure and support services can be minimal – otherwise why would they need volunteers?

So remember wherever you're sent, you can't count on much.

Regardless of the reputation of the voluntary work organisation you choose, or the competence of voluntary work coordinators in a particular country, it's about your skills and human qualities and those of the people you'll be with so there's bound to be an element of chance whether the school you are put in, for example, really values you or whether you get on with the family you stay with.

It's worth checking what training is given and what support there is in-country, but be aware that you may not get what you expect – you need to be adaptable and make the most of whatever situation you find yourself in.

What's the cost?

It varies hugely – some companies just expect you to pay for the airfare – others expect you to raise thousands of pounds for funding. It can be hard to combine raising money with studying for A levels, but there are a lot of ways to do it.

As usual, the earlier you start, the easier it will be. The organisation that you go with should be able to give advice, but options include organising sponsored events (abseiling down a tall building), writing to companies or trusts asking for sponsorship, car-boot sales, or even plain working and saving.

If approached, many local newspapers will do a short article about your plan if it's interesting enough – but it's better to write to them during the quieter news spells, like the summer holiday months, when they'll be more likely to welcome an additional story.

The last resort is to go cap-in-hand to your parents, either for a loan or a gift, but this can be unsatisfying and they may simply not be able to afford it. If your parents or relatives do want to help, you could ask for useful items for Christmas or birthday presents – like a rucksack.

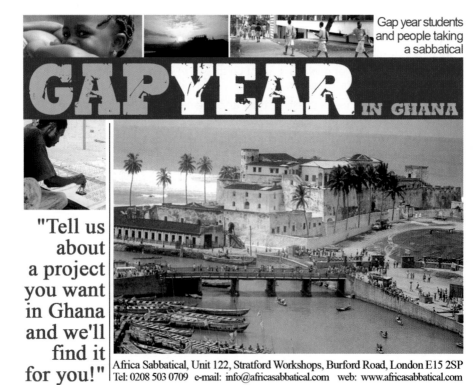

Safety first

If you're going with a good organisation they shouldn't send you anywhere too dangerous – but situations change quickly and it's always worth finding out about where you're going for yourself.

Check out the Foreign Office's Travel Advice pages on **www.fco.gov.uk** or via www.**gap**-year.com

The Foreign Office site also has lots of advice on visas, insurance and other things that need to be sorted out before you go, and advice on what to do in an emergency abroad.

Voluntary organisations

Adventure Alternative
31 Myrtledene Road,
Belfast, County Antrim BT8 6GQ

www.adventurealternative.com
Tel: +44 (0) 2890 701476

Email: office@adventurealternative.com

Teaching and volunteering in needy schools and orphanages in Kenya and in schools in Kathmandu (includes Himalayan trek). 2-3 months living locally with the communities, lots of interaction, independance and flexibility; big on professional, personal service. Very large network and strong support in-country with a highly fun and principled company dedicated to pro-poor tourism, which works alongside its own charity Moving Mountains. Opportunity to really help and make a difference. Reasonably priced.

Africa & Asia Venture
10 Market Place,
Devizes, Wiltshire SN10 1HT

www.aventure.co.uk
Tel: +44 (0) 1380 729009
Fax: +44 (0) 1380 720060
Email: av@aventure.co.uk

Africa Asia Venture is for motivated students and graduates of 18-24, who want to spend 3-5 months teaching a wide variety of subjects, especially English and sports in Africa (Tanzania, Kenya, Uganda, Malawi, Botswana) Mexico, Thailand, Nepal, and the Indian Himalayas. Excellent community and conservation projects are available for the same periods in Uganda. Departures are around September, January and May. A 3-week period of travel is included in all our Ventures and a 5-8 day safari is part of the scheme. Alternatively, shorter Ventures of 5 weeks that include building projects, safaris and adventure are also available in Kenya and Uganda (departures throughout the year but mainly in July, August, September). Full support and in-country back up is provided throughout. Costs range from £1830 to £2840 and include comprehensive training in TEFL, relevant languages, local religion, history, culture & customs, plus medical/equipment insurance (main scheme), accommodation, food, a local living allowance and a donation to your school/project. Check our website for relevant information and brochures.

Africa Sabbatical
Unit 122, Stratford Workshops, Burford Road
Stratford, London E15 2SP

www.africasabbatical.com
Tel: +44 (0) 208 503 0709

Email: info@africasabbatical.com

the gap-year guidebook 2007

African Conservation Experience
PO Box 206,
Faversham, Kent ME13 8WZ

www.ConservationAfrica.net
Tel: 0870 241 5816
Email: info@ConservationAfrica.net

African Conservation Experience have been sending volunteers to Africa for over five years and are the original, most experienced organisation for conservation placements in Southern Africa. ACE are able to offer each and every applicant the benefits of their personal experience, and all volunteers receive individual consideration. African Conservation Experience can offer you the chance to work on game and nature reserves alongside conservationists, zoologists, wildlife vets and reserve managers, making a real contribution to the conservation of African wildlife. Work can involve game capture for tagging and relocation, behavioural and population studies, wildlife veterinary work, anti-poaching patrols and animal rehabilitation. Volunteers become an integral part of the conservation project, many of which would not be able to run without their input. Placements are from one-three months, and cost from around £2700 for four weeks and up to £4000 for 12 weeks. This includes flights, accommodation, all meals and transfers.

African Conservation Trust
PO Box 310,
Linkhills, 3652 South Africa

www.projectafrica.com
Tel: +27 31 7675 044
Email: info@projectafrica.com

The mission of ACT is to provide a means for conservation projects to become self-funding through active participation by the public.

Africatrust Networks

Africatrust Chambers, P O Box 551,
Portsmouth, Hampshire PO5 1ZN

www.africatrust.org.uk
Tel: +44 (0) 1873 812453

Email: info@africatrust.gi

Africa work experience with disadvantaged young people. Minimum three months in English speaking West Africa or French speaking North Africa. FREE induction course. Help with funding.

AFS Community Projects Overseas

Leeming House, Vicar Lane,
Leeds LS2 7JF

www.afsuk.org
Tel: +44 (0) 113 242 6136
Fax: +44 (0) 113 243 0631
Email: info-unitedkingdom@afs.org

AFS is part of an international network with 54 partner countries that offers a range of intercultural learning opportunities. Every year AFS places young people, generally from the age of 18-29, on its International Volunteer Programme.

AIM International

Halifax Place,
Nottingham, Nottinghamshire NG1 1QN

www.aimeurope.net/synergy
Tel: +44 (0) 115 983 8120
Fax: +44 (0) 115 833 5156
Email: ukadmin@aimeurope.net

AIM International provides opportunities for Christian volunteers to use their skills in Africa. Join a summer team or use your gifts on an individual placement from 3-12 months.

Akha Heritage Foundation

Matthew McDaniel, Maesai, Chiangrai Thailand

www.akha.org
Email: akhalife@gmail.com

Based in northern Thailand the Foundation assists the Akha Hill tribe peoples with projects to aid clean water, nutrition, human rights, literacy and good governance. Opportunities range from one month to one year, involve solid, grass roots work and a very close level of community involvement and are for gappers who are very motivated and self-reliant.

Alliance Abroad Group LP

1221 South Mopac Expressway, Suite 250,
Austin, TX 78746 USA

www.allianceabroad.com
Tel: +1 (512) 457 8062
Fax: +1 (413) 460 3502
Email: info@allianceabroad.com

Alliance Abroad Group offers customised internship, work, teach and volunteer experiences around the world. Our services include guaranteed placement and 24/7 personal assistance.

ATD Fourth World

48 Addington Square,
London SE5 7LB

www.atd-uk.org
Tel: +44 (0) 20 7703 3231
Fax: +44 (0) 207 252 4276
Email: atd@atd-uk.org

ATD Fourth World is an international voluntary organisation working in partnership with people living in poverty worldwide.

Changing Worlds

**Volunteer
and
have fun**

CHINA
GHANA
HONDURAS
INDIA
KENYA
LATVIA
MADAGASCAR
THAILAND

telephone: 01883 340960
www.changingworlds.co.uk

YEAR OUT
GROUP

Azafady
Studio 7, 1a Beethoven Street,
London W10 4LG

www.madagascar.co.uk
Tel: +44 (0) 20 8960 6629
Fax: +44 (0) 20 8962 0126
Email: info@azafady.org

Pioneer Madagascar is a ten-week volunteer scheme that offers first-hand experience of frontline development and conservation work in beautiful and remote areas.

Blue Ventures
52 Avenue Road,
London N6 5DR

www.blueventures.co.uk
Tel: +44 (0) 208 341 9819
Fax: +44 (0) 208 341 4821
Email: enquiries@blueventures.org

Blue Ventures run award-winning research projects for those who want to become involved in marine conservation. Volunteers focus on both diving and land-based interests.

BMS World Mission
PO Box 49, 129 Broadway,
Didcot, Oxfordshire OX14 8XA

www.bmsworldmission.org
Tel: +44 (0) 1235 517653
Fax: +44 (0) 1235 517601
Email: shortterm@bmsworldmission.org

BMS World Mission is a Christian organisation which sends out volunteers in teams and as individuals to over 40 countries worldwide.

Brathay Exploration Group
Brathay Hall,
Ambleside, Cumbria LA22 0HP

www.brathayexploration.org.uk
Tel: +44 (0) 15394 33942
Fax: +44 (0) 15394 33942
Email: admin@brathayexploration.org.uk

Brathay provides 'challenging experiences for young people' aged 15-25. It runs a range of expeditions from one to five weeks long which vary each year.

Centre for Women and Children's Rights (HISANI)
PO Box 1817,
Mwanza Tanzania

www.crin.org
Tel: +255 28 156 2293
Fax: +255 28 250 3018
Email: brighttz@yahoo.co.uk

Aims to create awareness of women's and children's rights; provide training on civic education and legal rights; promote community based childcare; establish HIV/AIDS information centre; promote partnerships.

Changing Worlds
11 Doctors Lane,
Chaldon, Surrey CR3 5AE

www.changingworlds.co.uk
Tel: +44 (0) 1883 340 960
Fax: +44 (0) 870 990 9665
Email: welcome@changingworlds.co.uk

CMS (Church Mission Society)

157 Waterloo Road,
London SE1 8UU

www.cms-uk.org
Tel: +44 (0) 20 7928 8681
Fax: +44 (0) 20 7401 3215
Email: info@cms-uk.org

Offering more of a learning experience than a giving one, the CMS runs three- to four-week Encounter programmes in Africa, Asia, the Middle East and Eastern Europe for Christians aged 18-30.

Concordia International Volunteers

2nd Floor, 19 North Street,
Portslade, East Sussex BN41 1DH

www.concordia-iye.org.uk
Tel: +44 (0) 1273 422 218
Fax: +44 (0) 1273 421182
Email: info@concordia-iye.org.uk

Concordia organises international volunteer placements for 16-30 year olds working on conservation, renovation, arts/cultural based or social projects. Projects lasting 2-4 weeks are available worldwide.

Coral Cay Conservation

40-42 Osnaburgh Street,
London NW1 3ND

www.coralcay.org
Tel: +44 (0) 870 750 0668
Fax: +44 (0) 870 750 0667
Email: info@coralcay.org

Cross-Cultural Solutions

Tower Point 44, North Road,
Brighton, Sussex BN1 1YR

www.crossculturalsolutions.org
Tel: +44 (0) 1273 666 392

Email: infouk@crossculturalsolutions.org

Cross-Cultural Solutions' mission is to operate volunteer programmes around the world in partnership with sustainable community initiatives, bringing people together to work side-by-side while sharing perspectives and fostering cultural understanding. Our vision is of a world where people value cultures different from their own, are aware of global issues, and are empowered to effect positive change. It also operates year-round in Brazil, China, Costa Rica, Ghana, Guatemala, India, Peru, Russia, Tanzania, and Thailand. Volunteer work is in the areas of health, education, and social services. Programmes range from 1-12 weeks and fees start at £927 ($1,595).

Discover Nepal

GPO Box: 20209, Kathmandu, Nepal

www.discovernepal.com.np

Email: stt@mos.com.np

The aim of Discover Nepal is to provide opportunities for the involvement in the development process, and to contribute practically towards the socio-economic development of the country.

Earthwatch Institute (Europe)
267 Banbury Road,
Oxford, Oxfordshire OX2 7HT

www.earthwatch.org
Tel: +44 (0) 1865 318 838
Fax: +44 (0) 1865 311383
Email: info@earthwatch.org.uk

Earthwatch is an international environmental charity (registered charity number 1094467) which places conservation volunteers on scientific research expeditions around the world. Earthwatch currently supports 140 expeditions in about 50 countries, from looking at the impacts of climate change in the Arctic, to the protection of cheetah in Namibia. Volunteer field assistants are needed throughout the UK and worldwide. Earthwatch volunteers range in age from 16 to 85 – there is no maximum age limit.

Ecuador Volunteer
Reina Victoria, 1325 y Lizardo Garcia,
Quito, Ecuador

www.ecuadorvolunteer.com
Tel: +593 2 2564 488

Email: info@ecuadorvolunteer.com

Ecuador Volunteer Foundation is a non-profit organization that offers volunteer work opportunities abroad in social, environment, educational and community areas around Ecuador.

EIL (Experiment for International Living)
287 Worcester Road,
Malvern, Worcestershire WR14 1AB

www.eiluk.org
Tel: +44 (0) 168 456 2577
Fax: +44 (0) 168 456 2212
Email: info@eiluk.org

Worldwide Volunteering, give weeks to one year. European volunteering uses EU funding and placements involve no cost to the volunteer (6-12 months).

Equip Trust
55 Market Place,
Henley on Thames, Oxfordshire RG9 2AA

www.equip.org.uk
Tel: +44 (0) 1491 577 414
Fax: +44 (0) 1491 410 775
Email: office@equip.org.uk

Federation EIL International Office
PO Box 6141,
Brattleboro, VT 05302 USA

www.experiment.org
Tel: +1 802 258 3467
Fax: +1 802 258 3427
Email: federation@experiment.org

GAP Activity Projects
44 Queen's Road,
Reading, Berkshire RG1 4BB

www.gap.org.uk
Tel: +44 (0) 118 959 4914
Fax: +44 (0) 118 957 6634
Email: volunteer@gap.org.uk

The charity organisation GAP sends over 2000 volunteers overseas every year. Three to twelve month placements available include environmental, sports, teaching, caring and medical.

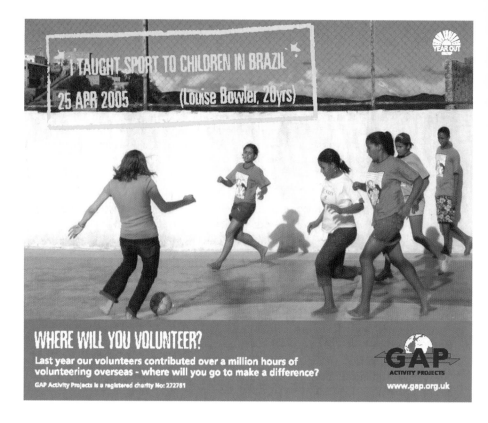

Gap Guru
1st Floor, Bankside House, West Mills
Newbury, RG14 5HP

www.gapguru.com
Tel: +44 (0) 8000 32 33 50
Fax: +44 (0) 1635 45596
Email: info@gapguru.com

Spend your time wisely by using your talents to help others. We have a wide range of opportunities, carefully selected to help you make the most of your gap year! The only hard part is deciding which project to choose from...

Gap Sports Ltd
Thamesbourne House, Station Road,
Bourne End, Buckinghamshire SL8 5QH

www.gapsports.com
Tel: +44 (0) 870 837 9797

Email: info@gapsports.com

GAPEA (Grupo de Apoyo y Proteccion a Especies y su Ambiente)
Libro de Texto Gratuito,
599 Jardines Residenciales P.C. 28030 Colima,
Mexico

www.gapea.org
Tel: 0052 312 134 8157

Email: jcmgx@hotmail.com

GIVE Foundation

c/o Credibility Alliance,
3rd Floor, Ketwadi Lane #5, Municipal School
Ketwadi, Mumbai 400004 India

www.givefoundation.org
Tel: +91 22 2389 4942
Fax: +91 22 3242 6400
Email: info@givefoundation.org

GIVE Foundation is a professionally governed and managed Indian nonprofit organisation dedicated to promote "giving". We help "good" NGOs raise funds and promote greater transparency & accountability in the voluntary sector.

Glencree Centre for Reconciliation

Glencree,
Enniskerry, County Wicklow, Eire

www.glenree.ie
Tel: +353 (01) 282 9711
Fax: +353 (01) 276 6085
Email: info@glencree.ie

Glencree welcomes international volunteers who provide practical help in exchange for a unique experience of working with those building peace in Ireland, Britain and beyond.

Global Action Nepal

Baldwins, Eastlands Lane,
Cowfold, West Sussex RH13 8AY

www.gannepal.org
Tel: +44 (0) 800 587 7138
Fax: +44 (0) 1403 864088

Global Action Nepal was founded in 1996 to improve the education of children in Nepal. GAN's projects and work are always closely in harness with grass roots level needs, focusing on community-led, participatory development.

Global Adventures Project

38 Queens Gate,
London SW7 5HR

www.globaladventures.co.uk
Tel: +44 (0) 800 085 4197
Fax: +44 (0) 207 7590 7444
Email: info@globaladventures.co.uk

Global Adventures Project is an exciting Gap Year programme that allows you to combine your own independent travel with worthwhile voluntary or paid work or a language course. It is organised by a division of the American Institute for Foreign Study (AIFS) and enjoys the benefit of the experience and resources that this worldwide organisation has from running cultural exchange programmes since 1964. For a one off fee, you get a 12-month round-the-world ticket and the opportunity to join up to four programmes (3 months each) in the USA, Brazil, Peru, Europe, South Africa, India, Australia, New Zealand, Canada and China with plenty of time for independent travel in between. Your trip could range from 3 months to the full year with departures in January, April, June and September.

Global Choices

Barkat House, 116-118 Finchley Road,
London NW3 5HT

www.globalchoices.co.uk
Tel: +44 (0) 207 433 2501
Fax: +44 (0) 870 330 5955
Email: info@globalchoices.co.uk

Global Choices offers Voluntary Work, Internships, Practical Training and Work Experience Worldwide from 2 weeks to 18 months. Placements are arranged all year round.

143

What's your passion?

Be all you can be as a
GapGuru Volunteer

Global Vision International

Amwell Farm House, Nomansland,
Wheathampstead
St Albans, Hertfordshire AL4 8EJ

www.gvi.co.uk
Tel: +44 (0) 870 608 8898
Fax: +44 (0) 870 609 2319
Email: info@gvi.co.uk

Critical conservation and humanitarian projects in over 30 countries rely on GVI for volunteers, promotion and direct funding. With unparalled in-country support, GVI volunteers benefit from exceptional training and a Careers Abroad job placement scheme. For more information call +44 (0) 870 608 8898, email info@gvi.co.uk, or visit www.gvi.co.uk.

Global Volunteer Network Ltd

PO Box 2231,
Wellington, New Zealand

www.volunteer.org.nz
Tel: +64 4 569 9080
Fax: +64 4 569 9081
Email: info@volunteer.org.nz

Volunteer through the Global Volunteer Network to support communities in need around the world. Volunteer placements include schools, refugee camps, wildlife sanctuaries and nature reserves.

Global Volunteers

375 East Little Canada Road,
St. Paul, MN 55117-1628 USA

www.globalvolunteers.org
Tel: +1 (651) 407 6100
Fax: +1 (651) 482 0915
Email: email@globalvolunteers.org

Global volunteers provide opportunities to work on over 70 different projects worldwide. The work is hard but very rewarding, and is diverse, from repairing old school houses in third world countries to social work within a Native American village.

Greenforce

11-15 Betterton Street,
Covent Garden, London WC2H 9BP

www.greenforce.org
Tel: +44 (0) 20 7470 8888
Fax: +44 (0) 207 379 0801
Email: info@greenforce.org

Do you want to live in an environment rather than just travel through? Amazing locations, conservation with the local peoples, helping UN, WWF, Red Cross, etc.

Habitat for Humanity (Great Britain)

11 Parsons Street,
Banbury, Oxfordshire OX16 5LW

www.hfhgb.org
Tel: +44 (0) 1295 264240
Fax: +44 (0) 1295 264230
Email: enquiries@hfhgb.org

The Habitat for Humanity's Global Village programme sends people all over the world to build housing for and with the local population. The aim is not only to provide homes, but also to raise awareness of the need for low cost housing. They are particularly looking for team leaders – training is given. Programmes last for between 3 and 4 weeks and costs obviously vary according to location.

145

Himalayan Light Foundation

GPO Box 12191,
Kathmandu Nepal

www.hlf.org.np
Tel: +977 (1) 4425 393
Fax: +977 (1) 4413 924
Email: info@hlf.mos.np

The Himalayan Light Foundation (HLF) is a Kathmandu-based non-profit NGO (non-governmental organisation) working to make renewable energy technologies more accessible to rural Nepal. HLF organises programmes that link energy with education, and income-generating activities such as sewing and weaving.

ICYE (Inter Cultural Youth Exchange) UK

Latin America House, Kingsgate Place,
London NW6 4TA

www.icye.co.uk
Tel: +44 (0) 870 774 3486
Fax: +44 (0) 20 7916 1246
Email: info@icye.co.uk

Each year ICYE sends young people aged between 18 and 30 to work in voluntary projects overseas in Africa, Asia, Europe and South America. Volunteers work in a range of projects including counselling centres, human rights NGOs, farms, orphanages and schools for the disabled.

Interserve

325 Kennington Road,
London SE11 4QH

www.interserveonline.org.uk
Tel: +44 (0) 20 7735 8227
Fax: +44 (0) 20 7820 5950
Email: enquiries@isewi.org

Interserve is a self-financing international missionary society, working mainly in Asia (Bangladesh, India, Mongolia, Nepal) and in the Arab world. Their gap year programme 'On Track' places volunteers with local churches and organisations in a variety of roles.

i-to-i

Woodside House, 261 Low Lane,
Leeds, Yorkshire LS18 5NY

www.i-to-i.com
Tel: +44 (0) 870 333 2332
Fax: +44 (0) 113 205 4619
Email: uk@i-to-i.com

i-to-i is the UK's leading provider of volunteer travel opportunities offering around 500 projects in 23 countries across the globe. Project types include plant and animal conservation, community development, teaching, sports, building and media as well as meaningful tours, self development trips and paid working holiday programmes. Placements range from panda conservation in China, to building homes in Costa Rica, to working with orphans in Kenya. i-to-i sends around 5,000 travellers of all ages and backgrounds to work on volunteer projects every year, with specialist packages available for school students and corporate groups.

IVCS

12 Eastleigh Avenue,
South Harrow, Middlesex HA2 0UF

www.ivcs.org.uk
Tel: +44 (0) 20 8864 4740
Fax: +44 (0) 20 8930 8338
Email: enquiries@ivcs.org.uk

IVCS is a small UK registered charity supporting sustainable development projects in rural India, and offering opportunities to stay in one. Reg Charity: 285872

i volunteer
D-134, 1st Floor, East of Kailash
New Delhi, 110065 India

www.ivolunteer.org.in
Tel: +91 11 262 174 60

Email: delhi@ivolunteer.org.in

IVS (International Voluntary Service)
Oxford Place Centre, Oxford Place,
Leeds, Yorkshire LS1 3AX

www.ivs-gb.org.uk
Tel: +44 (0) 113 246 9900
Fax: +44 (0) 113 246 9910
Email: ivsnorth@ivs-gb.org.uk

IVS exchanges volunteers with over 40 countries, mainly for international voluntary projects (living and working with a group on 2-4 week projects).

Josephite Community Aid
3 Nixon Avenue,
Ashfield, NSW 2131 Australia

www.jcaid.com
Tel: +61 (0) 2 9799 6990
Fax: +61 (0) 2 9716 9950
Email: help@jcaid.com

Kibbutz Representatives
Northside House, Mount Pleasant,
Barnet, Hertfordshire EN4 9EE

www.kibby.org.uk
Tel: +44 (0) 20 8216 2100
Fax: +44 (0) 20 8216 2101
Email: enquiries@kibbutz.org.uk

Kibbutz Representatives is officially part of the kibbutz movement. If you are 18-42 and both physically and mentally fit, KR will organise a place for you either as an individual or as a group.

Kings World Trust for Children
7 Deepdene,
Haslemere, Surrey GU27 1RE

www.kingschildren.org
Tel: +44 (0) 1428 653504
Fax: +44 (0) 1428 653504
Email: kwtc@haslemere.com

The Kings World Trust for Children is a UK-based charity which aims to provide a caring home, an education and skills training for orphaned and homeless children and young people in South India. Reg No. 1024872

L'Arche
GY07, Freepost BD 3209,
Keighley, West Yorkshire BD20 9BR

www.larche.org.uk
Tel: +44 (0) 800 917 1337
Fax: +44 (0) 1535 656426
Email: info@larche.org.uk

For further details see main listing under Volunteering in the UK/Voluntary Organisations.

Latin Link Step Teams
Latin Link, 87 London Street,
Reading, Berkshire RG1 4QA

www.stepteams.org
Tel: +44 (0) 118 957 7114
Fax: +44 (0) 118 957 7115
Email: step.uk@latinlink.org

Latin Link sends teams to work in mission with Latin American Christians every spring, from March to July (£2600), and summer, for seven weeks (£1850).

Madventurer
The Old Casino, 1-4 Forth Lane,
Newcastle upon Tyne, NE1 5HX

www.madventurer.com
Tel: T: +44 (0) 845 121 1996
Fax: F: +44 (0)191 269 9490
Email: team@madventurer.com

Madventurer offers award-winning projects and adventures throughout the developing world. Run in rural areas, off the tourist track, the projects combine teaching, building and conservation work for a worthwhile and truly unforgettable experience. Projects last from 2 weeks to 3 months, and are ideal for people on gap years, and students wanting to make the most of the long summer break. After the projects, Madventurer offers a wide-range of adventures so you can see more of your chosen destination. Trek the Andes, go white water rafting on the Nile or visit the magical city of Timbuktu. It's up to you...

Marlborough Brandt Group
The Upper Office, The Dutch Barn,
Elm Tree Park, Manton
Marlborough, Wiltshire SN8 1PS

www.mgb.org
Tel: +44 (0) 1672 861 116
Fax: +44 (0) 1672 861 211

Email: info@mgb.org

MBG was set up as a link between Marlborough and the village of Gunjur in the Gambia, and has been sending volunteers to teaching and rural development projects there since 1984. Individual volunteers (you don't have to come from Marlborough) go out for up to six months to the school or to work with TARUD, the local rural development NGO.

MondoChallenge

Malsor House, Gayton Road,
Milton Malsor, Northamptonshire NN7 3AB

www.mondochallenge.org
Tel: +44 (0) 1604 858225
Fax: +44 (0) 1604 859323
Email: info@mondochallenge.org

MondoChallenge is a not-for-profit organisation that runs volunteer programmes in India, Nepal, Sri Lanka, Tanzania, Kenya, The Gambia, Senegal, Chile and Ecuador. Projects are mainly teaching or business development, and last between 2 and 6 months. Most volunteers are post-graduate or career breakers. There is no upper age limit and we accept a few select gappers every year. All projects are community based - living and working with local people. The cost of a 3-month project is £1000 but doesn't include travel. Couples or friends applying together receive a 10% discount and all start dates are flexible.

Orangutan Foundation

7 Kent Terrace,
London NW1 4RP

www.orangutan.org.uk
Tel: +44 (0) 20 7724 2912

Email: info@orangutan.org.uk

Participate in hands-on conservation fieldwork that really makes a difference and see orangutans in their natural habitat. 6 weeks, £550 (excluding travel) in Kalimantan, Borneo.

Outreach International

Bartlett's Farm, Hayes Road,
Compton Dundon, Somerset TA11 6PF

www.outreachinternational.co.uk
Tel: +44 (0) 1458 274957
Fax: +44 (0) 1458 274957
Email: projects@outreachinternational.co.uk

Outreach International places committed volunteers in carefully selected projects on the Pacific coast of Mexico, Sri Lanka, Costa Rica, Cambodia, Ecuador and the Galapagos Islands. You can make a valuable contribution to them while experiencing the pleasures of living with local people. The projects are small, varied and handpicked by the Outreach International director. Immerse yourself in a fascinating foreign culture. Learn a language. Carry out an important project that will benefit a humble, local community.

- Orphanages & Street Children
- Teaching English, sports or computer skills
- Medicine
- Dance, Art & Craft
- Working at a centre for disabled children
- Conservation work with giant sea turtles
- Amazon rainforest conservation
- Humanitarian aid work

MONDO CHALLENGE
Volunteer · Projects Abroad

"A small step to a fairer world"

Volunteer programmes:

- teaching primary, secondary and adults
- from the Himalayas to the plains of Africa
- placements from 2 to 6 months

01604 858225
info@mondochallenge.org
www.mondochallenge.org

Oyster Worldwide Limited

Hodore Farm,
Hartfield, East Sussex TN7 4AR

www.oysterworldwide.com
Tel: +44 (0) 1892 770 771

Email: emailus@oysterworldwide.com

Oyster offers challenging voluntary work placements abroad. Those going to Tanzania, Chile and Nepal teach in schools and help make a real difference with extra curricular activities too. Those going to Romania and Brazil help at orphanages, community centres and hospitals. You'll go out as a group and will be met and supported by our local representative. Prices (£1,800 - £3000) include a preparation course, flights, accommodation, language tuition (extensive for Brazil and Chile) and expedition.

Peace River Refuge & Ranch

PO Box 1127, 2545 Stoner Lane,
Zolfo Springs, FL 33890 USA

www.peaceriverrefuge.org
Tel: +1 863 735 0804
Fax: +1 863 735 0805

Email: volunteer@peaceriverrefuge.org

Peace River Refuge & Ranch is a non-profit-making exotic animal sanctuary located in Florida. Its all-volunteer staff provides long-term care for confiscated, abused, neglected or unwanted exotic animals (from tigers to bats) to prevent them from being destroyed. Guided tours of the sanctuary are given to educate others about the cruelty that many exotic animals undergo in captivity and the plight of their wild counterparts. Contact the refuge direct for information about fees and accommodation.

Phenomena Academy

Takaro Lodge, PO Box 225,
Te Anau, New Zealand

www.phenomenaacademy.org
Tel: +64 3 249 1166
Fax: +64 3 249 1189

Email: sarah@phenomenaacademy.org

Phenomena Academy has a slightly different approach to volunteering: their aim, through the 30-week Life Design Foundation Course, is to teach you how to approach, enjoy and succeed in life in a completely different way, based on ancient Chinese ideas. An important part of the course is that you will help to build a new health centre for the local community.

Project Trust

The Hebridean Centre,
Isle of Coll, Argyll PA78 6TE

www.projecttrust.org.uk
Tel: +44 (0) 1879 230 444
Fax: +44 (0) 1879 230 357

Email: info@projecttrust.org.uk

Project Trust offers 12-month placements in over 20 countries departing in August or September. There are also some 8-month placements, departing in January. Projects include teaching English, teaching A-level/Higher subjects, work in children's homes, social work, outdoor activities instruction, journalism, conservation and medical projects.

Quest Overseas
North West Stables, Borde Hill Estate,
Balcombe Road
Hayward's Heath, West Sussex RH16 1XP

www.questoverseas.com
Tel: +44 (0) 1444 47 47 44
Fax: +44 (0) 1444 47 47 99

Email: emailus@questoverseas.com

Quest Overseas specialise in professionally managed Projects and Expeditions across Africa and South America for all ages.

Raleigh International
Raleigh House, 27 Parsons Green Lane,
London SW6 4HZ

www.raleighinternational.org
Tel: +44 (0) 20 7371 8585
Fax: +44 (0) 20 7371 5852
Email: info@raleigh.org.uk

"Be part of something amazing..." Raleigh International is a youth development charity committed to the personal development of young people and operates programmes in the UK and abroad. Our overseas programmes offer a unique variety of worthwhile and sustainable projects: community, environmental and adventure. Our full programmes in Costa Rica and Nicaragua, Namibia and Malaysia last 10 weeks, however 4-, 5- and 7-week alternatives are also available. You will support each other in small teams of diverse nationalities and backgrounds to achieve the project goals. You'll learn about different cultures, make new friends and develop self-confidence and soft skills.

Real Gap Experience

First Floor, 1 Meadow Road,
Tunbridge Wells, Kent TN1 2YG

www.realgap.co.uk
Tel: +44 (0) 1892 516 164
Fax: +44 (0) 1892 523 172
Email: info@realgap.co.uk

Leading Gap Year provider in the UK offering hundreds of programmes in over 35 countries - volunteering, paid work, sports, teaching, community and tailor-made itineraries.

Rempart

1 rue des Guillemites,
75004 Paris France

www.rempart.com
Tel: +33 (0) 1 42 71 96 55
Fax: +33 (0) 1 42 71 73 00
Email: contact@rempart.com

Rempart, a union of conservation associations organises short voluntary work in France. The projects are all based around restoration and maintenance of historic sites and buildings.

Senevolu

Golfe Atlantique, Cité Nations Unies n°175,
PO Box 26 557
Dakar, Senegal

www.senevolu.mypage.org
Tel: +221 559 67 35
Fax: +221 855 69 06
Email: senevolu@mypage.org

Senevolu run a Homestay programme covering Senegalese culture, language courses and excursions. During the week volunteers work in NGOs (non-governmental organisations), public services, community projects, or primary schools. During the weekend Senevolu organises cultural workshops (African dancing, cooking, djembé, kora, batik, etc.). Senevolu is also happy to organise weekend excursions for groups of five or more.

Skillshare International

UK Office, 126 New Walk,
Leicester, Leicestershire LE1 7JA

www.skillshare.org
Tel: +44 (0) 116 254 1862
Fax: +44 (0) 116 254 2614
Email: info@skillshare.org

Skillshare International recruits professionals from different sectors to share their skills, experience and knowledge with local partner organisations in Africa and Asia as volunteers.

SMLE Society

Udayrajpur, Madhyamgram, 9 no. railgate
Kolkata, West Bengal 700129 India

www.smilengo.org
Tel: +9 1933 973 1462
Fax: +9 1332 537 6621
Email: info@smilengo.org

SMILE Society invite international volunteers and students to join us in our welfare projects, International Work Camps, Summer Camps, Internship Programmes and Volunteer Projects in India.

Volunteering abroad | Voluntary organisations

SPW (Students Partnership Worldwide)   www.spw.org
2nd Floor, Faith House, 7 Tufton Street   Tel: +44 (0) 20 7222 0138
London SW1P 3QB   Fax: +44 (0) 20 7233 0008
    Email: spwuk@gn.apc.org

Students Partnership Worldwide (SPW) runs Health Education and Community Resource Programmes in South Asia (Nepal and India) and Africa (Zambia, Tanzania, Uganda and South Africa) for 5–11 months. Volunteers work as trained peer educators alongside local volunteers on sustainable grassroots projects addressing the real health, social and resource needs of rural communities. Volunteers are asked to fundraise £3,600 as a donation to the charity. Flights, insurance, all training and local allowances are covered by SPW. For a gap year with a difference, contact us on 0207 222 0138 or email info@spw.org. Alternatively, have a browse of our website www.spw.org.

Starfish Ventures Ltd   www.starfishventures.co.uk
PO Box 9061,   Tel: +44 (0) 800 197 4817
Epping, Essex CM16 7WU   Fax: +44 (0) 800 197 4817
    Email: enquiries@starfishventures.co.uk

Starfish has a volunteer placement for you, whatever your skills, they can be put to good use in our various projects in Thailand. From teaching English in schools, to helping conserve Thailand's turtle population, your work will not just touch the lives of those you meet, but will change your own forever.

Task Brasil Trust
PO Box 4901,
London SE16 3PP

www.taskbrasil.org.uk
Tel: +44 (0) 20 7735 5545
Fax: +44 (0) 20 7735 5675
Email: info@taskbrasil.org.uk

Charity helping impoverished children in Brazil. Reg No: 1030929

Teaching & Projects Abroad
Aldsworth Parade,
Goring, Sussex BN12 4TX

www.projects-abroad.co.uk
Tel: +44 (0) 1903 708300
Fax: +44 (0) 1903 501026
Email: info@tprojects-abroad.co.uk

Teaching & Projects Abroad organises voluntary work placements in such far flung places as Argentina, Bolivia, Cambodia, Chile, China, Costa Rica, Ghana, India, Mexico, Moldova, Mongolia, Nepal, Peru, Romania, Senegal, South Africa, Sri Lanka, Swaziland and Thailand.

The Leap Overseas Ltd
121 High Street,
Marlborough, Wiltshire SN8 1LZ

www.theleap.co.uk
Tel: +44 (0) 1672 519922
Fax: +44 (0) 1672 519944
Email: info@theleap.co.uk

Don't just walk through life: take the Leap. Voluntary placements in Africa, South America, Asia and Australia, combining work in exclusive safari camps/eco-lodges, with effective and life-changing conservation and community projects. Three contrasting experiences in any one placement. A Unique Leap... We are the only company to offer this fascinating mix. For example you can escort guests on safari, help stop poaching in game reserves and teach orphaned children.

The Year Out Group
Queensfield, 28 King's Road,
Easterton, Wiltshire SN10 4PX

www.yearoutgroup.org
Tel: +44 (0) 7980 395789

Email: info@yearoutgroup.org

ANIMALS, COMMUNITY, CONSERVATION, CULTURE, DRAMA, ENVIRONMENT, RELIGIOUS, RESEARCH/SCIENCE, TEACHING, TRAVEL Year Out Group (YOG) is an association of the UK's leading Year Out organisations that was launched in 2000 to promote the concepts and benefits of well-structured year out programmes, to promote models of good practice and to help young people and their advisers in selecting suitable and worthwhile projects. In 2005 the 34 members of the Group accounted for over 30,000 structured year out placements. The current members are listed below. The Group's member organisations provide a wide range of Year Out placements in the UK and overseas that cover courses and cultural exchanges, expeditions, volunteering and structured work placements. All members have agreed to adhere to the Group's Code of Practice and more detailed operational guidelines for each of the four sectors mentioned above. The Group's website also contains planning advice and guidelines for students and their advisers. These include questions that potential participants should ask providing organisations as they look for the programme that best suits their needs. Year Out Group monitors information published by its members for accuracy. Year Out Group members are expected to put potential clients and their parents in contact with those who have recently returned. Year Out Group

155

considers it important that these references are taken up at least by telephone and, where possible, by meeting face to face. Group members include their complaints procedure in their contracts. Year Out Group can advise on making complaints but is not itself able to deal with them, though half the members are now participating in the Independent Dispute Settlement scheme arranged by the group. Nor is Year Out Group able to 'police' the 30,000 placements provided by its members but it can take action if any member is shown to be consistently negligent. Since Year Out Group was formed its members have worked hard and continue to work hard to improve the service they offer their clients. However there will always be less-than-perfect organisations among members of a trade association and good associations that are not. There are some small specialist organisations with excellent reputations that cannot afford the membership fees. Whether or not an organisation is a member of YOG, the questions in the student guidelines can be used to advantage. YOG Membership (January 2006): Courses and Cultural Exchanges: Art History Abroad; BUNAC; Camp America; CESA Languages Abroad; Flying Fish; Nonstopski and Snowboard; Peak Leaders; St James's & Lucie Clayton College; Tante Marie School of Cooking; The International Academy; Year Out Drama. Expeditions: BSES; Blue Ventures; Coral Cay Conservation; Frontier; Greenforce; Quest Overseas; Raleigh International; Trekforce Expeditions; VentureCo; Wind Sand & Stars. Projects: Global Vision International; Oyster Worldwide. Structured Work Placements: The Year in Industry. Volunteering: Africa & Asia Venture; Africa Conservation Experience; Changing Worlds; CSV (Community Service Volunteers); GAP Activity Projects; Gap Sports; Global Adventures; i-to-i International Projects; Madventure; Outreach International; Project Trust; Teaching & Projects Abroad; The Leap; Travellers Worldwide.

Travellers Worldwide

7 Mulberry Close,
Ferring, West Sussex BN12 5HY

www.travellersworldwide.com
Tel: +44 (0) 1903 502595
Fax: +44 (0) 1903 500364
Email: info@travellersworldwide.com

Travellers Worldwide organises voluntary work placements abroad. You can participate in very worthwhile work in Australia, Argentina, Brazil, Brunei, Bolivia, China, Cuba, Ghana, Guatemala, India, Kenya, Malaysia, Peru, Russia, Sri Lanka, South Africa, Zambia, Zimbabwe. You can choose from over 200 projects from teaching and care to conservation work with endangered animals. The conservation projects include rehabilitation and research work. Work experience placements available in journalism, law, veterinary, medicine, architecture, hotel and catering, tourism and more. There are structured opportunities to learn languages and other skills such as capoeira in Brazil, tango in Argentina or meditation on Sri Lanka. Projects are flexible and tailored to suit you (2 weeks to one year) running throughout the year. No qualifications required. Prices start: £925 including accommodation, food and full support provided throughout.

Trekforce Expeditions

Naldred Farm Offices, Borde Hill Farm,
Haywards Heath, West Sussex RH16 1XR

www.trekforce.org.uk
Tel: +44 (0) 1444 474123
Fax: +44 (0) 1444 474101
Email: info@trekforce.org.uk

Trekforce is a long-established charity (Reg No: 1005452) that organises adventurous 8-20 week expeditions to Central and South America and East Malaysia. Working with local partners, their projects concentrate on rainforest conservation, scientific research and local communities.

UNA Exchange

Temple of Peace, Cathays Park,
Cardiff, Glamorgan CF10 3AP

www.unaexchange.org
Tel: +44 (0) 29 2022 3088
Fax: +44 (0) 29 2022 2540

UNA Exchange arranges international volunteer projects in over 60 countries: from Armenia to Zambia. Projects last 2-3 weeks and include environmental protection, construction, renovation, organising arts and cultural events, and projects working with disadvantaged children, refugees, and people with special needs.

VentureCo Worldwide

The Ironyard, 64-66 The Market Place,
Warwick, Warwickshire CV34 4SD

www.ventureco-worldwide.com
Tel: +44 (0) 1926 411 122
Fax: +44 (0) 1926 411 133
Email: mail@ventureco-worldwide.com

Learn about an indigenous culture and their customs; volunteer on a development project supported by the VentureCo Trust (Charity 1111268); and explore the deserts, jungles and mountains on an expedition.

Volunteer Galapagos

Ecuador House, 26 Sterne Street,
London W12 8AD

www.volunteergalapagos.com
Tel: +44 (0)700 593 8521
Fax: +44 (0) 871 2247284
Email: partner@volunteergalapagos.com

COMMUNITY, HEALTH, RESEARCH/SCIENCE, TEACHING, WORK PLACEMENTS The Galapagos Volunteer Programme places volunteers in a variety of vacancies which contribute to the development of the local community. Placements last from a month up to a year.

Volunteer Latin America

PO Box 465,
Brighton, East Sussex BN50 9AT

www.volunteerlatinamerica.com
Tel: +44 (0) 20 7193 9163
Email: info@volunteerlatinamerica.com

Volunteer Latin America provides a comprehensive and affordable solution to finding volunteering opportunities and Spanish language schools in Central and South America.

Volunteer Nepal National Group Kathmandu Nepal	www.eliabroad.org/choice/ nepal_programs.html Tel: +97 716 613 724
	Email: anishn@eliabroad.org

VSO (Voluntary Service Overseas) 317 Putney Bridge Road, London SW15 2PN	www.vso.org.uk/volunt/pdd Tel: +44 (0) 20 8780 7200 Fax: +44 (0) 20 8780 7254 Email: enquiry@vso.org.uk

VSO's Youth for Development programme (for ages 18-25) sends volunteers to placements in the developing world. You spend 10-12 months there. Participants are usually undergraduates from UK universities. VSO also runs the six-month World Youth programme for 17-25 year olds. Volunteers spend three months in the UK and three months in a developing country, living with a counterpart from a developing country with a local family and volunteering together with local community organisations.

Workaway.info

Workaway's philosophy is simple: 5 hours of work per day in exchange for food and accommodation with friendly hosts in varying situations and surroundings. The aim is to promote cultural understanding between different peoples and lands throughout the world and enable people travelling on a limited budget to fully appreciate living and working in a foreign environment. It's particularly good for language learners who can immerse themselves in their target language whilst living abroad.

Worldwide Experience

Ashley Adams Travel (UK) Ltd,
Guardian House, Borough Road
Godalming, Surrey GU7 2AE

www.worldwideexperience.com
Tel: +44 (0) 1483 860 560
Fax: +44 (0) 1483 860 391
Email: info@worldwideexperience.com

Worldwide Experience, formerly ECO AFRICA EXPERIENCE, specialises in offering enthusiastic groups of individuals year-round gap year placements in conservation, marine, teaching, medical and sports coaching projects, as well as general day to day activity-based projects, all around the globe.

WorldWide Volunteering for Young People

7 North Street Workshops,
Stoke sub Hamdon, Somerset TA14 6QR

www.wwv.org.uk
Tel: +44 (0) 1935 825588
Fax: +44 (0) 1935 825775
Email: wwv@wwv.org.uk

WorldWide Volunteering is a charity (Reg No: 1038253), set up to help people of all ages to find their ideal volunteering project either in the UK or in any country in the world. Their search-and-match database is the UK's most authoritative on-line database of volunteering opportunities. With over 1350 organisations and 350,000 projects, you can instantly match your choices with organisations needing volunteers. Projects last from a few hours a week to two years and range from those that cost nothing and provide pocket money to those that cost thousands of pounds. Much information about each organisation is available, including a profile, cost, accommodation, any benefits to volunteers and links to website and email.

WWOOF
(World Wide Opportunities
on Organic Farms)
PO Box 2675, Lewes,
East Sussex BN7 1RB

www.wwoof.org.uk & www.wwoof.org

Email: hello@wwoof.org.uk

WWOOF offers voluntary opportunities on over 300 organic farms, small holdings and gardens worldwide. WWOOF help is in exchange for food and accommodation.

159

YAP UK (Youth Action for Peace)
P.O.Box 43670,
London SE22 0XX

www.yap-uk.org
Tel: +44 (0) 8701 657 927

Email: action@yap-uk.org

YAP UK organises international work camps in the UK each summer and recruits volunteers (not necessarily young) to take part in short term work camps and a few longer term placements abroad. Volunteers going to Africa, Asia and Latin America attend a short orientation before departure.

everything you need to
know about taking a gap-year,
year out or career break

Chapter 6
Learning abroad

Mark, now 25, worked for a couple of years after university before taking a **gap-**.

He covered a lot of ground in his year out: South America (Peru, Bolivia, Chile, Argentina), New Zealand, Australia, Singapore, Malaysia, Thailand, Vietnam, Cambodia, Pakistan.

But he broke off from travelling to work in New Zealand to earn some more money then carried on and eventually went to Pakistan, where he volunteered to help the relief effort in a refugee camp following the devastating earthquake in Kashmir.

He said what he got from the whole experience was: "The skills to navigate myself around strange places with new people using little money and being confident in new situations."

But also: "I really realised how people around the world are so much worse off than Europeans and how politically the world is a messed up place. But inspite this people everywhere are overwhelmingly friendly, welcoming and helpful wherever you go."

He said when he got back around Christmas he felt: "Lost and emotionally flat. I returned around Christmas and after seeing friends and family over the holiday period, reality struck home, no money, no job and nothing to do. I desperately wanted to go back on the road. In fact I still long to move to NZ and I definitely plan to do some more long-term trips abroad."

It took him four or five months to come back to reality, he said, but even so: "I still dream about being there and friends who have just gone make me insanely jealous with their e-mails and postcards."

Learning abroad

Your **gap**-year is the ideal opportunity to combine the experience of living in a different culture and studying. You might want to continue learning something that interested you at school – a language or history. But 'learning' doesn't have to be academic; there are loads of sport 'schools' around the world that cater for all sports and all levels. For culture vultures, why not enrol on an art course in Florence or a film course in New York?

There's a huge variety of courses and you should be able to find something to fit your interests, budget and schedule. To make this chapter a bit easier to follow we've split it into sections by type: Academic year abroad; Arts & Culture (Art, Culture, Design & Fashion, Drama, Music, Photography); Languages (Language courses, TEFL); and Sport.

An academic year abroad

Another way of getting to know a place and its people in depth is to spend a whole year 'living the language and culture' at a foreign school, in Europe, the USA, or even further afield. You could spend the academic year before you go to university in a French Lycée or German Gymnasium, in a school in Spain, or a Spanish-speaking school in Argentina, for example – which still leaves several months free for travel.

The European Union website homepage has portals in the 20 different languages now spoken in the EU. Go to **http://europa.eu**.

EUROPASS

http://www.uknec.org.uk/

Europass is a method of recording the training carried out and skills acquired during a period of work experience, undertaken as part of an on-going training programme, in another European country.

Although it does not represent formal accreditation, the standard format of this passport-style document is intended to ensure a consistent framework for the recognition of skills by training providers and employers throughout Europe.

All the information contained within the Europass is endorsed by sending and receiving organisations. This information includes details such as the name and level of the course being followed in the UK and the training and practical work undertaken abroad.

Organisations offering academic placements abroad

Archaeology Abroad
Institute of Archaeology, University College,
31-34 Gordon Square
London WC1H OPY

www.britarch.ac.uk/archabroad
Tel: +44 (0) 20 8537 0849
Fax: +44 (0) 20 8537 0849

For info on digs abroad try the Archaeology Abroad bulletin and web pages.

Art History Abroad (AHA)
179c New Kings Road,
London SW6 4SW

www.arthistoryabroad.com
Tel: +44 (0) 20 7731 2231
Fax: +44 (0) 20 7731 2456

Art History Abroad (AHA) offer courses travelling throughout Italy studying the masterpieces of western art and civilization in the company of experts. Venice, Verona, Florence, Siena, Rome, Naples and Sicily. The courses are open to all of an enquiring mind. We have brilliant tutors who are clear, patient, energetic and great fun, and our method on on-site study in groups no larger than 9 is completely unique to AHA. Six week courses run in the Late Summer (Aug-Sept), Autumn (Oct-Dec), Spring (Jan-Mar) and Early Summer (Apr-May) to fit with your other Gap Year plans. We also offer two week long courses in the Summer (Jul-Aug). Prices range from £950 – £5700 per course and there is a scholarship worth £2350 (only applicable to Italian based courses). For further details please contact the office.

Bridge Year, Spanish Programs
Roman Diaz 297, Providencia,
Santiago Chile

www.bridgeyear.com
Tel: +44 (0) 20 7096 0369
Fax: 001 866 726 5705
Email: info@bridgeyear.com

Estancia Ranquilco
Estancia Ranquilco,
El Huecu, 8349 Argentina

www.ranquilco.com
Tel: +54 9 2942 66 4106

Email: ashleykentc@hotmail.com

Institute of International Education
1350 Edgmont Avenue, Ste 1100,
Chester, PA 19013 USA

www.iiepassport.org
Tel: +1 610 499 9200
Fax: +1 610 499 9205
Email: info@iiepassport.org

The Institute of International Education runs a service called IIEPassport which offers a comprehensive search for study programmes abroad. You can search for international education opportunities by country, language, subject and many other criteria; you then get a list of study abroad programmes that specifically match your needs as well as a list of other programmes you might be interested in.

InternationalStudent.com
15 Cottage Avenue, Fifth Floor,
Quincy, MA 02169 USA

www.internationalstudent.com

Information site for people considering becoming a student in another country.

Office of International Education, Iceland

Neshaga 16,
107 Reykjavík Iceland

www.hi.is
Tel: +354 525 4311
Fax: +354 525 5850
Email: ask@hi.is

The Office of International Education is a service organisation for all higher education institutions in Iceland. From their website you can find information on all the higher education institutions in the country, as well as practical things to do before arriving, visas, admissions, residence permits, etc.

Scuola Leonardo da Vinci

Via Bufalini 3,
Florence, 50122 Italy

www.scuolaleonardo.com
Tel: +39 055 261181
Fax: +39 055 294820
Email: florence@scuolaleonardo.com

Located in the centre of Florence, the school offers standard and intensive courses. Also have schools in Rome, Milan and Siena.

The English-Speaking Union

Dartmouth House, 37 Charles Street,
London W1J 5ED

www.esu.org
Tel: +44 (0) 20 7529 1550
Fax: +44 (0) 20 7495 6108
Email: esu@esu.org

The English-Speaking Union was set up to promote understanding between nations. It organises educational exchanges in high schools (mostly boarding) in the US and Canada, awarding up to 40 scholarships a year to gap year students. You could end up in a school in the middle of New York or in the middle of an Indiana field. Tuition and board are free, but you need to allow around £2500 for fares and spending money.

The US-UK Fulbright Commission

Fulbright House, 62 Doughty Street,
London WC1N 2JZ

www.fulbright.co.uk
Tel: +44 (0) 20 7404 6880
Fax: +44 (0) 20 7404 6834
Email: programmes@fulbright.co.uk

If you want to take a full four-year degree at a US university or college, you will need to start planning at least a year before entry. Get in touch with The Fulbright Commission's US Educational Advisory Service (EAS) in London the summer before you want to start a US degree. You will then need to write to US universities, applying for the fall (autumn) term starting at the end of August or beginning of September (application forms available from the university the previous year). Each October, The Fulbright Commission holds a 'College Day' for prospective undergraduates: more than 100 US universities are usually represented.

Where There Be Dragons

P O Box 4651,
Boulder, CO 80306 USA

www.wheretherebedragons.com
Tel: +1 303 413 0822

Email: info@wheretherebedragons.com

Where There Be Dragons runs overseas experiental education summer and semester programs, which are rugged and honest adventures that explore the people, landscapes, and issues of the ASIA, AFRICA and LATIN AMERICA.

Xplor Abroad
(Cultural Exchange Group of Argentina)
Avenida de Mayo, 4th Floor, Office 43,
Buenos Aires, C1085ABQ Argentina

www.xplorabroad.com
Tel: +54 11 43847070
Fax: +54 11 43847070
Email: info@xplorabroad.com

Arts and Culture

Attracted to art? Moved by music? Hooked on history? Fascinated by film? Designs on drama? Passion for photography? There are some mouth-watering courses across Europe and further afield for students interested in all sorts of cultural pleasures.

Art

Eastern Institute of Technology
Private Bag 1201, Taradale,
Napier, Hawke's Bay New Zealand

www.eit.ac.nz
Tel: +64 6 974 8000
Fax: +64 6 974 8910
Email: info@eit.ac.nz

Maori Culture. A variety of short courses for the community is run each year at the EIT marae, at our regional centres, at off campus locations and on air with Radio Kahungunu.

El Casal
Balmes 163, 3/1,
Barcelona, 8008 Spain

www.elcasalbarcelona.com
Tel: +34 93 217 90 38

Email: info@elcasalbarcelona.com

Based in Barcelona, El Casal offers the chance to soak in Catalan culture through a programme that combines study, travel and community service.

Istituto di Lingua e Cultura
Italiana Michelangelo
Via Ghibellina 88,
Florence, 50122 Italy

www.michelangelo-edu.it
Tel: +39 055 240 975
Fax: +39 055 240 997
Email: michelangelo@dada.it

Housed in the 15th-century Palazzo Gherardi close to Michelangelo's house and Florence University, the Michelangelo Institute offers cultural courses on Art History, Literature, Commerce and Commercial Correspondence, and 'L'Italia oggi', a current affairs course that covers the Italian political system, political parties, north/south issues, the media and EU/Italy relationships.

Italian Cultural Institute
(Istituto di Cultura Italiano)
39 Belgrave Square,
London SW1X 8NX

www.icilondon.esteri.it/IIC_Londra
Tel: +44 (0) 20 7235 1461
Fax: +44 (0) 20 7235 4618
Email: icilondon@esteri.it

The Italian Cultural Institute has a bookshelf brimming with free leaflets on courses of all sorts in Italy (including Italian cookery, musical, culture and fashion, for example).

TASIS, The American School in Switzerland

Montagnola, 6926 Switzerland

www.tasis.ch
Tel: +41 91 960 5151
Fax: +41 91 994 2364
Email: admissions@tasis.ch

Each year, the TASIS schools and summer programmes attract over 2400 students representing more than 40 nationalities who share in a caring, family-style international community.

The British Institute of Florence

Piazza Strozzi 2, Florence,
50123 Italy

www.britishinstitute.it
Tel: +39 (0) 55 2677 8200
Fax: +39 (0) 55 2677 8222

Located in the historic centre of Florence within minutes of all the main galleries, museums and churches, the British Institute offers courses in History of Art, Italian language, studio art and watercolour painting, as well as a wide ranging cultural programme. All students have access to the Institute's Harold Acton Library, with its magnificent views across the River Arno, and email and internet access, student support and accommodation service are available. Courses run throughout the year from 1 – 12 weeks, with a Summer School at Massa Marittima near the Tuscan coast during August.

The John Hall Pre-University Course

12 Gainsborough Road,
Ipswich, Suffolk IP4 2UR

www.johnhallvenice.co.uk
Tel: +44 (0) 1473 251 223
Fax: +44 (0) 1473 288 009
Email: info@johnhallpre-university.com

John Hall Pre-University Course, running from January to March, starts with an introductory week in London based at The National Gallery, and includes visits to Richard Rogers Studios (architecture), Christie's Auction House and Tate Modern. Then a party of about 50 students (mostly gappers) from the UK, several other European countries and the US, travels to Venice for six weeks of visits and lectures, given by nearly 30 different lecturers, on Italian history, European art (from Byzantine through Renaissance to Modern), Architecture, Literature, Music, Opera, World Cinema. Students can practise Life Drawing and Photography. Italian language is an optional extra. There's also an optional extra week in Florence and five days in Rome. The seven-week course costs £6,700, which includes travel, half-board, all entrance fees and a one-month vaporetto pass. Private visits to S.Marco, S.Giorgio Maggiore, Peggy Guggenheim Collection (Venice), Uffizi and Accademia (Florence) and in Rome to the Vatican Museums, Sistine Chapel, Villa Borghese Gallery and Keats-Shelley Memorial House. Visits to Ravenna, Padua and Villas and Gardens outside Venice, Florence and Rome are also included.

THE JOHN HALL
PRE-UNIVERSITY COURSE
FIRST IN THE FIELD AND **STILL** FIRST IN THE FIELD

London VENICE Florence Rome

- entirely different from any other cultural programme in Italy

January to March annually for Students of the Arts and Sciences.

Lectures / on-site visits given by a team of
writers, artists, musicians and university lecturers.
Art History, Music, Architecture, Conservation,
History, Opera, Literature, Design, Cinema.
Visits include Padua, Ravenna, Villas and
gardens near Venice, Florence and Rome.

Private visits in Venice to S.Marco, S.Giorgio Maggiore and
The Peggy Guggenheim Collection, in Florence to the
Uffizi Gallery and Accademia and in Rome to the
Vatican Museums, Sistine Chapel, Villa Borghese
Gallery and the Keats Shelley Memorial House.

Classes: Life Drawing, Photography, Italian Language.

Information from: The Secretary
12 Gainsborough Road, Ipswich IP4 2UR
Tel: 01473-251223 fax: 01473-288009

email: info@johnhallvenice.co.uk

www.johnhallvenice.co.uk

Travellers Worldwide
7 Mulberry Close,
Ferring, West Sussex BN12 5HY

www.travellersworldwide.com
Tel: +44 (0) 1903 502595
Fax: +44 (0) 1903 500364
Email: info@travellersworldwide.com

Xplor Abroad
(Cultural Exchange Group of Argentina)
Avenida de Mayo, 4th Floor, Office 43,
Buenos Aires, C1085ABQ Argentina

www.xplorabroad.com
Tel: +54 11 43847070
Fax: +54 11 43847070
Email: info@xplorabroad.com

Cultural Exchange Group of Argentina **www.gicarg.org:** GICArg specialises in intensive Spanish language programmes as well as other study abroad programmes and internships. GICArg offers programmes in partnership with five top universities in different locations throughout Argentina, Uruguay and Chile. GICArg also offers tango and cooking courses, internships and volunteer work placements.

Film, Theatre & Drama

Actors College of Theatre and Television
505 Pitt Street,
Sydney, NSW 2000 Australia

www.actt.edu.au
Tel: +61 (0) 2 9212 6000
Fax: +61 (0) 2 9281 3964
Email: info@actt.edu.au

Metropolitan Film School
Ealing Studios,
Ealing Green, London W5 5EP

www.metfilmschool.co.uk
Tel: +44 (0) 20 8280 9118
Fax: +44 (0) 20 8280 9111
Email: info@metfilmschool.co.uk

Practical courses for aspiring filmmakers. Short courses and one year intensive course available.

NYFA (New York Film Academy)
100 East 17th Street,
New York, NY 10003 USA

www.nyfa.com
Tel: +1 212 674 4300
Fax: +1 212 477 1414
Email: film@nyfa.edu

The New York Film Academy runs programmes all year round in New York City and at Universal Studios in Hollywood, as well as summer workshops worldwide.

PCFE Film School
Pstrossova 19,
Prague 1, /110 00 Czech Republic

www.filmstudies.cz
Tel: +420 257 534 013
Fax: +420 257 534 014
Email: info@filmstudies.cz

Prague-based PCFE Film School offers workshops, semester and year programmes in filmmaking including directing, screenwriting, cinematography, editing, and film history and theory.

171

Wildlife Film Academy
Oranjezicht,
Cape Town, South Africa

www.wildlifeacademy.com
Tel: +27 (0) 21 422 2644
Fax: +27 (0) 21 422 5363
Email: info@wildlifefilmacademy.com

Music

Travellers Worldwide
7 Mulberry Close,
Ferring, West Sussex BN12 5HY

www.travellersworldwide.com
Tel: +44 (0) 1903 502595
Fax: +44 (0) 1903 500364
Email: info@travellersworldwide.com

Photography

Nigel Turner Photographic Workshop
948 Osterville Street, Unit D,
Henderson, NV 89052 USA

www.nigelturnerphotography.com
Tel: +1 (702) 804 8962

Email: npturner@cox.net

Nigel Turner, a professional landscape photographer in the West of the US, offers one- and two-week workshops on photographic technique. You will be based in Las Vegas and have the chance to capture some of the most breathtaking scenery the US has to offer, from Death Valley to Yosemite National Park.

Steve Outram Crete Photo Tours & Workshops
D.Katsifarakis Street, Galatas,
Chania, Crete 73100 Greece

www.steveoutram.com
Tel: +30 28210 32201

Email: mail@steveoutram.com

Professional photographer Steve Outram uses his local knowledge of Zanzibar, Lesvos and Western Crete to show you how to make the most of photographic opportunities and develop your skill as a photographer.

Languages

Language is part of our everyday lives. We use it constantly to communicate with one another – but of course if we don't speak the same language as another person, it becomes a barrier rather than a bridge. Even if you don't want to study a language academically, being able to speak even the smallest amount of a foreign language opens opportunities. There's more to a language than just words: most language courses will include local culture, history, geography, religion, customs and current affairs – as well as traditional cuisine, eating and drinking habits. A language also involves more than just translating your own thoughts into someone else's words. A new language brings a whole new way of thinking with it, and therefore a much deeper understanding of the people who shaped it and use it. Why do some languages have no future tense – is there a different way time is conceived? Most people will know that the Icelanders have lots of words for 'snow', but did you know that they have 85 words for 'storm'?

Think laterally when you decide where you want to study. Spanish is spoken in many countries around the world, so you could opt for a Spanish course in Argentina, Chile or Ecuador, rather than Spain, and then go travelling around South America. The official language of Brazil being Portuguese, why not learn it in Sao Paulo instead of Lisbon. Many cities with a particularly international flavour will offer a variety of language courses: in Brussels, capital of the European Union, courses in other languages such as German, Spanish, Italian or even Russian can be found in a number of institutions. As everyone knows, Belgium is partly Dutch/Flemish-speaking and partly French-speaking: the Belgian Embassy in London will let you have a free list of Flemish and French language schools throughout Belgium.

Belgian Embassy, 103 Eaton Square,
London NW1 6PU, England
Tel: +44 (0) 207470 3700

Volunteer placements

Be aware though that if you learn a language outside its original country you may learn a particular accent and dialect that is spoken only there and may be considered inferior by some people (or even not be understood) elsewhere, e.g. Spanish in South America, Portuguese in Brazil, French in Belgium, Canada and Switzerland, German in Austria and Switzerland.

There's a whole section in this book about voluntary work abroad (see Volunteering Abroad), whether arranged under the umbrella of a **gap-**year organisation in the UK or independently and directly between the volunteer and the project itself. Some language course organisers also arrange volunteer placements after a language course, which can equip volunteers better for their work, and you can find details on their websites.

Living with a family

If enrolling on a language course sounds too much like school, another way of learning a language is staying with a family as an au pair or tutor (giving, say, English or music lessons to children) and going to part-time classes locally. (See Working Abroad, for more details on au pair work.)

Finding the right place to learn

You can try universities, which often have international summer school centres or courses for foreign students. For those who would prefer to dip their toes in gently, there is the popular network of British Institutes abroad. And there's a plethora of independent language colleges to choose from, either directly or through a language course organiser or agency in the UK. The advantage in dealing with a UK-based organisation is that if something goes wrong, it is easier to get it sorted out within easy reach and under UK law.

Language course organisers, consultancies and agencies will provide advice, book courses and organise your accommodation for you, usually getting their income from the commission they receive from language schools. Always ask the agency or language school to put you in contact with one or two students who have done the course you have in mind, so that you can get their views of what it's like before you sign up for anything.

Using the internet

As with most subjects the first place to go for extra information on language courses is the internet. Use search engines like **http://www.orange.co.uk/**, **www.google.com**, **www.lycos.com**, **www.msn.com** and **www.yahoo.com**. If you're looking for courses the following are some international language course websites that we have found:

www.europa-pages.co.uk   www.goabroad.com

www.ialc.org   www.languagesabroad.co.uk

www.languagecoursesabroad.co.uk   www.cesalanguages.com

Language courses

Courses at language schools abroad can be divided into as many as ten different levels, ranging from tuition for the complete beginner to highly technical or specialised courses at postgraduate level. The usual classification of language classes, however, into 'beginner' or 'basic', 'intermediate' and 'advanced' works well. Within each of these levels there are usually subdivisions, especially in schools large enough to move students from one class to another with ease. When you first phone a school from abroad or send in an application form, you should indicate how good your knowledge of the language is.

When you arrive, you may be tested before being allocated to your class, or you may be transferred from your original class to a lower or higher one as soon as they find you are worse or better than expected.

Different schools will use different methods of teaching: if you know that you respond well to one style, check that is what your course offers. Foreign language lessons are often attended by a variety of nationalities so they are almost always conducted in the language you are learning, forcing you to understand and respond without using English. In practice, however, most teachers can revert to English to explain a principle of grammar if a student is really stuck.

The smaller the class the better, though the quality of the teaching is most important – at more advanced levels, well-qualified graduate teachers should be available. Language schools and institutes show a mass of information, photographs and maps on their websites, so it's easy to find out if the school is near to other places that interest you, whether it's a city centre or a coastal resort. The admissions staff should be happy to give you references from previous students.

Over the next few pages we've listed some of the organisations offering language opportunities to gappers, from formal tuition to 'soaking it up' while you live with a family. We've split the organisations according to the languages they offer: **Chinese, French, German, Greek, Italian, Japanese, Portuguese, Russian, Spanish.** Some of the larger companies offer several languages – you'll find the full details of these companies listed under the Multi-languages section.

Chinese

WorldLink Education US Office
1904 3rd Avenue, suite 633,
Seattle, WA 98101 USA

www.worldlinkedu.com
Tel: +1 206 264 0941
Fax: +1 206 264 4932
Email: info@worldlinkedu.com

WorldLink Education's Chinese language programme immerses you in Mandarin Chinese through class instruction, after-class tutoring, language exchanges with native speakers and a range of optional extra activities.

French

Actilangue
2 rue Alexis Mossa,
Nice, 6000 France

www.actilangue.com
Tel: +33 (0) 493 96 3384
Fax: +33 (0) 493 44 3716
Email: contact@actilangue.com

Actilangue is located in the heart of Nice, near the beach and the famous Promenade des Anglais. Courses are conducted solely in French by experienced instructors.

Alliance Française
1 Dorset Square,
London NW1 6PU

www.alliancefrancaise.org.uk
Tel: +44 (0) 20 7723 6439

Email: info@alliancefrancaise.org.uk

Alliance Française is a non-profit-making organisation funded by a trust with a network of Alliances in 138 countries.

BLS French Courses
42 rue Lafaurie de Monbadon,
Bordeaux, 33000 France

www.bls-frenchcourses.com
Tel: +33 (0) 556 51 0076
Fax: +33 (0) 556 51 7615
Email: info@bls-frenchcourses.com

If you like the sound of the Bordeaux area, with its warm, open countryside and vineyards, you could try BLS French courses, based in the heart of Bordeaux. You will be put up in a modest hotel or, more likely, with a host family, perhaps with another student.

College Northside

CP 5158, 750 Chemin Pierre-Péladeau,
Sainte-Adèle PQ, J8B 1Z4 Canada

www.college-northside.qc.ca
Tel: +1 450 229 9889
Fax: +1 450 229 1715
Email: admin@college-northside.qc.ca

Northside offers an intensive French immersion camp through the summer geared towards gappers aged between 16 and 20, located in the mountains in the French-speaking village of Val-Morin about an hour's drive north of Montreal.

ELFCA (Institut d'Enseignement de la Langue Française sur la Côte D'Azur)

66 avenue de Toulon,
Hyères, 83400 France

www.elfca.com
Tel: +33 (0) 4 9465 0331
Fax: +33 (0) 4 9465 8122
Email: elfca@ elfca.com

The ELFCA institute is located in Hyères on the Mediterranean coast. Tuition is in small groups. Students can take the Alliance Française exams or prepare for the DELF exams.

Institut Cunéiforme

3, rue Maguelone,
Montpellier, 34000 France

www.cuneiforme.com
Tel: +33 467 065 690
Fax: +33 467 065 983
Email: info@cuneiforme.com

The Institut Cunéiforme runs intensive French courses, particularly for non-French speakers, in Montpellier lasting between two weeks and three months.

Institut Français

17 Queensberry Place,
London SW7 2DT

www.institut-francais.org.uk
Tel: +44 (0) 20 7073 1350

About 6000 students pass through the Institut Français each year – it's the official French government centre of language and culture in London.

Lyon Bleu International

54 Cours Lafayette,
Lyon, 69003 France

www.lyon-bleu.fr
Tel: +33 (0) 437 480 026
Fax: +33 (0) 478 607 326
Email: bonjour@lyon-bleu.fr

Lyon Bleu International is dedicated to teaching the French language and culture, located in Lyon, which has been classed part of "World heritage" by UNESCO since 1998; they provide a full range of language services.

Point3 Centre de Langues

404 St-Pierre Street, Suite 101,
Montréal PQ, H2Y 2M2 Canada

www.point-3.com
Tel: +1 514 840 7228

Email: info@point-3.com

If you like the idea of learning French in Canada, the Point3 language centre in Montréal, Quebec, runs courses ranging from two to 36 weeks.

Vis-A-Vis
2-4 Stoneleigh Park Road,
Epsom, Surrey KT19 0QT

www.visavis.org
Tel: +44 (0) 20 8786 8021

Email: info@visavis.org

Vis-A-Vis offer French courses in nine locations worldwide including Annecy, Bruxelles, Montréal, Montpellier, Nice, Royan, Vichy and Paris. Various other accommodation options are available, and there is the usual range of course length, level and intensity.

German

British-German Youth Exchange
34 Belgrave Square,
London SW1X 8QB

www.bgconnection.com
Tel: +44 (0) 20 7824 1574

Email: ute.paetzig@the-voyage.com

See their website for details of programmes.

BWS Germanlingua
Hackenstr. 7, Eingang C,
Munich 80331 Germany

www.bws-germanlingua.de
Tel: +49 (0) 89 599 892 00
Fax: +49 (0) 89 599 892 01
Email: info@bws-germanlingua.de

BWS Germanlingua is based in Munich and Berlin; all staff are experienced teachers, and classes have a maximum of 12 students.

BWS Germanlingua
Schlegelstr. 9,
Berlin, 10115 Germany

www.bws-germanlingua.de
Tel: +49 (0) 89 599 892 00
Fax: +49 (0) 89 599 892 01
Email: info@bws-germanlingua.de

BWS Germanlingua is based in Munich and Berlin; all staff are experienced teachers, and classes have a maximum of 12 students.

Deutsch-Institut Tirol
Am Sandhügel 2,
A-6370 Kitzbühel Austria

www.deutschinstitut.com
Tel: +43 53 56 71274
Fax: +43 53 56 72363
Email: office@deutschinstitut.com

The Deutsch-Institut Tirol has been offering German courses combined with skiing in Austria for over 20 years.

German Academic Exchange Service (DAAD)
871 United Nations Plaza,
New York, NY 10017 USA

www.daad.org
Tel: +1 212 758 3223
Fax: +1 212 755 5780
Email: daadny@daad.org

The German Academic Exchange Service is the largest academic exchange service in the world, granting over 50,000 scholarships per year. Has over 14 international offices.

177

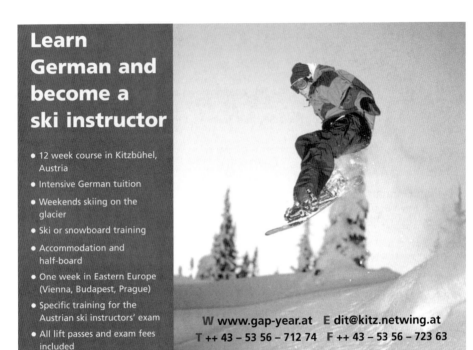
Goethe Institut
50 Princes Gate, Exhibition Road,
London SW7 2PH

www.goethe.de
Tel: +44 (0) 20 7596 4000
Fax: +44 (0) 20 7594 0240
Email: mail@london.goethe.org

The Goethe Institut is probably the best-known international German language school network.

Greek

DIKEMES - International Center for Hellenic and Mediterranean Studies
5 Plateia Stadiou,
Athens, GR - 10024 Greece

www.cyathens.org
Tel: +30 210 7560-749
Fax: +30 210 7561-497
Email: programs@dikemes.gr

Established in 1962 College Year in Athens, in association with the International Center for Hellenic and Mediterranean Studies, offers unparalleled opportunities to experience the unique historical and cultural contributions of Greece and the surrounding region.

Greek Embassy Education Office
1a Holland Park,
London W11 3TP

www.greekembassy.org.uk
Tel: +44 (0) 20 7221 0093
Fax: +44 (0) 20 7243 4212
Email: education@greekembassy.org.uk

Go to the Greek Embassy website to link to the Greek Ministry of Education. Here you can find a list of universities and schools in Athens, Thessalonika, Crete and the Greek islands among other places where modern Greek is taught, in combination with civilisation and culture courses (ancient and modern).

Italian

Accademia del Giglio
Via Ghibellina 116,
Florence, 50122 Italy

www.adg.it
Tel: +39 055 23 02 467
Fax: +39 055 23 02 467
Email: info@adg.it

This quiet, small school takes about 30 students, taught in small classes. As well as Italian language courses, they offer classes in drawing and painting.

Accademia Italiana
Piazza Pitti 15,
Florence, 50125 Italy

www.accademiaitaliana.com
Tel: +39 055 284 616
Fax: +39 055 284486
Email: inform@accademiaitaliana.com

An international design, art and language school, the Accademia Italiana puts on summer language courses as well as full-year and longer academic and Masters courses.

Centro Linguistico Italiano Dante Alighieri
Piazza della Repubblica 5,
Florence, 50123 Italy

www.clida.it
Tel: +39 055 21 0808
Fax: +39 055 28 7828
Email: study@clida.it

Recognised as a premier international language school and by the Italian Ministry of Public Education. Established 1965.

Centro Machiavelli
Piazza Santo Spirito 4,
Florence 50125, Italy

www.centromachiavelli.it
Tel: +39 (0) 55 2396 966
Fax: +39 (0) 55 280 800
Email: school@centromachiavelli.it

This is a delightful small language school in the Santo Spirito district of Florence, in a quiet square, 10 minutes away from the tourist-crammed Ponte Vecchio. Machiavelli has the normal range of language courses, quite reasonably priced. Apprenticeship courses can be organised in local artists' and artisans' workshops nearby and there is always the chance for conversation with local students.The school has a happy atmosphere, all ages, with mainly young continental European and some Japanese students.

179

Il Sillabo
Via Alberti, 31,
San Giovanni Valdarno (AR), 52027 Italy

www.sillabo.it
Tel: +39 055 91232 38
Fax: +39 055 9424 39
Email: info@sillabo.it

Il Sillabo, a small, family-run school, in San Giovanni Valdarno. Authorised by the Italian Ministry of Education.

Istituto Europeo
Piazza delle pallottole n. 1 (Duomo),
Florence, 50122 Italy

www.istitutoeuropeo.it
Tel: +39 05523 81071
Fax: +39 05528 9145
Email: info@istitutoeuropeo.it

Istituto Europeo offers Italian language courses lasting from a week to a year. There are three language schools: two in Italy (Florence and Chieti) and one in Japan (Osaka). As well as running courses on Italian wine and food, Istituto Europeo also has an art and music school.

Lorenzo de' Medici
Via de Giglio 15,
Florence, 50123 Italy

www.lorenzodemedici.it
Tel: +39 055 287 360

Email: ita@lorenzodemedici.it

The Lorenzo de' Medici offers a combination of language and cultural courses and has a large library in the adjoining San Iacopo di Corbolini church.

The John Hall Pre-University Course
12 Gainsborough Road,
Ipswich, Suffolk IP4 2UR

www.johnhallvenice.co.uk
Tel: +44 (0) 1473 251 223
Fax: +44 (0) 1473 288 009
Email: info@johnhallpre-university.com

Torre di Babele
Via Consenza 7,
Roma, 161 Italy

www.torredibabele.com
Tel: +39 06 4425 2578
Fax: +39 06 4425 1972
Email: info@torredibabele.com

Courses run all year round and are led by highly-qualified teachers. Also a teacher training centre, we aim to use dynamic teaching methods and stimulating texts in order to incorporate the personal interests of students as well as diverse aspects of Italian life.

Japanese

The Japan Foundation -
London Language Centre
6th Floor, Russell Square House,
10-12 Russell Square
London WC1B 5EH

www.jpf.org.uk/language
Tel: +44 (0) 20 7436 6698
Fax: +44 (0) 20 7323 4888
Email: info.language@jpf.org.uk

The Japan Foundation London Language Centre provides courses in Japanese. Also has regular newsletter and resource library.

Multi languages

Cactus Language
4 Clarence House, 30-31 North Street,
Brighton, East Sussex BN1 1EB

www.cactuslanguage.com
Tel: +44 (0) 1273 725200
Fax: +44 (0) 1273 775868
Email: info@cactuslanguage.com

Cactus Language offers language holidays in over 25 languages, and in 45 countries and 150 destinations, worldwide. Courses are available from one week upwards, for all ages and levels, and can be combined with other activities.

Caledonia Languages Abroad
The Clockhouse, Bonnington Mill,
72 Newhaven Road
Edinburgh, Midlothian EH6 5QG

www.caledonialanguages.co.uk
Tel: +44 (0) 131 621 7721/2
Fax: +44 (0) 131 621 6262
Email: courses@caledonialanguages.co.uk

Tailor-made advice and a personalised booking service for courses at 42 language schools around the world. Caledonia has 11 years experience and can organise your course and accommodation and give practical advice on all aspects of your trip. Short courses in French, Italian, German, Russian, Spanish and Portuguese in Europe and Latin America, for all levels, start all year round, most for a minimum of 2 weeks. Accommodation is usually with a local host family, half board. Residences and share flats are also often available. Volunteer work is available from 3 weeks to a year in Latin America, working with local schools, orphanages, social projects and nature reserves.

CERAN Lingua International
Avenue des Petits Sapins 27,
Spa, 4900 Belgium

www.ceran.com
Tel: +32 (0) 87 79 11 22
Fax: +32 (0) 87 79 11 88
Email: customer@ceran.com

CERAN runs weekly intensive residential language programmes in Dutch, French, German, Spanish and Japanese with 'complete immersion' in the language from 8am to 10pm.

181

CESA Languages Abroad
CESA House, Pennance Road,
Lanner, Cornwall TR16 5TQ

www.cesalanguages.com
Tel: +44 (0) 1209 211 800
Fax: +44 (0) 1209 211 830
Email: info@cesalanguages.com

CESA Languages Abroad are a family company. They arrange programmes in language colleges in Europe and beyond (Japan, Morocco and China for example), and offer advice on the most appropriate course for you. Of all the languages CESA offers, Spanish and Italian are most in demand. You can choose from Spanish courses in Costa Rica (San Jose), Ecuador (Quito and Cuenca), Mexico (Cuernavaca or Playa del Carmen) and Spain (Granada, Madrid, Marbella, Malaga, Nerja, Salamanca, Barcelona or Seville, for one week to nine months. CESA's German courses in Berlin are becoming increasingly popular, particularly the Work Experience option for gap and university students. Courses are also run in Cologne, Lindau, Munich (München) and Vienna or Kitzbuhel (Austria). Italian courses are offered in cities such as Rome, Milan and Florence and also smaller locations such as Viarregio and San Giovanni from one to 36 weeks. You can choose to improve your French in the Caribbean (Guadeloupe in January has definite attractions!) or in a wonderful selection of locations in France. If your language ambitions lie further afield, CESA also offers courses in Japanese, (Okazaki, near Nagoya), Russian (at language schools in St Petersburg and Moscow), Chinese (close to the Forbidden City, in Beijing) and Greek (in the capital city, Athens or the beautiful island of Crete).

EF International Language Schools
Dudley Hosue, 36-38 Southampton Street,
London WC2E 7HF

www.ef.com
Tel: +44 (0) 870 720 0780
Fax: +44 (0) 870 720 0767

On an EF International Language Schools programme you will immerse yourself in the language and culture of some of the world's most exciting cities.

Eurolingua Institute
Eurolingua House, 61 Bollin Drive,
Altrincham, Cheshire WA14 5QW

www.eurolingua.com
Tel: +44 (0) 161 972 0225
Fax: +44 (0) 161 972 0225

Eurolingua is a network of 70 institutes teaching nine languages in 35 countries. 'Group programmes' give 15 hours of tuition a week according to your level.

Inlingua International
Belpstrasse 11,
3007 Bern, Switzerland

www.inlingua.com
Tel: +41 31 388 7777
Fax: +41 31 388 7766
Email: service@inlingua.com

Inlingua International runs colleges throughout Europe.

Language Courses Abroad
67 Ashby Road,
Loughborough, Leicestershire LE11 3AA

www.languagesabroad.co.uk
Tel: +44 (0) 1509 211612

Email: info@languagesabroad.co.uk

Language Courses Abroad offers courses in French, German, Greek, Italian, Portuguese, Russian and Spanish in venues throughout Europe and South America, inluding Cuba. They specialise in arranging tailor-made course combinations to suit individual needs – so, for example, you could study one language in several locations, or several languages in one location. Many course venues offer excursions and supplementary courses.

Learn Languages Abroad
'Sceilig', Ballymorefinn,
Glenasmole, Dublin 24 Eire

www.languages.ie
Tel: +353 1 451 1674
Fax: +353 1451 1636
Email: info@languages.ie

Learn Languages Abroad will help you find the course best suited to your needs. They organise your application to the school and take care of the whole booking process for you. Courses available range from two weeks to a full academic year.

OISE Oxford
13-15 High Street,
Oxford, Oxfordshire OX1 4EA

www.oise.com
Tel: +44 (0)1865 247 272
Fax: +44 (0)1865 723 648
Email: oxford@oise.com

For over 30 years, OISE has developed and refined the concept of intensive language courses all over the world. Our unique teaching philosophy leads our students to gain confidence, fluency and accuracy when speaking another language taught by a native speaker.

Travellers Worldwide
7 Mulberry Close,
Ferring, West Sussex BN12 5HY

www.travellersworldwide.com
Tel: +44 (0) 1903 502595
Fax: +44 (0) 1903 500364
Email: info@travellersworldwide.com

Twin Languages Abroad
2nd Floor, 67-71 Lewisham High Street,
Lewisham, London SE13 5JX

www.twinlanguagesabroad.com
Tel: +44 (0) 20 8297 0505
Fax: +44 (0) 20 8297 0984
Email: languagesabroad@twinuk.com

Twin Languages has experience in arranging language courses from one week upwards for all ages and levels throughout Europe and South America.

Portuguese

CIAL Centro de Linguas
Av da Republica, 41 - 8th Floor,
Lisbon 1050-187, Portugal

www.cial.pt
Tel: +351 217 940 448
Fax: +351 217 960 783
Email: portuguese@cial.pt

With schools in Lisbon and Faro, CIAL organises courses in Portuguese including group courses with either 3 hours' tuition (€255 per week/€885 4 weeks) or 6 hours' tuition (€980 2 weeks/€1700 4 weeks), a two-week teachers' training course (€500), individual lessons (€33 per hour up to 60 hours/ €31 per hour more than 60 hours) and private groups of two (€40 per hour), as well as specialist courses in Brazilian or African Portuguese. Accommodation is in private homes at an extra cost of €116 per week, which includes breakfast.

Russian

Obninsk Humanities Centre
Dubravushka, 249020 Kaluga Oblast,
Obninsk, Pionersky Proezd 29, Russia

www.dubravushka.ru
Tel: +44 (0) 208 858 0614 (UK number)

Email: dubravushka@ok.ru

The Obninsk Humanities Centre is an independent boarding school two hours from Moscow offering intensive and reasonably priced Russian courses. A week's fees include 20-25 hours tuition, full board and lodging, emergency medical treatment, transport to and from the airport and sightseeing trips.

The Russian Language Centre
11 Coldbath Square,
London EC1R 5HL

www.russiancentre.co.uk
Tel: +44 (0) 20 7689 5400
Fax: +44 (0) 20 7689 5401
Email: info@russiancentre.co.uk

The Russian Language Centre in London offers a range of courses for groups and individuals: intensive, accelerated and private.

Academia Hispánica Córdoba
C/Rodríguez Sánchez, 15,
14003 Córdoba Spain

www.academiahispanica.com
Tel: +34 957 488 002
Fax: +34 957 488 199
Email: info@academiahispanica.com

Small-group language tuition to suit all levels.

AIL Madrid Spanish Language School
Doctor Esquerdo 33, 1a2,
28028 Madrid Spain

www.ailmadrid.com/gap-year/home
Tel: +34 91 725 6350
Fax: +34 91 725 4188
Email: gap.year@ailmadrid.com

AIL Madrid Spanish Language School Flexible Gap Year Programs tailored to your needs in Madrid, Spain. Combine learning Spanish with work placements in Spain. Travel around Latin America. Learn another language such as French, German or Catalan. Obtain the DELE certificate. Take Latin and Spanish dance classes. Be immersed in Spanish and Latin culture.

Amigos Spanish School
Zaguan de Cielo B-23,
Cusco, Peru

www.spanishcusco.com
Tel: +51 (84) 24 22 92
Fax: +51 84 242292
Email: amigos@spanishcusco.com

AMIGOS is the first non-profit SPANISH SCHOOL in Cusco-Peru. With every hour of your Spanish classes, you pay for education, food and medical care of a group of underprivileged children at our foundation.

Bridge Year, Spanish Programs
Roman Diaz 297, Providencia,
Santiago Chile

www.bridgeyear.com
Tel: +44 (0) 20 7096 0369
Fax: 001 866 726 5705
Email: info@bridgeyear.com

Study Spanish in Chile & Argentina! There are plenty of activities and excursions plus the homestay could be the most rewarding part of the experience.

Centro de Capacitación Simon Bolivar
Mariscal Foch E9-20 y Av. 6 de Diciembre,
Quito, Ecuador

www.simon-bolivar.com
Tel: +593 (2) 2234 708
,
Email: info@simon-bolivar.com

One of the biggest Spanish schools in Ecuador with an average of 40 students per month. Individual Spanish lessons are offered at the main building in Quito and group lessons are given at centres in the Amazon jungle and on the coast.

Don Quijote

PO Box 218,
Epsom, Surrey KT19 OYF

www.donquijote.org
Tel: +44 (0) 20 8786 8081
Fax: +44 (0) 20 8786 8086
Email: uk@donquijote.co.uk

Don Quijote has language schools in Spain and Latin America. In Spain the school offers courses in Barcelona, Granada, Madrid, Malaga, Salamanca, Seville, Puerto de la Cruz in Tenerife, and Valencia. There is also a Don Quijote school in Guanajuato, Mexico.

Escuela Internacional

Central Office, Calle Talamanca 10,
28807 Alcala de Henares
Madrid, Spain

www.escuelai.com
Tel: +34 91 883 1264
Fax: +34 91 883 1301
Email: info@escuelai.com

Gap Year Diver Ltd

Tyte Court,
Great Rollright, Oxfordshire OX7 5RS

www.gapyeardiver.com
Tel: +44 (0) 845 257 3292
Fax: +44 (0) 1608 730 574
Email: info@gapyeardiver.com.

Learn Spanish and dive in South America! Gap Year Diver offers a range of 2 to 6 month itineraries in Venezuela, Costa Rica and Panama. Courses range from introductory diving right the way through to instructor levels, with the added benefit of learning Spanish at the same time. Also included in these courses is the option to take advantage of overland trips (in the form of our travelling classroom) through some of the most breathtaking scenery and landscapes in South America. These are fun-packed and intensive trips designed for those that want to get the most out of their Gap Year. Discover the Blue with Gap Year Diver.

International House Madrid

C/Zurbano, 8,
Madrid, Spain 28010

www.ihmadrid.com
Tel: +34 91 319 7224
Fax: +34 91 308 5321
Email: spanish@ihmadrid.com

Spanish Study Holidays

67 Ashby Road,
Loughborough,
Leicestershire LE11 3AA

www.spanishstudy.co.uk
Tel: +44 (0) 1509 211 612
Fax: +44 (0) 1509 260 037
Email: spanishstudy.holidays@btinternet.com

Spanish Study Holidays offers Spanish courses throughout Spain and central and south America lasting from a week to nine months.

Universidad de Navarra - ILCE

Institute of Spanish Language and Culture,
Edificio Central,
Pamplona, Navarra 31080 Spain

www.unav.es
Tel: +34 948 425 600
Fax: +34 948 425 619
Email: ilce@unav.es

The Universidad de Navarra offers an educational Bridge Year program that allows students to learn Spanish in a university setting while earning college credits.

Xplor Abroad
(Cultural Exchange Group of Argentina)
Avenida de Mayo, 4th Floor, Office 43,
Buenos Aires, C1085ABQ Argentina

www.xplorabroad.com
Tel: +54 11 43847070
Fax: +54 11 43847070
Email: info@xplorabroad.com

Xplor Abroad specializes in intensive Spanish language programs as well as other study abroad programs and internships. Xplor Abroad offers programs in partnership with five top universities in different locations throughout Argentina, Uruguay and Chile. Xplor Abroad also offers tango and cooking courses, internships, ESL teaching positions and volunteer work placements.

TEFL

Academy of Prague Schools
Evropska 35,
Praha 6, Czech Republic

www.tefl.cz
Tel: +42 0 233 322 742
Fax: +42 0 233 323 779
Email: info@tefl.cz

Prague Schools is a dynamic private language school based in Prague 6, specializing in the Trinity Certificate in TESOL. Also accredited by the Ministry of Education.

Global Vision International
Amwell Farm House, Nomansland,
Wheathampstead
St Albans, Hertfordshire AL4 8EJ

www.gvi.co.uk
Tel: +44 (0) 870 608 8898
Fax: +44 (0) 870 609 2319
Email: info@gvi.co.uk

Join GVI's Mexico expedition, gain a TEFL qualification, and work with the local community in a Caribbean World Heritage Site. 100 or 50 hour TEFL.

i-to-i
Woodside House, 261 Low Lane,
Leeds, Yorkshire LS18 5NY

www.i-to-i.com
Tel: +44 (0) 870 333 2332
Fax: +44 (0) 113 205 4619
Email: uk@i-to-i.com

OxfordTEFL
C/Girona, 83,
08009 Barcelona, Spain

www.oxfordtefl.com
Tel: +34 934 580 111
Fax: +34 934 586 638
Email: tesol@oxfordtefl.com

Teach English worldwide

With 4 weeks top quality, practical training at OxfordTEFL, accredited by Trinity College London, you will get a Certificate in TEFL (Teaching English as a Foreign Language). As a qualified TEFL teacher you will be able to travel and teach English anywhere in the world, experience new cultures, learn new languages and improve your students' chances in life.

Hundreds of successful graduates teaching English around the world are our best guarantee. Visit our website and contact them directly.

Complete our 4 week Trinity Cert. TESOL course in Prague, Barcelona or Cadiz and find a job teaching English anywhere in the world.

OxfordTEFL .... experts in Teacher Training.

TEFL International
1200 Belle Passi Road,
Woodburn, OR 97071 USA

www.teflintl.com
Tel: +1 866 384 8854

Email: admin@teflintl.com

TEFL International are a leading provider of English Language Teacher Training courses and Volunteer placements.

TEFL Time
7 Mulberry Close,
Ferring, Sussex BN12 5HY

www.tefltime.com
Tel: +44 (0) 1903 573 679

Email: info@tefltime.com

TEFL Time UK-based weekend courses in TEFL: 20 hour certificate (£189) + 100 hour distance learning certificate (£288) available. Excellent support throughout + paid opportunities overseas available.

The Year Out Group
Queensfield, 28 King's Road,
Easterton, Wiltshire SN10 4PX

www.yearoutgroup.org
Tel: +44 (0) 7980 395789

Email: info@yearoutgroup.org

Sport

There are sports courses for all types at all levels, from scuba diving for beginners to advanced ski instructor qualification courses, in pretty much every country in the world. Of course if you manage to get qualified as an instructor you may be able to use it to get a job for the rest of your **gap**-year.

Make sure the course offers the qualifications that will be useful to you and check that the instructors are properly qualified. Most important is to make sure that you have the necessary insurance – take a look at any of the sport websites and you'll find out that accidents do happen (**www.bungeezone.com** disasters page is particularly scary) and if you slip whilst up a mountain, injuries tend to be a bit more serious – and expensive – than a sprained ankle. That said, learning a sport abroad is a great way to meet new people, experience the local culture and have a really energetic, fun **gap**-year.

Sport courses & organisations

Adventure Ireland
Bayview Avenue,
Bundoran, County Donegal, Eire

www.adventure-ireland.com
Tel: +353 7198 424 18
Fax: +353 7198 424 29
Email: info@adventure-ireland.com

Adventure Ireland Gap Year. Live and work in Ireland. Learn to surf, climb, kayak. Train as an outdoor sports instructor. Classes on Irish culture, history, language and literature.

Allaboard Sailing Academy
RYA Training Centre, 7 The Square,
Marina Bay, Gibraltar

www.asa.gi
Tel: +350 50202

Email: info@asa.gi

BASI (British Association of Snowsport Instructors)
Glenmore,
Aviemore, Inverness-shire PH22 1QU

www.basi.org.uk
Tel: 01479 861 403
Fax: 01479 861 718
Email: basi@basi.org.uk

The British Association of Snowsport Instructors (BASI) is the UK authority for training, examining and grading snowsport instructors and its qualifications are recognised worldwide.

Bear Creek Outdoor Centre
R R#3 Campbell's Bay,
Quebec J0X 1K0 Canada

www.bearcreekoutdoor.com
Tel: +1 819 453 2127
Fax: +1 819 453 2128
Email: info@bearcreekoutdoor.com

Bear Creek Outdoor Centre near Ottawa offers a ten-week outdoor adventure leadership programme aimed at all levels. You must be at least 18 years of age, be able to swim and consider yourself to be in good health.

Bermuda Sub Aqua Club
P. O. Box HM 3155,
Hamilton, Bermuda HM NX

www.bsac.com
Tel: + 1 441 291 5640

Email: bsac@callistoenterprises.com

The Bermuda Sub Aqua Club is a branch of the British Sub Aqua Club and offers members a varied programme of club-organised dives; a safe, structured, proven training programme (BSAC), social activities; access to the club's compressor for air fills and a club newsletter. The club is also active in the community, regularly participating in such events as the Keep Bermuda Beautiful Marine Clean-up dives.

6

Learning abroad | Sport

189

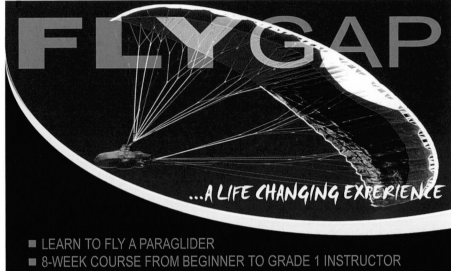
Cardrona Alpine Resort
PO Box 117,
Wanaka, New Zealand

www.cardrona.com
Tel: +64 3 443 7341

Email: jacollis@earthlink.net

Deutsch-Institut Tirol
Am Sandhügel 2,
A-6370 Kitzbühel Austria

www.deutschinstitut.com
Tel: +43 53 56 71274
Fax: +43 53 56 72363
Email: office@deutschinstitut.com

The Deutsch-Institut Tirol has been offering German courses combined with skiing, in Kitzbühel, Austria, for over 20 years.

Eurosail (UK) Ltd
Quinta da Rosa Linda, Malhao 218M,
Paderne, Alb. 8200-484 Portugal

www.euro-sail.co.uk
Tel: +351 289 366 993

Email: julian@euro-sail.co.uk

Come and enjoy sailing in the sunshine in Portugal with friendly skippers, modern yachts and excellent food!

Fly Gap

Chemin de la côte 15, Chalet Anguillita,
Villette, 1934 Switzerland

www.flygap.com
Tel: +41 (0) 79 313 5677
Fax: +41 (0) 27 776 1134
Email: stu@flygap.com

Fly Gap in Verbier is the only paragliding school worldwide whose flying courses are specifically designed for British gap year students. Our 8 week courses are not only designed to teach you how to fly but we also involve you in the running of the academy, teaching you priceless logistic skills. You will not just be a student here, but a valuable member of our team of instructors. Leave us with a pilot's licence, a Grade 1 instructor licence and numerous other qualifications that will look impressive on your CV as well as make you employable on the rest of your gap year as we can help you with work placements. We hope to see you in the skies above Verbier, Switzerland!

Gap Sports Ltd

Thamesbourne, Station Road,
Bourne End, Buckinghamshire SL8 5QH

www.gapsports.com
Tel: +44 (0) 870 837 9797

Email: info@gapsports.com

Gap year Diver Ltd

Tyte Court,
Great Rollright, Oxfordshire OX7 5RS

www.gapyeardiver.com
Tel: +44 (0) 845 257 3292
Fax: +44 (0) 1608 730 574
Email: info@gapyeardiver.com.

Learn to dive. Continue the adventure. Become a professional. Gap Year Diver are specialists in the field of recreational, professional and technical scuba diving. We cater for all types of "gappers", from school and university leavers to career breakers and early retirees. Whether you're after a short break to see what scuba diving is all about or an extended break to become a dive professional, Gap Year Diver is here to make your desired trip possible. Itineraries/courses range from 2 to 24 weeks and can be completed in Venezuela, Costa Rica, Panama and the Red Sea. Courses start frequently throughout the year, although we can also tailor-make courses to your exact requirements. Discover the Blue with Gap Year Diver.

Gap4U

6277, 35e Avenue,
Montréal PQ, H1T 3A4 Canada

www.gap4u.com
Tel: (UK) +44 (0) 20 8144 1844

Email: info@gap4u.com

Become a Ski or Snowboard Instructor whilst having the experience of a lifetime! Gain internationally recognised CASI/CSIA certification over a 12-week course commencing in January. Stay in the beautiful ski resort of Magog and train each day with our professional team. Our programmes include full board accommodation, lift passes and 4 hours instruction & training per day. Sharing our passion is what we do best, and the surroundings will blow you away!

Gibraltar Sailing Centre 10 The Square, Marina Bay, Gibraltar	www.straits-sail.com Tel: +350 51372 Fax: +350 51373 Email: info@straits-sail.com

Expert tuition with the full range of RYA courses.

Greenforce 11-15 Betterton Street, Covent Garden, London WC2H 9BP	www.greenforce.org Tel: +44 (0) 20 7470 8888 Fax: +44 (0) 207 379 0801 Email: info@greenforce.org

ICE Snowsports Ltd 3-4 Bath Place, Aberdovey, Gwynedd LL35 0LN	www.icesi.org Tel: +44 (0) 870 760 7360 Email: info@icesi.org

Marine Divers **(British Sub-Aqua Club School 388) Hong Kong** 3E, Block 18, Dynasty View, 11 Ma Wo Road, Tai Po New Territories, Hong Kong	www.marinedivers.com Tel: +852 2656 9399 Fax: +852 2656 9399 Email: info@marinedivers.com

Training and fun in Hong Kong, with optional 5-day trip to the Philippines. Various packages.

Mermaids Xtreme Diving
191/11 Pattaya Central Road, Banglamung,
20260, Chonburi, Thailand

www.pattayascubadiving.com
Tel: +66 38 420 411
Fax: +66 38 360 095
Email: info@pattayascubadiving.com

Join our Academy for two/six months and become a paid PADI Diving Instructor. All inclusive including equipment, fees, accomodation, dives, etc.

New Zealand Skydiving School
P O Box 21,
Methven, New Zealand

www.skydivingnz.com
Tel: +64 (03) 302 9143
Fax: +64 (03) 302 9140
Email: info@skydivingnz.com

Join the international skydiving industry by completing this unique skydiving qualification in New Zealand, the Adventure Capital of the Southern Hemisphere. The Diploma in Commercial Skydiving includes 200 skydives, a wide range of skydiving skills and knowledge including freefall photography, video editing, parachute packing, dedicated coaching camps and organised industry experience. The aim is to make students highly employable in the world of commercial skydiving; current graduate employment rates exceed 95%. The Skydiving School has a team of highly qualified and internationally respected instructors. The school is New Zealand Parachute Industry Association and New Zealand Qualifications Authority approved. Career Development Loans are available for UK students.

NONSTOP Adventure Ltd
Unit 3B, The Plough Brewery,
516 Wandsworth Road
London SW8 3JX

www.nonstopadventure.com
Tel: +44 (0) 870 241 8070

Email: info@nonstopadventure.com

Peak Leaders
Mansfield,
Strathmiglo, Fife-shire KY14 7QE

www.peakleaders.com
Tel: +44 (0) 1337 860 079
Fax: +44 (0) 1338 868 176
Email: info@peakleaders.com

Peak Leaders UK Ltd offer gap year ski and snowboard instructor training and improvement courses in Canada, Argentina, NZ, Switzerland and France. Check www.peakleaders.com.

Planet Subzero
20 Woodsyre, London SE26 6SS

www.planetsubzero.com

Email: info@planetsubzero.com

Improve your skiing/boarding and language skills. Includes avalanche courses, heli-skiing and involvement in the competition circuit.

Plas Menai
National Watersports Centre,
Caernarfon, Gwynedd LL55 1UE

www.plasmenai.co.uk
Tel: +44 (0) 1248 670964
Fax: +44 (0) 1248 673939
Email: info@plasmenai.co.uk

Plas Menai offers a range of courses training people to work as watersports, yachting and adventure instructors abroad and in the UK. Training courses last

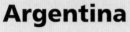

between 1 and 26 weeks and take place in Spain and UK. Courses for beginners and those with experience. Use your qualifications to train, work and travel in your gap year or longer term. - Start dates throughout the year - Weekend, 5 day and longer training courses - Professional Yacht Skipper: 17 weeks - Dinghy and Windsurf Instructor: 12 wks - Dinghy Instructor: 8 wks - Multi-Activity Instructor: 26 wks - Recruitment + work placements.

Polo Skool Ltd	www.poloskool.co.uk
Woodlands, The Straight Mile,	Tel: +44 (0) 1962 855 138
Romsey, Hampshire SO51 9BA	Fax: +44 (0) 1962 855 138
	Email: team@poloskool.co.uk

PoloSkool offers intensive polo tuition programmes in Argentina. Fully residential courses of two, four and ten weeks are available for players of all abilities.

Pro Dive Academy	www.prodive.com.au
120/35 Harrington Street, The Rocks,	Tel: +61 292 55 0300
Sydney, NSW 2000 Australia	
	Email: travel@prodive.com.au

Pro Dive Academy offers an extensive range of courses focussed on providing internationally-recognised qualifications.

Saracen Sailing
Correos 162,
Pollensa, Mallorca E-07460 Spain

www.saracensailing.com
Tel: +34 971 509 519
Fax: +34 971 509 064
Email: office@saracensailing.com

The Saracen Sailing School in Mallorca is an RYA approved sea school and offers a broad range of practical tidal sailing courses aboard their yachts based in North East Mallorca all year round.

Shoestring Polo Ltd
2 Street Cottages, Wheatsheaf Lane, Oaksey
Nr Malmesbury, Wiltshire SN16 9SZ

www.shoestringpolo.com
Tel: 01666 577898

Email: info@shoestringpolo.com

An enthusiastic, bilingual, well travelled team player is probably the most sought after individual in the working world - let Shoestring Polo broaden your CV. Playing polo in Argentina, the home of polo, is a fantastic opportunity for individuals regardless of previous experience. On average five hours a day are spent in the saddle stick and balling and playing instructed chukkas. Courses incorporate tournaments, regular talks, Spanish lessons, the chance to take part in gaucho work and other sports as well as enjoying the wildlife. Over twenty years polo experience has made us realise there isn't a better way of meeting like-minded people, or enjoying beef and red wine in such a relaxed environment!

Ski Instructor Training Co
Queenstown, Otago New Zealand

www.skiinstructortraining.co.nz

Email: info@skiinstructortraining.co.nz

Ski Instructor Training Co offers you the opportunity to train for your ski instructor qualification with the New Zealand Snow Sports Instructors Alliance Stage 1 ski instructors exam.

Ski le Gap
220 chemin Wheeler,
Mont-Tremblant PQ, J8E 1V3 Canada

www.skilegap.com
Tel: +1 819 429 6599
Fax: +1 819 425 7074
Email: info@skilegap.com

Ski le Gap offers ski and snowboard instructor training courses based at the popular Canadian resort of Tremblant. The three-month programme prepares you for the level I qualification through tuition in small groups, videos, clinics, seminars, lectures and individualised daily goals.

Ski-Exp-Air
913 Senneterre,
Québec PQ, G1X 3Y2 Canada

www.ski-exp-air.com
Tel: +1 418 204 6669
Fax: +1 418 654 9071
Email: info@ski-exp-air.com

Ski-exp-air is a Canadian ski and snowboard school serving an international clientele and offering quality, professional instruction in a fun atmosphere. They are located in the Quebec City Region, the wintersport capital of Canada. Using the four surrounding major mountain resorts and friendly, personalized instruction, they will teach you to be an excellent skier and snowboarder – regardless of whether

195

BECOME A SKI or/& SNOWBOARD INSTRUCTOR

THE FUN WAY

www.SKI-EXP-AIR.com

QUEBEC CITY, CANADA

you have ever been on snow or not! Ski-exp-air's three month programme is designed to ensure that you reach the level of certification of your choice as ski, snowboard instructor or racing coach. Canadian instructors and coaches have a world wide reputation of excellence. Ski-exp-air invite you to join them as a valued member of their team: "We have proven success in making dreams, your dreams, a reality."

Snow Skool	www.snowskool.co.uk
Woodlands, The Straight Mile,	Tel: +44 (0) 1962 855 138
Romsey, Hampshire SO51 9BA	Fax: +44 (0) 1962 855 138
	Email: team@snowskool.co.uk

Ski & Snowboard instructor courses in Canada and New Zealand. SnowSkool offers four, five, nine & eleven week programmes earning internationally recognised qualifications.

Sport Lived Ltd	www.sportlived.co.uk
The Hive, The Maudslay Building, Burton Street	Tel: 0870 950 3837
Nottingham, Nottinghamshire NG1 4BU	
	Email: info@sportlived.co.uk

Sport Lived is a sporting gap year company which arranges for young people to play sport overseas.

Sunsail
The Port House, Port Solent,
Portsmouth, Hampshire PO6 4TH

www.sunsail.com
Tel: +44 (0) 23 9222 2300

Email: yachting@sunsail.com

Sunsail offers the full range of RYA yacht courses as well as their own teaching programmes. Their instructors are RYA qualified.

Surfing Queensland
PO Box 233,
Burleigh Heads, QLD 4220 Australia

www.surfingqueensland.com.au
Tel: + 61 07 552 011 65
Fax: +61 07 557 624 33
Email: info@surfingqueensland.com.au

Surfing Queensland has a surf school system with 16 licensed surf schools operating on beaches from Coolangatta to Yeppoon.

Taupo Bungy
PO Box 919,
Taupo, New Zealand

www.taupobungy.co.nz
Tel: +64 7 377 1135

Email: jump@taupobungy.co.nz

Located in the Waikato River Valley, Taupo Bungy is considered one of the world's most spectacular bungy sites. Featuring the world's first cantilever platform and New Zealand's first 'splash cam'.

The International Academy
King's Place, 12-42 Wood Street,
Kingston Upon Thames, Surrey KT1 1JY

www.theinternationalacademy.com
Tel: +44 (0) 870 060 1381
Fax: +44 (0) 20 8939 0411
Email: info@theinternationalacademy.com

The International Academy is a unique organisation that combines travel, sport and training.

The Year Out Group
Queensfield, 28 King's Road,
Easterton, Wiltshire SN10 4PX

www.yearoutgroup.org
Tel: +44 (0) 7980 395789

Email: info@yearoutgroup.org

Whistler Snowboard Camps
Coast Mountain Snowboard Camps Ltd,
102-4369 Main Street, Suite 981
Whistler BC, V0N 1B4 Canada

www.whistlersnowboardcamps.com
Tel: +1 604 932 3259
Fax: +1 604 932 0565
Email: info@whistlersnowboardcamps.com

Conservation

Africa & Asia Venture
10 Market Place,
Devizes, Wiltshire SN10 1HT

www.aventure.co.uk
Tel: +44 (0) 1380 729009
Fax: +44 (0) 1380 720060
Email: av@aventure.co.uk

Africa Asia Venture is for motivated students and graduates of 18-24, who want to spend 3-5 months teaching a wide variety of subjects, especially English and sports in Africa (Tanzania, Kenya, Uganda, Malawi, Botswana) Mexico, Thailand, Nepal, and the Indian Himalayas. Excellent community and conservation projects are available for the same periods in Uganda. Departures are around September, January and May. A 3-week period of travel is included in all our Ventures and a 5-8 day safari is part of the scheme. Alternatively, shorter Ventures of 5 weeks that include building projects, safaris and adventure are also available in Kenya and Uganda (departures throughout the year but mainly in July, August, September). Full support and in-country back up is provided throughout. Costs range from £1830–£2840 and include comprehensive training in TEFL, relevant languages, local religion, history, culture & customs, plus medical/equipment insurance (main scheme), accommodation, food, a local living allowance and a donation to your school/project. Check our website for relevant information and brochures.

AFRICAN GAP YEAR
design your life!

"If you don't try to actively discover your purpose, you're likely to spend your life doing the wrong things." *John C. Maxwell, The Success Journey*

In association with

LAPALALA
WILDERNESS

During your gap year take <u>time out with a purpose</u> - spend 3 to 12 weeks letting us help you <u>create a plan for your future</u> based on your passions, whilst <u>in the South African bush!</u>

✧ Create your personalised **study and career path**
✧ Participate in special workshops with **futurists**
✧ Establish your unique **path to success**
✧ Make **friends** & develop life-long relationships
✧ Learn whilst experiencing the **beauty of Africa**, and
✧ Have a *Great time!*

www.africangapyear.com
info@africangapyear.com

Discover your Future of Work & Play - in South Africa

African Conservation Experience

PO Box 206,
Faversham, Kent ME13 8WZ

www.ConservationAfrica.net
Tel: 0870 241 5816

Email: info@ConservationAfrica.net

African Conservation Experience have been sending volunteers to Africa for over five years and are the original, most experienced organisation for conservation placements in Southern Africa. ACE are able to offer each and every applicant the benefits of their personal experience, and all volunteers receive individual consideration. African Conservation Experience can offer you the chance to work on game and nature reserves alongside conservationists, zoologists, wildlife vets and reserve managers, making a real contribution to the conservation of African wildlife. Work can involve game capture for tagging and relocation, behavioural and population studies, wildlife veterinary work, anti-poaching patrols and animal rehabilitation. Volunteers become an integral part of the conservation project, many of which would not be able to run without their input. Placements are from one-three months, and cost from around £2700 for four weeks up to £4000 for 12 weeks. This includes flights, accommodation, all meals and transfers.

African Conservation Trust

PO Box 310,
Linkhills, South Africa 3652

www.projectafrica.com
Tel: +27 31 7675 044

Email: info@projectafrica.com

The mission of ACT is to provide a means for conservation projects to become self-funding through active participation by the public.

African Gap Year

PO Box 1312,
Cresta, South Africa 2118

www.africangapyear.com
Tel: +27 (0) 118 887 117
Fax: +27 (0) 118 887 117
Email: info@africangapyear.com

Our programs are for school leavers and graduates who want to discover what they can do now to prepare to lead successful lives in the very challenging world of the future. Unique workshops and seminars are held which focus on the future of work and play, In addition, experts from different industries expose the career and work opportunities of the future. The Lapalala Wilderness School in South Africa is the base for the environmental part of the program. Each participant will be assessed to find the career and work options best suited to their preferences and abilities. Participants can choose between 3-week Core Programs or a 3-month program. In addition, any number of volunteering weeks can be added, during which volunteers work with conservation projects or local communities.

All Out

PO Box 153,
Lobamba, Swaziland

www.all-out.org
Tel: +268 550 4951
Fax: +268 416 8010
Email: info@all-out.org

We offer inspiring conservation, community, care, teaching and sport projects in southern Africa, plus exciting wildlife and adventure expeditions. If you're going, go All Out!

CREES The Rainforest Education
and Resource Centre
Calle San Miguel 250,
Cusco, Peru

www.crees-manu.org
Tel: +51 (0) 84 262433

Email: info@crees.manu.org

Fauna Forever programmes are practical training, team building and environmental monitoring initiatives located in strategically important and frequently threatened biologically and culturally diverse habitats. Fauna Forever Manu and Fauna Forever Ethnobiology are two programmes currently managed by The Rainforest Resource & Education Centre (CREES in Spanish). Both are based in the Manu Biosphere Reserve, a well known conservation area located in the Amazon rainforest of Peru, also known for its pristine habitats and exceptionally high levels of biological and cultural diversity. These programmes are an adventurous yet professional way to experience and learn first-hand about humid tropical ecosystems and indigenous Amazon cultures, and to contribute to useful on-going research.

Frontier
50-52 Rivington Street,
London EC2A 3QP

www.frontier.ac.uk
Tel: +44 (0) 20 7613 2422
Fax: +44 (0) 20 7613 2992
Email: info@frontier.ac.uk

Join Frontier's conservation expeditions and help save endangered wildlife and remote tropical environments on marine and terrestial projects in Cambodia, Madagasca, Tanzania, Nicaragua and Fiji.

Galapagos Conservation Trust
5 Derby Street,
London W1J 7AB

www.gct.org
Tel: +44 (0) 207 629 5049
Fax: +44 (0) 207 629 4149
Email: gct@gct.org

Greenforce
11-15 Betterton Street,
Covent Garden, London WC2H 9BP

www.greenforce.org
Tel: +44 (0) 20 7470 8888
Fax: +44 (0) 207 379 0801
Email: info@greenforce.org

Shumba Experience
6 Coventry Street,
Brighton, Sussex BN1 5PQ

www.shumbaexperience.com
Tel: +44 (0) 845 257 3205

Email: info@shumbaexperience.com

Shumba Experience offers a wide variety of conservation projects and community work in Africa for gap year students, career breakers and adventure enthusiasts. Join our conservation professionals and work directly on wildlife projects, ranging from 1-12 weeks. Conservation work can include game drives, wildlife research, game capture & relocation, wildlife rehabilitation and visits to the Born Free Big Cat Sanctuary. We have also developed a range of 'Mini Adventures' to suit people who have limited travelling time. So join Shumba Experience for an adventure of a lifetime and help conserve wildlife for future generations!

The Leap Overseas Ltd
121 High Street,
Marlborough, Wiltshire SN8 1LZ

www.theleap.co.uk
Tel: +44 (0) 1672 519922
Fax: +44 (0) 1672 519944
Email: info@theleap.co.uk

The Year Out Group
Queensfield, 28 King's Road,
Easterton, Wiltshire SN10 4PX

www.yearoutgroup.org
Tel: +44 (0) 7980 395789

Email: info@yearoutgroup.org

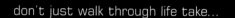

Chapter 7

Office skills

Many people temp to raise money for **gap**-year travels and projects. But it can also be a "breathing space", a good way of finding out what kind of a career you want to follow if you haven't really made up your mind where you're headed next.

Diana, 24, had GCSEs but then quit A level study to work in the jump and national hunt racing industry for 8 years, not only riding in races herself but managing a yard before completely turning her life around by becoming a Temp.

She's proof that there's more than one way to get work experience. "In the last year my heart wasn't in it any more and I knew there was no future in it for me."

She moved to London with some basic computer skills and touch typing and eventually became a temp working on reception for one company then in admin managing calls in a university: "I hadn't got much office experience. It's a new challenge."

"I love it. It's a major life change. It's a steep learning curve."

She did all the right things, dressing appropriately, wearing make-up and has discovered she particularly enjoys the communication side of the things she's been involved in. But, she said, she wanted to try several different settings to explore where she was headed and to learn more. She has also learned more about office culture, as she puts it to "get into the rhythm of how an office works."

She says: "Personality helps. You have to be friendly, to listen, and show you're enthusiastic."

Already, after only a few weeks, she'd noticed her typing beginning to speed up, and she's typed some correspondence.

"It's too soon to say where it's heading, but this is bliss. You get spoken to politely. The racing world is quite different."

visit: www.gap-year.com

Office skills

Office work is based on information technology, so being trained in this field is a great start to earning quick cash. Office temping is a very common job that pays reasonably well and there is plenty of it around.

Office skills are pretty basic to many careers and in an increasingly global market could lead to chances to work abroad – so you can even combine travel or living in another culture with work.

Already there's a substantial two-way interchange between some of the biggest call centre operators in India, like ICICI, and their client businesses in the UK, some of which are inviting skilled staff from the sub-continent to train staff here in their methods.

In this chapter we try and steer you in the right direction to getting that first job, including listings for colleges that run short information technology courses.

Work experience asap

The big question is 'how do I get work experience when everywhere I go rejects me because I haven't got work experience?' This could ruin your whole **gap**-year plan. For simple menial work, such as stacking shelves or fruit picking it shouldn't be too much of a problem, but those types of jobs don't pay particularly well.

If you need money fast then you might have to look elsewhere.

gap-year recruiters tend to expect their clients to have no work experience at all, so it could be a good idea to get ahead of the game and get some experience under your belt before you leave school.

If you're reading this while you're in the Year 12 then you have quite a lot of time left and we advise you to use it to get as much work experience as possible. This will seriously impress your future employers.

Even if the work is basic (filing, making the tea), it shows that you can function within a working environment.

We're not saying that you have to spend every week of your holidays working, although many teenagers do now combine weekend and holiday working – such as supermarket check-out operation – with study.

You can always do with a bit more cash. It may seem like a drag now, but think how much more impressive you'll be at job interviews later on with a fatter CV and references in hand.

Skills for work

What are the skills that you need in order to get that vital job? Don't forget that you only have a limited time, so you don't want to be training for too long as that will cut down on your earning time and therefore enjoyment time. This is why many people choose to go into trades such as bartending or retail, where the company tends to provide the training. Though this might not prove to be nearly as lucrative as office work.

If you've done a computer based course during Sixth form then that could well prove to be enough. If you can type at around 40-45 words per minute or you're comfortable designing websites then you stand a good chance of landing a fairly well-paid job.

"We have quite a lot of 18-year-olds, coming through us," says Louise Billington of Henderson Recruitment. "Most stay in a job for three or four months and save themselves a few thousand to go abroad with… The most important thing they need is 40-45 wpm touch-typing. You can teach yourself with a computer package… You'll be tested on your skills and you'll need to understand how to format a document as well. A good telephone manner and a knowledge of Microsoft Office software (Access, Excel, Powerpoint and Word) are a big help."

Qualifications – who needs them?

Qualifications are needed when you can't otherwise prove that you're capable of whatever the job involves. For example, if you're not French and have never lived in France, then you'll have to have a qualification showing that you can speak French, if that's what the job involves. In office work the agency that you go through will put you through some tests to show your skills to the employer.

"More important than any paper qualification is that your typing speed and accuracy are strong enough to take you through the tests which your agencies will ask you to undertake. Practice is vital in building up your speeds but don't despair if you don't reach that magic 45 words per minute in the test, there are other options available which will help you build up your speeds while you are working," says James Reed, Chief Executive, Reed Employment Services.

Many offices, especially the smaller ones, will offer a trial, for around three days, just to make sure that you have what it takes. This saves them from sorting through an array of paperwork and qualifications.

What if I'm just no good?

Well, you'll just have to get good then won't you. Training for information technology has dramatically changed recently. Skills that used to take a full year now can take as little as one month. The prices have dropped too.

Evening courses at a local FE college can be under £100 and public libraries also run courses on the internet. IT is already very firmly in schools' curricula so most of you should already have the skills to cope within the office. If not, then get going and get trained.

visit: www.gap-year.com

Which college?

There are lots of different things to look at when choosing a college.

Convenience (location, hours) is very important, along with price. However, you don't want to compromise the quality of qualification you will receive because of practical concerns. A good idea might be to check with an agency about the value of a qualification from particular colleges. Or check with the actual college on the employment record of their past students.

Finding the right course

Of course you want to start earning as soon as possible so is it worth spending a longer time studying for a qualification that you don't really need?

How do you know which course is best for you? Can you compare different word processing courses against each other; surely word processing is just word processing? Also, you don't want to pay to learn something that you already know how to do. To help with this little dilemma the City & Guilds, which awards over a million certificates a year, defines the levels of its qualifications (which continue up to Level 7).

Level 1: introductory awards for those new to the area covering routine tasks or basic knowledge and understanding

Level 2: qualifications for those with some knowledge of and ability in the areas which acknowledge individual responsibility

Level 3: qualifications that recognise complex work involving supervisory ability

If you think that you already know level two, for example, then its worth your while going straight onto level 3.

How much to pay?

The most important thing here is not to get ripped off. Of course the better the course the more expensive it's likely to be, but what things can you check for to make sure that you're not being conned? Be aware of the VAT and any other hidden costs that there might be. To test the value of the course compare the total hours of tuition to the price. Check out each course and just be sure that what you are going to do will be of benefit, before parting with any money.

Over the next pages you'll find a list of colleges from all over the country which run intensive business skills courses. It is only an indicator of what's available, not a guarantee of quality. We're happy to hear from (and report about) any training centres that offer short courses in office skills.

KEY

Size of college (number of full-time students):
L Large (100+) **M** Medium (50-100) **S** Small (0-50)

Course types:

I	Intensive, usually 12 weeks or less
Md	Modular
Flex	Mix of tuition and practice time with flexible timing
Cert	Lead to recognised certificated qualifications
DIY	One or two modules studied at college/training centre. Student can enter exam for individual elements or full set of modules including ones that have been self-taught

Course contents:

WP	Word processing		SS	Spreadsheets
TT	Touch-typing		EM	Email
DB	Databases		Web	Web design

UNITED KINGDOM

Aberdeen College of Further Education
Gallowgate Centre, Gallowgate,
Aberdeen, Aberdeenshire AB25 1BN
Tel:+44 (0) 1224 612 330

www.abcol.ac.uk
L/Cert
WP, DB, SS, Web

Abingdon and Witney College
Wootton Road,
Abingdon, Oxfordshire OX14 1GG
Tel:+44 (0) 1235 555 585

www.abingdon-witney.ac.uk
L/Cert, I
WP, TT, DB, SS, EM, Web

Accrington & Rossendale College
Sandy Lane Centre, Sandy Lane,
Accrington, Lancashire BB5 2AW
Tel:+44 (0) 1254 354 354

www.accross.ac.uk
L / Flex, Cert
WP, DB, SS, EM, Web

Alton College
Old Odiham Road,
Alton, Hampshire GU34 2LX
Tel:+44 (0) 1420 592 200

www.altoncollege.ac.uk
L/Cert, I
WP, TT, DB, SS, EM, Web

Amersham & Wycombe College
Chesham Campus, Lycrome Road,
Chesham, Buckinghamshire HP5 3LA
Tel:+44 (0) 1494 735 555

www.amersham.ac.uk
L/Cert
WP, DB, SS, EM, Web

Armagh College of Further Education
Lonsdale Road,
Armagh, County Armagh BT61 7JX
Tel:+44 (0) 28 3751 2205

www.armaghcollege.ac.uk
L/Cert
WP, TT, DB, SS, EM

Aylesbury College
Oxford Road,
Aylesbury, Buckinghamshire HP21 8PD
Tel:+44 (0) 1296 588 588

www.aylesbury.ac.uk
L/Cert
WP, TT, DB, SS, EM, Web

Ayr College
Dam Park,
Ayr, South Ayrshire KA8 0EU
Tel:+44 (0) 1292 265 184

www.ayrcoll.ac.uk
L/Flex, Cert
WP, TT, DB, SS, EM, Web

Banff & Buchan College
Henderson Road,
Fraserburgh, Aberdeenshire AB43 9GA
Tel:+44 (0) 1346 586 100

www.banff-buchan.ac.uk
L/Flex, Cert
WP, DB, SS, EM

Barking College
Dagenham Road,
Romford, Essex RM7 0XU
Tel:+44 (0) 1708 770 000

www.barkingcollege.ac.uk
L/Cert, I
WP, TT, DB, SS, EM, Web

Barnet College
Wood Street,
Barnet, Hertfordshire EN5 4AZ
Tel:+44 (0) 20 8200 8300

www.barnet.ac.uk
L / Cert, Md, I
WP, DB, SS, Web

Barnfield College
Rotherham Avenue,
Luton, Bedfordshire LU1 5PP
Tel:+44 (0) 1582 569 700

www.barnfield.ac.uk
L / Cert
WP, DB, SS, EM, Web

Barnsley College
Church Street,
Barnsley, South Yorkshire S70 2YW
Tel:+44 (0) 1226 216 216

www.barnsley.ac.uk
L/Cert
WP, TT

Barry College
Colcot Road,
Barry, Vale of Glamorgan CF62 8YJ
Tel:+44 (0) 1446 725 000

www.barry.ac.uk
L/Cert
WP, DB, SS, EM

Barton Peveril College Chestnut Avenue, Eastleigh, Hampshire SO50 5ZA Tel:+44 (0) 238 036 7200	www.barton-peveril.ac.uk L/Cert, I WP, TT, DB, SS, EM
Basingstoke College of Technology Worting Road, Basingstoke, Hampshire RG21 8TN Tel:+44 (0) 1256 354 141	www.bcot.ac.uk L/Cert, I WP, DB, SS, EM, Web
Bedford College Cauldwell Street, Bedford, Bedfordshire MK42 9AH Tel:+44 (0) 800 074 0234	www.bedford.ac.uk L/Cert WP, DB, SS, EM, Web
Belfast Institute College Square East, Belfast, County Antrim BT1 6DJ Tel:+44 (0) 28 9026 5000	www.belfastinstitute.ac.uk L/Cert, I WP, TT, DB, SS, EM, Web
Bexhill College Penland Road, Bexhill on Sea, East Sussex TN40 2JG Tel:+44 (0) 1424 214 545	www.bexhillcollege.ac.uk L/Cert, I BD, SS, EM, Web
Bexley College Tower Road, Belvedere, Kent DA17 6JA Tel:+44 (0) 1322 442 331	www.bexley.ac.uk L/Cert WP, SS
Bishop Auckland College Woodhouse Lane, Bishop Auckalnd, County Durham DL14 6JZ Tel:+44 (0) 1388 443 000	www.bacoll.ac.uk L/Cert WP, DB, SS, EM, Web
Blackburn College Feilden Street, Blackburn, Lancashire BB2 1LH Tel:+44 (0) 1254 551 44	www.blackburn.ac.uk L/Cert, I WP, DB, SS, EM, Web
Blackpool & The Fylde College Ashfield Road, Bispham, Blackpool, Lancashire FY2 0HB Tel:+44 (0) 1253 352 352	www.blackpool.ac.uk L/Cert WP, DB, SS, EM, Web

Bolton Community College
Manchester Road Centre, Manchester Road,
Bolton, Lancashire BL2 1ER
Tel:+44 (0) 1204 907 200

www.bolton-community-college.ac.uk
L/Cert
WP, TT, DB, SS, EM

Borders College
Melrose Road,
Galashiels, Borders TD1 2AF
Tel:+44 (0) 8700 505 152

www.borderscollege.ac.uk
L/Cert
WP, DB, EM

Boston College
Skirbeck Road,
Boston, Lincolnshire PE21 6JF
Tel:+44 (0) 1205 365 701

www.boston.ac.uk
L /Cert
WP, DB, SS, EM, Web

Bournemouth & Poole College
North Road,
Poole, Dorset BH14 0LS
Tel:+44 (0) 1202 205 205

www.thecollege.ac.uk
L/Flex, Cert, I
WP, DB, SS, EM, Web

Bournville College
Bristol Road South, Northfield,
Birmingham B31 2AJ
Tel:+44 (0) 121 483 1000

www.bournville.ac.uk
L / Cert
WP, DB, SS, EM, Web

Bracknell & Wokingham College
Church Road, Bracknell,
Bracknell Forest, Berkshire RG 12 1DJ
Tel:+44 (0) 845 330 3343

www.bracknell.ac.uk
L/Cert
WP, TT, DB, SS, EM

Bradford College
Great Horton Road,
Bradford, West Yorkshire BD7 1AY
Tel:+44 (0) 1274 433 004

www.bradfordcollege.ac.uk
L/Cert
WP, TT, DB, SS, EM, Web

Braintree College
Church Lane,
Braintree, Essex CM7 5SN
Tel:+44 (0) 1376 321 711

www.braintree.ac.uk
L/Cert, I
WP, DB, SS, EM, Web

Bridgwater College
Bath Road,
Bridgwater, Somerset TA6 4PZ
Tel:+44 (0) 1278 455464

www.bridgwater.ac.uk
L /Cert
BD, SS, EM

Brockenhurst College
Lyndhurst Road,
Brockenhurst, Hampshire SO42 7ZE
Tel:+44 (0) 1590 625 555

www.brock.ac.uk
L/Cert, I
WP, TT, DB, SS, EM, Web

Bromley College
Rookery Lane,
Bromley, Kent BR2 8HE
Tel:+44 (0) 20 8295 7000

www.bromley.ac.uk
L / Cert
WP, DB, SS, EM, Web

Budmouth Technology College
Chickerell Road,
Weymouth, Dorset DT4 9SY
Tel:+44 (0) 1305 530 500

www.budmouth.dorset.sch.uk
L/Cert
SS, EM

Burnley College
Shorey Bank, Ormerod Road,
Burnley, Lancashire BB11 2RX
Tel:+44 (0) 1282 711 200

www.burnley.ac.uk
L/Cert
WP, DB, SS, EM

Burton College
LIchfield Street,
Burton upon Trent, Staffordshire DE14 3RL
Tel:+44 (0) 1283 494 400

www.burton-college.ac.uk
L/Cert
WP, TT, DB, SS, EM

Bury College
Woodbury Centre, Market Street,
Bury, Lancashire BL9 0BG
Tel:+44 (0) 161 280 8280

www.burycollege.ac.uk
L/Flex, Cert, I
WP, DB, SS, EM

Cambridge Regional College
Kings Hedges Road,
Cambridge, Cambridgeshire CB4 2QT
Tel:+44 (0) 1223 418 200

www.camre.ac.uk
L/Cert
WP, DB, SS, Web

Cannock Chase Technical College
The Green,
Cannock, Staffordshire WS11 1UE
Tel:+44 (0) 1543 462 200

www.cannock.ac.uk
L /Cert
WP, DB, SS, EM, Web

Canterbury College
New Dover Road,
Canterbury, Kent CT1 3AJ
Tel:+44 (0) 1227 811 111

www.cant-col.ac.uk
L/Cert, I
WP, DB, SS, EM, Web

Cardonald College
690 Moss Park Drive,
Glasgow, Lanarkshire G52 3AY
Tel:+44 (0) 141 272 3333

www.cardonald.ac.uk
L/Flex, Cert
WP, TT, DB, SS, EM

Carlisle College
Victoria Place,
Carlisle, Cumbria LA1 1HS
Tel:+ 44 (0) 1228 822 703

www.carlisle.ac.uk
L/Cert
WP, DB, SS, EM

Castle College
Maid Marian Way,
Nottingham, Nottinghamshire NG1 6AB
Tel:+44 (0) 845 845 0500

www.castlecollege.ac.uk
L /Cert
WP, DB, SS, EM, Web

Causeway Institute
Union Street,
Coleraine, County Londonderry BT52 1QA
Tel:+44 (0) 28 7035 4717

www.causeway.ac.uk
L/Cert, I
WP, DB, SS, EM, Web

Central Sussex College
College Road,
Crawley, West Sussex RH10 1NR
Tel:+44 (0) 845 155 0043

www.centralsussex.ac.uk
L /Cert
WP, DB, SS, EM, Web

Chesterfield College
Infirmary Road,
Chesterfield, Derbyshire S41 7NG
Tel:+44 (0) 1246 500 500

www.chesterfield.ac.uk
L/Cert
WP, DB, SS, EM, Web

Cirencester College
Fosse Way Campus,
Stroud, Gloucestershire GL5 4AH
Tel:+44 (0) 1453 763 424

www.cirencestercollege.org.uk
L/Cert
WP, TT, DB, SS, EM, Web

City & Islington College
Dalby House, 396-398 City Road,
London EC1V 2QA
Tel:+44 (0) 207 833 2193

www.candi.ac.uk
L/Cert, I
WP, DB, SS, EM, Web

City College
University House, 55 East Road,
London N1 6AH
Tel:+44 (0) 20 7253 1133

www.citycollege.ac.uk
L /Cert
WP, DB, SS, Web

City College Brighton & Hove Pelham Street, Brighton, Sussex BN1 4FA Tel:+44 (0) 1273 667 788	www.ccb.ac.uk L, I WP, SS, EM, Web
City College Manchester Whitworth Street, Manchester, Lancashire M1 3HB Tel:+44 (0) 161 614 8000	www.ccm.ac.uk L/Cert WP, TT, DB, SS, EM
City College Norwich Ipswich Road, Norwich, Norfolk NR2 2LJ Tel:+44 (0) 1603 773 311	www.ccn.ac.uk L/Cert WP, DB, SS, Web
City College Southampton St Mary Street, Southampton, Hampshire SO14 1AR Tel:+44 (0) 023 8048 4848	www.southampton-city.ac.uk L/Flex, Cert WP, DB, SS, EM, Web
City Lit Keeley Street, London WC2B 4BA Tel:+44 (0) 207 492 2600	www.citylit.ac.uk L/Cert, I WP, TT, DB, SS, EM, Web
City of Bath College Avon Street, Bath, Somerset BA1 1UP Tel:+44 (0) 1225 312 191	www.citybathcoll.ac.uk L/Cert WP, DB, SS, EM
City of Bristol College College Green Centre, St George's Road, Bristol BS1 5UA Tel:+44 (0) 117 312 5000	www.cityofbristol.ac.uk L / Cert WP, DB, SS, EM, Web
City of Sunderland College Durham Road, Sunderland, Tyne & Wear SR3 4AH Tel:+44 (0) 191 511 6060	www.citysun.ac.uk L/Cert, I WP, DB, SS, EM, Web
City of Westminster College 25 Paddington Green, London W2 1NB Tel:+44 (0) 207 223 8826	www.cwc.ac.uk L/Cert, I WP, DB, SS, EM

City of Wolverhampton College
Bilston,
Wolverhampton, Staffordshire WV14 6BT
Tel:+44 (0) 1902 836 000

www.wolverhamptoncollege.ac.uk
L/Cert
WP, DB, SS, EM, Web

Clydebank College
Kilbowie Road, Clydebank,
Glasgow, Lanarkshire G81 2AA
Tel:+44 (0) 141 952 7771

www.clydebank.ac.uk
L/Flex, Cert
WP, DB, SS, EM

Coatbridge College
Kildonan Street,
Coatbridge, Lanarkshire ML5 3LS
Tel:+44 (0) 1236 422 316

www.coatbridge.ac.uk
L/Flex, Cert, I
WP, DB, SS, EM, Web

Colchester Institute
Sheepen Road,
Colchester, Essex CO3 3LL
Tel:+44 (0) 1206 518 000

www.colchester.ac.uk
L/Cert, I
WP, DB, SS, EM, Web

Coleg Abertawe
Tycoch Road, Tycoch,
Swansea, Glamorgan SA2 9EB
Tel:+44 (0) 1792 284 000

www.swancoll.ac.uk
L/Cert
WP, TT, DB, SS, EM

Coleg Castell Nedd
Dwr-y-Felin Road, Neath,
Port Talbot, Glamorgan SA10 7RF
Tel:+44 (0) 1639 648 000

www.nptc.ac.uk
L/Flex. Cert
WP, DB, SS, EM

Coleg Glannau Dyfrdwy
Kelsterton Road, Connah's Quay,
Deeside, Flintshire CH5 4BR
Tel:+44 (0) 1244 834 511

www.deeside.ac.uk
L/Cert
WP, TT, DB, SS, Web

Coleg Gorseinon
Belgrave Road, Gorseinon,
Swansea, Glamorgan SA4 6RD
Tel:+44 (0) 1792 890 777

www.gorseinon.ac.uk
L/Cert
WP, TT, DB, SS, EM

Coleg Gran Hafren
Trowbridge Road, Rumney,
Cardiff, Glamorgan CF3 1XZ
Tel:+44 (0) 845 045 0845

ww.glan-hafren.ac.uk
L/Cert
WP, DB, SS, EM, Web

Coleg Gwent The Rhadyr, Usk, Monmouthshire NP15 1XJ Tel:+44 (0) 1495 333 333	www.coleggwent.ac.uk L/Flex, Cert WP, DB, SS, EM
Coleg Llysfasi Ruthin, Denbighshire LU15 2LB Tel:+44 (0) 1978 790 263	www.llysfasi.ac.uk L/Cert, I WP, DB, SS, EM
Coleg Menai Ffriddoedd Road, Bangor, Gwynedd LL57 2TP Tel:+44 (0) 1248 370 125	www.menai.ac.uk L/Flex, Cert WP, DB, SS
Coleg Merthyr Tudfil Ynysfach, Merthyr Tydfil, Glamorgan CF48 1AR Tel:+44 (0) 1685 726 000	www.merthyr.ac.uk L/Cert WP, DB, SS, EM
Coleg Morgannwg Cwmdare Road, Aberdare, Rhondda Cynon, Glamorgan CF44 8BR Tel:+44 (0) 1685 887 511	www.morgannwg.ac.uk L/Cert WP, DB, SS, EM
Coleg Penybont Cowbridge Road, Bridgend, Glamorgan CF31 3DF Tel:+44 (0) 1656 302 302	www.bridgend.ac.uk L/Cert WP, DB, SS, EM
Coleg Sir Gâr Sandy Road, Pwll, Llanelli, Carmarthenshire SA15 4DN Tel:+44 (0) 1554 748 000	www.colegsirgar.ac.uk L/Cert WP, DB, SS, EM
College of North East London High Road, Tottenham, London N15 4RU Tel:+44 (0) 208 802 3111	www.conel.ac.uk L/Cert WP, DB, SS
College of North West London Willesden Centre, Dudden Hill Lane, London NW10 2XD Tel:+44 (0) 208 208 5000	www.cnwl.ac.uk L/Cert WP, DB, SS, EM, Web
College of West Anglia Tennyson Avenue, King's Lynn, Norfolk PE30 2QW Tel:+44 (0) 1553 761 144	www.col-westanglia.ac.uk L /Cert WP, DB, SS, EM, Web

Collyer's, The College of Richard Collyer
Hurst Road,
Horsham, West Sussex Rh12 2EJ
Tel:+44 (0) 1403 210 822

www.collyers.ac.uk
L/Cert
BD, SS, EM, Web

Cornwall College
Trevenson Road,
Redruth, Cornwall TR15 3RD
Tel:+44 (0) 1209 616 611

www.cornwall.ac.uk
L / Flex, Cert, I, Md
WP, TT

Coventry City College
Butts Centre,
Coventry, West Midlands CV1 3GD
Tel:+44 (0) 2476 791 000

www.covcollege.ac.uk
L /Cert
WP, DB, SS, EM, Web

Craven College
High Street,
Skipton, North Yorkshire BD23 1YJ
Tel:+44 (0) 1756 791 411

ww.craven-college.ac.uk
L/Cert, I
WP, DB, SS, Web

Cricklade College
Charlton Road,
Andover, Hampshire SP10 1EJ
Tel:+44 (0) 1264 360 000

www.cricklade.ac.uk
L
WP, TT, DB, SS, EM, Web

Croydon College
College Road,
Croydon, Surrey CR9 1DX
Tel:+44 (0) 208 686 5700

www.croydon.ac.uk
L/Cert
WP, DB, SS, EM, Web

CRTS International Study Centre
691-693 High Road,
Tottenham, London N17 8AD
Tel:+44 (0) 20 8801 0371

www.crts.co.uk
M/Cert
WP, DB, SS, EM

Cumbernauld College
Tryst Road, Cumbernauld,
Glasgow, Lanarkshire G67 1HU
Tel:+44 (0) 1236 731 811

www.cumbernauld.ac.uk
L/Cert
WP, DB, SS, EM

Darlington College of Technology
Central Park, Haughton Road,
Darlington, County Durham DL1 1DR
Tel:+44 (0) 1325 503 050

www.darlington.ac.uk
L/Cert, I
WP, DB, SS, EM, Web

Office skills | Colleges

Dearne Valley College
Manvers Park, Wath-upon-Dearne,
Rotherham, South Yorkshire S63 7EW
Tel:+44 (0) 1709 513 355

www.dearne-coll.ac.uk
L/Cert
WP, DB, SS, EM, Web

Derby College
Prince Charles Avenue, Mackworth,
Derby, Derbyshire DE22 4LR
Tel:+44 (0) 1322 520 200

www.derby-college.ac.uk
L / Cert
WB

Derwentside College
Front Street,
Consett, County Durham DH8 5EE
Tel:+44 (0) 1207 585 900

www.derwentside.ac.uk
L/Cert
WP, DB, SS, EM, Web

Dewsbury College
Halifax Road,
Dewsbury, West Yorkshire WF13 2AS
Tel:+44 (0) 1924 436 221

www.dewsbury.ac.uk
L /Cert
WP, DB, SS, EM, Web

Dudley College
The Broadway,
Dudley, West Midlands DY1 4AS
Tel:+44 (0) 1384 363 000

www.dudleycol.ac.uk
L /Cert
WP, DB, SS, EM, Web

Dumfries & Galloway College
Hernes Avenue, Heathall,
Dumfries, Dumfriesshire DG1 3QZ
Tel:+44 (0) 1387 261 261

www.dumgal.ac.uk
L/Cert
WP, DB, SS, EM

Dundee College
Old Glamis Road,
Dundee, Angus DD3 8LE
Tel:+44 (0) 1382 834 834

www.dundeecoll.ac.uk
L/Cert, I
WP, DB, SS, Web

Dunstable College
Kingsway,
Dunstable, Bedfordshire LU5 4HG
Tel:+44 (0) 1582 477 776

www.dunstable.ac.uk
L/Cert
WP, DB, SS, EM, Web

Ealing, Hammersmith & West London College
Gliddon Road, Barons Court,
London W14 9BL
Tel:+44 (0) 800 980 2185

www.wlc.ac.uk
L/Cert
WP, TT, DB, SS, EM, Web

East Antrim Institute of Further & Higher Education   www.eaifhe.ac.uk
Shore Road,   L/Cert
Newtownabbey, County Antrim BT37 9RS   WP, TT, DB, SS, EM, Web
Tel:+44 (0) 28 9085 5000

East Berkshire College   www.eastberks.ac.uk
Station Road, Langley,   L/Cert
Slough, Berkshire SL3 8BY   WP, DB, SS, EM
Tel:+44 (0) 800 923 0423

East Devon College   www.edc.ac.uk
Bolham Road,   L/Cert
Tiverton, Devon EX16 6SH   WP, DB, SS, EM, Web
Tel:+44 (0) 1884 235 264

East Down Institute of Further and Higher Education   www.edifhe.ac.uk
Market Street,   L / Cert, I, Md
Downpatrick, County Down BT30 6ND   WP, DB, SS, Web
Tel:+44 (0) 28 4461 5815

East Riding College   www.eastridingcollege.ac.uk
Gallows Lane,   L/Cert
Beverley, East Yorkshire HU17 7DT   WP, DB, SS, EM, Web
Tel:+44 (0) 845 120 0037

East Surrey College   www.esc.ac.uk
Gatton North Point, Claremont Road,   L/Flex, Cert
Redhill, Surrey RH1 2JX   WP, DB, SS, EM
Tel:+44 (0) 1737 788 391

East Tyrone College of Further & Higher Education   www.etcfhe.ac.uk
Circular Road,   L/Cert, I
Dungannon, County Tyrone BT71 6BQ   WP, DB, SS, EM, Web
Tel:+44 (0) 28 8772 2323

Eastleigh College   www.eastleigh.ac.uk
Chestnut Avenue,   L/Cert, I
Eastleigh, Hampshire SO50 5FS   WP, DB, SS, EM, Web
Tel:+44 (0) 238 091 1000

Edinburgh's Telford College   www.ed-coll.ac.uk
Crewe toll,   L/Flex, Cert, I
Edinburgh, Midlothian EH4 2NZ   WP, DB, SS, EM
Tel:+44 (0) 131 332 2491

Emma Hall Secretarial Business College   www.emmahallrecruitment.com
The Lodge, Knoll Hill, Sneyd Park,   S / Flex, Cert, I
Bristol, Somerset BS9 1QU
Tel:+44 (0) 117 904 3341

Enfield College   www.enfield.ac.uk
73 Hertford Road,   L /Cert, I
Enfield, Middlesex EN3 5HA   WP, DB, SS, EM, Web
Tel:+44 (0) 20 8443 3434

Epping Forest College   www.epping-forest.ac.uk
Borders Lane,   L/Cert, I
Loughton, Essex IG10 3SA   WP, DB, SS, EM, Web
Tel:+44 (0) 208 508 8311

Esher College   www.esher.ac.uk
Weston Green Road,   L/Cert, I
Thames Ditton, Surrey KT17 0JB   WP, DB, SS, EM, Web
Tel:+44 (0) 20 8398 0291

Evesham & Malvern Hills College   www.evesham.ac.uk
Davies Road,   L /Cert
Evesham, Worcestershire WR11 1LP   WP, TT, DB, SS, EM, Web
Tel:+44 (0) 1386 712 600

Exeter College   www.exe-coll.ac.uk
Victoria House, 33-36 Queen Street,   L/Cert
Exeter, Devon EX4 3SR   WP, DB, EM, Web
Tel:+44 (0) 1392 205 223

Fareham College   www.fareham.ac.uk
Bishopsfield Road,   L/Cert
Fareham, Hampshire PO14 1NH   WP, TT, DB, SS, EM, Web
Tel:+44 (0) 1329 815 200

Farnborough College of Technology   www.farn-ct.ac.uk
Boundary Road,   L/Cert, I
Farnborough, Hampshire GU14 6SB   WP, DB, SS, EM
Tel:+44 (0) 1252 407 040

Farnham College   www.farnham.ac.uk
Morley Road,   L/Cert
Farnham, Surrey GU9 8LU   WP, DB, SS, EM
Tel:+44 (0) 1252 716 988

Fermanagh College
Fairview, Dublin Road,
Enniskillen, County Fermanagh BT74 6AE
Tel:+44 (0) 28 6632 2431

www.fermanaghcoll.ac.uk
L/Cert, I
WP, TT, DB, SS, EM

Filton College
Filton Avenue,
Bristol, Gloucestershire BS34 7AT
Tel:+44 (0) 117 931 2121

www.filton.ac.uk
L/Cert
WP, DB, SS, EM, Web

Franklin College
Chelmsford Avenue,
Grimsby, Lincolnshire DN34 5BY
Tel:+44 (0) 1472 875 000

www.franklin.ac.uk
L/Cert
WP, TT, DB, SS, EM

Furness College
Channelside,
Barrow-in-Furness, Cumbria LA14 2PJ
Tel:+44 (0) 1229 825 017

www.furness.inter-base.net
L/Flex, Cert
WP, SS, EM, Web

Gateshead College
Durham Road, Low Fell,
Gateshead, County Durham NE9 5BN
Tel:+44 (0) 191 4900 300

www.gateshead.ac.uk
L/Cert
WP, DB, SS, EM

Gloscat
Princess Elizabeth Way,
Cheltenham, Gloucestershire GL51 7SJ
Tel:+44 (0) 1242 532 000

www.gloscat.ac.uk
L/Cert, I
WP, DB, SS, EM, Web

Godalming College
Tuesley Lane,
Godalming, Surrey GU7 1RS
Tel:+44 (0) 1483 423 525

www.godalming.ac.uk
L/Cert
WP, DB, SS, EM

Great Yarmouth College
Southtown,
Great Yarmouth, Norfolk NR31 0ED
Tel:+44 (0) 1493 655 261

www.gyc.ac.uk
L /Cert
WP, DB, SS, EM

GSC Corporate Training
17 Chapel Street,
Guildford, Surrey GU1 3UL
Tel:+44 (0) 1483 564 885

www.g-s-c.co.uk
M/Cert
WP, DB, SS, EM, Web

221

Guildford College
Stoke Park Campus, Stoke Road,
Guildford, Surrey GU1 1EZ
Tel:+44 (0) 1483 448 500

www.guildford.ac.uk
L/Cert
WP, DB, SS, EM, Web

Halesowen College
Whittingham Road,
Halesowen, Worcestershire B64 3NA
Tel:+44 (0) 121 602 7777

www.halesowen.ac.uk
L/Cert
WP, DB, SS, EM, Web

Halton College
Kingsway,
Widnes, Cheshire WA8 7QQ
Tel:+44 (0) 151 257 2800

www.haltoncollege.ac.uk
L/Cert
WP, DB, SS, EM, Web

Harrogate College
Hornbeam Park Campus,
Hornbeam, North Yorkshire HG2 8QT
Tel:+44 (0) 1423 879 466

www.leedsmet.ac.uk/harrogate
L/Cert, I
WP, TT, DB, SS, EM, Web

Hartlepool College of Further Education
Stockton Street,
Hartlepool, County Durham TS24 7NT
Tel:+44 (0) 1429 295 000

www.hartlepoolfe.ac.uk
L/Cert
WP, DB, SS, EM, Web

Hartpury College
Hartpury House, Hartpury,
Gloucester, Gloucestershire GL19 3BE
Tel:+44 (0) 1452 700 283

www.hartpury.ac.uk
L / I
WP, DB, SS, EM, Web

Havant College
New Road,
Havant, Hampshire PO9 1QL
Tel:+44 (0) 23 9248 3856

www.havant.ac.uk
L / Cert, I
WP, DB, SS, EM, Web

Havering College
Ardleigh Green Road,
Hornchurch, Essex RM11 2LL
Tel:+44 (0) 1708 455 011

www.havering-college.ac.uk
L / Cert
WP, DB, SS, EM, Web

Herefordshire College of Technology
Folly Lane,
Hereford, Herefordshire HR1 1LS
Tel:+44 (0) 800 032 1986

www.hereford-tech.ac.uk
L/Cert, I
WP, TT, DB, SS, EM, Web

Highbury College
Dovercourt Road,
Portsmouth, Hampshire PO6 2SA
Tel:+44 (0) 23 9238 3131

www.highbury.ac.uk
L / Cert
WP, DB, SS, EM, Web

Holy Cross Sixth Form College
Manchester Road,
Bury, Lancashire BL9 9BB
Tel:+44 (0) 161 762 4500

www.holycross.ac.uk
L/Cert
WP, DB, SS

Hopwood Hall College
Rochdale Road,
Middleton, Lancashire M24 6XH
Tel:+44 (0) 161 643 7560

www.hopwood.ac.uk
L/Cert
WP, TT, DB, SS, EM

Hove College
Medina House, 41 Medina Villas,
Hove, East Sussex BN3 2RP
Tel:+44 (0) 1273 772577

www.hovecollege.co.uk
M / Cert
WB

Huddersfield Technical College
New North Road,
Huddersfield, North Yorkshire HD1 5NN
Tel:+44 (0) 1484 536 521

www.huddcoll.ac.uk
L/Cert
WP, DB, SS, EM

Hull College
Queen's Gardens Centre, Wilberforce Drive,
Hull, East Yorkshire HU1 3DG
Tel:+44 (0) 1482 329 943

www.hull-college.ac.uk
L / Cert, I
WP, DB, SS

Huntingdonshire Regional College
California Road,
Huntingdon, Cambridgeshire PE18 1BL
Tel:+44 (0) 1480 379 100

www.huntingdon.ac.uk
L / Cert
WP, DB, SS, EM, Web

Interlink College of Technology
22 Sutherland Road,
Walthamstow, London E17 6JW
Tel:+44 (0) 208 531 1118

www.interlinktech.co.uk
S/Cert
WP

Inverness College
3 Longman Road,
Inverness, Highland IV1 1SA
Tel:+44 (0) 1463 273 000

www.inverness.uhi.ac.uk
L/Cert
WP, DB, SS, EM

223

Isle College
Ramnoth Road,
Wisbech, Cambridgeshire PE13 2JE
Tel:+44 (0) 1945 582 561

www.isle.ac.uk
L / Cert
WP, DB, EM

Isle of Man College
Homefield Road,
Douglas, Isle of Man IM2 6RB
Tel:+44 (0) 1624 648 200

www.iomcollege.ac.im
L/Cert, I
WP, TT, DB, SS, EM

Isle of Wight College
Medina Way,
Newport, Isle of Wight PO30 5TA
Tel:+44 (0) 1983 526 631

www.iwightc.ac.uk
L/Cert
WP, TT, DB, SS, EM, Web

Itchen College
Middle Road, Bitterne,
Southampton, Hampshire SO19 7TB
Tel:+44 (0) 23 8043 5636

www.itchen.ac.uk
L/Cert
WP, TT, DB, SS, Web

Jewel & Esk Valley College
Milton Road East,
Edinburgh, Midlothian EH15 2PP
Tel:+44 (0) 131 660 1010

www.jevc.ac.uk
L/Cert
WP, DB, SS, EM

John Wheatley College
1346 Shettleston Road,
Glasgow, Lanarkshire G32 9AT
Tel:+44 (0) 141 778 2426

www.jwheatley.ac.uk
L/Cert
WP, DB, SS, EM

Josiah Mason College
Slade Road, Erdington,
Birmingham, Warwickshire B23 7JH
Tel:+44 (0) 121 603 4757

www.jmc.ac.uk
L/Cert
WP, TT, DB, SS, EM, Web

Keighley College
Cavendish Street,
Keighley, West Yorkshire BD21 3DF
Tel:+44 (0) 1535 618 600

www.keighley.ac.uk
L/Cert, I
WP, TT, DB, SS, Web

Kendal College
Milnthrope Road,
Kendal, Cumbria LA9 5AY
Tel:+44 (0) 1539 814 709

www.kendal.ac.uk
L/Cert, I
WP, DB, SS, EM

Kensington & Chelsea College
Hortensia Road,
London SW10 0QS
Tel:+44 (0) 207 573 3600

www.kcc.ac.uk
L/Cert, I
WP, DB, SS, Web

Kidderminster College
Market Street,
Kidderminster, Worcestershire DY10 1LX
Tel:+44 (0) 1562 820 811

www.kidderminster.ac.uk
L/Cert, I
WP, DB, SS, EM, Web

Kilmarnock College
Holehouse Road,
Kilmarnock, East Ayrshire KA3 7AT
Tel:+44 (0) 1563 523 501

www.kilmarnock.ac.uk
L/Cert
WP, DB, SS, EM

Kingston College
Kingston Hall Road,
Kingston Upon Thames, Surrey KT1 2AQ
Tel:+44 (0) 208 546 2151

www.kingston-college.ac.uk
L/Cert
WP, DB, SS, EM

Knowsley Community College
Cherryfield Drive,
Kirkby, Merseyside L32 8SF
Tel:+44 (0) 845 155 1055

www.knowsleycollege.ac.uk/
L/Cert
WP, DB, SS, EM

Lakes College
Hallwood Road, Lillyhall Business Park,
Workington, Cumbria LA14 4JN
Tel:+44 (0) 1946 839 300

www.lcwc.ac.uk
L/Cert
WP, DB, SS, EM

Lambeth College
56 Brixton Hill,
London SW2 1QS
Tel:+44 (0) 207 501 5281

www.lambeth.ac.uk
L/Cert
WP, TT, EM

Lancaster & Morecambe College
Morecambe Road,
Lancaster, Lancashire LA1 2TY
Tel:+44 (0) 1524 66 215

www.lmc.ac.uk
L/Cert
WP, TT, DB, SS, EM

Langside College
50 Prospecthill Road,
Glasgow, Lanarkshire G42 9LB
Tel:+44 (0) 141 649 4991

www.langside.ac.uk
L/Flex, Cert
WP, SS, EM

Office skills | Colleges

the gap-year guidebook 2007

Lauder College
Halbeath,
Dunfermline, Fifeshire KY11 8DY
Tel:+44 (0) 1383 845 000

www.lauder.ac.uk
L/Cert
BD, SS

Leeds College of Technology
Cookridge Street,
Leeds, West Yorkshire LS2 8BL
Tel:+44 (0) 113 297 6464

www.lct.ac.uk
L/Cert
WP, DB, SS, EM, Web

Leeds Thomas Danby
Roundhay Road,
Leeds, West Yorkshire LS7 3BG
Tel:+44 (0) 113 249 4912

www.leedsthomasdanby.ac.uk
L/Cert
WP, DB, SS, EM, Web

Leicester College
Freeman's Park Campus, Aylestone Road,
Leicester, Leicestershire LE2 7LW
Tel:+44 (0) 116 224 2240

www.leicestercollege.ac.uk
L / Cert, I
WP, DB, SS, EM, Web

Lewisham College
Lewisham Way,
London SE4 1UT
Tel:+44 (0) 208 692 0353

www.lewisham.ac.uk
L/Cert, I
WP, SS, Web

Lews Castle College
Stornaway,
Isle of Lewis, Highland HS2 0XR
Tel:+44 (0) 1851 770 000

www.lews.uhi.ac.uk
L/Cert
WP, TT, DB, SS, EM

Limavady College of Further & Higher Education
Main Street,
Limavady, County Londonderry BT49 0EX
Tel:+44 (0) 28 7776 2334

www.limavady.ac.uk
L/Cert
WP, DB, SS, Web

Lincoln College
Monks Road,
Lincoln, Lincolnshire LN2 5HQ
Tel:+44 (0) 1522 876 000

www.lincolncollege.ac.uk
L/Cert
WP, TT, DB, SS, EM, Web

Lisburn Institute
39 Castle Street,
Lisburn, County Antrim BT27 4SU
Tel:+44 (0) 28 9267 7225

www.liscol.ac.uk
L/Cert, I
WP, DB, SS, EM, Web

Liverpool Community College
Old Swan, Broad Green Road,
Liverpool, Merseyside L13 5SQ
Tel:+44 (0) 151 252 3000

www.liv-coll.ac.uk
L/Cert
WP, DB, SS, EM, Web

Loughborough College
Radmoor Road,
Loughborough, Leicestershire LE11 3BT
Tel:+44 (0) 845 166 2952

www.loucoll.ac.uk
L/Cert
WP, DB, SS, EM, Web

Lowestoft College
St Peters Street,
Lowestoft, Suffolk NR32 2NB
Tel:+44 (0) 1502 583 521

www.lowestoft.ac.uk
L/Cert, Mod
WP, TT, DB, SS, EM

Ludlow College
Castle Square,
Ludlow, Shropshire SY8 1GD
Tel:+44 (0) 1584 872 846

www.ludlow-college.ac.uk
L/Cert
WP, DB, SS, EM, Web

Macclesfield College
Park Lane,
Macclesfield, Cheshire SK11 8LF
Tel:+44 (0) 1625 410 000

www.macclesfield.ac.uk
L/Cert, I
WP, DB, SS, EM, Web

Manchester College of Arts & Technology
Ashton Old Road, Openshaw,
Manchester, Lancashire M11 2WH
Tel:+44 (0) 161 953 5995

www.mancat.ac.uk
L /Cert
WP, EM, Web

Matthew Boulton College
of Further & Higher Education
Jennens Road,
Birmingham, Warwickshire B4 7PS
Tel:+44 (0) 121 446 455

www.matthew-boulton.ac.uk
L/Cert
WP, DB, SS, EM

Merton Adult Education
Whatley Avenue,
London SW20 9NS
Tel:+44 (0) 20 8543 9292

www.merton-adult-education.ac.uk
L /Cert, I
WP, TT, DB, SS, EM, Web

Merton College
Morden Park, London Road,
Morden, Surrey SM4 5QX
Tel:+44 (0) 20 8408 6500

www.merton.ac.uk
L /Cert, I
WP, DB, SS, EM, Web

Office skills | Colleges

7

Middlesbrough College
Marton Campus, Marton Road,
Middlesbrough, North Yorkshire TS4 3RZ
Tel:+44 (0) 1642 333 333

www.mbro.ac.uk
L/Cert, I
WP, TT, DB, SS, EM

Mid-Kent College
Horsted Centre, Maidstone Road,
Chatham, Kent ME5 9UQ
Tel:+44 (0) 1634 402 020

www.midkent.ac.uk
L / Cert
WP, DB, SS, EM, Web

Milton Keynes College
Chaffron Way Campus, Leadenhall,
Milton Keynes, Buckinghamshire MK6 5LP
Tel:+44 (0) 1908 684 444

www.mkcollege.ac.uk
L/Flex, Cert, I
WP, TT, DB, SS, EM

Moray College
Moray Street, Elgin,
Moray, Highland IV30 1JJ
Tel:+44 (0) 1343 576 000

ww.moray.ac.uk
L/Cert
WP, DB, SS, EM, Web

Morley College
61 Westminster Bridge Road,
London SE1 7HT
Tel:+44 (0) 207 450 1889

www.morleycollege.ac.uk
L/Cert, I
WP, DB, SS, EM, Web

Motherwell College
Dalzell Drive,
Motherwell, Lanarkshire ML1 2DD
Tel:+44 (0) 1698 232 425

www.motherwell.ac.uk
L/Cert, I
WP, DB, SS

Nelson & Colne College
Scotland Road,
Nelson, Lancashire BB9 7YT
Tel:+44 (0) 1282 440 200

www.nelson.ac.uk
L/Cert
WP, DB, SS, Web

Nescot
Reigate Road, Ewell,
Epsom, Surrey KT17 3DS
Tel:+44 (0) 20 8394 1731

www.nescot.ac.uk
L / I
WP, DB, SS, EM, Web

New College - Swindon
New College Drive,
Swindon, Wiltshire SN3 1AH
Tel:+44 (0) 808 172 1721

www.newcollege.ac.uk
L/Flex, Cert
WP, DB, SS, EM

New College - Pontefract
Park Lane,
Pontefract, West Yorkshire WF8 4QR
Tel:+44 (0) 1977 702 139

www.newcollpont.ac.uk
L/Cert
WP, TT

New College Durham
Framwellgate Moor Campus, Framwellgate Moor,
Durham, County Durham DH1 5ES
Tel:+44 (0) 191 375 4000

www.newdur.ac.uk
L/Cert, I
WP, DB, SS, EM, Web

New College Nottingham
The Adams Building, Stoney Street,
Nottingham, Nottinghamshire NG1 1NG
Tel:+44 (0) 115 9100 100

www.ncn.ac.uk
L/Cert, I
WP, TT, DB, SS, EM, Web

Newark & Sherwood College
Friary Road,
Newark on Trent, Nottinghamshire NG24 1PB
Tel:+44 (0) 1636 680 680

www.newark.ac.uk
L/Flex, Cert
WP, TT, DB, SS, EM

Newbury College
Monks Lane,
Newbury, Berkshire RG14 7TD
Tel:+44 (0) 1635 845 000

www.newbury-college.ac.uk
L/Cert, I
WP, DB, SS, Web

Newham College of Further Education
East Ham Campus, High Street South,
London E6 6ER
Tel:+44 (0) 208 257 4000

www.newham.ac.uk
L/Cert, I
WP, TT, SS, EM, Web

Newry Institute
Patrick Street,
Newry, County Down BT35 8DN
Tel:+44 (0) 3026 1071

www.nkifhe.ac.uk
L/Cert
WP, DB, SS, EM, Web

North Devon College
Old Sticklepath Hill,
Barnstaple, Devon EX31 2BQ
Tel:+44 (0) 1271 345 291

www.ndevon.ac.uk
L/Cert, I
WP, DB, SS

North Downs & Ards Institute
Castle Park Road,
Bangor, County Down BT20 4TF
Tel:+44 (0) 28 9127 6600

www.ndai.ac.uk
L/Cert
WP, DB, SS, EM, Web

North East Institute of Further & Higher Education
Fountain Street,
Antrim, County Antrim BT41 4AL
Tel:+44 (0) 28 9446 3916

www.nei.ac.uk
L/Cert
WP, TT, DB, SS, EM, Web

North East Worcestershire College
Peakman Street,
Redditch, Worcestershire B98 8DW
Tel:+44 (0) 1527 570 020

www.ne-worcs.ac.uk
L/Flex, Cert
WP, TT, DB, SS, Web

North Glasgow College
110 Flemington Street, Springburn,
Glasgow, Lanarkshire G21 4BX
Tel:+44 (0) 141 558 9001

www.north-gla.ac.uk
L/Cert
WP, TT, DB, SS

North Hertfordshrie College
Stevenage Centre, Monkswood Way,
Stevenage, Hertfordshire SG1 1LA
Tel:+44 (0) 1462 424 242

www.nhc.ac.uk
L/Cert, I
WP, DB, SS, EM, Web

North Nottinghamshire College
Carlton Road,
Worksop, Nottinghamshire S81 7HP
Tel:+44 (0) 1909 504 504

www.nnotts-col.ac.uk
L/Cert
WP, DB, SS, EM

North Trafford College
Talbot Road Centre, Stretford,
Manchester, Lancashire M32 0XH
Tel:+44 (0) 161 886 7070

www.ntc.ac.uk
L/Cert
WP, TT, DB, SS, EM

North Warwickshire & Hinckley College
Hinckley Road,
Nuneaton, Warwickshire CV11 6BH
Tel:+44 (0) 24 7624 3000

www.nwhc.ac.uk
L/Cert
WP, TT, DB, SS, EM

North West Institute of Further & Higher Education
Strand Road,
Londonderry, County Londonderry BT48 7AL
Tel:+44 (0) 28 7127 6000

www.nwifhe.ac.uk
L /Cert
WP, DB, SS, EM, Web

North West Kent College
Oakfield Lane,
Dartford, Kent DA12 2JT
Tel:+44 (0) 1322 629 400

www.nwkcollege.ac.uk
L/Cert
WP, TT, DB, SS, EM, Web

Northampton College
Booth Lane,
Northampton, Northamptonshire NN3 3RF
Tel:+44 (0) 1604 734 567

www.northamptoncollege.ac.uk
L/Cert
WP, DB, SS, Web

Northumberland College
college Road,
Ashington, Northumberland NE63 9RG
Tel:+44 (0) 1670 841 200

www.northland.ac.uk
L/Cert, I
WP, TT, DB, SS, EM

Norton Radstock College
South Hill Park,
Radstock, Somerset BA3 3RW
Tel:+44 (0) 1761 433 161

www.nortcoll.ac.uk
L/Cert
WP, DB, SS, EM, Web

Oaklands College

St Albans, Hertfordshire AL4 0JA
Tel:+44 (0) 1727 737 000

www.oaklands.ac.uk
L/Cert, I
WP, DB, SS, EM, Web

Omagh College
2 Mountjoy Road,
Omagh, County Tyrone BT79 7AH
Tel:+44 (0) 28 8224 5433

www.omagh.ac.uk
L/Cert, I
WP, DB, SS, EM, Web

Orkney College
Kirkwall,
Orkney Islands, Highland KW15 1LX
Tel:+44 (0) 1856 569 000

www.orkney.uhi.ac.uk
L/Cert
WP, DB, SS, EM

Ormskirk College
Hants Lane,
Ormskirk, Lancashire L39 1PX
Tel:+44 (0) 1695 577 140

www.skelmersdale.ac.uk
L/Cert
WP, DB, SS, EM

Orpington College
The Walnuts,
Orpington, Kent BR6 0TE
Tel:+44 (0) 1689 899 700

www.orpington.ac.uk
L /Cert, I
WP, DB, SS, EM, Web

Oxford & Cherwell College
Oxpens Road,
Oxford, Oxfordshire OX1 1SA
Tel:+44 (0) 1865 550 550

www.ocvc.ac.uk
L/Cert, I
WP, DB, SS, EM

231

Oxford Media & Business School
Rose Place, St Aldates,
Oxford, Oxfordshire OX1 1SB
Tel:+44 (0) 1865 240 963 Fax:+44 (0)1865 242 783,

www.oxfordbusiness.co.uk
L/Cert, I
WP, DB, SS, EM, Web

Email: courses@oxfordbusiness.co.uk

Palmer's College
Chadwell Road,
Grays, Essex RM17 5TD
Tel:+44 (0) 1375 370 121

www.palmers.ac.uk
M/Cert
WP, DB, SS, EM, Web

Park Lane College
Park Lane,
Leeds, West Yorkshire LS3 1AA
Tel:+44 (0) 845 045 7275

www.parklanecoll.ac.uk
L /Cert
WP, DB, SS, EM, Web

Paston College
Grammar School Road,
North Walsham, Norfolk NR28 9JL
Tel:+44 (0) 1692 402 334

www.paston.ac.uk
L/Cert
WP, DB, SS, EM

Penwith College
St Clare Street,
Penzance, Cornwall TR18 2SA
Tel:+44 (0) 1736 335 000

www.penwith.ac.uk
L / Cert, Web
BD, SS, EM

Perth College
Crieff Road,
Perth, Perth & Kinross PH1 2NX
Tel:+44 (0) 1738 877 000

www.perthcollege.co.uk
L/Cert
WP, DB, SS, EM

Peterborough Regional College
Park Crescent,
Peterborough, Cambridgeshire PE1 4DZ
Tel:+44 (0) 1733 767 366

www.peterborough.ac.uk
L / Cert
WP, DB, SS, EM, Web

Pitmans Training Group
UK Head Office, Sandown House, Sandbeck Way,
Wetherby, West Yorkshire LS22 7DN
Tel:+44 (0) 1937 548500

www.pitman-training.com
M / Flex, Cert, DIY
WP, TT, DB, SS, EM, Web

Plymouth College of Further Education
Kings Road, Devonport,
Plymouth, Devon PL1 5QG
Tel:+44 (0) 1752 305 300

www.pcfe.ac.uk
L / Cert
WP, DB, Web

Portsmouth College
Tangier Road,
Portsmouth, Hampshire PO3 6PZ
Tel:+44 (0) 23 9266 7521

www.portsmouth-college.ac.uk
L/Cert
WP, DB, SS, EM

Prior Pursglove College
Church Walk,
Guisborough, Cleveland TS14 6BU
Tel:+44 (0) 1287 280 800

www.pursglove.ac.uk
L/Cert
WP, TT, DB, SS, EM

Queen Mary's College
Cliddesdon Road,
Basingstoke, Hampshire RG21 3HF
Tel:+44 (0) 1256 417 500

www.gmc.ac.uk
L/Cert, I
WP, DB, SS, EM

Queen's Business & Secretarial College
24 Queensberry Place,
London SW7 2DS
Tel:+44 (0) 20 7589 8583

www.qbsc.ac.uk
L /Cert, I, Md
WP, TT, DB, SS, EM

Redcar & Cleveland College
Corporation Road,
Redcar, Cleveland TS10 1EZ
Tel:+44 (0) 1642 473 132

www.cleveland.ac.uk
L /Cert
WP, DB, SS, EM, Web

Reid Kerr College
Renfrew Road,
Paisley, Renfrewshire PA3 4DR
Tel:+44 (0) 800 052 7343

www.reidkerr.ac.uk
L/Cert
WP, DB, SS

Royal Forest of Dean
Berry Hill,
Cinderford, Gloucestershire GL16 7JT
Tel:+44 (0) 1594 833 416

www.rfdc.ac.uk
L/Cert
WP, SS

Salisbury College
Southampton Road,
Salisbury, Wiltshire SP1 2LW
Tel:+44 (0) 1722 344 344

www.salisbury.ac.uk
L / Flex, Cert, I
WP, DB, SS, EM, Web

Sandwell College
Pound Road,
Oldbury, Worcestershire B68 8NA
Tel:+44 (0) 121 556 6000

www.sandwell.ac.uk
L/Cert
WP, TT, DB, SS, EM

7

Office skills | Colleges

233

Selby College
Abbott's Road,
Selby, North Yorkshire YO8 8AT
Tel:+44 (0) 1757 211 000

www.selbycollege.co.uk
L /Cert
WP, DB, SS, Web

Shipley College
Exhibition Road,
Saltaire, West Yorkshire BD18 3JW
Tel:+44 (0) 1274 327 222

www.shipley.ac.uk
L / Flex, Cert
WP, DB, SS, EM, Web

Skelmersdale College
Westbank Campus, Yewdale,
Skelmersdale, Lancashire WN8 6JA
Tel:+44 (0) 1695 728 744

www.skelmersdale.ac.uk
L/Cert
WP, DB, SS, EM

Solihull College
Blossomfield Road,
Solihull, Warwickshire B91 1SB
Tel:+44 (0) 121 678 7000

www.solihull.ac.uk
L/Cert
WP, TT, Web

South Cheshire College
Dane Bank Avenue,
Crewe, Cheshire CW2 8AB
Tel:+44 (0) 1270 654 654

www.s-cheshire.ac.uk
L/Cert
WP, DB, SS, EM, Web

South Devon College
Vantage Point, Long Road,
Paignton, Devon TQ4 7EJ
Tel:+44 (0) 1803 540 540

www.southdevon.ac.uk
L/Cert, I
WP, TT, EM, Web

South Downs College
College Road,
Waterlooville, Hampshire PO7 8AA
Tel:+44 (0) 23 9279 7979

www.southdowns.ac.uk
L / Cert
WP, DB, SS, EM, Web

South Kent College
Ashford Sixth Form Centre, Jemmett Road,
Ashford, Kent TN23 4RJ
Tel:+44 (0) 1233 655 524

www.southkent.ac.uk
L/Cert, I
WP, DB, SS, EM

South Lanarkshire College
Hamilton Road, Cambuslang,
Glasgow, Lanarkshire G72 7NY
Tel:+44 (0) 141 641 6600

www.south-lanarkshire.ac.uk
L/Cert
WP, DB, SS, EM

South Leicestershire College
Station Road,
Wigston, Leicestershire LE18 2DW
Tel:+44 (0) 116 288 5051

www.wigston-college.ac.uk
L/Cert
WP, DB, SS, Web

South Nottingham College
West Bridgford Centre, Greythorn Drive,
West Bridgford, Nottinghamshire NG2 7GA
Tel:+44 (0) 115 914 6400

www.snc.ac.uk
L/Cert
WP, TT, DB, SS, EM, Web

South Thames College
Wandsworth High Street,
London SW18 2PP
Tel:+44 (0) 208 918 7777

www.south-thames.ac.uk
L/Flex, Cert, I
WP, TT, DB, SS, EM

South Trafford College
Manchester Road, West Timperley,
Altrincham, Cheshire WA14 5PQ
Tel:+44 (0) 161 952 4600

www.stcoll.ac.uk
L / Flex, Cert, Md
WP, TT, DB, SS, EM, Web

South Tyneside College
St George's Avenue,
South Shields, Tyne & Wear NE34 6ET
Tel:+44 (0) 191 427 3500

www.stc.ac.uk
L/Flex, Cert
WP, TT, DB, SS, EM, Web

South-East Essex College
Luker Road,
Southend on Sea, Essex SS1 1ND
Tel:+44 (0) 1702 200 400

www.southend.ac.uk
L / Cert
WP, DB, SS, EM, Web

Southgate College
High Street,
Southgate, London N14 6BS
Tel:+44 (0) 208 982 5050

www.southgate.ac.uk
L/Cert, I
WP, DB, SS, EM, Web

Southport College
Mornington Road,
Southport, Lancashire PR9 0TT
Tel:+44 (0) 1704 500 606

www.southport-college.ac.uk
L/Cert, I
WP, DB, SS, EM, Web

Southwark College
Waterloo Centre, The Cut,
London SE1 8LE
Tel:+44 (0) 207 815 1500

www.southwark.ac.uk
L/Flex, Cert
WP, DB, SS, EM, Web

Spelthorne College
Church Road,
Ashford, Middlesex TW15 2XD
Tel:+44 (0) 1784 248 666

www.spelthorne.ac.uk
L/Cert, I
WP, DB, SS, EM, Web

St David's Catholic College
Ty Gwyn Road, Penylan,
Cardiff, Glamorgan CF23 5QD
Tel:+44 (0) 29 2049 8555

www.st-davids-coll.ac.uk
L/Cert
WP, DB, SS, EM

St Helens College
Brook Street,
St Helens, Merseyside WA10 1PZ
Tel:+44 (0) 1744 733 766

www.sthelens.ac.uk
L/Cert
WP, TT, DB, SS, EM

St James's & Lucie Clayton College
4 Wetherby Gardens,
London SW5 OJN
Tel:+44 (0) 20 7373 3852

www.sjlc.co.uk
M /Md, I
WP, TT, DB, SS, EM

St Mary's College
Shear Brow,
Blackburn, Lancashire BB1 8DX
Tel:+44 (0) 1254 580 464

www.stmarysblackburn.ac.uk
L/Cert
WP, DB, SS, EM, Web

St Vincent College
Mill Lane,
Gosport, Hampshire PO12 4QA
Tel:+44 (0) 239 258 8311

www.stvincent.ac.uk
L/Cert
WP, TT, DB, SS

Stafford College
Earl Street,
Stafford, Staffordshire ST16 2QR
Tel:+44 (0) 1785 223 800

www.staffordcoll.ac.uk
L/Cert
WP, DB, SS, EM, Web

Stamford College
Drift Road,
Stamford, Lincolnshire PE9 1XA
Tel:+44 (0) 1780 484 300

www.stamford.ac.uk
L/Cert
WP, DB, SS, EM, Web

Stanmore College
Elm Park,
Stanmore, Middlesex HA7 4BQ
Tel:+44 (0) 20 8420 7700

www.stanmore.ac.uk
L / Cert
WP, TT, DB, SS, EM, Web

Stockport College
Wellington Road South,
Stockport, Cheshire SK1 3UQ
Tel:+44 (0) 161 958 3100

www.stockport.ac.uk
L/Cert
WP, TT, DB, SS, EM

Stockton Riverside College
Harvard Avenue,
Stockton on Tees, County Durham TS17 6FB
Tel:+44 (0) 1642 865 400

www.stockton.ac.uk
L/Cert
WP, TT, DB, SS

Stoke on Trent College
Stoke Road, Shelton,
Stoke on Trent, Staffordshire ST4 2DG
Tel:+44 (0) 1782 208 208

www.stokecoll.ac.uk
L/Cert
WP, TT, DB, SS, EM, Web

Stourbridge College
Hagley Road,
Stourbridge, Worcestershire DY8 1QU
Tel:+44 (0) 1384 344 344

www.stourbridge.ac.uk
L/Cert
WP, TT, DB, SS, EM

Stow College
43 Shamrock Street,
Glasgow, Lanarkshire G4 9LD
Tel:+44 (0) 141 332 1786

www.stow.ac.uk
L/Flex, Cert
WP, DB, SS, EM, Web

Stratford-upon-Avon College
The Willows North, Alcester Road,
Stratford-upon-Avon, Warwickshire CV37 9QR
Tel:+44 (0) 1789 266 245

www.strat-avon.ac.uk
L /Cert
WP, DB, SS, EM, Web

Strode College
Church Road,
Street, Somerset BA16 0AB
Tel:+44 (0) 1458 844 400

www.strode-college.ac.uk
L/Cert, I
WP, DB, SS, Web

Stroud College
Stratford Road,
Stroud, Gloucestershire GL5 4AH
Tel:+44 (0) 1453 763 424

www.stroud.ac.uk
L/Flex, Cert, I
WP, TT, DB, SS, EM, Web

Sussex Downs College
Mountfield Road,
Lewes, West Sussex BN7 2XH
Tel:+44 (0) 1273 483 188

www.sussexdowns.ac.uk
L/Cert, I
WP, TT, DB, SS, EM, Web

237

Sutton Coldfield College
Lichfield Road,
Sutton Coldfield, Warwickshire B74 2NW
Tel:+44 (0) 121 362 1109

www.sutcol.ac.uk
L/Cert
WP, TT, DB, SS, EM, Web

Swindon College
North Star Avenue,
Swindon, Wiltshire SN2 1DY
Tel:+44 (0) 1793 491 591

www.swindon-college.ac.uk
L/Cert
EM, Web

Tameside College
Beaufort Road,
Ashton Under Lyne, Lancashire OL6 6NX
Tel:+44 (0) 161 908 6789

www.tameside.ac.uk
L/Cert
WP, DB, SS, EM

Tamworth & Lichfield College
Croft Street, Upper Gungate,
Tamworth, Staffordshire B79 8AE
Tel:+44 (0) 1827 310 202

www.tamworth.ac.uk
L/Cert, I
WP, TT, DB, SS, EM, Web

Taunton's College
Hill Lane,
Southampton, Hampshire SO15 5RL
Tel:+44 (0) 23 8051 1811

www.tauntons.ac.uk
L/Cert
WP, DB, SS

Thames Valley University
Kings Road,
Reading, Berkshire RG1 4HJ
Tel:+44 (0) 118 967 5000

www.tvu.ac.uk
L/Cert
WP, DB, SS, EM, Web

Thanet College
Ramsgate Road,
Broadstairs, Kent CT10 1PN
Tel:+44 (0) 1843 605 040

www.thanet.ac.uk
L/Cert
WP, TT, DB, SS, EM, Web

The Adam Smith College
Stenton Road,
Glenrothes, Fifeshire KY6 2RA
Tel:+44 (0) 1592 772 233

www.adamsmithcollege.ac.uk
L/Cert
WP, DB, SS, EM

The Blackpool Sixth Form College
Blackpool Old Road,
Blackpool, Lancashire FY3 7LR
Tel:+44 (0) 1253 394 911

www.blackpoolsixth.ac.uk
L/Cert
BD, SS

The College Ystrad Mynach
Twyn Road, Ystrad Mynach,
Hengoed, Powys CF82 7XR
Tel:+44 (0) 1443 816 888

www.ystrad-mynach.ac.uk
L/Cert
WP, DB, SS, EM

The Community College Hackney
Shoreditch Campus, Falkirk Street,
London N1 6HQ
Tel:+44 (0) 207 613 9123

www.tcch.ac.uk
L/Cert, I
WP, TT, DB, SS, EM

The Henley College
Deanfield Avenue,
Henley on Thames, Oxfordshire RG9 1UH
Tel:+44 (0) 1491 579 988

www.henleycol.ac.uk
L/Cert, I
WP, TT, DB, SS, Web

The North Highland College
Ormlie Road,
Thurso, Highland KW14 7EE
Tel:+44 (0) 1847 889 000

www.nhcscotland.com
L/Cert, I
WP, TT, DB, SS

The Oldham College
Rochdale Road,
Oldham, Lancashire OL9 6AA
Tel:+44 (0) 161 624 5214

www.oldham.ac.uk
L/Cert, I
WP, DB, SS, EM, Web

The Sheffield College
Granville Road,
Sheffield, South Yorkshire S2 2RL
Tel:+44 (0) 114 260 2600

www.sheffcol.ac.uk
L/Cert
WP, DB, SS, EM

Thomas Rotherham College
Moorgate Road,
Rotherham, West Yorkshire S60 2BE
Tel:+44 (0) 1709 300 600

www.thomroth.ac.uk
L/Cert
WP, DB, SS

Thurrock & Basildon College (FE)
Woodview,
Grays, Essex RM16 2YR
Tel:+44 (0) 845 601 5746

www.thurrock.ac.uk
L / Cert
WP, DB, SS, EM, Web

Totton College
Calmore Road, Totton,
Southampton, Hampshire SO40 3ZX
Tel:+44 (0) 2380 874 874

www.totton.ac.uk
L/Cert
WP, TT, DB, SS, EM, Web

Tower Hamlets College
Poplar High Street,
London E14 0AF
Tel:+44 (0) 207 510 7510

www.tower.ac.uk
L/Cert
WP, DB, SS, EM, Web

Tresham Institute of Further & Higher Education
Kettering Campus, St Marys Road,
Kettering, Northamptonshire NN15 7BS
Tel:+44 (0) 845 658 8990

www.tresham.ac.uk
L/Flex, Cert
WP, DB, SS, EM

Truro College
College Road,
Truro, Cornwall TR1 3XX
Tel:+44 (0) 1872 267 000

www.trurocollege.ac.uk
L/Cert
WP, DB, SS, EM, Web

Tyne Metropolitan College
Embleton Avenue, Wallsend,
Newcastle upon Tyne, Northumberland NE28 9NJ
Tel:+44 (0) 191 229 5000

www.ntyneside.ac.uk
L/Cert
WP, TT, DB, SS, EM, Web

University of Derby - Buxton
Devonshire Road,
Buxton, Derbyshire SK17 6RY
Tel:+44 (0) 1298 71100

www.derby.ac.uk
L/Cert
WP, TT, DB, SS, EM, Web

University of East Anglia - Suffolk College
Ipswich, Suffolk IP4 1LT
Tel:+44 (0) 1473 255 885

www.suffolk.ac.uk

WP, DB, SS, EM, Web

Upper Bann Institute
Castlewellan Road,
Banbridge, County Down BT32 4AY
Tel:+44 (0) 28 3839 7700

www.ubi.ac.uk
L/Cert
WP, TT, DB, SS, EM

Uxbridge College
Park Road,
Uxbridge, Middlesex UB8 1NQ
Tel:+44 (0) 1895 853 333

www.uxbridgecollege.ac.uk
L/Cert, I
WP, DB, SS, EM, Web

Varndean College
Surrenden Road,
Brighton, Sussex BN1 6WQ
Tel:+44 (0) 1273 508 011

www.varndean.ac.uk
L/Cert
WP, DB, SS, EM, Web

Wakefield College
Margaret Street,
Wakefield, West Yorkshire WF1 2DH
Tel:+44 (0) 1924 789 789

www.wakcoll.ac.uk

WP, TT, DB, SS, EM, Web

Walsall College
St Paul's Street,
Walsall, Staffordshire WS1 1WY
Tel:+44 (0) 1922 657 000

www.walsallcollege.ac.uk
L/Cert
WP, DB, SS, EM

Waltham Forest College
Forest Building, Forest Road,
Walthamstow, London E17 4JB
Tel:+44 (0) 208 501 8000

www.waltham.ac.uk
L/Cert, I
WP, TT, DB, SS

Warrington Collegiate
Winwick Road,
Warrington, Cheshire WA2 8QA
Tel:+44 (0) 1925 494 494

www.warr.ac.uk
L/Cert, I
WP, TT, DB, SS, Web

Warwickshire College
Warwick New Road,
Leamington Spa, Warwickshire CV32 5JE
Tel:+44 (0) 1926 318 000

www.warkscol.ac.uk
L /Cert
WP, DB, SS, EM, Web

West Cheshire College
Handbridge Centre, Eaton Road,
Chester, Cheshire CH4 7ER
Tel:+44 (0) 1244 677 677

www.west-cheshire.ac.uk
L/Cert, I
WP, DB, SS, EM

West Kent College
Brook Street,
Tonbridge, Kent TN9 2PW
Tel:+44 (0) 1732 358 101

www.wkc.ac.uk
L / Flex, Cert, DIY
WP, DB, SS, EM, Web

West Lothian College
Almondvale Cresent,
Livingston, West Lothian EH54 7EP
Tel:+44 (0) 1506 418181

www.west-lothian.ac.uk
L/Flex, Cert, I
WP, DB, SS, EM, Web

West Nottinghamshire College
Derby Road,
Mansfield, Nottinghamshire NG18 5BH
Tel:+44 (0) 1623 627 191

www.wnc.ac.uk
L/Cert, I
WP, TT, DB, SS, Web

West Thames College
London Road,
Isleworth, Middlesex TW7 4HS
Tel:+44 (0) 20 8326 2000

www.west-thames.ac.uk
L /Cert
WP, DB, SS, EM, Web

Westfield College
Margaret Street,
Wakefield, West Yorkshire WF1 2DH
Tel:+44 (0) 1924 789 789

www.wakcoll.ac.uk
L /Cert, I
WP, DB, SS, EM, Web

Westminster Kingsway College
Victoria Centre, Vincent Square,
London SW1P 2PD
Tel:+44 (0) 870 060 9800

www.westking.ac.uk
L/Cert, I
WP, TT, DB, SS

Weston College
Knightstone Road,
Weston Super Mare, Somerset BS23 2AL
Tel:+44 (0) 1934 411 411

www.weston.ac.uk
L/Flex, Cert, I
WP, TT, DB, SS, EM, Web

Weymouth College
Cranford Avenue,
Weymouth, Dorset DT4 7LQ
Tel:+44 (0) 1305 761 100

www.weymouth.ac.uk
L/Cert
WP, SS, EM

Wigan & Leigh College
PO Box 53, Parsons Walk,
Wigan, Lancashire WN1 1RS
Tel:+44 (0) 1942 761 600

www.wigan-leigh.ac.uk
L/Cert
WP, DB, SS, EM

Wiltshire College
Cocklebury Road,
Chippenham, Wiltshire SN15 3QD
Tel:+44 (0) 1249 464 644

www.wiltscoll.ac.uk
L / Flex, Cert
WP, DB, SS, EM, Web

Wirral Metropolitan College
Europa Boulevard, Conway Park,
Birkenhead, Cheshire CH41 4NT
Tel:+44 (0) 151 551 7777

www.wmc.ac.uk
L/Flex, Cert
WP, DB, SS, EM

Woking College
Rydens Way,
Woking, Surrey GU22 9DL
Tel:+44 (0) 1483 761 036

www.woking.ac.uk
L/Cert
WP, SS, EM

Worcestershire College of Technology
Deansway,
Worcester, Worcestershire WR1 2JF
Tel:+44 (0) 1905 725 555

www.wortech.ac.uk
L/Cert, I
WP, TT, DB, SS, Web

Yale College
Grove Park Road,
Wrexham, Denbighshire LL12 7AB
Tel:+44 (0) 1978 311 794

www.yale-wrexham.co.uk
L/Cert
WP, DB, SS, EM

visit: www.gap-year.com

Yeovil College
Mudford Road,
Yeovil, Somerset BA21 4DR
Tel:+44 (0) 1935 423 921

www.yeovil.ac.uk
L/Flex, Cert
WP, TT, DB, SS, EM

Yorkshire Coast College
Lady Edith's Drive,
Scarborough, North Yorkshire YO12 5RN
Tel:+44 (0) 1723 372 105

www.yorkshirecoastcollege.ac.uk
L/Cert
WP, TT, SS, EM

Office skills | Colleges

the gap-year guidebook 2007

Chapter 8
Learning in the UK

Chris spent 7 months travelling through Malaysia, India, Nepal, South Africa, Zambia and Tanzania and in that time completed two volunteer projects, one in Nepal, the other in Tanzania.

"I spent two months teaching in a Nepalese village in Northern India near Darjeeling and a week on a project at Arusha."

He took a break: "from seven years climbing the career ladder – simply an opportunity to take some time out and try something different instead."

It gave him, "Great experience working in the Nepalese village – completely different environment, lovely people, amazing location. Teaching was rewarding – working with kids was a first."

He said when he first returned it was: "Strange to see so clearly the wealth of the UK – people, houses, clothes, etc. Realisation that life in the UK is not the norm – but very privileged in comparison to areas in India and Africa".

He lists the benefits of volunteering: "It helps to demonstrate that there's always another way, another opportunity open to you....it shows you that with a bit of effort you can change your own path and make a difference.

"It's also helped me think about what I want to do next – to add a bit of structure to what I want to do rather than 'drifting on'.

246

Learning in the UK

You don't have to spend your **gap-**year travelling the globe if that doesn't appeal to you. The point about taking a **gap-** is to try out new experiences that leave you feeling refreshed and stimulated, to learn something new and possibly come up with some new ideas about where you want your life to head next.

So if you're frustrated that hardly anything you were taught at school seems relevant to your life, why not use your **gap-**year to learn new skills that you choose yourself? You can make them as useful as you want.

Archaeology

Are you fascinated by relics from the past? Would you love to find one? You could get yourself on an actual archaeological dig. One good place to start is with your local county council's Archaeology Department, which may know of local digs you could join. Nowadays, whenever a major building development is going through the planning application process, it regularly happens that permission to build includes a condition allowing for archaeological surveys before any work can begin, so another source of information could be the planning departments of local district councils.

Archaeological organisations

Council for British Archaeology
St Mary's House, 66 Bootham,
York, Yorkshire YO30 7BZ

www.britarch.ac.uk
Tel: +44 (0) 1904 671 417
Fax: +44 (0) 1904 671 384

The best starting point for archaeological digs in the British Isles is a magazine called British Archaeology which contains information about events and courses as well as digs.

Museum of London
London Wall,
London EC2Y 5HN

www.museumoflondon.org.uk
Tel: +44 (0) 870 444 3850

The Museum of London runs several archaeology courses for adults in partnership with Birbeck Collge. Please visit **www.museumoflondon.org.uk** for full information.

247

Art

If you're seriously interested in painting, sculpting or other artistic subjects, but don't know if you want to carry it through to a full degree, there is the useful option of a one-year art foundation course, available from a wide variety of art colleges.

A foundation course at art college doesn't count towards an art degree in the sense that you can then skip the first year of your three-year degree course.

But it can help you find out whether you are interested in becoming a practising artist, maybe an illustrator, an animator, a graphic designer, or are more interested in things like art history, or perhaps working in a gallery or a museum or in a field like interior design.

If you do want to go onto the three-year art school degree, competition for undergraduate places is based on the volume and standard of work in a candidate's 'entry portfolio'. Having a portfolio from your foundation course puts you at a natural advantage. Course providers also advise against specialising in one discipline, say sculpture, before covering the more wide-ranging syllabus of a foundation course.

Art

Blake College
162 New Cavendish Street,
London W1W 6YS

www.blake.ac.uk
Tel: +44 (0) 20 7636 0658
Fax: +44 (0) 20 7436 0049

Part-time courses available of between 6 weeks and one year. Can study towards a Diploma in Art & Design by combining four daytime part-time courses.

Bristol School of Animation
UWE, Faculty of Art, Media and Design,
Bower Ashton, Kennel Lodge Rd
Bristol, BS3 2JT

www.uwe.ac.uk
Tel: +44 (0)117 328 4810

Run by UWE's Faculty of Art, Media and Design, The Bristol School of Animation runs a wide range of animation courses aimed at budding animators of all levels and abilities.

Camberwell College of Arts
Peckham Road,
London SE5 8UF

www.camberwell.arts.ac.uk
Tel: +44 (0) 20 7514 6302
Fax: +44 (0)20 7514 6310

Established 100 years ago, Camberwell College of Arts, London, has a long tradition of teaching art, design and conservation. Today it offers a blend of heritage and new thinking at foundation studies, undergraduate and postgraduate level.

Heatherley School of Art
80 Upcerne Road,
Chelsea, London SW10 0SH

www.heatherleys.org
Tel: +44 (0) 20 7351 4190
Fax: +44 (0) 20 7351 6945

The Heatherley School of Art in Chelsea is the oldest independent art school in London. It is one of the few art schools Britain to focus purely on portraiture, figurative painting and sculpture.

The Prince's Drawing School	www.princesdrawingschool.org
19-22 Charlotte Road,	Tel: +44 (0) 207 6138527
London EC2A 3SG	

The Prince's Drawing School is an educational charity dedicated to teaching drawing from observation. Daytime, evening and summer school courses are run for artists and the general public.

University College London -	www.ucl.ac.uk/slade
Slade School of Fine Art	Tel: +44 (0) 20 7679 2313
Gower Street,	
London WC1E 6BT	

University of the Arts - Central Saint Martins	www.csm.linst.ac.uk
College of Art and Design	
Southampton Row, Holborn, London WC1B 4AP	

University of the Arts London -	www.chelsea.arts.ac.uk
Chelsea College of Art and Design	Tel: +44 (0) 20 7514 7751
16 John Islip Street,	Fax: +44 (0) 20 7514 7777
London SW1P 4JU	

University of Wales Institute - Cardiff School of Art and Design	
www.uwic.ac.uk/csad	
Howard Gardens,	Tel: +44 (0) 29 2041 6070
Cardiff, Glamorgan CF24 0SP	Fax: +44 (0) 29 2041 6286

Wimbledon School of Art	www.wimbledon.ac.uk
Main Building, Merton Hall Road,	Tel: +44 (0) 20 8408 5000
London SW19 3QA	Fax: +44 (0) 20 8408 5050

Cookery

Can you cook? There are really two types of cookery courses for gappers: basic skills and how to earn money.

The basic skills courses are for those who want to be able to feed themselves more than baked beans or packet soup. These courses can take you from boiling water through to quite a reasonable level - you may not be able to cook for a dinner party of 12, but you should leave being able to cook a variety of tasty meals without poisoning anyone. Cheap and cheerful cookery courses (standard, ethnic, exotic) can be found at day or evening classes at local colleges of further education. Usually the fees are low but you have to pay for ingredients.

The second type of course is aimed at teaching you the skills needed to work as a cook during your **gap**-year. Working as a cook in ski resorts, on yachts in the Caribbean or in villas in Tuscany or the South of France not only allows you to see the world, but pays you while you see it.

249

"The majority of those who want to work after doing our Essential Cookery course do find cooking work," says Hilary McFarland from Cookery at the Grange. "What's involved in being a chalet cook depends on what a ski company or employer wants. Usually the day starts with cooked breakfast for the ski party, then possibly a packed lunch, tea and cake when hungry skiers get back, possibly canapés later, and a three- or four-course supper. The food does need more than the usual amount of carbohydrate."

That doesn't mean dropping a large pile of pasta on a plate - ski companies expect high standards and may ask for sample menus when you apply for chalet cooking jobs. Sometimes the menus are decided in advance and the shopping done locally by someone else; sometimes the cook has to do the shopping.

Perhaps surprisingly, ski companies and agencies rarely ask about language skills - the cooks seem to manage without (see Chapter 4: Working Abroad for ideas on making use of your new skills).

Cookery

Aldeburgh Cookery School
84 High Street,
Aldeburgh, Suffolk IP15 5AB

www.aldeburghcookeryschool.com
Tel: +44 (0) 1728 454 039

Courses range from one to five days and cover a range of themes, from shellfish and pacific cuisine to exotic spices.

Belle Isle School of Cookery
Lisbellaw,
Enniskillen, County Fermanagh BT94 5HG

www.irishcookeryschool.com
Tel: 028 6638 7231
Fax: 028 6638 7261

Essential Cooking is an intensive four week course designed for people who are interested in learning the key skills for a gap year job in cooking.

CookAbility
Sherlands, 54 Stonegallows,
Taunton, Somerset TA1 5JS

www.residentialcookery.com
Tel: +44 (0) 1823 461374
Fax: +44 (0) 1884 432419

Cookery at The Grange
The Grange, Whatley,
Frome, Somerset BA11 3JU

www.cookeryatthegrange.co.uk
Tel: +44 (0) 1373 836 579

Cookery at the Grange in Somerset offers immensely popular four week residential cookery courses. Working in kitchens around a Somerset farmhouse courtyard, local and home grown organic ingredients are used wherever possible. A sense of fun and plenty of hands-on work ensures a good understanding of food and cooking by the end of the month. The course leads on to cooking for family and friends or to working professionally – in chalets, on boats or outside catering – ideal for generating a little cash. The intensive Essential Cookery Course costs £2850 to £3220 (depending on the time of year), including accommodation in twin-bedded rooms, en-suite rooms and particularly suits gap year students.

Cookery School at Little Portland Street

15B Little Portland Street,
London W1W 8BW

www.cookeryschool.co.uk
Tel: +44 (0) 20 7631 4590

Cookery School aims to turn out confident, inspired cooks not chefs. Courses for university and pre-university students are run during the summer holidays.

Cutting Edge

Food & Wine School
Hackwood Farm,
Robertsbridge, East Sussex TN32 5ER

www.cuttingedgefoodandwineschool.co.uk
Tel: +44 (0) 1580 881 281

Based in a 16th century farmhouse at Robertsbridge vineyard, Cutting Edge offers a range of cookery courses, from foundation to a chalet course, in modern kitchens. You will be taught in small groups by Tom Kime, who has an excellent reputation and who cooked for Jamie Oliver's wedding!

Edinburgh School of Food and Wine

The Coach House, Newliston,
Edinburgh, Midlothian EH29 9EB

www.esfw.com
Tel: +44 (0) 131 333 5001

Courses of interest to gappers are the four week Intensive Certificate Course which is geared towards chalet work, and the 1-week Survival Course which is ideally suited to those leaving home for the first time.

Food of Course

Middle Farm House, Sutton,
Shepton Mallet, Somerset BA4 6QF

www.foodofcourse.co.uk
Tel: +44 (0) 1749 860116

Le Cordon Bleu

114 Marylebone Lane,
London W1U 2HH

www.lcblondon.com
Tel: +44 (0) 800 980 3503

Le Cordon Bleu has courses ranging from their famous diplomas in 'Cuisine and Pâtisserie', to the shorter Gourmet Sessions featuring regional French cuisine, fusion, pâtisserie à la carte and bread baking. They also run an intensive four-week Essentials Course, geared specifically to gappers, which is full time and includes a trip to Paris. The price is £1940 and includes the minimum uniform required.

Leith's School of Food & Wine

21 St Alban's Grove,
London W8 5BP

www.leiths.com
Tel: +44 (0) 20 7229 0177

Leiths runs a four-week Foundation Course (£2355) starting in mid-July, five days a week. The most popular gap year courses, useful for chalet-people-to-be, are the three-month Beginner's Certificate in Food and Wine (£5350, September to December) and the Basic Certificate in Practical Cookery (£2290, four weeks, full-time from August.

Murray School of Cookery

Glenbervie House, Holt Pound,
Farnham, Surrey GU10 4LE

www.cookeryschool.net
Tel: +44 (0) 1420 23049
Fax: +44 (0) 1420 23049

The Murray School of Cookery offers two non-residential courses for gappers:
1. The intensive 4-week Cookery Certificate Course covers the skills required to work on luxury yachts, at premier ski chalets or at small restaurants and hotels. The course costs £1600.
2. The one-week Chalet Chef Course, designed in conjunction with major ski operators, teaches students to prepare recipes ideal for catered ski chalets and other knowledge needed to be a successful chalet host. The course costs £420 per person. Successful students also have access to the Murray School of Cookery database of ski companies and job vacancies.

Tante Marie School of Cookery Ltd

Woodham House, Carlton Road,
Woking, Surrey GU21 4HF

www.tantemarie.co.uk
Tel: +44 (0) 1483 726957
Fax: +44 (0) 1483 724173

Tante Marie, accredited by the BAC and member of the Year Out Group, offers various courses suitable for gap year students. The 11-week Cordon Bleu Certificate course (£4995 to include recipe file, knife set, uniform and 3-day wine course) starting September, January and April provides graduates with an internationally recognised qualification suitable to work the ski and yacht seasons and beyond. The 4-week Essential Skills course (£2300 to include recipe file, knife set and uniform) starting September, October, January and July offers an excellent foundation in cookery and a skill for life helpful in gaining short term employment.

The Bertinet Kitchen

12 St Andrew's Terrace,
Bath, BA1 2QR

www.thebertinetkitchen.com
Tel: 01225 445531
Fax: 01225 337533

The Gables School of Cookery

Pipers Lodge, Bristol Road,
Falfield, South Gloucestershire GL12 8DF

www.thegablesschoolofcookery.co.uk
Tel: 01454 260 444

The School of Cookery

40b Wincombe Business Park,
Shaftesbury, Dorset SP7 9QJ

www.theschoolofcookery.com
Tel: +44 (0) 1747 854800

Three Week Beginners – This course is designed to cover all areas needed to be able to work professionally for private parties, ski chalets or on a yacht.

The Year Out Group

Queensfield, 28 King's Road,
Easterton, Wiltshire SN10 4PX

www.yearoutgroup.org
Tel: +44 (0) 7980 395789

Drama

Abingdon Touring Theatre
"Sycamores", Station Yard,
Steventon, Oxon OX13 6RX

www.attc.org.uk
Tel: 07747 038410

A touring company for talented gap year students hoping to pursue careers in theatre after university or drama school.

Company of Angels
126 Cornwall Road,
London SE1 8TQ

www.companyofangels-uk.org
Tel: +44 (0) 020 7928 2811

DramaScene
25 Bristol Mews, Little Venice,
London, W9 2JF

www.dramascene.com
Tel: +44 (0) 20 7870 7547

Summer course: Students prepare with a dedicated director for performance in a London venue and learn about the reality of the professional drama scene.

Emerson College	www.emerson.org.uk
East Grinstead, Forest Row,	Tel: +44 (0) 1342 822238
East Sussex RH18 5JX	

Emerson College Orientation Gap Year Programme: Emerson College is an international centre for adult education and research based on the work of Rudolf Steiner (after whom Steiner schools are named), set in beautiful grounds in the Ashdown Forest area of rural Sussex. The Orientation Gap Year is an organised gap year for young people who want to be part of an international group engaged in activities such as study, volunteer work, arts drama and crafts. The year includes opportunities to develop creative skills, examine questions of our time and to make contributions to initiatives through volunteer work in placement sites around the world. The course also addresses self-development and orientation for the future.

RADA (Royal Academy of Dramatic Art)	www.rada.org
62-64 Gower Street,	Tel: +44 (0) 20 7636 7076
London WC1E 6ED	Fax: +44 (0) 20 7323 3865

This legendary drama college runs summer school courses. No audition is needed for the RADA Summer School (July-Aug) with its four weeks of intensive 'Shakespeare-based' workshops.

The Oxford School of Drama	www.oxforddrama.ac.uk
Sansomes Farm Studios,	Tel: +44 (0) 1993 812883
Woodstock, Oxfordshire OX20 1ER	Fax: +44 (0) 1993 811220

The Oxford School of Drama runs a six-month Foundation Course, including acting, voice, movement, music and stage fighting.

The Year Out Group	www.yearoutgroup.org
Queensfield, 28 King's Road,	Tel: +44 (0) 7980 395789
Easterton, Wiltshire SN10 4PX	

Driving

There are two reasons to learn to drive: first, unless you're intending to live in an inner city indefinitely, you'll need a driver's licence to get a job; secondly, it will give you independence and you won't have to rely on everyone else (especially your parents) to give you lifts everywhere. Even though you might not be able to afford the insurance right now, let alone an actual car, your **gap**-year is an ideal time to take driving lessons.

The test comes in two parts, theory and practical: and you need to pass the theory test before you apply for the practical one. However, you can start learning practical driving before you take the theory part, but to do that you need a provisional driving licence. You need to complete a driving licence application form and photocard application form D1 (formerly D750) - available from most post offices. Send the forms, the fee of £38 and original documentation confirming your identity such as your passport or birth certificate (make sure you keep a photocopy) and a passport-sized colour photograph to the DVLA.

You also need to check that you are insured for damage to yourself, other cars or

255

other people, and if you are practising in the family car, your parents will have to add cover for you on their insurance.

The DSA (Driving Standards Authority) is responsible for driving tests.

Information can be found on **www.dsa.gov.uk.**

Theory

The theory test is in two parts: a multiple choice part and a hazard perception section. You have to pass both. If you pass one and fail the other, you have to do both again.

The multiple choice is a 40-minute touch-screen test where you have to get 30 out of 35 multiple-choice questions right. You don't have to answer the questions in turn and the computer shows how much time you have left. You can have 15 minutes practice before you start the test properly. If you have special needs you can get extra time for the test – ask for this when you book it.

In the hazard test, you are shown a number of video clips filmed from a car, each containing one or more developing hazards. You have to indicate as soon as you see a hazard developing which may result in the driver taking some action, such as changing speed or direction. The sooner a response is made the higher the score.

Test results and feedback information are given within half-an-hour of finishing. The fee for the standard theory test is currently £21.50.

Your driving school, instructor or local test centre should have an application form, although you can book your test over the phone (0870 240 0009) or online at DSA Online booking.

Practical test

You have two years to pass the practical test once you have passed the theory part. The practical test for a car will cost £48.50, unless you choose to take it in the evening or on Saturday in which case the cost will increase to £58. You can book the practical test in the same way as the theory test. The bad news is that the tests are tough and it's quite common to fail twice or more before a pass. The practical test requires candidates to drive on faster roads than before - you'll need to negotiate a dual carriageway as well as a suburban road. You'll fail if you commit more than 15 driving faults. Once you pass your practical test, you can exchange your provisional licence for a full licence free.

Instructors

Of course some unqualified instructors (including parents) are experienced and competent, as are many small driving schools – but some checking out is a good idea if a driving school is not a well-known name. You can make sure that it is registered with the Driving Standards Agency and the instructor is qualified. AA and BSM charges can be used as a benchmark if you're trying other schools.

Driving

AA (Automobile Association)
Contact Centre, Lambert House, Stockport Road
Cheadle, Cheshire SK8 2DY

www.theaa.co.uk
Tel: +44 (0) 161 495 8945
Fax: +44 (0) 161 488 7300

Routes you to an AA centre near you. The website has lots of useful information on driving in the UK and abroad, including stuff about breakdown, insurance and travel planning. You can find hotels, good places to stop whilst driving and you're even able to find out about up-to-date traffic news.

Driving Standards Agency
Stanley House, 56 Talbot Street,
Nottingham, Nottinghamshire NG1 5GU

www.dsa.gov.uk
Tel: +44 (0) 115 901 2500

Information on theory and practical driving tests, fees and other relevant information.

DVLA (Driver and Vehicle Licencing Agency)
Swansea, Glamorgan SA6 7JL

www.dvla.gov.uk

RAC Motoring Services
8 Surrey Street, Norwich, Norfolk NR1 3NG

www.rac.co.uk

The RAC website has lots of useful information on driving in the UK and abroad, with breakdown, insurance and other services.

Languages

Even if the job you are applying for doesn't require them, employers are often impressed by language skills. With the growth of the internet, most companies like to think of themselves as having international potential at the very least. If you didn't enjoy language classes at school, that shouldn't necessarily put you off. College courses and evening classes are totally different – or at least they should be. If in doubt ask to speak to the tutor or to someone who has already been on the course before you sign up.

And even if you don't aspire to learn enough to be able to use your linguistic skills in a job, you could still take conversation classes so you can speak a bit of the language when you go abroad on your holidays. It is amazing what a sense of achievement and self confidence you can get when you manage to communicate the simplest things to a local in their own language: simply ordering a meal or buying stamps for your postcards home.

The best way to improve your language skills is to practice speaking, preferably to a native speaker in their country. But if you don't have the time or the money to go abroad yet, don't worry. There are plenty of places in the UK to learn a wide variety of languages, from Spanish to Somali. We've listed some language institutions below, but also find out what language courses your local college offers, and what evening classes there are locally.

Languages

Canning House
2 Belgrave Square,
London SW1X 8PJ

www.canninghouse.com
Tel: +44 (0) 20 7235 2303
Fax: +44 (0) 20 7838 9258

The Canning House Education and Cultural Department provides information about Latin America, Portugal and Spain.

Instituto Cervantes
326/330 Deansgate, Campfield Avenue Arcade,
Manchester, Lancashire M3 4FN

www.cervantes.org.uk
Tel: +44 (0) 161 661 42 00
Fax: +44 (0) 161 661 42 03

Instituto Cervantes is a Spanish government-funded 'ambassador' for Spanish culture in the UK. Its database provides information about language course locations. The Instituto runs its own Spanish language and cultural courses throughout the academic year in Leeds and Manchester.

University of London -
School of Oriental and African Studies
Thornhaugh Street, Russell Square,
London WC1H 0XG

www.soas.ac.uk
Tel: +44 (0) 20 7898 4888
Fax: +44 (0) 20 7436 3844

The SOAS (part of the University of London) runs courses for numerous languages, inluding all levels in Arabic language, culture and civilization.

Online learning

Companies offering language courses have cottoned on to the fact that many of us are welded semi-permanently to our computers.

You can now get very comprehensive language courses on CD-ROM which include booklets or pages that can be printed off. The better ones use voice recognition as well, so you can practise your pronunciation. These can also be found in book stores.

The internet itself is also a good source of language material. There are many courses, some with free access, some that need a very healthy credit card. If all you want is a basic start, then take a look at **www.bbc.co.uk/education/languages/** which offers you the choice of beginner's French, German and Spanish complete with vocab lists to download, all for free.

As well as courses, there are translation services, vocab lists and topical forums - just do a web search and see how many sites come up. Lots of them are free.

Practice makes perfect

When you need to practise, find out if there are any native speakers living in your town - you could arrange your own language and cultural evenings.

Terrestrial TV stations run some language learning programmes, usually late at night. If you have satellite or cable TV you can also watch foreign shows though this can be a bit frustrating if you're a beginner.

It's best to video the programmes so you can replay any bits that you didn't understand the first time round. Once you're getting a bit more advanced then you can try tuning your radio in to foreign speech-based shows from the relevant countries. This is a good way to keep up to date with current affairs in your chosen country, as well as keeping up your listening and understanding skills. Subjects are wide-ranging, and there's something to interest everyone.

The tapes have been well-received by teachers and reviewers, but are a bit expensive for the average **gap**-year student. It costs extra for the glossy booklet containing a transcript of the programme and help with vocabulary.

Music

Perhaps you always wanted to learn the saxophone, but never quite got round to it? Now would be an ideal time to start. If you're interested, your best bet is to find a good private tutor. Word of mouth is the best recommendation, but some teachers advertise in local papers, and you could also try an online search engine like Musicians' Friend **www.musiciansfriend.co.uk**.

the gap-year guidebook 2007

If you already play an instrument, you could broaden your experience by going on a residential course or summer school. These are available for many different ability levels, although they tend to be quite pricey. Here are a few of the courses we've heard about.

Music

Lake District Summer Music
Stricklandgate House, 92 Stricklandgate,
Kendal, Cumbria LA9 4PU

www.ldsm.org.uk
Tel: +44 (0) 845 6 44 21 44
Fax: +44 (0) 845 6 44 25 06

The Lake District Summer Music School is an ensemble-based course for string players and pianists intending to pursue careers as professional musicians. Coaching is given by top instrumentalists and ensembles.

London Music School
9-13 Osborn Street,
London E1 6TD

www.tlms.co.uk
Tel: +44 (0) 20 7247 1311
Fax: +44 (0) 20 9202 0574

The London Music School offers a Diploma in Music Technology, open to anyone with musical ability aged 17 or over. The course explores professional recording and you get to use a 24-track studio.

North London Piano School
78 Warwick Avenue,
Edgware, Middlesex HA8 8UJ

www.nlps.org
Tel: +44 (0) 20 8958 5206
Fax: +44 (0) 20 8366 9665

The North London Piano School offers a residential Summer Course.

Oxford Flute Summer School
12 Jesse Terrace,
Reading, Berkshire RG1 7RT

www.oxford-flutes.co.uk
Tel: +44 (0) 118 950 7865

The Oxford Flute Summer School runs from mid-August. Tuition is available at different levels to suit your standard.

Photography

There are lots of photography courses available, from landscape photography to studio work. Don't kid yourself that a photography course is going to get you a job and earn you pots of money, but there's nothing to stop you enjoying photography as a hobby or sideline.

Photography

Experience Seminars
Unit 4, Hill Farm, Wennington,
Huntingdon, Cambridgeshire PE28 2LU

www.experience-seminars.co.uk
Tel: +44 (0)1487 772804

Experience Seminars hosts a range of workshops throughout the UK, which are designed to provide a fast track way of learning photography and digital imaging techniques.

The Royal Photographic Society
Fenton House, 122 Wells Road,
Bath, Somerset BA2 3AH

www.rps.org
Tel: +44 (0) 1225 325 733

The Royal Photographic Society holds photography courses, from landscape photography to studio work, throughout the year.

Sport

After all that studying maybe all you want to do is get out there and do something. If you're the energetic type and hate the thought of spending your **gap**-year stuck behind a desk, why not get active and do some sport?

There are sports courses for all types at all levels, from scuba diving for beginners to advanced ski instructor qualification courses. Of course if you manage to get an instructor's qualification you may be able to use it to get a job (see Working Abroad).

If you hated sport at school, try giving it another chance during your **gap**-year – you may be surprised how much you like it.

Sport

Big Squid Scuba Diving Training and Travel
72 Hubert Grove,
Clapham, London SW9 9PD

www.bigsquid.co.uk
Tel: +44 (0) 20 7733 6966

Big Squid offers a variety of dive courses using the PADI and TDI systems of diver education. Beginners can start with Discover Scuba courses (a trial dive in the pool) or go straight on to the Open Water Diver course.

British Mountaineering Council
177-179 Burton Road,
Manchester, Lancashire M20 2BB

www.thebmc.co.uk
Tel: +44 (0) 870 010 4878

BMC travel insurance covers a range of activities and is designed by experts to be free from unreasonable exclusions or restrictions, for peace of mind wherever you travel.

British Offshore Sailing School - BOSS
Hamble Point Marina, School Lane,
Hamble, Hampshire SO31 4NB

www.boss-sail.co.uk
Tel: +44 (0) 23 8045 7733
Fax: +44 (0) 23 8045 6744

BOSS offers complete 5-day and weekend RYA shore-based and practical training courses from Hamble Point Marina.

British Sub Aqua Club
Telford's Quay, South Pier Road,
Ellesmere Port, Cheshire CH65 4FL

www.bsac.com
Tel: +44 (0) 151 350 6200
Fax: +44 (0) 151 350 6215

Why not discover scuba diving or snorkelling during your gap year? After obtaining some initial training from one of our recognised Branches or Centres you could be qualified to teach snorkelling to others.

Explorers Tours
8 Minster Court, Tuscam Way,
Camberley, Surrey GU15 3YY

www.explorers.co.uk
Tel: +44 (0) 845 644 7090
Fax: +44 (0) 1276 406 854

Gap Sports Ltd
Thamesbourne, Station Road,
Bourne End, Buckinghamshire SL8 5QH

www.gapsports.com
Tel: +44 (0) 870 837 9797

Kiteboarding UK
301 London Road South,
Lowestoft, Suffolk NR33 0DX

www.kiteboardinguk.com
Tel: +44 (0) 1502 512768

Kiteboarding UK offer kiteboarding lessons on their council-approved training area at Kesslingland beach near Lowestoft.

Lawn Tennis Association
Palliser Road,
West Kensington, London W1H 9EG

www.lta.org.uk
Tel: +44 (0) 20 7381 7000
Fax: +44 (0) 20 7381 5965

The LTA runs coaching courses with three levels of qualification: Development, Club and Performance, all running for 14 days over five months.

London Scuba Diving School
Raby's Barn, Newchapel Road,
Lingfield, Surrey RH7 6LE

www.londonscuba.com
Tel: +44 (0) 1342 837 711
Fax: +44 (0) 1342 837 722

The London Scuba Diving School walks you underwater on the floors of swimming pools in Battersea and Bayswater.

National Mountaineering Centre
Plas y Brenin, Capel Curig,
Conwy, Caernarfonshire LL24 OET

www.pyb.co.uk
Tel: +44 (0) 1690 720 214
Fax: +44 (0) 1690 720 394

For those hoping to reach dizzy heights, the National Mountaineering Centre offers a vast range of activities and courses.

Plas Menai
National Watersports Centre,
Caernarfon, Gwynedd LL55 1UE

www.plasmenai.co.uk
Tel: +44 (0) 1248 670964
Fax: +44 (0) 1248 673939

Plas Menai offers a range of courses training people to work as watersports, yachting and adventure instructors abroad and in the UK. Training courses last between 1 and 26 weeks and take place in Spain and UK. Courses for beginners and those with experience. Use your qualifications to train, work and travel in your gap year or longer term.

• Start dates throughout the year
• Weekend, 5 day and longer training courses
• Professional Yacht Skipper: 17 wks
• Dinghy and Windsurf Instructor: 12 wks
• Dinghy Instructor: 8 wks
• Multi-Activity Instructor: 26 wks
• Recruitment + work placements.

ProAdventure Limited
23 Castle Street,
Llangollen, Denbighshire LL20 8NY

www.adventureholiday.com
Tel: +44 (0)1978 861912

Based in Wales, ProAdventure offers different activity courses around the UK, including canoeing, kayaking, rock climbing and mountain biking.

The Talland School of Equitation
Dairy Farm, Ampney Knowle,
Cirencester, Gloucestershire GL7 5ED

www.talland.net
Tel: 01285 740155
Fax: 01285 740153

World renowned BHS and ABRS approved equestrian centre offering top class training for professional qualifications. Variety of courses including competition training on quality horses.

Wellington Riding
Heckfield,
Hook, Hampshire RG27 OLJ

www.wellington-riding.co.uk
Tel: +44 (0) 118 932 6308
Fax: +44 (0) 118 932 6661

Wellington Equestrian Education offers training towards BHS exams in exchange for work.

X-rated

If you want a real adrenalin rush, go for one of the extreme sports like street luge or skyboarding. Skyboarding is basically a combination of skydiving and snowboarding – you throw yourself out of a plane wearing a parachute and perform acrobatic stunts on a board. Or you could try street luge – where you hurtle down a street on nothing but a narrow aluminium rail, with no brakes!

Or if you like company when you're battling against the elements, then you could get involved in adventure racing: teams race each other across rugged terrain without using anything with a motor, for example skiing, hiking, sea kayaking. Team members have to stay together throughout the race. Raid Gauloises (five-person teams, two weeks, five stages, half the teams don't finish!) and Eco-Challenge (ten days, 600km, several stages and an environmental project) are the two most well-known adventure race events.

The annual X Games feature a wide range of extreme sports and take place during one week in summer (including aggressive in-line skating) and another week in winter (including mountain bike racing on snow). Check out their website http://expn.go.com/ for the full details.

If you want to get wet, then try diving, kayaking, sailing, surfing, water polo, windsurfing, or whitewater rafting.

And if those don't appeal then there's always abseiling, badminton, baseball, basketball, bungee jumping, cavediving, cricket, fencing, football, golf, gymnastics, hang gliding, hockey, horse riding, ice hockey, ice skating, jet skiing, motor racing, mountain biking, mountain boarding, netball, parachuting, polo, rock climbing, rowing, rugby, running, skateboarding, skating, ski jumping, skiing, skydiving, skysurfing, snooker, snow mobiling, snowboarding, squash, stock car racing, tennis or trampolining! If the sport you are interested in isn't listed below then try contacting the relevant national association (eg. the LTA for tennis) and asking them for a list of course providers.

TEFL

TEFL

Teaching English as a Foreign Language qualifications are always useful for earning money wherever you travel abroad. The important thing to check is that the qualification you will be gaining is recognised by employers. Most courses should also lead on to help with finding employment.

Intensive TEFL Courses　　　　　　　　www.tefl.co.uk
26 Cockerton Green,　　　　　　　　　　Tel: 08456 445464
Darlington, County Durham DL3 9EU　　Fax: 01325 366167

ITC are recognised as one of the forerunners of approved intensive weekend TEFL courses in the UK. Established for more than a decade, we have trained many students who have since found new careers teaching English in the UK and abroad. Fully qualified and experienced tutors run our weekend courses throughout the UK, enabling our students to attend without the inconvenience of taking time away from their work or study. All of our courses are held in conference venues of major towns and cities throughout Great Britain, and these are easily accessible by road or rail.

TEFL Training

Friend's Close, Stonefield,
Witney, Oxfordshire OX29 8PH

www.tefltraining.co.uk
Tel: +44 (0) 1993 891 121
Fax: +44 (0) 1993 891 996

Our TEFL courses:

• Practical

• Flexible

• Fun

• Academically accredited

• Cashflow friendly: Choose how much training you want

• You set the pace of your study

• Work Worldwide!

Weekend TEFL courses (£210) in 30 different UK locations & Paris. 80 hour add-on self-study (£135) leads to the Certificate of Educational Studies (TESOL) from the College of Teachers (**www.collegeofteachers.ac.uk**). You can also get this qualification by doing our 100 hour full distance learning TEFL/TESOL course. Consolidate and practise your new knowledge by adding on a 40-hour Teaching Practice Week (£250) in a UK language school.

Chapter 9
Working in the UK

Ben, 19, has been working as a customer services consultant in a motor insurance call centre for a large financial services organisation for the last year.

He'd worked weekends for two years in a discount retail store while studying for A levels at school, and was undecided about going to university straight after. He also knew he wanted to go to the USA eventually.

He suspected that his grades were not going to be good enough to read film studies at uni and decided to take a **gap-**. He started job-hunting for a full-time post as soon as he left school after A levels.

He said: "I wasn't sure what I wanted to do when I left school so I decided to look for a full-time position to give me some time to think and put some money in my pocket".

Ben signed up with job agencies, wrote a proper CV that emphasised his IT skills and work experience, bought a suit, and after interviews with just two companies was offered a job.

Almost a year later, he still hopes to go to University but is concerned about the cost and the debt he could be left with.

So what does he feel he's learned during his **gap-** spent working in the UK?

"I have learnt an abundance of financial related information, and also experienced what it's like to have a full-time job for an extended period of time. I'm also in a more comfortable position financially if I want to take time out for further education."

Does he feel it's changed him?

"Not really, it was more of a stop-gap or a stepping stone onto bigger and better things. I still have every intention of going to university and getting a job more suited to my personal tastes."

What does he plan to do next and when?

"University in the next year, followed by hopefully a job in the media industry."

Why work on a year out?

If you're not working to raise money for **gap-**year travel working might be the last thing on your mind during a time where the world seems to be your oyster.

Unfortunately, it could well prove necessary or perhaps even desirable.

Some industries (especially media, medicine and law) are very competitive and any experience, paid or unpaid, might make all the difference down the line when you have to prove to a potential employer that you really are committed.

Another consideration is the frequency with which people applying for jobs report being rejected at interview "because of lack of work experience".

A **gap-**year is a great time to build up that initial experience of work culture as well as getting a foot in the door and getting recognised; in fact many students go back to the same firms after graduation. If you're not sure what you want to do as a career, then a **gap-**year could be a great time to try out different jobs, to get a feel for what you might want to do in the future.

Going to university is an expensive thing to do. The vast majority of graduates are heavily in debt, recent estimates put the figure as high as £25,000, which can prove to be a true burden later on in their lives.

So earning just a little bit now could really help your bank balance in the future.

Whatever the reason, start looking early, rather than late, to avoid disappointment.

Getting the job

How do you get that first job with no prior experience? What can you possibly offer? The key is creativity. Show the company you're applying so that you can offer them something that nobody else can, and do this by giving them an example.

If you're applying to an advertising firm, for instance, then mock up some adverts to show them. Want to go into journalism? Write some specimen articles and send them to local newspapers. Write to the editor and ask whether you could volunteer to help out in the newsroom to get a feel for the environment and the skills you'll need – a kind of extended work experience to add to the two you should have had via school.

You could try this with companies in other fields you're interested in. Be proactive and persevering. It will show you have initiative and commitment and whatever your eventual career it will also help you learn the basics of acting professionally in a professional environment.

Whatever your chosen field, find out about the company and show your knowledge about the industry.

If you are going for an industry, such as medicine or law, then showing that you are more than competent and willing is all that you can really do. Saying this, you have to make sure that you stick out from other applicants.

At one time the advice was to include a photo (one that doesn't make you look like a criminal) with your CV but recently employment agencies have said many employers now specifically ask them not to supply photos.

If in doubt, call the company and ask to speak to someone in personnel/HR, or if you're using an employment agency ask their advice.

Contacts

Over the next few pages we list some companies that specifically employ **gap-**year students or companies that we think are worth contacting. But, take this as a starting point – the tip of the iceberg – there are hundreds of other companies out there waiting to be impressed by you.

Research is key. Tailor each application towards that specific company, and never just expect to get a job; you have to work at it. The general rule is that nobody will call you back – be the one who gets in contact with them.

Job surfing

Most major job agencies, and many smaller ones, now have websites.

You don't get the personal touch from a website that you do by going into a local branch and getting advice or registering face-to-face, but recruitment websites are really useful if you know what you want to do and you have a 'skills profile' that one of their customers is looking for. Some of them are aimed at graduates and students, others at a general audience, others at specific areas of work (IT, for example). Here are a few to start with:

www.activate.co.uk	www.milkround.co.uk
www.excite.co.uk	www.monster.com
www.fish4jobs.co.uk	www.peoplebank.com
www.ft.com	www.reed.co.uk
www.gradunet.co.uk	www.search.co.uk
www.jobserve.com	www.stepstone.com
www.jobsunlimited.co.uk	

On spec

If contacts, advertisements, agencies or the internet all fail there is always DIY job-hunting. Just walk into shops and restaurants to ask about casual work or use a phone directory (e.g. Yellow Pages) to phone businesses (art galleries, department stores, zoos...) and ask what is available.

Ring up, ask to speak to the personnel manager, and ask if and when they have jobs available and how you should apply. If they ask you to write in, you can do it after the call. If you go in, make sure you look smart.

Opportunities in the big professional firms are not always well-publicised.

Temporary jobs (except agency-filled ones) are often filled by personal contact. If you have a burning desire to work for an architects' or lawyers' firm, for example, and you find nothing advertised, you could try phoning through a list to ask if work is available.

Banking: approach your local branches for work experience.

Education: Most educational work experience is tied in with travelling abroad, to places like Africa or Asia, mostly to teach English. However, there are ways of gaining experience back home in England. A very popular way is to see if the school that you have just left would like classroom helpers, or perhaps help teaching a younger sports team. The key to this is to ask around and see what might be available. As well as straight teaching, any experience with children can be very useful, so try looking at camps and sports teams that may need help – there are a few contacts for camps within the Seasonal Work section.

Legal and medical: As everybody knows, these two professions are extremely hard to pursue, so any amount of work experience could prove to be very useful. There's plenty of work experience available, but lots of competition for the places so start looking early. Nearly all NHS hospitals look for volunteer staff if you can't find anything worthwhile that you could get paid for, so just contact the HR (Human Resources) Manager at your local hospital.

Media, publishing and advertising: Working on television or the radio is a very popular and highly competitive career, and it is because of this that the media is one of the hardest industries to break into. Work experience is highly recommended. Many companies are very willing to try out **gap**-year students as trainees, as raw talent is such a limited commodity they want to nurture it as much as possible – plus it's cheap.

Theatre: Many theatres provide work experience for **gap**-year students, so it's definitely worthwhile contacting your nearby production company. This industry recognises creativity and application probably more than any other, so starting out early and fiercely is the only way to do it.

Interviews

Your persistence has got you an interview, now how do you go about impressing your potential employers? Confidence and knowledge is probably top of the list for employers, so that is what you must portray, even if you're a bag of nerves and haven't got a clue.

Make sure you are dressed appropriately (cover tattoos, remove nose piercings etc, don't show too much flesh, have clean and brushed hair - all the stuff that your teachers/parents tell you and really annoys you). If you're going for a creative job (advertising, art, etc.) then you can probably be a little more casual - when you phone the secretary to confirm your interview time and venue, you can ask whether you'll be expected to dress formally.

Stand straight, keep eye contact with the interviewer and smile.

Be well prepared to answer the question: "So, why do you want this job?"

Finally, be positive about yourself - don't lie, but focus on your good points rather than your bad ones.

Gap-year specialists

If you would like to get a work placement from a **gap-**year specialist, a good starting point is The Year Out Group, an association of organisations formed to promote the concept and benefits of well-structured year out programmes and to help people select suitable and worthwhile projects. The Group's member organisations are listed on the website and provide a wide range of year out placements in UK and overseas including structured work placements.

Year Out Group members are expected to put potential clients and their parents in contact with those who have recently returned. Year Out Group considers it important that these references are taken up at least by telephone and, where possible, by meeting face to face.

The Year Out Group
Queensfield, 28 King's Road
Easterton, Wiltshire SN10 4PX
Tel: 07980 395789
www.yearoutgroup.org

Money, money, money
So you got the job, you've put in the hours and you are just waiting for the cash to roll in...

Pay, tax and National Insurance

You can expect to be paid in cash for casual labour, by cheque (weekly or monthly) in a small company and by bank transfer in a large one. Always keep the payslip that goes with your pay, along with your own records of what you earn (including payments for casual labour) during the tax year: from 6 April one year to 5 April the next. You need to ask your employer for a P46 form when you start your first job and a P45 form when you leave (which you take to your next employer).

If you are out of education for a year you are not treated as a normal taxpayer.

Personal allowances - that is the amount you can earn before paying tax, are reviewed in the budget each year in April. To find out the current tax-free personal allowance rate call the Inland Revenue helpline or go to:

www.inlandrevenue.gov.uk

Minimum wages, maximum hours

Since we published our last edition the Government has reviewed the minimum wage rate again and the rates are:

From October 1 2006, workers aged 16 to 18 a 'development rate' of should get £3.30 an hour, 18 to 21-year-old workers should receive £4.45 an hour and workers aged 22 and over should get £5.35 per hour.

To check on how the National Minimum Wage applies to you, use the TIGER interactive website at **www.dti.gov.uk/er/nmw/** or phone the National Minimum Wage Helpline on 0845 6000 678. This is also the number to ring if you think you are being underpaid and want to complain. All complaints about underpayment of the National Minimum Wage are treated in the strictest confidence.

There is also a law on working hours which the UK has had to put into force to comply with European Union legislation. This says that (with some exemptions for specific professions) no employee should be expected to work more than 48 hours a week. Good employers do give you time off 'in lieu' if you occasionally have to work more than 48 hours a week. Others take no notice, piling a 60-hour-a-week workload on you. This is against the law and, unless you like working a 12-hour day, they must stop. You are also entitled to four weeks paid leave per year, a day off each week and an in-work rest break if the working day is longer than six hours.

Gap-year employers

Over the next few pages we list companies that either have specific **gap**-year employment policies or that we think are worth contacting. We've split them into three groups: arts festivals, seasonal work and general employers. This isn't a comprehensive list, so it's still worth checking the internet and your local companies (in the Yellow Pages, for example).

Arts festivals

Whether musical, literary or dramatic, there are loads of festivals taking place up and down the country every year. You need to apply as early as possible, as there aren't that many placements. Satellite organisations spring up around core festivals, so if you are unsuccessful at first, try to be transferred to another department. The work can be paid or on a voluntary basis. Short-term work, including catering and stewarding, is available mainly during the summer. Recruitment often starts on a local level, so check the local papers and job agencies.

Arts festivals

Brecon Jazz Festival
Festival Office, Brecon, Powys LD3 7EF

www.breconjazz.co.uk

This sleepy mid-Wales town turns into New Orleans in August every year as jazz bands and singers from all over the world congregate.

Brighton Literary Festival
Brighton, East Sussex BN1 1UE

www.brighton-festival.org.uk

Email: info@brightonfestival.org

A handful of volunteer posts are open during the festival in May, working in the education and press office departments.

Cheltenham Festivals
Cheltenham, Gloucestershire GL50 1QA

www.cheltenhamfestivals.co.uk

This company runs festivals throughout the year, including jazz, science, music, folk, fringe and literary events. There are usually a number of placements available, although they tend to be unpaid.

Edinburgh International Festival
Edinburgh, EH1 2NE

www.eif.co.uk

Big and long-established late summer festival that has managed to stay cutting-edge.

Hay Festival
The Drill Hall, 25 Lion Street,
Hay-on-Wye, Herefordshire HR3 5AD

www.hayfestival.co.uk
Tel: +44 (0) 870 787 2848
Fax: +44 (0) 1497 821066

One of the most famous literary festivals in the UK. Most departments take on extra workers for the festival fortnight, including stewards, extra staff for the box-office and the bookshop and three interns.

Seasonal work

A great way to make some quick cash, either to save up for travelling or to spend at home, is seasonal work. There are always more jobs going at Christmas in the Post Office sorting office or in local shops. In the summer it can be a lot of fun to fruit pick for example – and also a great way to work on your tan (try **www.pickingjobs.com**) which links farms worldwide with students looking for holiday work.

Camp Beaumont
5-7 John Prince's Street,
London W1G 0JN

www.campbeaumont.com
Tel: +44 (0) 870 499 8787

Email: enquiries@campbeaumont.com

Have the Summer of your life working at Camp Beaumont Summer Camps! We need vibrant and energetic people to work as Group Leaders, responsible for the round-the-clock welfare of a group of children.

Facilities Management Catering
Church Road, Wimbledon,
London SW19 5AE

www.fmccatering.co.uk
Tel: +44 (0) 20 8947 7430
Fax: +44 (0) 20 8944 6362
Email: resourcing@fmccatering.co.uk

The official caterers to the Wimbledon Tennis Championships, FMC employ keen, hard-working gappers from mid-June to early July. Contact the company for an application pack.

Kingswood Group
Kingswood House, Alkmaar Way,
Norwich, Norfolk NR6 6BF

www.kingswoodjobs.co.uk
Tel: +44 (0) 870 499 7744
Fax: +44 (0) 870 240 7465
Email: jobs@kingswood.co.uk

Kingswood offer and provide leading IT, Educational and Adventure Activity Courses to schools throughout the UK.

General companies

Abbey National
Abbey National House, 2 Triton Square,
Regent's Place
London NW1 3AN

www.abbeynational.co.uk
Tel: +44 (0) 870 607 6000
Fax: +44 (0) 1908 349 187

Check the local press or ask your local branch about short term employment opportunities. Take a look at **www.jobsatabbeynational.co.uk** for jobs nationally.

Alliance & Leicester plc
Carlton Park,
Narborough, Leicestershire LE19 0AL

www.alliance-leicester-group.co.uk
Tel: +44 (0) 116 201 1000
Fax: +44 (0) 116 200 4040

A&L can't guarantee work but it will keep your CV on file in case a project comes up that needs extra staff, usually at the Narborough customer services centre.

Arcadia Group plc
Training Programmes Team, 70 Berners Street,
London W1T 3NL

www.arcadiagroup.co.uk
Tel: +44 (0) 20 7927 1112

Email: resourcing.manager@arcadiagroup.co.uk

For jobs in branches (Burton Menswear, Dorothy Perkins, Evans, Hawkshead, Principles, Racing Green, Topshop/Topman), apply directly to your local branch.

Army
HQ Recruiting Group, Room 107,
Building 38B, Trenchard Lines
Upavon, Wiltshire SN9 6BE

www.army.mod.uk
Tel: 0845 7300 111

The Undergraduate Army Placement offers undergraduates a course that includes compulsory work experience, gaining life experience as an officer without any obligation to join the Army on completion of the placement.

Bierrum International Ltd
Bierrum House, High Street, Houghton Regis
Dunstable, Bedfordshire LU5 5BJ

www.bierrum.co.uk
Tel: +44 (0) 1582 845 745
Fax: +44 (0) 1582 845 746
Email: solutions@bierrum.co.uk

A civil engineering firm which takes one gap year student a year through YINI. You can also contact them direct for other short-term work.

Cadbury Schweppes plc
25 Berkeley Square,
London W1J 6HB

www.cadburyschweppes.com
Tel: +44 (0) 20 7409 1313
Fax: +44 (0) 20 7830 5200

Cadbury Schweppes places people on work experience in response to specific business needs. Contact the business units direct.

Demos

Third Floor, Magdalen House, 136 Tooley Street
London SE1 2TU

www.demos.co.uk
Tel: +44 (0) 845 458 5949
Fax: +44 (0) 20 7367 4201
Email: hello@demos.co.uk

Independent social policy think tank and charity (Reg No: 1042046) examining societal change and exploring public policy solutions. Internships available. Send CV and letter.

DialogueDirect Ltd

MacMillan House, 38 St Aldates,
Oxford, OX1 1BN

www.funjobs4u.co.uk
Tel: +44 (0) 8451 307 255
Fax: +44 (0) 1865 297529
Email: jobs@dialoguedirect.co.uk

Dialogue Direct are the UK's leading fundraising agency, with extensive national and international experience of face-to-face fundraising. Our high-street fundraisers recruit thousands of long-term supporters for our charity partners every week, these include: The British Red Cross, Amnesty International, Shelter and Mencap. We currently have two types of charity fundraising vacancies:

- Residential – fundraise across London
- Roaming – fundraise whilst travelling around the UK with accommodation and transport included. We are looking for hardworking, team-spirited people with excellent communication skills, and a passion for the causes we represent. This is an excellent opportunity if you are looking for an ethically paid gap year job, to launch your career in the charity sector, broaden your skills, and help generate millions of pounds for leading charities!

EMI Group plc

27 Wrights Lane, London W8 5SW

www.emicareers.com

See website for details.

Foreign & Commonwealth Office

King Charles Street,
London SW1A 2AH

www.fco.gov.uk
Tel: +44 (0) 20 7008 1500

See their website for more about careers and opportunities in the Diplomatic Service.

Future Publishing Ltd

Beauford Court, 30 Monmouth Street,
Bath, Somerset BA1 2BW

www.futurenet.com
Tel: +44 (0) 1225 442244
Fax: +44 (0) 1225 446019
Email: recruit@futurenet.co.uk

HSBC Holdings plc

8 Canada Square,
London E14 5HQ

www.hsbc.com
Tel: +44 (0) 20 7991 8888

Working in the UK | General companies

I Found Work Ltd
PO Box 2085,
Worthing, West Sussex BN12 9AB

www.ifoundwork.com
Tel: +44 (0) 870 419 1970
Fax: +44 (0) 870 419 1971
Email: enquiries@ifoundwork.com

IMI plc
Lakeside, Solihull Parkway,
Birmingham Business Park
Birmingham, Warwickshire B37 7XZ

www.imi.plc.uk
Tel: +44 (0) 121 717 3700

Email: info@imiplc.com

IMI operates a global graduate development programme and offers vacation work from June to September to penultimate year engineering (mechanical, electrical or manufacturing) students leading to possible sponsorship through the final year at university.

Modern Painters
3rd Floor, 52 Bermondsey Street,
London SE1 3UD

www.modernpainters.co.uk
Tel: +44 (0)20 7407 9246

Email: info@modernpainters.co.uk

Modern Painters magazine has a limited amount of internships in its sales and editorial departments. This could be a very good option if you are particularly artistic. The internships last for three months.

PGL Recruitment Team
Alton Court, Penyard Lane,
Ross-on-Wye, Herefordshire HR9 5GL

www.pgl.co.uk
Tel: +44 (0) 870 401 4411
Fax: +44 (0) 870 401 4444
Email: recruitment@pgl.co.uk

PGL runs activity holidays and courses for children. Each year the company employs over 2000 young people to work as instructors, group leader, catering and support staff at its centre in the UK, France and Spain.

PricewaterhouseCoopers
Southwark Towers, 32 London Bridge Street,
London SE1 9SY

www.pwc.com/uk/careers
Tel: +44 (0) 808 100 1500

The National Magazine Company Ltd
National Magazine House, 72 Broadwick Street,
London W1F 9EP

www.natmags.co.uk
Tel: +44 (0) 20 7439 5000
Fax: +44 (0) 20 7439 6886
Email: hr.recruitment@natmags.co.uk

The National Magazine Company runs many of the UK's leading magazines, including Esquire, Cosmo and Good Housekeeping. There is quite a lot of work experience available and it can all be accessed by their website.

Unilever plc
Unilever House,
Blackfriars, London EC4P 4BQ

www.ucmds.com
Tel: +44 (0) 20 7822 5252

Unipart
Unipart House,
Cowley, Oxfordshire OX4 2PG

www.unipart.co.uk
Tel: +44 (0) 1865 77 89 66

United Biscuits
Human Resources, Hayes Park, Hayes End Road
Hayes, Middlesex UB4 8EE

www.unitedbiscuits.co.uk
Tel: +44 (0) 20 8234 5000
Fax: +44 (0) 20 8734 5555

Although there are no gap year placements, sandwich (degree) students should contact the Graduate Resourcing Department for an updated list of placements.

Virgin Radio
Gareth & Alysia, Work Experience, Virgin Radio
1 Golden Square, London W1F 9DJ

www.virginradio.co.uk

Virgin Radio offers unpaid work experience for between two and four weeks. These places are hotly sought after and if you have any experience at all it will help a lot. Hospital radio is smiled upon, as is any other type of radio volunteer work.

Chapter 10
Volunteering UK

Brian, 33, went on a week's post-tsunami house-building project in Sri Lanka through his company HBOS's charitable foundation.

Volunteers had to raise money to contribute to the project if they wanted to go and the foundation then matched their contribution.

He said: "Our group of 20 volunteers was rotated round various building and decorating tasks during the week, including roofing, rendering, foundation filling and painting. Habitat for Humanity, and the organisation Community Challenge based in London laid on evening events to introduce us to the culture of the area, and to visit the people affected by the disaster. It was a real emotional roller coaster.

"I raised over £2000 for the Tsunami victims, and rather than worry about the funds being swallowed up in red tape or corrupt officialdom, I could see that a real difference was being made to the victims of such a horrific tragedy."

When he returned he said: "I was glad that I was going on a short holiday a week later because when I got back to the office I really felt like nothing we did at work was that important.

"I tried to remain professional of course, but after seeing the difference I could make to people's lives with a smile and some hammer bashing it was a bit tortuous to be faced with a mountain of spreadsheets or an I.T. problem."

"I kept daydreaming, wondering if the families we had visited would be happy with their new houses, and how long it would be until their neighbours were housed too."

"It was useful to test myself albeit for a short time, to see if I could actually handle the hard graft, or would be able to face the emotional elements of dealing with disadvantaged people, while knowing that my own life in the

UK is relatively stress free. I think that if I ever do have the resources to spend a year out, at least 50% of the time will be spent doing voluntary work."

"Since the project I have been keen to help out with other volunteering initiatives through work, including a recent trip to renovate a drugs rehabilitation centre in Edinburgh."

Volunteering UK

Volunteering doesn't have to be done in a developing country among the poorest on the planet to bring a sense of satisfaction.

There are many deserving cases right on your doorstep. You might also find that if you do voluntary work close to home it will make you more involved in your own community.

If you spend at least some of your **gap-**year doing something for the benefit of others here in the UK you'll still get both a satisfying sense of achievement and an opportunity to learn about other people as well as a lot about yourself.

Although the definition for 'voluntary work' is, strictly-speaking, work that you're not paid for, voluntary schemes (especially the government-inspired ones) will often pay you some 'pocket money' and may also give you free meals and accommodation. Each scheme varies in what it provides – there are no rules. The point is that these are not 'jobs'; what you will be doing is altruistic: helping someone or a specific cause, usually a charity, whether you're working directly with children with special needs or doing the office filing for a charity.

Volunteering can also be an opportunity to gain relevant work experience. If you know, for example, that you want a career in retail, a stint with Oxfam will teach you a surprising amount. Many charity shops recognise this and offer training. Or perhaps you could find yourself helping to develop a charity's website.

Below we list the contact details of a number of charities and organisations that are grateful for volunteers - go to **www.gap-year.com** for a direct link to their websites and emails. If you can't find anything that interests you here, then there are a number of organisations which place people with other charities or with a wide national network of their own - an internet search should give you a good list.

The following websites provide useful links and information about volunteering:

www.do-it.org.uk

www.ncvo-vol.org.uk

www.timebank.org.uk

www.vois.org.uk

You have nothing to lose and so much to gain!

Voluntary organisations

Barnabas Adventure Centres Head Office
Carroty Wood, Higham Lane,
Tonbridge, Kent TN11 9QX

www.barnabas.org.uk
Tel: +44 (0) 1732 366 766
Fax: +44 (0) 1732 366 767
Email: enquiries@barnabas.org.uk

Opportunities are available to assist in the practical running of the Barnabas Trust centres. Reg Charity No: 1107724

BREAK
Residential Volunteers' Co-ordinator,
Davison House, 1 Montague Road
Sheringham, Norfolk NR26 8WN

www.break-charity.org
Tel: +44 (0) 1263 822161
Fax: +44 (0) 1263 822181
Email: office@break-charity.org

BREAK charity has special care residential holiday/respite centres in Norfolk, offering children and adults with learning and physical disabilities week-long holiday breaks. Reg Charity No: 286650

BTCV
Sedum House, Mallard Way, Potteric Carr
Doncaster, Yorkshire DN4 8DB

www.btcv.org
Tel: +44 (0) 1302 388 883

Email: information@btcv.org.uk

BTCV runs working conservation holidays in the UK and in more than 25 countries abroad working in partnership with other organisations.

BTCV Scotland
Balallan House, 24 Allan Park,
Stirling, Stirlingshire FK8 2QG

www.btcv.org.uk
Tel: +44 (0) 1786 479697

Email: scotland@btcv.org.uk

BTCV Scotland provides all-year-round environmental volunteering opportunities for over 6000 people a year. No skills are required, just an interest in the environment and people. BTCV Scotland provides expenses for all regular volunteers, and accommodation for those working from the Inverness office.

Camphill Communities in the UK
55 Cainscross Road,
Stroud, Gloucestershire GL5 4EX

www.camphill.org.uk
Tel: +44 (0) 1453 753142
Fax: +44 (0) 1453 767469
Email: coworker@camphill.org.uk

Camphill is a worldwide network of communities dedicated to work and life with children, adolescents or adults with developmental and other disabilities.

Careforce
35 Elm Road,
New Malden, Surrey KT3 3HB

www.careforce.co.uk
Tel: +44 (0) 20 8942 3331
Fax: +44 (0) 20 8942 3331
Email: enquiry@careforce.co.uk

Each year Careforce recruits Christians aged 17 to 30 and places them at churches and community projects across the UK.

Central Scotland Forest Trust

Hillhouseridge, Shottskirk Road,
Shotts, Lanarkshire ML7 4JS

www.csct.co.uk
Tel: +44 (0) 1501 822 015

Email: enquiries@csft.co.uk

CSCT organises volunteers to help with ecological improvements in Central Scotland. Work includes fence repairing and path building.

Centre for Alternative Technology

Machynlleth, Powys SY20 9AZ

www.cat.org.uk
Tel: +44 (0) 1654 705 950
Fax: +44 (0) 1654 702782

The Centre for Alternative Technology (CAT) runs one-week programmes throughout the summer, as well as a full-time 'long term volunteer' (LTV) programme which usually lasts for six months. Anyone can apply to be an LTV but those with specific skills and experience to offer have a head start (biology, building, engineering, gardening, information, media, publications and site maintenance).

Children's Country Holidays Fund

Head Office, 42-43 Lower Marsh,
London SE1 7RG

www.childrensholidays-cchf.org
Tel: +44 (0) 20 7928 6522
Fax: +44 (0) 20 7401 3961
Email: helen.cchf@staffordhouse.org.uk

The Children's Country Holidays Fund (registered charity number 206958) provides holidays for London children who would otherwise not get one. Volunteers are required to be activity holiday camp supervisors in the summer school holidays. Training is provided and all travel, board and accommodation costs are met.

Children's Trust

Tadworth Court,
Tadworth, Surrey KT20 5RU

www.thechildrenstrust.org.uk
Tel: +44 (0) 1737 365000
Fax: 0) 1737 365001
Email: rturner@thechildrenstrust.org.uk

The Children's Trust run a residential centre for about 80 severely disabled children, and is currently expanding. Volunteers help with the day-to-day needs of the children.

Churchtown Outdoor Adventure Centre

Churchtown, Lanlivery,
Bodmin, Cornwall PL30 5BT

www.vitalise.org.uk/
Tel: +44 (0) 1208 872 148
Fax: +44 (0) 1208 873 377
Email: mwarren@vitalise.org.uk

The Churchtown Outdoor Adventure Centre is an activity holiday centre for people of all ages, many disabled. Volunteers stay for a minimum of one month, looking after the visitors and helping with activities; you get pocket money and board.

Conservation Volunteers Northern Ireland
Beech House, 159 Ravenhill Road,
Belfast, County Antrim BT10 0BP

www.cvni.org
Tel: +44 (0) 28 906 45169
Fax: +44 (0) 28 906 44409
Email: cvni@btcv.org.uk

Conservation Volunteers, part of BTCV, provides all-year-round volunteering opportunities on a broad range of practical environmental projects across Northern Ireland.

CSV (Community Service Volunteers) www.csv.org.uk/Volunteer/Full-time/
237 Pentonville Road,
London N1 9NJ

Tel: +44 (0) 800 374 991

Email: volunteer@csv.org.uk

CSV is the largest volunteering organisation in the UK. CSV's full time volunteering programme provides hundreds of free gap year placements at social care projects throughout the UK. Placements are away from home and last for 4-12 months with accommodation, food (or a food allowance of £36.50 p/wk) and pocket money of £30 p/wk provided, along with out-of-pocket expenses such as travel costs. No specific qualifications or experience are required. The types of placements available are wide ranging but could include supporting people with disabilities to live independently, mentoring young offenders, helping in schools and supporting homeless people.

Friends of The Earth
26-28 Underwood Street,
London N1 7JQ

www.foe.co.uk
Tel: +44 (0) 20 7490 1555
Fax: 0) 20 7490 0881
Email: info@foe.co.uk

ENVIRONMENT:

Committed to raising awareness of global enviromental issues Friends of The Earth welcome volunteers at their head office in London, or at any of their regional offices. Work may involve administrative work – from helping with mailouts and press cuttings to research and information gathering. Wherever possible, FoE aim to identify specific roles providing opportunity for the development and acquisition of skills.

HiPACT
PO Box 770, York House, Empire Way
Wembley, Middlesex HA9 0PA

http://hipact.sentral.co.uk
Tel: +44 (0) 208 900 1221
Fax: 0) 208 900 0330
Email: hipact@hipact.ac.uk

TEACHING:

HiPACT is an association of British Universities which aims to widen participation in higher education. It offers opportunities to volunteer both in the UK and abroad. In the UK you could help at one of the summer schools run each year at various universities throughout the country. The summer schools are attended by students from schools that rarely send their pupils on to higher education. As a current undergraduate or recent graduate, you could help lead workshops on career choice, self-confidence or overcoming difficulties.

ILA (Independent Living Alternatives)
Trafalgar House, Grenville Place,
London NW7 3SA

www.ILAnet.co.uk
Tel: +44 (0) 20 8906 9265
Fax: +44 (0) 20 8959 1910
Email: enquiry@ILAnet.co.uk

Independent Living Alternatives (ILA) was established in May 1989 and promotes the right to independence and freedom of disabled people.

- ILA aims to enable people who need personal assistance, to be able to live independently in the community and take full control of their lives and thereby have individuality and spontaneity.

- ILA establishes the necessary personal assistance as a direct part of an individual's life to enable disabled people to have direct control over their own lives.

- ILA is managed by disabled people who are personal assistance users.

 **L'ARCHE**

L'Arche
GY07, Freepost BD 3209,
Keighley, West Yorkshire BD20 9BR
   Email: info@larche.org.uk

www.larche.org.uk
Tel: +44 (0) 800 917 1337
Fax: +44 (0) 1535 656426

L'Arche (French for 'The Ark') is an international movement with 130 communities in over 30 countries. It aims to provide local communities – a cluster of houses, usually within walking distance of each other and with access to a workshop – for adults with learning disabilities. The work could be weaving, for example, or making candles. Volunteer assistants are 'welcome to share life with those who need help to learn' both in communities in the UK and abroad. To volunteer abroad you need to contact communities direct; L'ARCHE can supply you with a list of their communities worldwide.

Millennium Volunteer Programme
Youth Volunteering Team,
Department for Education and Skills,
Room E4C, Moorfoot
Sheffield, West Yorkshire S1 4PQ

www.mvonline.gov.uk
Tel: +44 (0) 870 000 2288

Email: millennium.volunteers@dfes.qsi.gov.uk

Launched in 1999 for 16- to 24-year olds the Millennium Volunteer programme is still going strong. The idea is that you volunteer your time to help others, doing something you enjoy.

NSPCC

West House, 42 Curtain Road,
London EC2A 3NH

www.nspcc.org.uk
Tel: +44 (0) 20 7825 2500
Fax: +44 (0) 20 7825 2525

COMMUNITY, CHILDREN, FUNDRAISING, OFFICE WORK:

Volunteers can either do (primarily) fundraising work in their local area (see your local branch for details), or office work at head office in London. Reg Charity No: 216401

Rainforest Concern

8 Clanricarde Gardens,
London WC2 4NA

www.rainforestconcern.org
Tel: +44 (0) 20 7229 2093
Fax: +44 (0) 20 7221 4094
Email: info@rainforestconcern.org

FUNDRAISING Rainforest Concern has office work placements in London to help in the fundraising department. Ideally volunteers should be able to work for longer than two months. Rainforest Concern also runs a scheme with Quest Overseas sending volunteers to projects in Ecuador and Costa Rica to help in the construction of rainforest corridors.

RSPB (Royal Society for the Protection of Birds)

The Lodge,
Sandy, Bedfordshire SG19 2DL

www.rspb.org.uk/volunteering
Tel: +44 (0) 1767 680 551
Fax: +44 (0) 1767 683262
Email: volunteers@rspb.org.uk

Conservation/Environment Working holidays from one to four weeks on 39 sites around the UK. Good experience towards a career in conservation. Reg Charity No: 207076

SHAD

5 Bedford Hill,
Wandsworth, London SW12 9ET

www.shad.org.uk
Tel: +44 (0) 20 8675 6095
Fax: +44 (0) 20 8673 2118
Email: info@shad.org.uk

COMMUNITY, SOCIAL CARE:

Volunteers needed in London! Are you aged over 18 years, with 4 months (or more) to spare? Personal Assistants are needed to enable physically disabled adults to live independently in their own homes.

Student Volunteering England

Oxford House, Derbyshire Street,
London E2 6HG

www.studentvol.org.uk/
Tel: 0800 0182 146

Email: info@studentvolunteering.org.uk

The Blackie

Great Georges Community Cultural Project,
Great George Street,
Liverpool,
Lancashire L1 5EW

www.theblackie.org.uk
Tel: +44 (0) 151 709 5109
Fax: +44 (0) 151 709 4922
Email: gamesforthe21stcentury@theblackie.org.uk

The Blackie, one of Britain's longest-running community cultural projects, invites volunteers for innovative projects - co-operative games, publications, youth arts - home and touring. Accommodation available.

The Monkey Sanctuary Trust

Looe, Cornwall PL13 1NZ

www.monkeysanctuary.org
Tel: +44 (0) 1503 262 532

Email: info@monkeysanctuary.org

Monkey Sanctuary provides a home to a colony of Amazonian woolly monkeys and rescued ex-pets. Volunteers help all year round, making monkey food, cleaning enclosures, helping serve the public in the summer, and maintenance and other projects in the winter. Volunteers do not work directly with the monkeys.

The National Trust for Scotland

Wemyss House, 28 Charlotte Square,
Edinburgh, Midlothian EH2 4ET

www.nts.org.uk
Tel: +44 (0) 131 243 9300
Fax: +44 (0) 131 243 9301
Email: information@nts.org.uk

CONSERVATION, ENVIRONMENT:

The National Trust for Scotland is a conservation charity (No: SCO07410) that protects and promotes Scotland's natural and cultural heritage for present and future generations to enjoy. Contact them to find out about volunteering opportunities.

The Shaftesbury Society

16 Kingston Road,
London SW19 1JZ

www.shaftesburysoc.org.uk
Tel: +44 (0) 845 330 6033
Fax: +44 (0) 20 8239 5580
Email: info@shaftesburysoc.org.uk

COMMUNITY, CARING:

The Shaftesbury Society provides care and education services for people with physical and learning disabilities, and support for people who are disadvantaged or on a low income. Contact them direct for volunteering opportunities.

The Simon Community

Office F2, 89-93 Fonthill Road,
London N4 3JH

www.simoncommunity.org.uk
Tel: +44 (0) 20 7561 8270
Fax: +44 (0) 20 7619 3589
Email: info@simoncommunity.org.uk

COMMUNITY:

The Simon Community is a partnership of homeless people and volunteers living and working with London's street homeless. They need full-time residential volunteers all year round. This is a real challenge which offers work experience in many areas, especially if you intend to work professionally with vulnerable people. Volunteers need to be 19+, and to commit for between six months to two years. Pocket money, time off, paid leave and training are provided.

Time for God Training

Chester House, Pages Lane,
Muswell Hill, London N10 1PR

www.timeforgod.org
Tel: +44 (0) 20 8883 1504
Fax: +44 (0) 8365 2471
Email: office@timeforgod.org

Time for God co-ordinates national and international projects, including youth and community work, homeless and rehabilitation projects.

UNICEF (United Nations Childrens Fund)

Africa House, 64-78 Kingsway,
London WC2B 6NB

www.unicef.org.uk
Tel: +44 (0) 20 7405 5592
Fax: +44 (0) 20 7405 2332

UNICEF campaigns and sets up initiatives to promote better health, education and sanitation for children around the world. It normally has two or three volunteers working in its main office at any one time, and local offices will always need help: apply to them direct.

Vitalise

12 City Form, 250 City Road,
London ECIV 8AF

www.vitalise.org.uk
Tel: +44 (0) 845 345 1792
Fax: +44 (0) 845 345 1978
Email: info@vitalise.org.uk

Vitalise runs centres providing holiday and respite opportunities for people with disabilities and their carers. Volunteers are welcomed and needed, and will receive accommodation and board.

Volunteer Reading Help

Charity House, 14-15 Perseverance Works,
38 Kingsland Road
London E2 8DD

www.vrh.org.uk
Tel: +44 (0) 20 7729 4087
Fax: +44 (0) 20 7729 7643
Email: info@vrh.org.uk

VRH is a national charity (No: 296454) that helps primary school children who find reading a struggle. Training takes 6 hours and volunteers work with the same children every week, giving at least an hour of their time.

Whizz-Kidz

Elliott House, 10-12 Allington Street,
London SWIE 5EH

www.whizz-kidz.org.uk
Tel: +44 (0) 20 7233 6600
Fax: +44 (0) 20 7233 6611
Email: info@whizz-kidz.org.uk

Whizz-Kidz aims to improve the lives of disabled under-18s by providing wheelchairs, trikes, walking aids and so on. Contact them direct to find out about overseas challenge events such as climbing Kilimanjaro or walking the Great Wall of China.

Young People's Trust for the Environment and Nature Conservation

43 South Street,
South Petherton, Somerset TA13 5AE

www.yptenc.org.uk
Tel: +44 (0) 1460 249 163

Email: ypteinfo@btconnect.com

The Young People's Trust for the Environment and Nature Conservation provides free lectures and information to local schools in Surrey, Dorset and the Lake District. Contact them direct if you would like to help them with some of your time and energy.

Youth Hostel Association

Trevelyan House,
Matlock, Derbyshire DE4 3YH

www.yha.org.uk
Tel: +44 (0) 1629 592 600
Fax: +44 (0) 1629 592 702
Email: recuitment@yha.org.uk

The YHA has 230 Youth Hostels around the country and needs volunteers to help with running them and maintaining the local environment and paths, as well as fundraising.

Chapter 11
Re-entry

It only takes a week on a project to shake up your thinking, as HBOS manager Joe, 34, found out when he did a week with the finance group's Foundation in Galle, Sri Lanka, helping build homes for tsunami survivors who had lost everything.

Before becoming a HBOS manager Joe had worked for 7 years in the construction industry in Africa and S Asia, but he said this experience was completely different.

He went just 6 months after the tsunami and issues about fair and even-handed aid distribution between the local authorities and the larger aid organisations were still being thrashed out, but the small charity HBOS was linked with was able to avoid much of that and get on with the practical.

He had been sceptical about how much good going out there for a week would do. But he found hard physical work using building skills without any of the technology available in the West and working with local people changed all that.

His verdict? "I think everything we did was worthwhile."

On their return he and many colleagues found they'd been as profoundly affected as people taking a longer time out would have been: "I couldn't face going into the office on the Monday morning." Elsewhere a branch manager who'd been on the project walked into his branch on the first day and "burst into tears". Many other colleagues had reported feeling tearful, he said.

"It's a combination of the intensity of the work – it felt like a month rather than a week – and the absurdity of existence over here; all the unnecessary stuff. You start to question just how much of what we do is absolutely necessary."

A couple of his colleagues have now taken longer career breaks and more have talked about it and shelved but not abandoned the idea as they gradually returned to "normal" life.

Joe summed up the experience: "It's qualitatively different. How you feel about yourself, what you learn, the intensity of the relationships you form and more than anything the impact when you come home."

visit: www.gap-year.com

Re-entry

You expected a last jolt to your system when you started all this didn't you?

Well, maybe you didn't, but we've talked to enough people who've taken a **gap-** to know a kind of reverse culture shock takes hold within a few days of your return home. Returning to ordinary life takes time.

It doesn't matter when you took your **gap-** you're likely to still go through the same sequence of feelings over the three-months it generally takes to readjust.

How you respond will, though, depend on what you are returning to – if you went between school and uni you might find yourself switching courses or storing up something else to explore later. Or you might be quite content to take up your course with renewed enthusiasm after a travelling break from study.

Coming back from a properly-structured **gap-** immediately after uni is a great addition to a cv, but you already knew that when you used this guidebook to help you plan it, didn't you?

It's different again for people mid-career or over-50 mature travellers, but the pattern of adjustment is pretty much the same.

Kate, 31, returned from her second **gap-** in April 2006. She'd done one immediately post uni and then took a career break at age 30 so she's clocked up a total of three years covering N America, NZ, Australia & SE Asia, and, on her latest trip, S America.

She said: "Both times, I planned to come back in Spring so that the weather should be good."

"It was nice to come back & see friends and family. But also there's the realisation that absolutely nothing had changed at home. Two years is very little in the lives of normal working people – you have to remember not to talk about travelling too much as they don't understand and get irritated with 'when I was in…, we did/saw, etc.'

Mark, 25, worked for two years and completed a Masters degree before taking a year out to travel and explore South America (Peru, Bolivia, Chile, Argentina), New Zealand, Australia, Singapore, Malaysia, Thailand, Vietnam, Cambodia and Pakistan. Though mostly travelling he worked in New Zealand to top up funds to continue his travels, then helped out at a refugee camp in Pakistan after the earthquake.

After he returned, he said: "I felt lost and emotionally flat. I returned around Christmas and after seeing friends and family over the holiday period, reality struck home, no money, no job and nothing to do. I desperately wanted to go back on the road. In fact I still long to move to NZ and I definitely plan to do some more long-term trips abroad."

Minesh, 32, **gap-**year.com's online diarist for 2005-06 returned in March 2006 after a year's globe trotting. He described feeling very disoriented and "speedy" for the first ten days or so. Sensibly he had a list of things to do – keeping in touch with and arranging meetings with people he met on his travels, catching up with friends and the like.

Chetal, 22, was on a **gap-** for six months before taking up a graduate trainee job with a law firm: "The last week of my travels, I was counting down the days until I returned home; I couldn't wait! I was longing for my home comforts, seeing my family and friends and most of all sleeping in my bed.

"I had a grin from ear to ear when I returned, I was on such a high from my travels it was unreal. I was on cloud nine. So many stories and tales had accrued from the last 6 months of my life, memories that would be with me for a lifetime. I could not wait to share my experiences."

Judith, 42, went to Tanzania to teach 11-14 year-olds for three months. This is her account of her first few days back: "I felt like an alien at first – a sense of disgust at our material world – it was hard going into supermarkets and seeing how easily people buy things. I felt ashamed at having so many possessions, which I didn't really need. Have still not really got into watching TV. I missed the human contact, which I had out there – so much value was placed on your interaction with people. When I came back to London it was so obvious how most people just get on with their own lives and often don't bother to even make eye contact with others."

Prepare for crash-landing

To start with, the body's decelerating but the brain's still on the move - a common phenomenon and one our career-breaker diarist, Minesh, certainly reported.

Chetal's experience also confirms that the length of time you've been away makes no difference to the feelings you go through on your return and even after 6 months or less you still need time to adjust.

After the first three weeks of initial euphoria and sharing be prepared to come down to earth with a bump.

At around that point Minesh reported feeling flat as reality started to intrude and with it the realisation that he had to bite the bullet and start serious job hunting. Then the football world cup intervened and that was a great distraction for a footie fanatic!

Here's Chetal, again:

"Before long reality struck! My friends had warned me that it would not be long until my feet touched the ground. Three weeks into my return, it had dawned on me, I had just had the adventure of a lifetime and now I was back at home. There is no feeling quite like it, I keep thinking about my next trip to keep me going!"

It seems to take about three months on average between stepping off that last plane after a **gap-** and getting back into life's routines.

Kate returned in April 2006 and she too spent the first three months re-adjusting. This is what she said three months after she got back: "I could have stayed away another year if I wanted but one year seemed enough. Probably should work after that length of time anyway. I wanted to work in the same field as I was doing before – and will apply for those jobs soon."

Judith said it took her two months at least to feel comfortable again, and: "I knew I would need to get a job and earn some money. I started looking for a permanent job in teaching but in the meantime did some supply teaching – a real shock after the experience of teaching 60+ pupils in a class in Tanzania with no behavioural problems!"

What do you do now?

This one depends on what you had planned before you left and whether the option's still there – and you still want to do it – once you're back.

Taking time out:

Several people advise that, if you can manage it, putting aside some money for about three months of living expenses for your return as part of pre-**gap-** preparations takes off the pressure if you're going to be job hunting.

As we've already seen, Kate and Minesh both allowed themselves some leeway before picking up the threads of pre-**gap-** life.

While he was on the move, Minesh kept up to date with former colleagues and with developments in the IT fields he worked in before his one-year **gap-**.

Family commitments meant he didn't seriously start job-hunting for about three months after his return, but his "on the road networking" meant he had options and offers to consider. He only really got seriously stuck into the job hunt in mid-late July 2006.

Chetal, on the other hand, had it all sorted before she left:

"Before I went travelling, I knew what I was doing for the next four years of my life. After travelling I have been working, then I have London to look forward to. I will be studying for my Legal Practice Course for a year to enable me to practise as a solicitor. In 2007, I have a training contract for a law firm for two years and after that, who knows. So far so good. I have managed to stick to my original plans."

Her view? "Just remember, if you fail to plan, you plan to fail!"

No time for time out? Don't panic!

If you already have work to go back to you may have to combine the post trip elation with a fairly quick return to the "rat race".

You'll need to think about how you interact with your colleagues. How much do you say about your trip?

A spokeswoman from Halifax Group (HBOS), which supports its staff in taking time out and also has a foundation on whose projects they can do voluntary work, had this advice:

"When you are returning to work it is important to have a plan. Returning to work after 18 weeks or more can prove difficult on both a psychological and logistical level.

"Keep your line manager up to date with the timings of your return to work. This will ensure that they can factor you into their resource planning and also help you integrate back into the working environment.

"Do not rule out a degree of retraining when you return to work. Refreshing your skills will benefit most people in the work place, and, if you have been away from work for a long period of time, you should use the opportunity to familiarise yourself with new systems, procedures and practices.

"When you return to work take into consideration reverse culture shock. Whilst you might be keen to talk about your travels for many months to come, your colleagues may not be so keen to listen."

If the need to start earning soon after your return is an issue but you were not able to take a year out from your old job and took the plunge anyway, or you've come back unsettled and thinking in terms of a career change, Sarah Reynolds, operations manager at Reed Executive, the recruitment agency, has some words of advice:

"If you feel lost when you return home and you really don't know which direction your career is going in, it is always a good idea to consider temporary work.

"You can usually secure a temporary job quite quickly, which will help to keep your funds healthy, and temporary work is flexible enough that you will be able to take time to look around the market place, apply for permanent positions and find one that you really fancy.

"The danger is that you will be desperate for some money and therefore take the first job you're offered – temping takes away that feeling of 'panic' and allows you some time to weigh up your options."

BT also offers support to returning career breakers. A spokesman said: "Line managers and HR can offer support to individuals returning from a career break, helping them to settle back into working life in the UK. This is particularly important if someone has been out of the western world for some time as it can be quite an adjustment to return to the UK."

How is it now? Deciding what next...

While taking up the threads of life, on you've no doubt been trying to process everything you've learned from your **gap-** experience.

How do you feel? What's changed? What's been confirmed? Where to now? Is there something new you want to do next as a result? How to go about it?

You'll almost certainly still be in touch with friends you made on your travels, maybe even had a couple of after **gap-** reminiscence meetings. Others may still be travelling and keeping you restless!!

You may also still be in touch with the projects you worked on. It's a fairly common feeling to want to keep a link to something that's been a life-changing, learning experience. Is this you?

Chetal: "The experience has altered the way I look at things in life. No longer

am I pre-occupied with the smaller things in life, rather I have an appreciation and real understanding of the world as it is today. I know it sounds rather cliché, but travelling has made me a bigger and better person."

"My year out was meant to provide me with an insight into different cultures. It was primarily a backpacking experience, but we did do some work experience (legal work in Gujarat) and voluntary work (working in an orphanage that looks after homeless children with disabilities and Aids in Kenya) along the way."

Here's Mark: "I gained the skills to navigate myself around strange places with new people using little money and being confident in new situations.

"I really realised how people around the world are so much worse off than Europeans and how politically the world is a messed up place. But inspite of this people everywhere are overwhelmingly friendly, welcoming and helpful wherever you go."

Judith: "I would like to think it has changed the way I look at things but I have to work at keeping hold of the experience and remind myself by looking at my photos of the school, the area and the family I lived with. It has made me more aware of what is really important in life – the things that money can't buy.

"I start a new job in September and ironically am going to work in the Private sector which I have never done before and never thought I would – I have decided I want to teach pupils who *want* to learn and I don't want to be in an aggressive or hostile environment which I think is sadly all too often the case in state schools."

Good advice from gappers

The best piece of advice on dealing with the consequences of any life-changing experience is to be patient, give it time. Nothing but time can make things settle into some kind of perspective and help you work out whether you are in the grip of a sudden enthusiasm or something deeper and more long-lasting.

The first reaction most people report is that it's whetted their appetites to hit the road again.

It's certainly given Chetal the urge to travel again. She said: "I am planning a trip to South America in the next five years – that should give me enough time to polish up on my Spanish!"

Mark, too, hankers to be on the move: "I still long to move to NZ and I definitely plan to do some more long-term trips abroad."

As a second string while job-hunting in his former field of work, Minesh toyed with the idea of working as a tour guide in Latin America, a place he fell in love with and wanted to explore further, but at the time of writing had not taken it to the stage of serious planning – though, ever efficient, he does have contact numbers and names if he should choose to do so later.

Here's Kate's reflection on taking a **gap-** : "Do it. Don't put it off, do it now.

"Make sure that you are doing it for the right reason. There seemed to be a lot of lost souls who were running away from reality at home rather than going travelling for positive reasons. The problems will still be there when they get back home, and in many cases putting them off will only make things worse.

"If there is nobody to go with, go alone. I did and made many more friends because of it. However, I would advise not trekking alone as some of the places are very remote and I didn't pass another person all day."

Chetal too: "You cannot be prepared for everything, expect the worst and then nothing will seem so bad when it happens. Do it while you can, it is the opportunity of a lifetime. Once you have experienced it once you will be hooked."

And Judith: "Now when I look back I wish I had planned to stay for longer in Tanzania – I think 6 months would have been really good.

"Go for it!! Have an open mind when you go and be prepared for anything but throw yourself in as a human being and you can't go wrong."

Change of direction?

In time you'll know whether your urge to travel has also become an urge to keep the links with the communities you visited now you're back.

What level of involvement do you want? Is it going to be something local like fundraising – doing local talks, letters to newspapers – or are you seriously looking to change career?

If you have come back with the germ of an idea for a career change as a result of a volunteer placement, for example, there's nothing to stop you slowly exploring the options and possibilities.

Have a look at your CV. Try to talk to people working in the field you're considering moving into.

Armed with some basic information you could also consider talking through issues like what transferable skills you have to add to your volunteer experience, what training you might need and how affordable it is with a, careers counsellor or recruitment specialist – preferably with an organisation that specialises in aid/charity or NGO positions.

Try this link. It's the "not for profit sector" of totaljobs.com:

http://www.totaljobs.com/IndustrySearch/NotForProfitCharities.aspx

There's a wealth of information about how to go about working in the aid and not for profit sectors on:

http://www.support4learning.org.uk/jobsearch/voluntary_work__voluntary_organisations__ngos__gap_year.cfm

and it also has links to recruitment sites like:

http://www.charitynet.org/

http://www.charitypeople.co.uk/

http://peopleandplanet.org/ethicalcareers/

To keep you going you should also never underestimate the power of synchronicity. You may find unexpected connections and information come your way while you're getting on with other things.

If it's meant to be, you'll find ways to make it happen.

And finally

Here are some last words of wisdom on coping with your return from Anthony Lunch, MD of Mondo Challenge, specialists in volunteer placements for young gappers, career breakers and mature travellers.

"Returning to a normal life after a gap year can sometimes be just as much of a challenge as the **gap-** itself!

"Initially most people are busy catching up with family, friends and colleagues, with lots of opportunity to share their experiences. Also, when you first return, depending on what you did whilst you were away, you may be preoccupied with enjoying some of the home comforts that you missed on your travels - a hot shower, cupboards full of food, a clean western toilet…!

"However as you settle back into your normal routine you may find that life feels a bit mundane and you miss the constant new experiences and stimulus that you were having on your **gap-**, but there are ways of easing this transitional period, and making sure that you reap the benefits of your experience."

Here are Anthony's suggestions:

• Make the most of everything you will have learnt. For example, if you have returned from a teaching placement, you may feel more confident about speaking in public than you did before your **gap-**. Talk to your manager about incorporating any new skills into your role.

• Ensure that your managers/employees are aware of what you have been doing. Giving a short presentation will help people understand that you haven't returned from a long holiday (anything but!). It will also showcase the benefits to you and your job, and you may even find that you inspire others to go on and do something similar.

• Write a short report on your time away, emphasising how it has helped you develop your skills. It might feel like you will never forget all the things you learnt and achieved, but putting it on paper while it is still fresh in your mind will prove useful a year or so down the line when you are applying for promotion or a new job.

• Keep helping! Many volunteer organisations support the project where you will have been working financially. In the case of MondoChallenge we also run the MondoChallenge Foundation so that we can back up the work of our volunteers by providing equipment, buildings and grants. Past volunteers are a fantastic source of money and support for this and raise funds through sponsored events, themed parties, and even just by pestering family and friends.

• Depending on which organisation you worked with, you may find that they organise reunions and/or fundraising events. This is a great chance to meet and share your experiences with other people who have done something similar to you.

• Keep in touch. Many volunteers keep in contact with friends and colleagues where they were working by email and letter. Some even go back for a short visit after a year or so. If you decide to this, contact the organisation that arranged your original placement – it may be that you could do something useful, even on a short visit.

• Go back for another stint! It might not be possible in the short term, but after a few years you may find yourself in the position where you could take some more time to do something different.

Appendices

Choosing a tutorial college

Standards vary and it's best to check out two or three colleges before you choose. Here are some things to check before you decide:

- Does the college get results? For the last few years *The Daily Telegraph* has regularly published a table in early September giving the average A level retake grade improvements at tutorial colleges.

- Does the college have a good reputation? Get references from former students – the college should be happy to supply you with contact names.

- Has the college been inspected by the Department for Education and Skills (DfES) or an independent body such as BAC (the British Accreditation Council for Independent Further and Higher Education) or CIFE (the Council for Independent Further Education?

- Does the college teach the right subjects?

- Does the college teach the same syllabus (*eg* OCR/French) that you studied at school?

- What time of year are the courses run? (this affects what you can do during the rest of your year out).

- Who will be teaching you? Check their qualifications and how familiar they are with the syllabus.

- Is the place up-to-date? near transport? does it have quiet study rooms and good facilities?

- What does it cost? What are the hourly rates?

- What do get for your money? How many hours of group teaching each week and how many one-to-one tutorials?

Please note: The information contained in these appendices is for guidance only. We would advise that you talk to your school or college examination officer, chosen university or exam board for up-to-the-minute advice and information.

1a Retakes

There are several reasons why you might find yourself considering retakes: maybe because your grades are too low to meet a conditional offer (and the university won't negotiate with you to admit you on lower grades), or because illness interfered with exams, for example.

But beware, getting better grades second time round doesn't guarantee you a university place – often unis will demand even higher grades if it's taken you two bites at the cherry (unless of course you've got a really good excuse, like illness).

Grade appeals

The now almost habitual media comment about the devaluation of A level marks has left many people wondering just how much we can trust exam results. If you really think you've been done down by a tired exam marker, a misleading or misprinted question or some other factor, you can appeal against your result.

You appeal first to the examination board that set the exam, and if you don't think the adjudication is just, you can go on to appeal to the Examination Appeals Board (EAB). Be warned: this process takes a long time and there's no guarantee the appeal will go your way.

Retake timing

Now that modular A levels are firmly entrenched you may be able to retake the modules you did badly in while you are still at school instead of having to retake them in your year out.

However, you need to check with both your exam board and chosen university before you make any plans.

Every exam board has its own timetable for retakes (see below for contact details) and universities too vary considerably in their regulations on retakes.

You need to make sure your chosen university course doesn't set higher entry grades for exams taken at a second sitting. And under the new A level system, retaking a module more than once is no longer allowed.

In some cases you may find that when you retake a certain exam you have to change exam board – this can be a problem in some subjects (eg languages

307

with set texts) and you may therefore have to resit your A levels a whole year after the original exams, which can seriously disrupt your **gap**-year. Check with your exam board as early as you can.

Tutorial colleges like to keep students working on A levels for a full year. That keeps the college full and tutors paid. But many agree that the best thing is to get resits over before work already done is forgotten. So the best timing, if you are academically confident and want to enjoy your **gap**-year, is to go to a tutorial college in September and resit the whole exam or the relevant modules in January – if sittings are available then.

Languages

If you have only language AS levels, A2 levels or A levels to retake, there are several options:

- Take an extra course or stay in the country of the relevant language and return to revise for a summer resit, choosing the same exam board (courses abroad, however, are not usually geared to A level texts).

- Check with tutorial colleges how much of your syllabus module or modules (the chosen literature texts are crucial) overlap with those of other exam boards. This may give you the chance to switch exam boards and do a quick retake in January.

- Cram for as long as necessary at a specialist language college. Some British tutorial colleges and language course organisers have links with teaching centres in France so it's worth checking this out before signing on.

Retake results

Those who sit A level retakes in January and get the grades needed for a chosen place will not have to wait until August for that place to be confirmed.

Examining boards will feed the result directly into UCAS so you will know your place has been clinched. A technicality, but comforting for **gap**-year students who want to go away.

And don't forget that if you have a firm choice conditional offer and you make the grades asked for, the university can't back out. It has an obligation to admit you.

A level examining boards

There are six A level examining boards: AQA (Assessment and Qualifications Alliance), Edexcel, IBO (International Baccalaureate Organization), OCR (Oxford, Cambridge & RSA), Northern Ireland (CCEA) and Wales (WJEC). All these boards now provide their exam timetables on the internet about nine months in advance: we've provided their details below, along with those of other exam-related organisations.

AQA (Assessment and Qualifications Alliance)
Stag Hill House,
Guildford, Surrey GU2 7XJ

www.aqa.org.uk
Tel: +44 (0) 1483 506506
Fax: +44 (0) 1483 300152

CCEA (Northern Ireland Council for the Curriculum, Examinations and Assessment)
Clarendon Dock, 29 Clarendon Road,
Belfast, County Antrim BT1 3BG

www.ccea.org.uk
Tel: +44 (0) 28 9026 1200
Fax: +44 (0) 28 9026 1234
Email: info@ccea.org.uk

EAB (Examination Appeals Board)
83 Piccadilly,
London, London W1J 8QA

www.theeab.org.uk
Tel: +44 (0) 20 7509 5995

This is the final court of appeal for exam grades. Centres and private candidates only go to the EAB if an appeal to the relevant examination board for an exam paper has failed. The EAB website has a notice board showing when appeals are going to be heard.

EDEXCEL
190 High Holborn,
London, London WC1V 7BH

www.edexcel.org.uk
Tel: +44 (0) 870 240 9800

IBO (International Baccalaureate Organization)
Route des Morillons 15, CH-1218,
Grand-Saconnex, GenevaFax: +41 22 791 0277

www.ibo.org
Tel: +41 22 791 7740

Email: ibhq@ibo.org

Central body for the development, administration and assessment of the International Baccalaureate Diploma Programme.

OCR (Oxford Cambridge & RSA Examinations)
1 Hills Road,
Cambridge, Cambridgeshire CB1 2EU

www.ocr.org.uk
Tel: +44 (0) 1223 553 998
Fax: +44 (0) 1223 552 627
Email: general.qualifications@ocr.uk

QCA (Qualifications and Curriculum Authority)
83 Piccadilly,
London, London W1J 8QA

www.qca.org.uk
Tel: +44 (0) 20 7509 5555
Fax: +44 (0) 20 7509 6666
Email: info@qca.org.uk

The QCA is the body that (along with the Qualifications, Curriculum and Assessment Authority for Wales: ACCAC) approves all syllabuses and monitors exams (grading standards, for example).

SQA (Scottish Qualifications Authority)
The Optima BUilding, 58 Robertson Street,
Glasgow, Lanarkshire G2 8DQ

www.sqa.org.uk
Tel: +44 (0) 845 279 1000
Fax: +44 (0) 845 213 5000
Email: customer@sqa.org.uk

Central body for the development, administration and assessment of Scottish qualifications, including Standard Grade, Highers, Advanced Highers, HNCs, HNDs and SVQs.

WJEC (Welsh Joint Education Committee)   www.wjec.co.uk
245 Western Avenue,   Tel: +44 (0) 29 2026 5000
Cardiff, Glamorgan CF5 2YX

The QCA is the body that (along with the Qualifications, Curriculum and Assessment Authority for Wales: ACCAC) approves all syllabuses and monitors exams (grading standards, for example).

You can get some basic explanations of the new A level system on its website, though much QCA information is aimed at teachers rather than those who are going to sit the exams.

Colleges accredited by BAC and CIFE

The following independent Sixth form and tutorial colleges offering A level tuition (one-year, two-year, complete retakes, modular retakes or intensive coaching) are recognised by the British Accreditation Council (BAC, Tel: 0207224 5474, **www.the-bac.org**) and/or the Council for Independent Further Education (CIFE, Tel: 020 8767 8666, **www.cife.org.uk**). Of course a college can have a good reputation and achieve excellent results without accreditation.

Abacus College (Oxford)	BAC	Tel:+44 (0) 1865 240 111
Abbey College Birmingham	BAC/CIFE	Tel:+44 (0) 121 236 7474
Abbey College Cambridge	BAC/CIFE	Tel:+44 (0) 1223 578 280
Abbey College London (SW1)	BAC/CIFE	Tel:+44 (0) 20 7824 7300
Abbey College Manchester	BAC/CIFE	Tel:+44 (0) 161 817 2700
Acorn Independent College (Southall)	CIFE	Tel:+44 (0) 20 8571 9900
Albany College (London, NW4)	BAC/CIFE	Tel:+44 (0) 20 8202 5965
Ashbourne Independent Sixth Form College, (London W8)	BAC/CIFE	Tel:+44 (0) 20 7937 3858
Bales College (London W10)	BAC/CIFE	Tel:+44 (0) 20 8960 5899
Basil Paterson Tutorial College (Edinburgh)	BAC	Tel:+44 (0) 131 225 3802
Bath Academy (Bath)	BAC	Tel:+44 (0) 1225 334 577
Bellerbys College (Hove)	BAC/CIFE	Tel:+44 (0) 1273 323374
Bosworth Independent College (Northampton)	BAC/CIFE	Tel:+44 (0) 1604 239 995

Brampton College (London NW4)	BAC	Tel:+44 (0) 20 8203 5025
Brooke House College (Market Harborough)	BAC/CIFE	Tel:+44 (0) 1858 462 452
Cambridge Arts and Sciences (Cambridge)	BAC	Tel:+44 (0) 1223 314 431
Cambridge Centre for Sixth Form Studies (Cambridge)	CIFE	Tel:+44 (0) 1223 716 890
Cambridge Seminars (Cambridge)	BAC	Tel:+44 (0) 1223 313 464
Cambridge Tutors College (Croydon)	BAC/CIFE	Tel:+44 (0) 20 8688 5284
Cardiff Academy (Cardiff)	CIFE	Tel:+44 (0) 29 2040 9630
Cherwell College (Oxford)	BAC/CIFE	Tel:+44 (0) 1865 242 670
College of International Education (Oxford)	BAC	Tel:+44 (0) 1865 202238
Collingham (London SW5)	BAC/CIFE	Tel:+44 (0) 20 7244 7414
Commonwealth College (London, E1)	BAC	Tel:+44 (0) 20 7247 8082
Concord College (Shrewsbury)	CIFE	Tel:+44 (0) 1694 731 631
David Game College (London W11)	BAC	Tel:+44 (0) 20 7221 6665
Davies, Laing & Dick (London, W1)	BAC	Tel:+44 (0) 20 7935 8411
Dean College (London N7)	BAC	Tel:+44 (0) 20 7281 4461
Duff Miller College (London SW7)	BAC/CIFE	Tel:+44 (0) 20 7225 0577
E F Brittin College (Torquay)	BAC	Tel:+44 (0) 1803 202 932
Ealing Independent College (London, W5)	BAC	Tel:+44 (0) 20 8579 6668
Exeter Tutorial College (Exeter)	BAC/CIFE	Tel:+44 (0) 1392 278 101
Harrogate Tutorial College (Harrogate)	BAC/CIFE	Tel:+44 (0) 1423 501 041
Holborn College (SE7)	BAC	Tel:+44 (0) 20 8317 6000
International College Britain (Edinburgh)	BAC	Tel:+44 (0) 131 315 7631
King's School, Oxford	BAC	Tel:+44 (0) 1865 711 829

Kingsbridge College of Management & Technology (London, N1)	BAC	Tel:+44 (0) 20 7923 7466
Lansdowne College (London W2)	BAC/CIFE	Tel:+44 (0) 20 7616 4400
London College, Wimbledon (London, SW19)	BAC	Tel:+44 (0) 20 8417 1185
London School of Management (London W5)	BAC	Tel:+44 (0) 20 8567 4355
London School of Science & Technology (Wembley)	BAC	Tel:+44 (0) 870 414 0004
Mander Portman Woodward (Birmingham)	BAC/CIFE	Tel:+44 (0) 121 454 9637
Mander Portman Woodward (London SW7)	BAC/CIFE	Tel:+44 (0) 20 7835 1355
Mander Portman Woodward (Cambridge)	BAC/CIFE	Tel:+44 (0) 1223 350 158
Modes Study Centre (Oxford)	BAC/CIFE	Tel:+44 (0) 1865 245 172
Oxford Business College (Oxford)	BAC	Tel:+44 (0) 1865 791 908
Oxford Tutorial College (Oxford)	BAC/CIFE	Tel:+44 (0) 1865 793 333
Padworth College (Reading)	BAC/CIFE	Tel:+44 (0) 118 983 2644
Pinnacle International College (London, N15)	BAC	Tel:+44 (0) 20 8826 5911
Rayat London College (Heston)	BAC	Tel:+44 (0) 20 8754 3330
Regent College (Harrow)	BAC/CIFE	Tel:+44 (0) 20 8966 9900
Rochester Independent College (Rochester)	BAC	Tel:+44 (0) 1634 828 115
St Andrew's (Cambridge)	BAC	Tel:+44 (0) 1223 360 040
St Andrew's (London, SE19)	BAC	Tel:+44 (0) 20 8653 7285
St Dominic's (London, SE1)	BAC	Tel:+44 (0) 20 7378 9061
Stafford House College (Canterbury)	BAC	Tel:+44 (0) 1227 866 540
Sterling College (London, NW2)	BAC	Tel:+44 (0) 20 8830 7555

Surrey College (Guildford)	BAC/CIFE	Tel:+44 (0) 1483 565 887
The Abbey College (Malvern)	BAC	Tel:+44 (0) 1684 892300
Tudor College (London, WC1H)	BAC	Tel:+44 (0) 20 7837 8382
Wentworth Tutorial College (London NW11)	BAC	Tel:+44 (0) 20 8458 8524

1A

Appendix | 1A

the gap-year guidebook 2007

The number of students taking up university and college places in Autumn 2005 was the highest ever, according to annual figures released by UCAS. The total number of applications rose in 2005 to 522,155 from 486,028 in 2004, which was up 7.4%. The figures for those accepted increased in a similar way from 377,544 in 2004 to 405,369 in 2005.

For some the decision to take a year off is made well in advance. Often they make the decision to defer their entry into higher education with specific projects in mind. In the 2005 UCAS application cycle there was a 9.2% increase in the number of applicants being accepted on a deferred entry basis to 2006, with 31,059 applicants representing 7.7% of the total number of acceptances. However, application figures in 2005 were undoubtedly inflated by the change in tuition fees facing those applying in 2006. Current UCAS figures for 2006 (up to July), as a result, show a 3.5% decrease in the numbers of students applying (17,184).

Some students choose not to apply at all until after their A level results. Others find themselves taking a **gap**-year at much shorter notice once they receive their grades. If they have not met the conditions of the offers they are holding then a **gap**-year can allow them to reassess their plans. Equally those who have done better than expected can use the time to aim for something they had originally considered beyond them.

Application process

UCAS (the Universities and Colleges Admissions Service) handles applications to all UK universities (except the Open University) as well as to most other institutions that offer full-time undergraduate higher education courses. This includes applications for Oxford, Cambridge and for degrees in medicine, dentistry and veterinary science/medicine, although they have to be in earlier than for other universities and colleges and for other subjects.

UCAS	**www.ucas.com**
Rosehill,	Tel: 0870 1122211
New Barn Lane,	
Cheltenham GL52 3LZ	

If you have hearing difficulties, you can call RNID the Typetalk service on 18001 0870 1122211 from within the UK or on +44 151494 1260 from outside the UK. There is no extra charge for this service. Calls are charged at normal rates.

UCAS offers a distribution service to companies who wish to send promotional material to students. UCAS handles the distribution itself and does not pass on your personal details, which remain confidential. If you prefer not to receive this kind of material however, you can opt out when completing

315

your UCAS application.

You can apply for six different courses at any UCAS institution, except for medical courses A100, A101, A102, A103, A104, A106, dentistry courses: A200, A203, A204, A205, A206 and veterinary science courses: D100, D101 for which you can make just four choices. If you are using the 'two-track' application procedure for art and design courses you can use up to three of your choices in Route B. If you are applying for art and design through Route B, you can still only apply to a maximum of six choices overall. The different combinations that you can use are listed on the UCAS website. You can hold on to two of the offers you get: one 'firm (first) choice' and one 'insurance (second choice) place'. So you may have to be cautious about the courses you pitch for.

Online application

UCAS has a secure, web-based application system called Apply. Each school, college, careers agency or British Council Office that has registered with UCAS to use Apply appoints a coordinator who manages the way it is used. For students, registering to the new system takes a few minutes and costs nothing. Once a student has registered, they are given a username and are asked to choose a password that they will need to use each time they want to access their application. Applicants can use this system anywhere that has access to the web. The service works in tandem with the online course search service. Check out the UCAS website for more information at www.ucas.com

Students who are not at a school or college also make their applications online using a different pathway of the Apply system. Individual applicants cut and paste in a reference which has been sent to them and send the completed application together with payment to UCAS themselves.

A level results

A level results come out in mid-August. Depending on your grades one of the following will happen:

• Firm (first) choice uni confirms offer of a place

• Insurance (second choice) uni confirms offer of a place

• Clearing

• Retakes

Before you make any decisions make sure you know all the angles: retakes may be the only way for you to get to university, but most universities will demand even higher results the second time around, an expectation confirmed by Glasgow university: "We expect slightly higher requirements if you don't get good enough grades in one A level attempt".

The UCAS Tariff

The UCAS Tariff was first used for those applying to enter HE in 2002. Since its introduction it has expanded to cover additional qualifications. It is a points-based system, which establishes agreed equivalences between different types of qualifications. It provides admissions tutors with a way of comparing applicants with different types and volumes of achievement.

UCAS is keen to encourage all universities and colleges to use the Tariff to make the application system more uniform across the country. Three quarters of universities and colleges now use the Tariff, but some admissions tutors choose to make offers in terms of grades.

More information and a copy of the latest Tariff is available at

http://www.ucas.com/candq/tariff/index.html

There is also a tariff calculator online to help you work out the value of your qualifications.

QUALIFICATION	GRADE	POINT SCORE
A2, Scottish Advanced Higher	A	120
and Vocational A level*	B	100
	C	80
	D	60
	E	40
Note: there is no grade E in Scottish Advanced Higher,		
AS Level and	A	60
Vocational AS level	B	50
	C	40
	D	30
	E	20
Scottish Higher	A	72
	B	60
	C	48
	D	42

Key dates

In 1999 and 2000, UCAS met with universities and colleges to agree a number of changes to the UCAS application system. The last two, Extra and Invisibility of Choices, were put in place for 2003 entry.

This is what will happen if you apply for a university course starting in autumn 2006 or deferred entry to 2007 so if you are thinking of taking a **gap**-year you'll need to know that:

- The main deadline for applications for all universities (except Oxford, Cambridge, Medicine, Dentistry, Veterinary Medicine or Veterinary Science courses and Route B Art and Design programmes) is 15 January.

- There is a 'commitment to clear, transparent admissions policies'. Universities include 'Entry Profiles' on their own and UCAS' websites to tell students about entry requirements, including skills, personal qualities, or experience not necessarily connected with academic qualifications.

- Extra has been designed for applicants who have been considered at all six of their choices, but who do not have a place. Extra allows them to make additional choices through UCAS, one at a time. The service runs from mid-March to the end of June, so you won't have to wait until Clearing to find a place. If you are eligible for Extra, UCAS will tell you how to refer your application using the Track service on its website to a university or college with vacancies.

- 'Invisibility of choices' means that universities and colleges cannot see which other universities or colleges a student has applied to until that applicant has replied to an offer or goes into UCAS Extra.

The autumn term is when Year 13 students usually begin to apply for university and college places through the UCAS system (though some super-organised schools and students start preparations in the summer of Year 12).

The information you need for applying to university or college is online at www.ucas.com where an up-to-date list of courses is always available.

Here are some key dates:

- University open days organised from spring each year.

- Applications for 2007 entry which include any Oxford or Cambridge choices or any Medicine courses: A100, A101, A102, A103, A104, A106, Dentistry courses: A200, A203, A204, A205, A206 or Veterinary Science courses: D100, D101 must be at UCAS by 15 October 2006.

- Other applications for 2007 entry (except Route B applications for art and design courses: see How to Apply) should be sent to UCAS by 15 January 2007 at the latest but early application is advised.

- When your application is received UCAS contacts you stating your choices, and application number. If there seems to be a mistake, call UCAS immediately, quoting your application number.

Universities and colleges start to notify UCAS of their decisions for 2007 entry after October 2006. Applicants receive decisions via UCAS (interview, unconditional offer, conditional offer or unsuccessful application).

You should reply to offers by the deadline given when you receive all your university decisions from UCAS.

- UCAS has two main deadlines. 15 January is the initial closing date. Applications received after 15 January are marked 'late'. After 15 January the university or college you have applied to does not guarantee that it will consider your application. 30 June is the final closing date. Applications received after this date go straight into Clearing.

- A level results will be published on Thursday, 16 August 2007.

318

- Note that UCAS advises that applicants should confirm their acceptance of an offer of a university place as quickly as possible.

- After the A level results are released, UCAS automatically notifies all applicants about clearing who have who have missed their grades and have been turned down, who have not received offers earlier in the year, who have declined all offers made to them, who have applied after the final closing date 'late' (see above), or who haven't found a place using Extra.

- A list of vacancies for degrees, HNDs and other undergraduate courses is published on the UCAS website at www.ucas.com as soon as results are released. This on-line vacancy service is updated several times a day. Vacancy listings are also published by some of the national daily newspapers from A level results day.

Clearing closes at the end of September.

Track

The Track facility on the UCAS website enables those who have applied not only to check the progress of their application, but also to reply to offers online, to cancel choices from which they no longer wish to hear and even to change their address for correspondence. It is an invaluable tool for managing an application, but particularly useful to those who apply during a **gap**-year and are overseas when important decisions are being made.

Deferred entry, rescheduled entry, or post A level application?

There are three ways to handle university entrance if you want to take a **gap**-year. The safest is usually to apply for deferred entry, but not all courses accept deferred entry candidates.

Our advice is to talk to the admissions office before making a decision about taking a **gap**-year.

For more information visit **www.dfes.gov.uk/studentsupport**, or contact your LEA.

1 Deferred entry

- Check first with the appropriate department of the university you want to go to that they are happy to take students after a **gap**-year. If it's a popular course, preference may go to the current year applications.

- On your UCAS application there is a specific 'Defer entry' column in the key 'Courses' section. Click in the 'Defer entry' box for all (or some) of the courses you apply for, having checked that they will still be available a year later. Talk to your teachers first and follow instructions in How to Apply.

- If you are planning to take a **gap**-year, you will need to explain why in your Personal Statement on the UCAS application. You need to convince the university that a year off will make you a better applicant, so give an outline of what you plan to do and why.

- Send your completed application to UCAS, like any other student applying

319

for entry without taking a **gap**-year. Those who do so well before the 15 January deadline, however, may be among the first to start receiving replies (via UCAS). You will get a call for selection interview(s), a rejection or an offer which is conditional on getting specific A level grades or total point score.

- From the 15 January deadline to 30 June, UCAS will forward 'late' applications to universities 'for consideration at their discretion'. Applications received after 30 June go straight into Clearing.

- NOTE: Some academics are not happy with deferred entry because it means it might be nearly two years before you reach higher education. During that time a course may have changed, or you may have changed. So your application may be looked on unfavourably without you knowing why. Most departments at many universities are in favour of a **gap**-year but they are not all in favour of deferred entry. If they interview you in November 2006 for a place in October 2008 it will be 23 months before they see you again. Check it out with the university department first.

2. Deferring entry after you have applied

If you apply for a place in the coming university year and after A level results decide to defer, you can negotiate direct with the university or college at which you are holding a place.

NOTE: Some admissions tutors say that to give up a place on a popular course is risky, because the university will not be happy after you have messed them about. Others say that if a course has over-recruited, your deferral will be welcome. Tread carefully.

3. Post A level applications

If you take A levels in June 2007, you can still apply through UCAS after the results come out in August. You will go straight into Clearing. If you do not send in a UCAS application before the end of the 2007 entry cycle, (20 September 2007) you should apply – between 1 September 2007 and 15 January 2008 - for entry in the following year.

Universities and colleges will not accept those who do not apply through UCAS. Those who ring up at the last minute to try to get a place will either be told how to apply via the normal UCAS application or given a Record of Prior Acceptance form if the university is sure it wants to accept.

Faculty check: all subjects

If you want to take a **gap**-year, remember (before you apply) to contact the appropriate department or faculty at the university you would like to go to, and find out if they approve of a **gap**-year or not. Prepare a good case for it before you phone. It is advisable to do this even if you are an absolutely outstanding candidate, because on some courses a year off is considered a definite disadvantage. This is usually the case where a degree course is very long or requires a large amount of remembered technical knowledge at the start.

320

Art and design

Applying through UCAS to your chosen college of Art and Design might involve applying by two different routes (Route A and Route B). You must make your Route A application by 15 January and your Route B application between 1 January and 24 March. You can apply to only three Route B choices. When you send off your UCAS form with your Route A choices, remember to indicate that you intend to apply through Route B as well, so that you can make route choices later.

Medicine, dentistry and veterinary science/medicine

If you hope to pursue a career in medicine, dentistry or veterinary science/medicine, you can use no more than four (of your possible six) choices in any one of those three subject areas. The courses involved are:

Medical courses: A100, A101, A102, A103, A104, A106

Dentistry courses: A200, A203, A204, A205, A206

Veterinary Science/Medicine courses: D100, D101

Don't forget that UCAS must receive ALL applications for these courses by 15 October.

Foundation degrees

The Foundation Degree (not to be confused with a foundation year), started in autumn 2001. It is a two-year 'vocational' degree – in other words, a degree in work-related subjects like computing or business studies rather than purely academic subjects. Students (of any age) do work experience as part of the course, and the degree will be convertible to an honours degree by adding further study afterwards. This makes getting a degree more flexible, and adds another opportunity to take a **gap-**year – you could take a Foundation Degree, then have a **gap-**year, then restart studies later to convert your Foundation Degree into a full Honours Degree.

Financing Your Studies

Most Students apply to the Students Loans Company www.slc.co.uk for a loan and the amount received depends on their family's income.

Loans don't have to be paid back until your income reaches £15,000 a year before tax. Repayments are linked to salary.

A new Higher Education Grant of up to £1,000 a year is available to new students from lower-income families and some grant assistance is also be available to those whose families earn up to £20,000.

Applications are made through your local education authority (LEA) and should be made early (certainly before July). Your LEA will assess how much you get depending on your family's income.

Useful reading

You can get booklets on student loans and on financial support for higher education students from your LEA, or **www.dfes.gov.uk/studentsupport**, or by calling 0800 731 9133

Bursaries, scholarships and sponsorship

Many organisations still offer sponsorship to students to study for a degree. This is sometimes on condition that they join the sponsoring company or institution for a period when they graduate. The Army is one example from the public sector, information is available on **http://www.armyjobs.mod.uk /RegularArmy/Grants/EducationAndGrants/HigherEducation/**

If you're looking for sponsorship, The Year in Industry improves your chances and removes the need to write endless letters go to www.yini.org.uk, or you may be interested in the offer from the Smallpeice Trust **www.smallpeicetrust.org.uk** (Tel: 01926 333200).

Anglia Ruskin University	www.anglia.ac.uk Tel: +44 (0) 845 271 3333
Aston University	www.aston.ac.uk Tel: +44 (0) 121 204 3000
Bath Spa University	www.bathspa.ac.uk Tel: +44 (0) 1225 875 875
Bournemouth University	www.bournemouth.ac.uk Tel: +44 (0) 1202 524 111
Brunel University, West London	www.brunel.ac.uk Tel: +44 (0) 1895 274 000
Buckinghamshire Chilterns University College	www.bcuc.ac.uk Tel: +44 (0) 1494 522 141
Canterbury Christ Church University	www.canterbury.ac.uk Tel: +44 (0) 1227 767 700
City University, London	www.city.ac.uk Tel: +44 (0) 20 7040 5060
Coventry University	www.coventry.ac.uk Tel: +44 (0) 2476 88 76 88
Cranfield University	www.cranfield.ac.uk Tel: +44 (0) 1234 750 111
De Montfort University	www.dmu.ac.uk Tel: +44 (0) 116 255 1551
Durham University	www.durham.ac.uk Tel: +44 (0) 191 334 2000
Edge Hill University	www.edgehill.ac.uk Tel: +44 (0) 1695 575 171
Glasgow Caledonian University	www.caledonian.ac.uk Tel: +44 (0) 141 331 3000
Heriot-Watt University	www.hw.ac.uk Tel: +44 (0) 131 449 5111
Institute for System Level Integration	www.sli-institute.ac.uk Tel: +44 (0) 506 469 3000

Keele University	www.keele.ac.uk Tel: +44 (0) 1782 621 111
Kingston University	www.kingston.ac.uk Tel: +44 (0) 20 8547 2000
Lancaster University	www.lancs.ac.uk Tel: +44 (0) 1524 65201
Leeds College of Music	www.lcm.ac.uk Tel: +44 (0) 113 222 3400
Leeds Metropolitan University	www.leedsmet.ac.uk Tel: +44 (0) 113 283 2600
Liverpool Hope University	www.hope.ac.uk Tel: +44 (0) 151 291 3000
Liverpool John Moores University	www.ljmu.ac.uk Tel: +44 (0) 151 231 2121
London Metropolitan University	www.londonmet.ac.uk Tel: +44 (0) 20 7423 0000
London South Bank University	www.lsbu.ac.uk Tel: +44 (0) 20 815 7815
Loughborough University	www.lboro.ac.uk Tel: +44 (0) 1509 263 171
Manchester Metropolitan University	www.mmu.ac.uk Tel: +44 (0) 161 247 2000
Middlesex University	www.mdx.ac.uk Tel: +44 (0) 20 8411 5000
Napier University	www.napier.ac.uk Tel: +44 (0) 500 353 570
Newcastle University	www.ncl.ac.uk Tel: +44 (0) 191 222 6000
Northumbria University	www.northumbria.ac.uk Tel: +44 (0) 191 232 6002
Nottingham Trent University	www.ntu.ac.uk Tel: +44 (0) 115 941 8418
Oxford Brookes University	www.brookes.ac.uk Tel: +44 (0) 1865 741 111
Queen Margaret University College	www.qmuc.ac.uk Tel: +44 (0) 131 317 3000

visit: www.gap-year.com

Queen's University Belfast	www.qub.ac.uk Tel: +44 (0) 28 9024 5133
Roehampton University	www.roehampton.ac.uk Tel: +44 (0) 20 8392 3000
Royal College of Art	www.rca.ac.uk Tel: +44 (0) 20 7590 4444
Royal College of Music	www.rcm.ac.uk Tel: +44 (0) 20 7589 3643
Sheffield Hallam University	www.shu.ac.uk Tel: +44 (0) 114 225 5555
Southampton Solent University	www.solent.ac.uk Tel: +44 (0) 23 8031 9000
Staffordshire University	www.staffs.ac.uk Tel: +44 (0) 1782 294 000
Thames Valley University	www.tvu.ac.uk Tel: +44 (0) 118 967 5000
The Arts Institute at Bournemouth	www.aib.ac.uk Tel: +44 (0) 1202 533 011
The Liverpool Institute for Performing Arts	www.lipa.ac.uk Tel: +44 (0) 151 330 3000
The Open University	www.open.ac.uk Tel: +44 (0) 870 333 4340
The Robert Gordon University	www.rgu.ac.uk Tel: +44 (0) 1224 262 000
The University of Birmingham	www.bham.ac.uk Tel: +44 (0) 121 414 3344
The University of Bolton	www.bolton.ac.uk Tel: +44 (0) 1204 900 600
The University of Edinburgh	www.ed.ac.uk Tel: +44 (0) 131 650 1000
The University of Greenwich	www.gre.ac.uk Tel: +44 (0) 20 8331 8000
The University of Hull	www.hull.ac.uk Tel: +44 (0) 1482 346 311
The University of Manchester	www.manchester.ac.uk Tel: +44 (0) 161 306 6000

The University of Northampton	www.northampton.ac.uk Tel: +44 (0) 1604 735500
The University of Nottingham	www.nottingham.ac.uk Tel: +44 (0) 115 951 5151
The University of Reading	www.reading.ac.uk Tel: +44 (0) 1189 875 123
The University of Sheffield	www.sheffield.ac.uk Tel: +44 (0) 114 222 2000
The University of Strathclyde	www.strath.ac.uk Tel: +44 (0) 141 552 4400
The University of Winchester	www.winchester.ac.uk Tel: +44 (0) 1962 841515
Trinity College of Music	www.tcm.ac.uk Tel: +44 (0) 20 8305 4444
UCE Birmingham	www.uce.ac.uk Tel: +44 (0) 121 331 5000
University College for the Creative Arts	
• Canterbury	www.ucreative.ac.uk Tel: +44 (0) 1227 817302
• Epsom	www.ucreative.ac.uk Tel: +44 (0) 1372 728811
• Farnham	www.ucreative.ac.uk Tel: +44 (0) 1252 722441
• Rochester	www.ucreative.ac.uk Tel: +44 (0) 1634 888702
University of Aberdeen	www.abdn.ac.uk Tel: +44 (0) 1224 272 000
University of Abertay Dundee	www.abertay.ac.uk Tel: +44 (0) 1382 308 000
University of Bath	www.bath.ac.uk Tel: +44 (0) 1225 388 388
University of Bradford	www.bradford.ac.uk Tel: +44 (0) 1274 232 323
University of Brighton	www.brighton.ac.uk Tel: +44 (0) 1273 600 900
University of Bristol	www.bristol.ac.uk Tel: +44 (0) 117 928 9000

visit: www.gap-year.com

University of Buckingham	www.buckingham.ac.uk Tel: +44 (0) 1280 814 080
University of Cambridge	www.cam.ac.uk Tel: +44 (0) 1223 337 733
University of Central Lancashire	www.uclan.ac.uk Tel: +44 (0) 1772 201 201
University of Chester	www.chester.ac.uk Tel: +44 (0) 1244 375444
University of Chichester	www.ucc.ac.uk Tel: +44 (0) 1243 816000
University of Derby - Derby	www.derby.ac.uk Tel: +44 (0) 1332 590 500
University of Dundee	www.dundee.ac.uk Tel: +44 (0) 1382 344 000
University of East Anglia	www.uea.ac.uk Tel: +44 (0) 1603 456 161
University of East London	www.uel.ac.uk Tel: +44 (0) 20 8223 3333
University of Essex	www.essex.ac.uk Tel: +44 (0) 1206 873 333
University of Exeter	www.exeter.ac.uk Tel: +44 (0) 1392 661 000
University of Glamorgan	www.glam.ac.uk Tel: +44 (0) 144 3828 812
University of Glasgow	www.gla.ac.uk Tel: +44 (0) 141 330 2000
University of Gloucestershire	www.glos.ac.uk Tel: +44 (0) 8707 210 210
University of Hertfordshire	www.herts.ac.uk Tel: +44 (0) 1707 284 800
University of Huddersfield	www.hud.ac.uk Tel: +44 (0) 1484 422 288
University of Kent	www.kent.ac.uk Tel: +44 (0) 1227 764 000
University of Leeds	www.leeds.ac.uk Tel: +44 (0) 113 243 1751

| University of Leicester | www.le.ac.uk |
| | Tel: +44 (0) 116 252 2522 |

| University of Lincoln | www.lincoln.ac.uk |
| | Tel: +44 (0) 1522 882 000 |

| University of Liverpool | www.liv.ac.uk |
| | Tel: +44 (0) 151 794 2000 |

| University of London (contact colleges directly) | www.london.ac.uk |
| | Tel: +44 (0) 20 7862 8360 |

- Barts and The London — www.mds.qmw.ac.uk
  Tel: +44 (0) 20 7377 7611

- Birkbeck College — www.bbk.ac.uk
  Tel: +44 (0) 845 601 0174

- Courtauld Institute of Art — www.courtauld.ac.uk
  Tel: +44 (0) 20 7848 2777

- Goldsmith's College — www.goldsmiths.ac.uk
  Tel: +44 (0) 20 7919 7171

- Heythrop College — www.heythrop.ac.uk
  Tel: +44 (0) 20 7795 6600

- Imperial College — www.imperial.ac.uk
  Tel: +44 (0) 20 7589 5111

- Institute in Paris — www.bip.lon.ac.uk
  Tel: +33 1 44 11 73 73

- King's College London — www.kcl.ac.uk
  Tel: +44 (0) 20 7836 5454

- London School of Hygiene and Tropical Medicine — www.lshtm.ac.uk
  Tel: +44 (0) 20 7636 8636

- Queen Mary — www.qmul.ac.uk
  Tel: +44 (0) 800 376 1800

- Royal Academy of Music — www.ram.ac.uk
  Tel: +44 (0) 20 7873 7373

- Royal Free and University College Medical School — www.ucl.ac.uk/medicalschool
  Tel: +44 (0) 20 7679 2000

- Royal Holloway, — www.rhul.ac.uk
  Tel: +44 (0) 1784 434 455

- School of Pharmacy — www.pharmacy.ac.uk
  Tel: +44 (0) 20 7753 5800

- School of Slavonic
  and East European Studies
  www.ssees.ac.uk
  Tel: +44 (0) 20 7679 8801

- St George's
  www.sgul.ac.uk
  Tel: +44 (0) 20 8672 9944

- The Institute of Education
  www.ioe.ac.uk
  Tel: +44 (0) 20 7612 6000

- The London School of Economics
  and Political Science
  www.lse.ac.uk
  Tel: +44 (0) 20 7405 7686

- The Royal Veterinary College
  www.rvc.ac.uk
  Tel: +44 (0) 20 7468 5000

- The School of Oriental
  and African Studies
  www.soas.ac.uk
  Tel: +44 (0) 20 7637 2388

- University College London
  www.ucl.ac.uk
  Tel: +44 (0) 20 7679 2000

University of Luton	www.luton.ac.uk Tel: +44 (0) 1582 734 111
University of Oxford	www.ox.ac.uk Tel: +44 (0) 1865 270 000
University of Paisley	www.paisley.ac.uk Tel: +44 (0) 141 848 3000
University of Plymouth	www.plymouth.ac.uk Tel: +44 (0) 1752 600 600
University of Portsmouth	www.port.ac.uk Tel: +44 (0) 2392 84 84 84
University of Salford	www.salford.ac.uk Tel: +44 (0) 161 295 5000
University of Southampton	www.soton.ac.uk Tel: +44 (0) 23 8059 5000
University of St Andrews	www.st-andrews.ac.uk Tel: +44 (0) 1334 476 161
University of Stirling	www.stir.ac.uk Tel: +44 (0) 1786 473 171
University of Sunderland	www.sunderland.ac.uk Tel: +44 (0) 191 515 2000
University of Surrey	www.surrey.ac.uk Tel: +44 (0) 1483 300 800

University of Sussex	www.sussex.ac.uk Tel: +44 (0) 1273 606 755
University of Teesside	www.tees.ac.uk Tel: +44 (0) 1642 218 121
University of the West of England, Bristol	www.uwe.ac.uk Tel: +44 (0) 117 965 6261
University of Ulster	www.ulster.ac.uk Tel: +44 (0) 8 700 400 700
University of Wales (contact colleges directly)	www.wales.ac.uk Tel: +44 (0) 29 2038 2656

• University of Wales - Cardiff University www.cardiff.ac.uk
Tel: +44 (0) 29 2087 4000

• University of Wales - North East Wales Institute www.newi.ac.uk
of Higher Education Tel: +44 (0) 1978 290 666

• University of Wales - Royal Welsh College www.rwcmd.ac.uk
of Music and Drama Tel: +44 (0) 29 2034 2854

• University of Wales - www.sihe.ac.uk
Swansea Institute of Higher Education Tel: +44 (0) 1792 481 000

• The University of Wales, Aberystwyth www.aber.ac.uk
Tel: +44 (0) 1970 623 111

• University of Wales - www.trinity-cm.ac.uk
Trinity College Carmarthen Tel: +44 (0) 1267 237 971

• University of Wales College, Newport www.newport.ac.uk
Tel: +44 (0) 1633 430 088

• University of Wales Institute, Cardiff www.uwic.ac.uk
Tel: +44 (0) 29 2041 6070

• University of Wales, Bangor www.bangor.ac.uk
Tel: +44 (0) 1248 351 151

• University of Wales, Lampeter www.lamp.ac.uk
Tel: +44 (0) 1570 422 351

• University of Wales, Swansea www.swansea.ac.uk
Tel: +44 (0) 1792 205 678

University of Warwick	www.warwick.ac.uk Tel: +44 (0) 2476 523 523
University of Westminster	www.wmin.ac.uk Tel: +44 (0) 20 7911 5511

University of Wolverhampton	www.wlv.ac.uk
	Tel: +44 (0) 1902 321 000
University of Worcester	www.worcester.ac.uk
	Tel: +44 (0) 1905 855 000
University of York	www.york.ac.uk
	Tel: +44 (0) 1904 430 000

Once you have chosen where you want to go, whether one country or a dozen, do some research. It would be a shame to travel to the other side of the world and then miss what it has to offer. There are loads of websites giving interesting and useful factual advice (weather, geographical, political, economic) as well as those that are more touristy.

Foreign Office warnings

It's worth bearing in mind that economic and political situations can change rapidly in countries, so check with the Foreign and Commonwealth Office that the country is still safe to travel to before you go. There's a link to their website on **www.gap-year.com**. It's important to look at the lists of specific areas which travellers should avoid. It's also worth noting the phone numbers of all British embassies and consulates in areas where you may be travelling in case you need to contact them for help.

Telephone or email home regularly to save your family a lot of worry and British embassies a lot of wasted time. Just to give you a taste, the following pages contain data for individual countries: make sure you check with the FCO for up-to-date information.

Afghanistan

- Population: estimated to be 28 million (UNHCR 2004)
- Location: South Asia
- Capital: Kabul
- Currency: Afghani (AFN)
- Religion: mainly Sunni Muslim, Shi'a Muslim
- Languages: Farsi (Dari), Pashtu (Pashto or Pukhto), Turkic languages (primarily Uzbek and Turkmen), 30 minor languages (primarily Balochi and Pashayi), also Tajiki and Eastern Farsi, much bilingualism
- British Embassy, Kabul: +93 (0) 70 102 000

Albania

- Population: estimated to be 3.5 million
- Location: South-east Europe
- Capital: Tirana
- Currency: Lek (ALL)
- Religion: Sunni Muslim, Albanian Orthodox, Roman Catholicism
- Languages: Albanian (Tosk is the official dialect), Greek
- British Embassy, Tirana: +355 4 2 34973/4/5

333

Algeria

- Population: 32 million
- Location: North Africa
- Capital: Algiers
- Currency: Algerian Dinar (DZD)
- Religion: Sunni Muslim, Christianity, Judaism
- Language: Arabic (official language), French and Amazigh
- British Embassy, Algiers: +213 21 23 00 68

Andorra

- Population: 67,159
- Location: South-west Europe
- Capital: Andorra la Vella
- Currency: Euro (EUR)
- Religion: Roman Catholicism
- Language: Catalan (official), French, Spanish
- British Consulate-General, Barcelona: +34 933 666 200

Angola

- Population: 14.3 million (2005 estimate)
- Location: Southern Africa
- Capital: Luanda
- Currency: Kwanza (AOA)
- Religion: Indigenous beliefs, Roman Catholicism, Christianity, Muslim
- Language: Portuguese (official), local African languages
- British Embassy, Luanda: +244 (222) 334582

Antigua and Barbuda

- Population: 75,000 (Census 2001 Estimates) including about 1,200 Montserratians living in Antigua.
- Location: Caribbean
- Capital: Saint John's City
- Currency: East Caribbean dollar (XCD)
- Religion: Anglican, Moravian, Methodist and Roman Catholicism
- Language: English
- British High Commission, St John's: +1 268 462 0008/9

visit: www.gap-year.com

Argentina

- Population: 36.2 million
- Location: Southern South America
- Capital: Buenos Aires
- Currency: Peso (ARS)
- Religion: Roman Catholicism, Protestant, Judaism and Muslim
- Language: Spanish
- British Embassy, Buenos Aires: +54 (11) 4808 2200

Armenia

- Population: 3.2 million
- Location: South-west Asia
- Capital: Yerevan
- Currency: Dram (AMD)
- Religion: Armenian Orthodox
- Language: Armenian, Russian
- British Embassy, Yerevan: +374 (10) 264 301

Australia

- Population: 20.2 million
- Location: Australasia
- Capital: Canberra
- Currency: Australian dollar (AUD)
- Religion: Christianity, Buddhism, Judaism, Muslim
- Language: English, Aboriginal
- British High Commission, Canberra: +61 (2) 6270 6666

Austria

- Population: 8.2 million
- Location: Central Europe
- Capital: Vienna
- Currency: Euro (EUR)
- Religion: Roman Catholicism, Muslim and Protestant
- Language: German
- British Embassy, Vienna Tel: +43 (1) 716 130

Azerbaijan

- Population: 8.3 million
- Location: South-west Asia

the gap-year guidebook 2007

- Capital: Baku
- Currency: Manat (AZM)
- Religion: Muslim, Russian Orthodox, Armenian Orthodox,
- Language: Azeri, Russian, Armenian
- British Embassy, Baku: +994 (12) 497 5188/89/90

Bahamas

- Population: 303,770 (2006 estimate)
- Location: Caribbean, chain of islands in the North Atlantic Ocean
- Capital: Nassau
- Currency: Bahamian Dollar (BSD)
- Religion: Baptist, Anglican, Roman Catholicism, Methodism, Church of God, Evangelical Protestants
- Language: English, Creole (among Haitian immigrants)
- refer to British High Commission, Kingston, Jamaica: +1 (876) 510 0700

Bahrain

- Population: 666,442 (including Expatriate residents)
- Location: Middle East
- Capital: Manama (Al Manamah)
- Currency: Bahraini Dinar (BHD)
- Religion: Muslim
- Language: Arabic, English
- British Embassy, Manama: +973 1757 4100;
  +973 1757 4167 (Information Hot-Line);
  +973 3960 0274 (Emergency Number)

Bangladesh

- Population: 135 million (2003 estimate)
- Location: South Asia
- Capital: Dhaka
- Currency: Taka (BDT)
- Religion: Muslim, Hinduism, Buddhism, Christianity
- Language: Bangla, English
- British High Commission, Dhaka: +880 (2) 882 2705

Barbados

- Population: 272,400 (2004)
- Location: Caribbean
- Capital: Bridgetown

visit: www.gap-year.com

- Currency: Barbados Dollar (BBD)
- Religion: Protestant, Roman Catholicism, Judaism, Muslim
- Language: English
- British High Commission, Bridgetown: +1 (246) 430 7800

Belarus
- Population: 9.8 million (2004 estimate)
- Location: Eastern Europe
- Capital: Minsk
- Currency: Belorusian Ruble (BYR)
- Religion: Eastern Orthodox Christian, Roman Catholicism, Protestant, Judaism, Muslim
- Language: Belorusian, Russian
- British Embassy, Minsk: +375 (17) 210 5920/1

Belgium
- Population: 10.25 million
- Location: Central Europe
- Capital: Brussels
- Currency: Euro (EUR)
- Religion: Roman Catholicism, Protestant
- Language: Dutch, French, German
- British Embassy, Brussels: +32 (2) 287 6211

Belize
- Population: 291,600 (2005)
- Location: Central America
- Capital: Belmopan
- Currency: Belizean Dollar (BZD)
- Religion: Roman Catholicism, Protestant, Muslim, Buddhism, Hinduism, Bahá'í
- Language: English, Creole, Spanish
- British High Commission, Belmopan: +501 822 2146

Benin
- Population: 6.9 million
- Location: West Africa
- Capital: Porto-Novo
- Currency: CFA Franc BCEAO (XOF)

- Religion: Indigenous beliefs, Christianity, Muslim
- Language: French, Fon, Yoruba
- Community Liaison Officer, Contonou (consular emergencies only): +229 21 30 32 65
  British Ambassador, Abuja, Nigeria: +234 (9) 413 2010

Bhutan
- Population: estimated to be 600,000
- Location: South Asia
- Capital: Thimphu
- Currency: Ngultrum (BTN)
- Religion: Drukpa Kagyupa (Buddhism), Hinduism, Muslim, Christianity
- Language: Dzongkha
- UK has no diplomatic representative in Bhutan. Contact British Deputy High Commission, Kolkata (Calcutta), India: +91 33 2288 5172

Bolivia
- Population: 9 million (2004)
- Location: Central South America
- Capital: La Paz
- Currency: Boliviano (BOB)
- Religion: Roman Catholicism, Evangelical Methodism
- Language: Spanish, Quechua, Aymara
- British Embassy, La Paz: +591 (2) 243 3424

Bosnia and Herzegovina
- Population: 4 million
- Location: South-east Europe
- Capital: Sarajevo
- Currency: Convertible Mark (BAM)
- Religion: Roman Catholicism, Orthodox, Mulim
- Language: Bosnian, Serbian, Croatian
- British Embassy, Sarajevo Tel: +387 33 282 200

Botswana
- Population: 1.7 million
- Location: Southern Africa
- Capital: Gaborone
- Currency: Pula (BWP)
- Religion: Christianity, indigenous beliefs

visit: www.gap-year.com

- Language: English, Setswana
- British High Commission, Gabarone: +267 395 2481

Brazil
- Population: 182.1 million (2006)
- Location: Eastern South America
- Capital: Brasilia
- Currency: Reai (BRL)
- Religion: Roman Catholicism, Pentecostal, Animism
- Language: Portuguese
- British Embassy, Brasilia: +55 61 3329 2300

Brunei
- Population: 357,800 (2004 estimate)
- Location: South-east Asia
- Capital: Bandar Seri Begawan
- Currency: Brunei Dollar (BND)
- Religion: Muslim
- Language: Malay, English, Chinese
- British High Commission, Bandar Seri Begawan: +673 (2) 222 231

Bulgaria
- Population: 7.45 million
- Location: South-east Europe
- Capital: Sofia
- Currency: Leva (BRL))
- Religion: Bulgarian Orthodox, Muslim, Roman Catholicism, Judaism
- Language: Bulgarian
- British Embassy, Sofia: +359 (2) 933 9222

Burkina Faso
- Population: 13 million (2003 estimate)
- Location: West Africa
- Capital: Ouagadougou
- Currency: CFA Franc BCEAO (XOF)
- Religion: Animism, Muslim, Christianity, indigenous beliefs
- Language: French, tribal languages
- British Honorary Consul, Ouagadougou: +226 (50) 30 73 23

Burma

- Population: 52 million
- Location: North Africa
- Capital: Rangoon
- Currency: Kyat (MMK)
- Religion: Buddhism, Christianity, Muslim, Animism
- Language: Burmese
- British Embassy, Rangoon: +95 (1) 370 863

Burundi

- Population: 6.8 million
- Location: Central Africa
- Capital: Bujumbura
- Currency: Burundi Franc (BIF)
- Religion: Christianity, Muslim, indigenous beliefs
- Language: Kirundi, French, Swahili
- British Embassy, Liaison Office, Bujumbura: +257 827 602

Cambodia

- Population: 14.1 million (2003)
- Location: South-east Asia
- Capital: Phnom Penh
- Currency: Riel (KHR)
- Religion: Buddhism, Muslim
- Language: Khmer, Cambodian
- British Embassy, Phnom Penh : +855 23 427124; +855 23 428295

Cameroon

- Population: 16.3 million
- Location: West Africa
- Capital: Yaounde
- Currency: CFA Franc BEAC (XAF)
- Religion: Christianity, Muslim, indigenous beliefs
- Language: French, English
- British High Commission, Yaounde: +237 222 05 45; +237 222 07 96

Canada

- Population: 32.5 million (2006)
- Location: North America

visit: www.gap-year.com

- Capital: Ottawa
- Currency: Canadian Dollar (CAD)
- Religion: Roman Catholicism, Protestant
- Language: English, French
- British High Commission, Ottawa: +1 (613) 237 1530

Cape Verde
- Population: 511,000 (2005 estimate)
- Location: West Africa
- Capital: Praia
- Currency: Escudo (CVE)
- Religion: Roman Catholicism
- Language: Portuguese, Crioulo
- British Honorary Consulate, Sao Vincente: +238 232 2830; refer to British Embassy, Dakar, Senegal: +221 823 7392/9971

Central African Republic
- Population: 3.8 million
- Location: Central Africa
- Capital: Bangui
- Currency: CFA Franc BEAC (XAF)
- Religion: Christianity, Muslim, indigenous beliefs
- Language: French
- refer to British High Commission, Yaounde, Cameroon: +237 222 05 45; +237 222 07 96

Chad
- Population: 8.6 million (2002 estimate)
- Location: Central Africa
- Capital: N'Djamena
- Currency: CFA Franc BEAC (XAF)
- Religion: Muslim, Christianity, traditional beliefs
- Language: French, Arabic, Tribal languages
- refer to British High Commission, Yaounde, Cameroon: +237 222 05 45; +237 222 07 96

Chile
- Population: 15.8 million (2004 estimate)
- Location: Southern South America
- Capital: Santiago de Chile

- Currency: Peso (CLP)
- Religion: Roman Catholicism, Evangelical, Judaism, Muslim
- Language: Spanish, Mapuche, Aymara, Quechua
- British Embassy, Santiago: +56 (2) 370 4100

China

- Population: 1.29 billion
- Location: East Asia
- Capital: Beijing
- Currency: Yuan Renminbi (CNY)
- Religion: Officially atheist. Daoism, Buddhism, Muslim, Roman Catholicism, Protestant
- Language: Putonghua (Mandarin), many local Chinese dialects
- British Embassy, Beijing: +86 (10) 5192 4000

Colombia

- Population: 44 million
- Location: Northern South America
- Capital: Bogotá
- Currency: Peso (COP)
- Religion: Roman Catholicism
- Language: Spanish
- British Embassy, Bogotá: +57 (1) 326 8300

Comoros

- Population: 575,660 (2003)
- Location: Southern Africa, group of islands in the Mozambique Channel
- Capital: Moroni (Ngazidja)
- Currency: Comoros Franc (KMF)
- Religion: Sunni Muslim, Roman Catholicism
- Language: Comoran, French, Arabic
- refer to British High Commission, Port Louis, Mauritius: +230 202 9400

Congo, The Republic of

- Population: 2.9 million (2005)
- Location: West Africa,
- Capital: Brazzaville
- Currency: CFA Franc BEAC (XAF)
- Religion: Roman Catholicism, Christianity, Muslim, traditional beliefs

- Language: French (official), Lingala, Kingongo, Munakutuba
- refer to British Embassy, Kinshasa, Democratic Republic of Congo: +242 620 893

Congo, The Democratic Republic of the
- Population: 58.7 million
- Location: Central Africa
- Capital: Kinshasa
- Currency: Franc (CDF)
- Religion: Roman Catholicism, Protestant, Kimbanguist, Muslim, indigenous beliefs
- Language: French (official), Lingala (trade language), Swahili, Kikongo, Tshiluba
- British Embassy, Kinshasa: +243 81 715 0761; (emergencies only) +243 81 715 0724

Costa Rica
- Population: 4.2 million
- Location: Central America
- Capital: San José
- Currency: Colon (CRC)
- Religion: Roman Catholicism, Evangelical Protestant
- Language: Spanish
- British Embassy, San José: +506 258 2025

Côte d'Ivoire
- Population: 16.4 million (2001)
- Location: West Africa
- Capital (economic): Abidjan
- Currency: CFA Franc BCEAO (XOF)
- Religion: Muslim, Christianity, indigenous beliefs
- Language: French (official), Dioula, Baoule and other local native dialects
- refer to British High Commission, Accra, Ghana: +233 (21) 221 665

Croatia
- Population: 4.5 million (2004 estimate)
- Location: South-east Europe
- Capital: Zagreb
- Currency: Kuna (HRK)
- Religion: Roman Catholicism, Orthodox

- Language: Croatian
- British Embassy, Zagreb: +385 (1) 6009 100;
  +385 (1) 6009 122 (Visa and Consular)

Cuba

- Population: 11.2 million
- Location: Caribbean
- Capital: Havana
- Currency: Convertible Peso (CUC) or Peso (CUP)
- Religion: Roman Catholicism, Santeria, Protestant
- Language: Spanish
- British Embassy, Havana: +53 (7) 204 1771

Cyprus

- Population: 754,064
- Location: Mediterranean
- Capital: Nicosia
- Currency: Cyprus Pound (CYP)
- Religion: Greek Orthodox, Muslim, Maronite, Armenian Apostolic
- Language: Greek, Turkish, English
- British High Commission, Nicosia: +357 22 861100

Czech Republic

- Population: 10.3 million
- Location: Central Europe
- Capital: Prague
- Currency: Czech Koruna (CZK)
- Religion: Roman Catholicism, Protestant, Orthodox, Atheism
- Language: Czech
- British Embassy, Prague: +420 257 402 111

Denmark

- Population: 5.4 million
- Location: Northern Europe
- Capital: Copenhagen
- Currency: Danish Krone (DKK)
- Religion: Evangelical Lutheran
- Language: Danish, Faroese, Greenlandic (an Inuit dialect), German (small minority), English is the predominant second language

- British Embassy, Copenhagen: +45 35 44 52 00

Djibouti
- Population: 700,000 (2003 estimate)
- Location: East Africa
- Capital: Djibouti
- Currency: Djiboutian Franc (DJF)
- Religion: Muslim, Christianity
- Language: French (official), Arabic (official), Somali, Afar
- British Consulate, Djibouti: +253 (3) 85007 (staff resident in Addis Ababa)

Dominica, The Commonwealth of
- Population: 71,000
- Location: Caribbean
- Capital: Roseau
- Currency: East Caribbean Dollar (XCD)
- Religion: Roman Catholicism, Protestant
- Language: English (official), French patois (Creole)
- British High Commission, Roseau: +246 430 7800

Dominican Republic
- Population 8.9 million (2005 estimate)
- Location: Caribbean
- Capital: Santo Domingo
- Currency: Dominican Peso (DOP)
- Religion: Roman Catholicism
- Language: Spanish
- British Embassy, Santo Domingo: +1 809 472 7111

East Timor - see Timor-Leste

Ecuador
- Population: 12.65 million
- Location: Western South America
- Capital: Quito
- Currency: US Dollar (USD)
- Religion: Roman Catholicism
- Language: Spanish (official), Amerindian languages (especially Quechua)
- British Embassy, Quito: +593 (2) 2970 800/1

345

Egypt
- Population: 70.5 million (2004)
- Location: North Africa
- Capital: Cairo
- Currency: Egyptian Pound (EGP)
- Religion: Muslim (mostly Sunni), Coptic Christianity, Bahá'í
- Language: Arabic (official), English and French
- British Embassy, Cairo: +20 (2) 794 08 50/52/58

El Salvador
- Population: 6.7 million
- Location: Central America
- Capital: San Salvador
- Currency: US Dollar (USD), Colon (SVC)
- Religion: Roman Catholicism
- Language: Spanish
- refer to British Embassy, Guatemala City, Guatemala: +502 2367 5425/6/7/8/9

Equatorial Guinea
- Population: 523.051 (2004)
- Location: West Africa
- Capital: Malabo
- Currency: CFA Franc BEAC (XAF)
- Religion: Christianity (predominantly Roman Catholicism), indigenous religions
- Language: Spanish (official), French (official), Fang, Bubi, Ibo
- Refer to British High Commission, Yaounde, Cameroon: +237 222 05 45; +237 222 07 96

Eritrea
- Population: 3.5 million
- Location: East Africa
- Capital: Asmara
- Currency: Nafka (ERN)
- Religion: Christianity, Muslim
- Language: Tigrinya, Tigre, Arabic, English
- British Embassy, Asmara: +291 1 12 01 45

Estonia

- Population: 1.35 million
- Location: East Europe
- Capital: Tallinn
- Currency: Kroon (EEK)
- Religion: Lutheran, Orthodox Christianity
- Language: Estonian (official), Russian
- British Embassy, Tallinn: +372 667 4700

Ethiopia

- Population: 70.7 million (2003)
- Location: East Africa
- Capital: Addis Ababa
- Currency: Ethiopian Birr (ETB)
- Religion: Orthodox Christianity, Muslim, Animist
- Language: Amharic, Tigrinya, Oromigna, Guaragigna, Somali, Arabic, other local dialects, English (major foreign language taught in schools)
- British Embassy, Addis Ababa: +251 (11) 661 2354

Fiji

- Population: 801,500 (1999)
- Location: Pacific Ocean
- Capital: Suva
- Currency: Fijian Dollar (FJD)
- Religion: Christianity, Hinduism, Muslim
- Language: English (official), Fijian, Hindustani
- British High Commission, Suva: +679 3229 100

Finland

- Population: 5.2 million
- Location: Northern Europe
- Capital: Helsinki
- Currency: Euro (EUR)
- Religion: Lutheran, Orthodox
- Language: Finnish (official), Swedish (official), small Lapp- and Russian speaking minorities
- British Embassy, Helsinki: +358 (0) 9 2286 5100

France
- Population: 61.2 million
- Location: West Europe
- Capital: Paris
- Currency: Euro (EUR)
- Religion: Roman Catholicism, Protestant, Judaism, Muslim
- Language: French
- British Embassy, Paris: +33 1 44 51 31 00

Gabon
- Population: 1.4 million
- Location: West Africa
- Capital: Libreville
- Currency: CFA Franc BEAC (XAF)
- Religion: Christianity, Muslim, indigenous beliefs
- Language: French (official), Fang, Myene, Bateke, Bapounou/Eschira, Bandjabi
- British Consulate, Libreville: +241 762200 (all staff resident at Yaounde, Cameroon)

Gambia, The Republic of
- Population: 1.4 million
- Location: West Africa
- Capital: Banjul
- Currency: Dalasi (GMD)
- Religion: Muslim, Christianity, indigenous beliefs
- Language: English (official), Mandinka, Wolof, Fula, indigenous vernaculars
- British High Commission, Banjul: +220 449 5133

Georgia
- Population: 4.4 million
- Location: South-west Asia
- Capital: Tbilisi
- Currency: Lari (GEL)
- Religion: Georgian Orthodox, Muslim, Russian Orthodox, Armenian Apostolic
- Language: Georgian (official), Russian, Armenian, Azeri
- British Embassy, Tbilisi: +995 32 274 747

Germany

- Population: 82.5 million
- Location: Central Europe
- Capital: Berlin
- Currency: Euro (EUR)
- Religion: Protestant, Roman Catholicism, Muslim
- Language: German
- British Embassy, Berlin: +49 (3) 0 20457-0

Ghana

- Population: 20.3 million (2003 estimate)
- Location: West Africa
- Capital: Accra
- Currency: Cedi (GHC)
- Religion: Muslim, Christianity, indigenous beliefs
- Language: English (official), African languages (incl Akan, Mossi, Ewe, and Hausa)
- British High Commission, Accra: +233 (21) 221 665

Greece

- Population: 10.94 million
- Location: South-east Europe
- Capital: Athens
- Currency: Euro (EUR)
- Religion: Greek Orthodox, Muslim
- Language: Greek
- British Embassy, Athens: +30 210 727 2600

Grenada

- Population: 89,502 (2005 estimate)
- Location: Caribbean
- Capital: St George's
- Currency: East Caribbean Dollar (XCD)
- Religion: Roman Catholicism, Anglican
- Language: English (official), French patois
- British High Commission, St George's: +1 473 440 3222/3536 (resides in Barbados)

Guatemala
- Population: 14.6 million (2005 estimate)
- Location: Central America
- Capital: Guatemala
- Currency: Quetzal (GTQ)
- Religion: Roman Catholicism, Protestant, Judasim, Muslim, indigenous Mayan beliefs
- Language: Spanish, 22 officially recognized Mayan languages including K'iche, Kakchiquel, K'ekchi and Mam
- British Embassy, Guatemala City: +502 2367 5425/6/7/8/9

Guinea
- Population: 9.4 million
- Location: West Africa
- Capital: Conakry
- Currency: Guinean Franc (GNF)
- Religion: Muslim, Christianity, traditional beliefs
- Language: French (official), eight local languages taught in schools (Basari, Pular, Kissi, Koniagi, Kpelle, Loma, Malinke and Susu)
- British Embassy, Conakry: +224 30 45 58 07

Guinea-Bissau
- Population: 1.3 million
- Location: West Africa
- Capital: Bissau
- Currency: CFA Franc BCEAO (XOF)
- Religion: Muslim, Christianity, indigenous beliefs
- Language: Portuguese (official), Crioulo, indigenous African languages
- Honorary British Consulate (limited emergency service): +245 20 12 24/16; refer to British Embassy, Dakar, Senegal: +221 823 7392/9971

Guyana
- Population: 751,000
- Location: Northern South America
- Capital: Georgetown
- Currency: Guyanese Dollar (GYD)
- Religion: Christianity, Hinduism, Muslim
- Language: English, Amerindian dialects, Creole, Hindi, Urdu
- British High Commission, Georgetown: +592 226 58 81/82/83/84

Haiti

- Population: 8.1 million (2005 estimate)
- Location: Caribbean
- Capital: Port-au-Prince
- Currency: Gourde (HTG)
- Religion: Roman Catholicism, Protestant, Baptist, Pentecostal, Adventist, also Voodoo
- Language: French (official), Creole (official)
- British Consulate, Port-au-Prince: +509 257 3969

Holy See, Rome

- Population: 890
- Location: Italy
- Capital: Vatican City
- Currency: Euro (EUR)
- Religion: Roman Catholicism
- Language: Latin, Italian, English and French
- British Embassy, Rome: +39 06 4220 0001

Honduras

- Population: 7.2 million
- Location: Central America
- Capital: Tegucigalpa
- Currency: Lempira (HNL)
- Religion: Roman Catholicism, Protestant
- Language: Spanish, English (business), Amerindian dialects
- refer to British Embassy, Guatemala City: +502 2367 5425/6/7/8/9

Hong Kong (The Hong Kong Special Administration of China)

- Population: 6.8 million
- Location: East Asia
- Currency: Hong Kong Dollar (HKD)
- Religion: Buddhism, Taoism, Christianity, Muslim, Hinduism, Sikhism, Judaism
- Language: Chinese (Cantonese), English
- British Consulate General, Hong Kong: +852 2901 3000

Hungary
- Population: 10.1 million (2005)
- Location: Central Europe
- Capital: Budapest
- Currency: Forint (HUF)
- Religion: Roman Catholicism, Calvinist, Lutheran, Judaism, Atheism
- Language: Hungarian
- British Embassy, Budapest: +36 (1) 266 2888

Iceland
- Population: 300,000 (2006)
- Location: North Europe
- Capital: Reykjavik
- Currency: Icelandic Krona (ISK)
- Religion: Evangelical Lutheran, Protestant, Roman Catholicism
- Language: Icelandic
- British Embassy, Reykjavik: +354 550 5100

India
- Population: 1.1 billion (2005 estimate)
- Location: South Asia
- Capital: New Delhi
- Currency: Rupee (INR)
- Religion: Hinduism, Muslim, Christianity, Sikhism, Buddhism, Jain, Parsi
- Language: Hindi (official), 18 main and regional official state languages, plus 24 further languages, 720 dialects and 23 tribal languages, English (officially an associate language, is used particularly for political, and commercial communication)
- British High Commission, New Delhi: +91 (11) 2687 2161

Indonesia
- Population: 221 million (estimated projection for 2003)
- Location: South-east Asia
- Capital: Jakarta
- Currency: Rupiah (IDR)
- Religion: Muslim, Protestant, Roman Catholicism, Hinduism, Buddhism
- Language: Bahasa Indonesia (official), over 583 languages and dialects
- British Embassy, Jakarta: +62 (21) 315 6264; +62 811 802435 (Out of hours emergencies)

visit: www.gap-year.com

Iran

- Population: 70 million
- Location: Middle East
- Capital: Tehran
- Currency: Rial (IRR)
- Religion: Shi'a Muslim, Sunni Muslim, Zoroastrian, Judaism, Christianity, and Bahá'íí
- Language: Persian (Farsi), Azeri, Kurdish, Arabic, Luri, Baluchi
- British Embassy, Tehran: +98 (21) 6670 5011

Iraq

- Population: 24.6 million (2003 estimate)
- Location: Middle East
- Capital: Baghdad
- Currency: New Iraqi Dinar (IQD)
- Religion: Muslim, Christianity
- Language: Arabic, Kurdish, Assyrian, Armenian, Turkoman
- British Embassy, Bagdad: +964 (0) 7901 926 280 (emergency number for British Nationals only: (1) 914 360 9060 – mobile)

Ireland, Republic of

- Population: 3.9 million
- Location: West Europe
- Capital: Dublin
- Currency: Euro (EUR)
- Religion: Roman Catholicism, Church of Ireland, Presbyterian, Methodism, Judaism
- Language: Irish, English
- British Embassy, Dublin: +353 (1) 205 3700

Israel

- Population: 7 million
- Location: Middle East
- Capital: Tel Aviv
- Currency: New Israeli Shekel (ILS)
- Religion: Judaism, Muslim, Christianity
- Language: Hebrew, Arabic, English, Russian
- British Embassy, Tel Aviv: +972 (3) 725 1222
  British Consulate-General, Jerusalem: +972 (02) 541 4100

the gap-year guidebook 2007

Italy
- Population: 57.5 million
- Location: South Europe
- Capital: Rome
- Currency: Euro (EUR)
- Religion: Roman Catholicism, Judaism, Protestant, Muslim
- Language: Italian (official), German, French, Slovene
- British Embassy, Rome: +39 06 4220 0001; +39 06 4220 2603 (out of hours)

Ivory Coast - see Côte d'Ivoire

Jamaica
- Population: 2.7 million (2005 estimate)
- Location: Caribbean
- Capital: Kingston
- Currency: Jamaican Dollar (JMD)
- Religion: Anglican, Baptist and other Protestant, Roman Catholicism, Seven Day Adventist, Rastafarian, Judaism, Bahá'í
- Language: English, Patois
- British High Commission, Kingston: +1 (876) 510 0700

Japan
- Population: 12.7 million
- Location: East Asia
- Capital: Tokyo
- Currency: Yen (JPY)
- Religion: Shinto, Buddhism, Christianity
- Language: Japanese
- British Embassy, Tokyo: +81 (3) 5211 1100

Jordan
- Population: 5.3 million
- Location: Middle East
- Capital: Amman
- Currency: Jordanian Dinar (JOD)
- Religion: Sunni Muslim, Christianity
- Language: Arabic (official), English
- British Embassy, Amman: +962 6 590 9200

Kazakhstan

- Population: 15.1 million (2005)

- Location: Central Asia

- Capital: Astana

- Currency: Kazakh Tenge (KZT)

- Religion: Muslim, Russian Orthodox, Protestant

- Language: Kazakh, Russian

- British Embassy, Almaty: +7 573 150 2200

Kenya

- Population: 31.5 million

- Location: East Africa

- Capital: Nairobi

- Currency: Kenyan Shilling (KES)

- Religion: Protestant (including Evangelical), Roman Catholicism, indigenous beliefs, Muslim

- Language: English (official), Kiswahili, numerous indigenous languages

- British High Commission, Nairobi: +254 (20) 284 4000

Kiribati

- Population: 94,149

- Location: Pacific Ocean

- Capital: Tarawa

- Currency: Australian Dollar (AUD)

- Religion: Roman Catholicism, Protestant (Congregational), Seventh-Day Adventist, Bahá'í, Latter-day Saints, Church of God

- Language: English (official), I-Kiribati

- British High Commission, Tarawa: +679 322 9100

Korea, DPR (North Korea)

- Population: 22.5 million (2003)

- Location: East Asia

- Capital: Pyongyang

- Currency: North Korean Won (KPW)

- Religion: Buddhism, Christianity, Chondo

- Language: Korean

- British Embassy, Pyongyang: +850 2 381 7980 (International); 02 382 7980/2 (Local dialling)

355

Korea, Republic of (South Korea)

- Population: 48.3 million (2002 estimate)
- Location: East Asia
- Capital: Seoul
- Currency: South Korean Won (KRW)
- Religion: Shamanism, Buddhism, Confucianism, Chondogyo, Roman Catholicism, Protestant
- Language: Korean
- British Embassy, Seoul: +82 (2) 3210 5500

Kuwait

- Population: 2.31 million
- Location: Middle East
- Capital: Kuwait City
- Currency: Kuwaiti Dinar (KWD)
- Religion: Muslim, Christianity
- Language: Arabic (official), English widely spoken
- British Embassy, Dasman: +965 240 3335

Kyrgyzstan

- Population: 4.8 million
- Location: Central Asia
- Capital: Bishkek
- Currency: Som (KGS)
- Religion: Muslim, Russian Orthodox
- Language: Kyrgyz, Russian
- British Honorary Consul, Bishkek: +996 312 680 815

Laos

- Population: 5.5 million (2002 estimate)
- Location: South-east Asia
- Capital: Vientiane
- Currency: Kip (LAK)
- Religion: Buddhism, Animism, Christianity
- Language: Lao
- British Embassy, Vientiane: +856 (21) 413606

Latvia

- Population: 2.31 million
- Location: East Europe
- Capital: Riga
- Currency: Lat (LVL)
- Religion: Lutheran, Roman Catholicism, Russian Orthodox
- Language: Latvian, Russian
- British Embassy, Riga: +371 777 4700

Lebanon

- Population: 3.6 million
- Location: Middle East
- Capital: Beirut
- Currency: Lebanese Pound (LBP)
- Religion: Muslim, Christianity, and 18 regular sects
- Language: Arabic (official), English, French, Armenian
- British Embassy, Beirut: +961 (1) 990 400 (24 hours)

Lesotho

- Population: 1.8 million (2005 estimate)
- Location: Southern Africa
- Capital: Maseru
- Currency: Loti (LSL)
- Religion: Christianity, indigenous beliefs
- Language: Sesotho, English
- refer to British High Commission, Pretoria, South Africa: +27 (12) 421 7500

Liberia

- Population: 3.36 million (2004 estimate)
- Location: West Africa
- Capital: Monrovia
- Currency: Liberian Dollar (LRD), US Dollar (USD)
- Religion: Christianity, Muslim, indigenous beliefs
- Language: English (official), indigenous languages
- British Honorary Consulate, Monrovia: +231 226 056; +37747 651 6973 (mobile)

the gap-year guidebook 2007

Libya

- Population: 5.41 million
- Location: North Africa
- Capital: Tripoli
- Currency: Dinar (LYD)
- Religion: Sunni Muslim
- Language: Arabic, Italian and English understood in major cities
- British Embassy, Tripoli: +218 (21) 335 1084

Liechtenstein
- Population: 34,000 (2004)
- Location: Central Europe
- Capital: Vaduz
- Currency: Swiss Franc (CHF)
- Religion: Roman Catholicism, Protestant
- Language: German (official), Alemannic dialect
- refer to British Embassy, Berne, Switzerland: +41 (31) 359 7700

Lithuania
- Population: 3.4 million (2005)
- Location: East Europe
- Capital: Vilnius
- Currency: Litas (LTL)
- Religion: Roman Catholicism
- Language: Lithuanian (official), Russian
- British Embassy, Vilnius: +370 5 246 29 00

Luxembourg
- Population: 451,000
- Location: Central Europe
- Capital: Luxembourg
- Currency: Euro (EUR)
- Religion: Roman Catholicism, Protestant, Judaism, Muslim
- Language: Luxembourgish, German, French
- British Embassy, Luxembourg: + 352 22 98 64; +021 186 653 (out of hours duty officer)

visit: www.gap-year.com

Macedonia

- Population: 2 million (2004 estimate)
- Location: East Europe
- Capital: Skopje
- Currency: Macedonian Denar (MKD)
- Religion: Orthodox, Muslim
- Language: Macedonian, Albanian, Turkish, Serbian
- British Embassy, Skopje: + 389 (2) 3299 299

Madagascar

- Population: 18 million (2005 estimate)
- Location: Southern Africa
- Capital: Antananarivo
- Currency: Ariary (MGA)
- Religion: Christianity, indigenous beliefs, Muslim
- Language: Malagasy (official), French (official)
- refer to British High Commission Port Louis, Mauritius (limited Consular Services): +230 202 9400

Malawi

- Population: 12.1 million (2004 estimate)
- Location: Southern Africa
- Capital: Lilongwe
- Currency: Kwacha (MWK)
- Religion: Protestant, Roman Catholicism, Muslim, indigenous beliefs
- Language: English, Chichewa
- British High Commission, Liongwe: +265 (1) 772 400

Malaysia

- Population: 26 million (2005)
- Location: South-east Asia
- Capital: Kuala Lumpur
- Currency: Ringgit (MYR)
- Religion: Muslim, Buddhism, Taoism, Christianity, Hinduism, Animism
- Language: Bahasa Malay (national language), Iban, English widespread, Chinese, Tamil
- British High Commission, Kuala Lumpur: +60 (3) 2170 2200

Maldives

- Population: 400,000 (2004 estimate)
- Location: South Asia
- Capital: Malé
- Currency: Rufiyaa (MVR)
- Religion: Sunni Muslim (other religions illegal)
- Language: Dhivehi, but English widely spoken in Malé and resort islands
- refer to British High Commission, Colombo, Sri Lanka: +94 (11) 2437336

Mali

- Population: 10.67 million
- Location: West Africa
- Capital: Bamako
- Currency: CFA Franc BCEAO (XOF)
- Religion: Muslim, Christianity, indigenous beliefs
- Language: French (official), Bambara, and numerous other African languages
- British Embassy Liaison Office, Bamako: +223 277 46 37
  refer also to British Embassy, Dakar, Sengal, for Visa applications: +221 823 7392

Malta

- Population: 402,700
- Location: South Europe
- Capital: Valletta
- Currency: Maltese Lira (MTL)
- Religion: Roman Catholicism
- Language: Maltese (official), English (official)
- British High Commission, Valletta: +356 2323 0000

Marshall Islands

- Population: 60,422 (2006 estimate)
- Location: Pacific Ocean
- Capital: Majuro
- Currency: US Dollar (USD)
- Religion: Christianity (mostly Protestant)
- Language: English, 2 major Marshallese dialects, Japanese
- refer to British Embassy, Suva, Fiji: +679 322 9100

Mauritania

- Population: 3 million (2003 estimate)
- Location: North Africa
- Capital: Nouakchott
- Currency: Ouguiya (MRO)
- Religion: Muslim
- Language: Hassaniya Arabic (official), Pulaar, Soninke, Wolof, French widely used in business
- British Honorary Consul, Nouakchott: +222 525 83 31

Mauritius

- Population: 1.23 million (2004 estimate)
- Location: Southern Africa
- Capital: Port Louis
- Currency: Mauritian Rupee (MUR)
- Religion: Hinduism, Christianity, Muslim
- Language: English, French, Creole
- British High Commission, Port Louis: +230 202 9400; +230 252 8006 (Duty Officer, for general emergency out of hours)

Mexico

- Population: 105 million (2004 estimate)
- Location: Central America
- Capital: Mexico City
- Currency: Mexican Peso (MXN)
- Religion: Roman Catholicism, Protestant
- Language: Spanish, at least 62 other regional languages
- British Embassy, Mexico City: +52 (55) 5242 8500

Micronesia

- Population: 108,004 (2006 estimate)
- Location: Pacific Ocean
- Capital: Palikir
- Currency: US Dollar (USD)
- Religion: Roman Catholicism, Protestant
- Language: English, Turkese, Pohnpeian, Yapese, Kosrean, Ulithian, Woleaian, Nukuoro, Kapingamarangi
- refer to British Embassy, Suva, Fiji: +679 322 9100

Moldova

- Population: 4.29 million
- Location: East Europe
- Capital: Chisinau
- Currency: Moldovan Leu (MDL)
- Religion: Eastern Orthodox, Judaism, Baptist
- Language: Moldovan, Russian (official), Gagauz, Ukranian
- British Embassy, Chisinau: +373 22 25 59 02;
  out of hours +373 69 10 44 42

Monaco

- Population: 32,020
- Location: West Europe
- Capital: Monaco
- Currency: Euro (EUR)
- Religion: Roman Catholicism
- Language: French (official), English, Italian, Monegasque
- British Consulate, Monaco: +377 93 50 99 54

Mongolia

- Population: 2.5 million (estimated)
- Location: North Asia
- Capital: Ulaanbaatar
- Currency: Togrog (Tughrik) (MNT)
- Religion: Tibetan Buddhism, Shamanism, Muslim (south-west)
- Language: Khalkh Mongol, Kazakh
- British Embassy, Ulaanbaatar: +976 (11) 458 133

Morocco

- Population: 32.2 million (2004 estimate)
- Location: North Africa
- Capital: Rabat
- Currency: Moroccan Dirham (MAD)
- Religion: Muslim, Christianity, Judaism
- Language: Arabic (official), Berber dialects, French (commerce, diplomacy and government)
- British Embassy, Rabat: +212 (37) 63 33 33

visit: www.gap-year.com

Mozambique

- Population: 19.2 million (2004)
- Location: Southern Africa
- Capital: Maputo
- Currency: Metical (MZN)
- Religion: Roman Catholicism, Christianity, Muslim, indigenous beliefs
- Language: Portuguese (official), over 30 African languages
- British High Commission, Maputo: +258 21 356 000

Myanmar (see Burma)

Namibia

- Population: 1.9 million (2003)
- Location: Southern Africa
- Capital: Windhoek
- Currency: Namibian Dollar (NAD)
- Religion: Christianity
- Language: English (official), Afrikaans, German, and several indigenous languages
- British High Commission, Windhoek: +264 (61) 274800

Nauru, The Republic of

- Population: 12,088 (2001 estimate)
- Location: Pacific Ocean
- Capital: Yaren District
- Currency: Australian Dollar (AUD)
- Religion: Protestant, Roman Catholicism
- Language: Nauruan (official), English (commerce and government, widely understood)
- refer to British High Commission, Suva, Fiji: +679 322 9100

Nepal

- Population: 23.7 million (estimated)
- Location: South Asia
- Capital: Kathmandu
- Currency: Nepalese Rupee (NPR), Chinese Yuan Renminbi (CNY)
- Religion: Hinduism, Buddhism, Muslim
- Language: Nepali (official), Newari (mainly in Kathmandu), Tibetan languages (mainly hill areas), Indian languages (mainly Terai areas). Nepal has over 30 languages and many dialects

- British Embassy, Kathmandu: +977 (1) 4410583

The Netherlands
- Population: 16.3 million (2006)
- Location: North Europe
- Capital: Amsterdam
- Currency: Euro (EUR)
- Religion: Roman Catholicism, Protestant, Muslim
- Language: Dutch
- British Embassy, The Hague: +31 (0) 70 4270 427

New Zealand
- Population: 4.1 million (2005)
- Location: Pacific Ocean
- Capital: Wellington
- Currency: New Zealand Dollar (NZD)
- Religion: Anglican, Presbyterian, Roman Catholicism, Methodism, Baptist
- Language: English, Maori
- British High Commission, Wellington: +64 (4) 924 2888

Nicaragua
- Population: 5.1 million
- Location: Central America
- Capital: Managua
- Currency: Cordoba (NIO)
- Religion: Roman Catholicism, Evangelical Protestant
- Language: Spanish (official), English, Miskito, Creole, Mayanga, Garifuna, Rama
- British Honorary Consul, Managua: +505 254 5454
  refer to British Embassy, San José: +506 258 2025

Niger
- Population: 12 million (2005 estimate)
- Location: West Africa
- Capital: Niamey
- Currency: CFA Franc BCEAO (XOF)
- Religion: Muslim
- Language: French (official), Arabic, local languages widely spoken
- British Honorary Consul, Niamey: +227 725 046
  refer to British High Commission, Ghana: +233 (21) 221 665

visit: www.gap-year.com

Nigeria

- Population: 133 million (estimate)
- Location: West Africa
- Capital: Abuja
- Currency: Naira (NGN)
- Religion: Muslim, Christianity, traditional beliefs
- Language: English (official), Hausa, Yoruba, Igbo
- British High Commission, Abuja: +234 (9) 413 2010

Norway

- Population: 4.6 million (2006)
- Location: North Europe
- Capital: Oslo
- Currency: Norwegian Kroner (NOK)
- Religion: Church of Norway (Evangelical Lutheran)
- Language: Norwegian
- British Embassy, Oslo: +47 23 13 27 00

Oman

- Population: 2.3 million (2003)
- Location: Middle East
- Capital: Muscat
- Currency: Oman Rial (OMR)
- Religion: Ibadhi Muslim, Sunni Muslim, Shi'a Muslim, Hinduism, Christianity
- Language: Arabic (official), English, Farsi, Baluchi, Urdu
- British Embassy, Muscat: +968 24 609 000; (out of hours emergencies) +968 9920 0865

Pakistan

- Population: 162.4 million
- Location: South Asia
- Capital: Islamabad
- Currency: Rupee (PKR)
- Religion: Muslim, Hinduism, Christianity
- Language: Punjabi, Sindhi, Pashtun, Urdu, Balochi, English and other local languages
- British High Commission, Islamabad: +92 51 201 2000

Palau, Republic of

- Population: 18,400
- Location: Pacific Ocean
- Capital: Koror
- Currency: US Dollar (USD)
- Religion: Roman Catholicism, Seven Day Adventist, Jehovah's Witness, Assembly of God, Liebenzell Mission, Latter-day Saints, indigenous faiths
- Language: English, Palauan
- refer to British Ambassador, Suva, Fiji: +679 3229 100

Palestine (Palestinian National Authority)

- Population: 2.9 million
- Location: Middle East
- Currency: New Israeli Shekel (ILS), Jordanian Dinar (JOD) (West Bank Only)
- Religion: Muslim, Christianity
- Language: Arabic, English
- British-Consulate General, Jerusalem: +972 (02) 541 4100 (24-hour switchboard)

Panama

- Population: 3.2 million (2005)
- Location: Central America
- Capital: Panama City
- Currency: US Dollar (USD) (known locally as the Balboa (PAB))
- Religion: Roman Catholicism, Protestant, Judaism, Muslim
- Language: Spanish (official), English
- British Embassy, Panama City: +507 269 0866

Papua New Guinea

- Population: 6 million
- Location: South-east Asia,
- Capital: Port Moresby
- Currency: Kina (PGK)
- Religion: Christian according to its constitution, Roman Catholicism, Evangelical Lutheran, Evangelical Alliance, Pentecostal, Baptist, Anglican, Buddhism, Muslim, Hinduism, Seventh Day Adventist, United Church
- Language: English, Pidgin English, Hiri Motu, over 820 different languages
- British High Commission, Port Moresby: +675 325 1677; +675 683 1627 (mobile - emergencies only)

Paraguay

- Population: 5.6 million

- Location: Central South America

- Capital: Asunción

- Currency: Guarani (PYG)

- Religion: Roman Catholicism, Mennonite, Protestant, Latter-day Saints, Judaism, Russian Orthodox

- Language: Spanish (official), Guarani (official)

- British High Commission, Asunción: +595 (21) 210 405
  refer to British Embassy, Buenos Aires, Argentina: +54 (11) 4808 2200

Peru

- Population: 27.1 million (2004 estimate)

- Location: Western South America

- Capital: Lima

- Currency: Nuevo Sol (PEN)

- Religion: Roman Catholicism

- Language: Spanish (official), Quechua (official), Aymara and several minor Amazonian languages

- British Embassy, Lima: +51 (1) 617 3000

Philippines

- Population: 86.7 million (2005 estimate)

- Location: South-east Asia

- Capital: Metro Manila

- Currency: Peso (PHP)

- Religion: Roman Catholicism, Protestant, Muslim

- Language: Filipino (official), English (official)

- British Embassy, Manila: +63 (2) 816 7116

Poland

- Population: 38.6 million

- Location: Central Europe

- Capital: Warsaw

- Currency: Zloty (PLN)

- Religion: Roman Catholicism, Eastern Orthodox, Protestant

- Language: Polish

- British Embassy, Warsaw: +48 (22) 311 00 00

Portugal

- Population: 10.3 million
- Location: South-west Europe
- Capital: Lisbon
- Currency: Euro (EUR)
- Religion: Roman Catholicism, Protestant
- Language: Portuguese
- British Embassy, Lisbon: +351 21 392 4000

Qatar, State of

- Population: 585,000 (2000 estimate)
- Location: Middle East
- Capital: Doha
- Currency: Qatar Riyal (QAR)
- Religion: Muslim
- Language: Arabic (official), English, Urdu
- British Embassy, Doha: +974 442 1991

Romania

- Population: 22.6 million
- Location: South-east Europe
- Capital: Bucharest
- Currency: New Lei (Leu) (RON)
- Religion: Orthodox, Roman Catholicism, Protestant, Reformed, Greek Catholicism, Unitarian
- Language: Romanian (official), English, French, German
- British Embassy, Bucharest: +40 (21) 201 7200

Russia Federation

- Population: 143.5 million (2005)
- Location: North Asia
- Capital: Moscow
- Currency: Ruble (RUB)
- Religion: Orthodox, Christianity, Muslim, Judaism
- Language: Russian
- British Embassy, Moscow: +7 (495) 956 7200

visit: www.gap-year.com

Rwanda

- Population: 8 million (estimated)
- Location: Central Africa
- Capital: Kigali
- Currency: Rwandan Franc (RWF)
- Religion: Roman Catholicism, Protestant, Muslim, indigenous beliefs
- Language: Kinyarwanda (official), French (official), English (official), Kiswahili (used in commercial centres and by army)
- British Embassy, Kigali: +250 584 098

Saint Christopher & Nevis

- Population: 42,000
- Location: Caribbean
- Capital: Basseterre
- Currency: East Caribbean Dollar (XCD)
- Religion: Anglican, Roman Catholicism, Evangelical Protestant
- Language: English
- British High Commission, St John's Antigua: +268 462 0008/9

Saint Lucia

- Population: 160,145 (2002 estimate)
- Location: Caribbean
- Capital: Castries
- Currency: East Caribbean Dollar (XCD)
- Religion: Roman Catholicism, Anglican, Methodist, Baptist, Judaism, Hinduism, Muslim
- Language: English (official), French patois (Kweyol)
- British High Commission, Castries: +1 (758) 45 22484/5

Saint Vincent and the Grenadines

- Population: 116,394 (2002 estimate)
- Location: Caribbean
- Capital: Kingstown
- Currency: East Caribbean Dollar (XCD)
- Religion: Anglican, Methodism, Roman Catholicism, Seventh Day Adventist, Hinduism, other Protestant
- Language: English
- British High Commission, Kingstown: +784 457 1701

Samoa

- Population: 176,710 (2001)
- Location: South Pacific
- Capital: Apia
- Currency: Samoan Tala (WST)
- Religion: Roman Catholicism, Methodism, Latter-day Saints
- Language: Samoan, English
- British High Commission, Apia: +64 (4) 924 2888

Sao Tomé & Príncipe

- Population: 1.16 million (2005 estimate)
- Location: West Africa
- Capital: Sao Tomé
- Currency: Dobra (STD)
- Religion: Christianity
- Language: Portuguese, Lungwa Santomé, and other creole dialects
- British Consulate, Sao Tomé: +239 (12) 21026/7

Saudi Arabia

- Population: 24.3 million (2003 estimate)
- Location: Middle East
- Capital: Riyadh
- Currency: Saudi Riyal (SAR)
- Religion: Muslim (Sunni, Shia). The public practice of any other religion is forbidden
- Language: Arabic, English
- British Embassy, Riyadh: +966 (0) 1 488 0077

Senegal

- Population: 11.6 million (2005 estimate)
- Location: West Africa
- Capital: Dakar
- Currency: CFA Franc BCEAO (XOF)
- Religion: Muslim, Christianity, indigenous beliefs
- Language: French (official), Wolof, Malinke, Severe, Soninke, Pular
- British Embassy, Dakar: +221 823 7392

visit: www.gap-year.com

Serbia & Montenegro (formerly Federal Republic of Yugoslavia)

- Population: 9.4 million (2002)

- Location: South-east Europe

- Capital: Belgrade

- Currency: New Yugoslav Dinar (CSD), Euro (EUR)

- Religion: Serbian Orthodox, Muslim, Roman Catholicism, Protestant

- Language: Serbian, Romanian, Hungarian, Slovak, Croatian, Albania (Kosovan)

- British Embassy, Belgrade: +381 (11) 2645 055

Seychelles

- Population: 82,472 (2004 estimate)

- Location: Indian Ocean

- Capital: Victoria

- Currency: Seychelles Rupee (SCR)

- Religion: Roman Catholicism, Anglican, Muslim, Hinduism

- Language: English, French, Creole (Seselwa)

- British High Commission, Mahe: +248 283 666

Sierra Leone

- Population: 5 million (2003 estimate)

- Location: West Africa

- Capital: Freetown

- Currency: Leone (SLL)

- Religion: Muslim, Christianity, indigenous beliefs

- Language: English (official), Krio (English-based Creole), indigenous languages widely spoken

- British High Commission, Freetown: +232 (22) 232 961

Singapore

- Population: 4.2 million (2003 UN)

- Location: South-east Asia

- Capital: Singapore

- Currency: Singapore Dollar (SGD)

- Religion: Taoism, Buddhism, Muslim, Christianity, Hinduism

- Language: Mandarin Chinese, English, Malay, Tamil

- British High Commission, Singapore: +65 6424 4200

Slovakia

- Population: 5.39 million (2002)
- Location: Central Europe
- Capital: Bratislava
- Currency: Slovak Crown (Koruna) (SKK)
- Religion: Roman Catholicism, Atheism, Protestant, Orthodox
- Language: Slovak (official), Hungarian
- British Embassy, Bratislava: +421 (2) 5998 2000

Slovenia

- Population: 2 million
- Location: Central Europe
- Capital: Ljubljana
- Currency: Tolar (SIT)
- Religion: Roman Catholicism
- Language: Slovene, Italian, Hungarian, English
- British Embassy, Ljubljana: +386 (1) 200 3910

Solomon Islands

- Population: 450,000
- Location: Pacific Ocean
- Capital: Honiara
- Currency: Solomon Islands Dollar (SBD)
- Religion: Christianity, traditional beliefs
- Language: English, Pidgin, 92 indigenous languages
- British Embassy, Honiara: +677 21705/6

Somalia

- Population: 10.4 million
- Location: East Africa
- Capital: Mogadishu
- Currency: Somali Shilling (SOS)
- Religion: Sunni Muslim
- Language: Somali (official), Arabic, Italian, English
- British Embassy, Mogadishu: +252 (1) 20288/9
  NB British Embassy staff in Somalia withdrawn from post (August 2006)

South Africa

- Population: 45.3 million (2005 UN)
- Location: Southern Africa
- Capital: Pretoria
- Currency: Rand (ZAR)
- Religion: Predominately Christianity but all principal religions are represented in South Africa
- Language: 11 official languages: Afrikaans, English, Ndebele, Sepedi, Sesotho, Swati, Tsonga, Tswana, Venda, Xhosa, Zulu
- British High Commission, Pretoria: +27 (12) 421 7500

Spain

- Population: 44 million
- Location: South-westn Europe
- Capital: Madrid
- Currency: Euro (EUR)
- Religion: Roman Catholicism, Protestant
- Language: Castilian Spanish (official), Catalan, Galician, Basque
- British Embassy, Madrid: +34 (91) 700 8200

Sri Lanka

- Population: 19.5 million (2004)
- Location: South Asia
- Capital: Colombo
- Currency: Rupee (LKR)
- Religion: Buddhism, Hinduism, Muslim, Christianity
- Language: Sinhalese, Tamil, English
- British High Commission, Colombo: +94 (11) 2437336

Sudan

- Population: 33.61 million (2003)
- Location: North Africa
- Capital: Khartoum City
- Currency: Dinar (SDD)
- Religion: Muslim, Christianity, indigenous religions
- Language: Arabic (official), Nubian, Ta Bedawie, diverse dialects of Nilotic, Nilo- Hamitic, Sudanic languages, English
- British Embassy, Khartoum: +249 (183) 777 105

Suriname
- Population: 438,000 (2003 estimate)
- Location: Northern South America
- Capital: Paramaribo
- Currency: Suriname Dollar (SRD)
- Religion: Hinduism, Muslim, Roman Catholicism, Dutch Reformed, Moravian, Judaism, Bahá'í
- Language: Dutch (official), English, Sranan Tongo (Creole), Hindustani, Javanese
- British Honorary Consulate (resides in Georgetown): +597 402 558

Swaziland
- Population: 1.1 million (2004)
- Location: Southern Africa
- Capital: Mbabane
- Currency: Lilangeni (SZL)
- Religion: Christianity, indigenous beliefs
- Language: English, Siswati
- British High Commission, Mbabane: +27 (12) 421 7500

Sweden
- Population: 9 million
- Location: North Europe
- Capital: Stockholm
- Currency: Swedish Krona (SEK)
- Religion: Lutheran, Roman Catholicism, Orthodox, Baptist, Muslim, Judaism, Buddhism
- Language: Swedish
- British Embassy, Stockholm: +46 (8) 671 3000

Switzerland
- Population: 7.4 million (2005)
- Location: Central Europe
- Capital: Berne
- Currency: Swiss Franc (CHF)
- Religion: Roman Catholicism, Protestant
- Language: Swiss German (official), French, Italian, Rhaeto-Rumantsch
- British Embassy, Berne: +41 (31) 359 7700

Syria (The Syrian Arab Republic)

- Population: 18.6 million
- Location: Middle East
- Capital: Damascus
- Currency: Syrian Pound (also called Lira) (SYR)
- Religion: Sunni Muslim, Alawite, Druze, other Muslim sects, Christianity, Judaism
- Language: Arabic (official), Kurdish, Armenian, Aramaic, Circassian, some French, English
- British Embassy, Damascus: +963 (11) 373 9241/2/3/7

Taiwan

- Population: 22.7 million (2005)
- Location: East Asia
- Capital: Taipei
- Currency: New Taiwan Dollar (TWD)
- Religion: Buddhism, Taoism, Christianity
- Language: Mandarin Chinese (official), Taiwanese, Hakka
- British Trade & Cultrual Office, Taipei: +886 (2) 2192 7000
  refer to British Consul General, Shanghai, China: +86 (21) 6279 7650

Tajikistan

- Population: 6.34 million (2004)
- Location: Central Asia
- Capital: Dushanbe
- Currency: Somoni (TJS), Russian Ruble (RUB)
- Religion: Sunni Muslim, Ismal, Shiites, Orthodox Christianity, Judaism
- Language: Tajik, Russian
- British Embassy, Dushanbe: +992 372 24 22 21

Tanzania

- Population: 36 million
- Location: East Africa
- Capital: Dodoma
- Currency: Tanzania Shilling (TZS)
- Religion: Christianity, Muslim, indigenous beliefs
- Language: Kiswahili, English
- British High Commission, Dar es Salaam: +255 (22) 211 0101;
  (emergencies only) +255 (0) 744 242 242

the gap-year guidebook 2007

Thailand

- Population: 62 million (2004)
- Location: South-east Asia
- Capital: Bangkok
- Currency: Baht (THB)
- Religion: Buddhism, Muslim, Christianity, Hinduism
- Language: Thai
- British Embassy, Bangkok: +66 (0) 2 305 8333

Tibet – see China

Timor-Leste

- Population: 925,000 (estimated)
- Location: South-east Asia
- Capital: Dili
- Currency: US Dollar (USD)
- Religion: Roman Catholicism, Protestant, Muslim, Hinduism, Buddhism
- Language: Tetum (official), Portuguese (official), Bahasa Indonesian, English
- British Embassy, Dili: +670 332 2838; (out of hours emergency only) +670 723 1606

Togo

- Population: 4.7 million
- Location: West Africa
- Capital: Lome
- Currency: CFA Franc BCEAO (XOF)
- Religion: Christianity, Muslim, indigenous beliefs
- Language: French, Kabiye, Ewe
- British Commission Office, Lomé: +228 271 141

Tonga

- Population: 100,200 (2000)
- Location: Pacific Ocean
- Capital: Nuku'alofa
- Currency: Pa'anga (TOP)
- Religion: Christianity
- Language: Tongan, English
- refer to British High Commission, Suva, Fiji: +679 322 9100

Trinidad and Tobago

visit: www.gap-year.com

- Population: 1.3 million (2003)
- Location: Caribbean
- Capital: Port of Spain
- Currency: Trinidad and Tobago Dollar (TTD)
- Religion: Roman Catholicism, Hinduism, Anglican, Muslim, Presbyterian
- Language: English (official), Spanish
- British High Commission, Port of Spain: +1 (868) 622 2748

Tunisia
- Population: 9.92 million (2003)
- Location: North Africa
- Capital: Tunis
- Currency: Tunisian Dinar (TND)
- Religion: Muslim, Christianity
- Language: Arabic, French
- British Embassy, Tunis: +216 71 108 700

Turkey
- Population: 67.8 million (1999)
- Location: South-east Europe
- Capital: Ankara
- Currency: New Turkish Lira (TRY)
- Religion: Muslim
- Language: Turkish, Kurdish
- British Embassy, Ankara: +90 (312) 455 3344

Turkmenistan
- Population: 4.2 million (2004 UN)
- Location: Central Asia
- Capital: Ashgabat
- Currency: Manat (TMM)
- Religion: Sunni Muslim
- Language: Russian, Turkmen
- British Embassy, Ashgabat: +993 (12) 363 462/63/64

Tuvalu
- Population: 10,200
- Location: Pacific Ocean
- Capital: Funafuti

- Currency: Australian Dollar (AUD), Tuvaluan Dollar (TVD) (coinage only)

- Religion: Church of Tuvalu, Seventh-Day Adventist, Bahá'í

- Language: Tuvaluan, English

- refer to British High Commission, Suva, Fiji: +679 322 9100

Uganda
- Population: 25.5 million (2003)

- Location: Central Africa

- Capital: Kampala

- Currency: Uganda Shilling (UGX)

- Religion: Christianity, Muslim

- Language: English (official national language), Luganda, Swahili

- British High Commission, Kampala: +256 (31) 231 2000;
  (emergency and out of hours): +256 (0) 75 276 7777

Ukraine
- Population: 47.8 million (estimate)

- Location: East Europe

- Capital: Kyiv (Kiev)

- Currency: Hryvna (UADH)

- Religion: Ukrainian Orthodox, Ukrainian Catholicism , Ukrainian Greek

- Language: Ukrainian, Russian, Romanian, Polish, Hungarian

- British Embassy, Kyiv: +380 44 490 3660

United Arab Emirates
- Population: 3.48 million (2002 estimate)

- Location: Middle East

- Capital: Abu Dhabi

- Currency: Dirham (AED)

- Religion: Muslim, Hinduism

- Language: Arabic (official)

- British Embassy, Abu Dhabi: +971 (2) 6101 100

visit: www.gap-year.com

United Kingdom

- Population: 60.6 million (2006 estimate)
- Location: West Europe
- Capital: London
- Currency: British pound (GBP)
- Religion: Christian (Anglican, Roman Catholic, Presbyterian, Methodist) Muslim, Hindu, other/unspecified
- Language: English, Welsh, Scottish Gaelic
- Foreign & Commonwealth Office (FCO): +44 (0)20 7008 1500

United States of America

- Population: 298 million (2006 estimate)
- Location: North America
- Capital: Washington, DC
- Currency: US Dollar (USD)
- Religion: Protestant, Roman Catholicism, Latter-day Saints, Judaism, Muslim
- Language: English, Welsh, Scottish form of Gaelic
- British Embassy, Washington DC: +1 (202) 588 6500

Uruguay

- Population: 3.24 million (2004)
- Location: Southern South America
- Capital: Montevideo
- Currency: Peso Uruguayan (UYU)
- Religion: Roman Catholicism, Protestant, Judaism
- Language: Spanish
- British Embassy, Montevideo: +598 (2) 622 36 30/50

Uzbekistan

- Population: 26.5 million (2004 UN)
- Location: Central Asia
- Capital: Tashkent
- Currency: Som (UZS)
- Religion: Sunni Muslim
- Language: Uzbek, Russian, Tajik
- British Embassy, Tashkent: +99871 120 78 52

Vanuatu, Republic of

- Population: 204,000

the gap-year guidebook 2007

- Location: South Pacific
- Capital: Port Vila
- Currency: Vatu (VUV)
- Religion: Presbyterian, Anglican, Roman Catholicism, some Muslim
- Language: Bislama (offical), English (official), French (official), plus over 130 vernacular languages
- refer to British High Commission, Suva, Fiji: +679 322 9100

Venezuela
- Population: 25 million
- Location: Northern South America
- Capital: Caracas
- Currency: Bolivar (VEB)
- Religion: Roman Catholicism
- Language: Spanish
- British Embassy, Caracas: +58 (212) 263 8411

Vietnam
- Population: 83 million
- Location: South-east Asia
- Capital: Hanoi
- Currency: Vietnamese Dong (VND) (US dollar widely accepted)
- Religion: Buddhism, Roman Catholicism, Protestant, Cao Dai, Hoa Hao
- Language: Vietnamese
- British Embassy, Hanoi: +84 (4) 936 0500; (Duty Officer's mobile for emergencies only) +84 90340 4919

Yemen
- Population: 20 million (estimate)
- Location: Middle East
- Capital: Sana'a
- Currency: Yemeni Rial (YER)
- Religion: Muslim
- Language: Arabic
- British Embassy, Sana'a: +967 (1) 2640 81/82/83/84

Yugoslavia - see Serbia & Montenegro

visit: www.gap-year.com

Zambia

- Population: 10.7 million (2003)
- Location: Southern Africa
- Capital: Lusaka
- Currency: Kwacha (ZMK)
- Religion: Christianity, Muslim, Hindu, indigenous beliefs
- Language: English (official language of government), plus seven further official languages
- British High Commission, Lusaka: +260 (1) 251133

Zimbabwe

- Population: 12.9 million (2002)
- Location: Southern Africa
- Capital: Harare
- Currency: Zimbabwean Dollar (ZWD)
- Religion: Christianity, indigenous beliefs, small communities of Hinduism, Muslim and Judaism
- Language: English (official), Shona, Ndebele
- British Embassy, Harare: +263 (4) 772990; +263 (4) 774700

NOTES | Your ideas & plans

2

NOTES | Your ideas & plans